Good Jews

The Holocaust is now widely recognized as a central event in twentieth-century Europe. But how did the genocide of the Jews affect European attitudes toward Jews, Judaism, and Jewishness after 1945? While many histories of antisemitism exist, *Good Jews* offers a broad investigation of philosemitism – defined here as a politics of a priori friendship and valorization. Gerard Daniel Cohen presents a critical exploration of the languages of philosemitism in mainstream European politics and culture from 1945 to October 7, 2023, with particular emphasis on Germany and France. Within this framework, Cohen explores how the "Jewish question," or the problem of Jewish difference and incorporation in Western countries during the postwar decades, has been distinctively foregrounded in the language of philosemitism. Ultimately, *Good Jews* demonstrates that philosemitic Europe is not an idealized love story, but a reflection of European attitudes toward Jews from the Holocaust to the present.

Gerard Daniel Cohen is the Samuel W. & Goldye Marian Spain Associate Professor of Modern European History and Jewish Studies at Rice University. He specializes in the history of forced displacement after 1945, humanitarianism, and philosemitism in European thought and politics since the Holocaust.

Good Jews

Philosemitism in Europe since the Holocaust

Gerard Daniel Cohen

Rice University

Shaftesbury Road, Cambridge CB2 8EA, United Kingdom

One Liberty Plaza, 20th Floor, New York, NY 10006, USA

477 Williamstown Road, Port Melbourne, VIC 3207, Australia

314–321, 3rd Floor, Plot 3, Splendor Forum, Jasola District Centre, New Delhi – 110025, India

103 Penang Road, #05–06/07, Visioncrest Commercial, Singapore 238467

Cambridge University Press is part of Cambridge University Press & Assessment, a department of the University of Cambridge.

We share the University's mission to contribute to society through the pursuit of education, learning and research at the highest international levels of excellence.

www.cambridge.org
Information on this title: www.cambridge.org/9781009370912

DOI: 10.1017/9781009370905

© Gerard Daniel Cohen 2025

This publication is in copyright. Subject to statutory exception and to the provisions of relevant collective licensing agreements, no reproduction of any part may take place without the written permission of Cambridge University Press & Assessment.

When citing this work, please include a reference to the
DOI 10.1017/9781009370905

First published 2025

Cover credit: Brandenburg Gate, Berlin, 9th January 2017. Michael Kappeler/DPA/AFP via Getty Images.

A catalogue record for this publication is available from the British Library

A Cataloging-in-Publication data record for this book is available from the Library of Congress

ISBN 978-1-009-37091-2 Hardback
ISBN 978-1-009-37089-9 Paperback

Cambridge University Press & Assessment has no responsibility for the persistence or accuracy of URLs for external or third-party internet websites referred to in this publication and does not guarantee that any content on such websites is, or will remain, accurate or appropriate.

For EU product safety concerns, contact us at Calle de José Abascal, 56, 1°, 28003 Madrid, Spain or email eugpsr@cambridge.org.

Contents

Acknowledgments		*page* vi
1	"Philosemitic Europe": A Contradiction in Terms?	1
2	From Antisemitism to Tactical Philosemitism (1945–1960)	25
3	Genesis of a Struggle: Anti-antisemitism (1945–1948)	60
4	From Humanism to Israelophilia (1945–1967)	95
5	Birth Pangs: "Judeo-Christian Europe" (1945–1965)	135
6	"The Long 1960s" and the Jews (1960–1980)	171
7	Archetypal Friends: Euro-Philosemitism (1980–2020)	215
	Epilogue: New Philosemitism and Its Critics: From the Turn of the Twenty-First Century to October 7, 2023	253
Select Bibliography		270
Index		283

Acknowledgments

I am deeply grateful to the colleagues and friends who generously offered their insights on all or part of this manuscript. They are too numerous to name individually, but this study would not have come to fruition without them. My deepest thanks go to Liz Friend-Smith, my editor at Cambridge University Press, whose unwavering support in overseeing the book's publication was truly invaluable.

I have been fortunate to receive support from various institutions. At Rice University, I am indebted to the Boniuk Institute, the Program in Jewish Studies, the Department of History, and Kathleen Canning, Dean of the School of Humanities, for enabling me to conduct research in France, the United Kingdom, Germany, the Netherlands, Italy, and Austria since 2017. My sincere appreciation goes to Anna Shparberg, Humanities Librarian, and the interlibrary staff at Rice's Fondren Library, who diligently sourced the publications and archival materials essential to completing this volume.

This project began with a EURIAS research fellowship at the Institute for Human Sciences (IWM) in Vienna (2017–18), an institution I have been connected with since my graduate school days. I extend my gratitude and friendship to its extraordinary staff and permanent members. Conversations with Ivan Krastev, Timothy Snyder, Ludger Hagedorn, and Ivan Vejvoda, along with numerous visiting fellows, have been indispensable to my work. Additionally, a six-month senior research fellowship at the Vienna Wiesenthal Institute for Holocaust Studies (August 2018–January 2019) was instrumental in shaping this book. I am grateful to Béla Rásky, Eva Kovács, and Marianne Windsperger for their warm welcome. My appreciation also goes to the Ustinov Institute (Vienna) for appointing me as the Peter Ustinov Guest Professor at the Institute for Contemporary History at the University of Vienna in the spring of 2024.

Early – and highly tentative – versions of my ideas on the politics and culture of post-Holocaust philosemitism were presented at the Pears Institute for the Study of Antisemitism (Birkbeck College, London), the

Center for Research on Antisemitism at Technical University (Berlin), the Watson Institute at Brown University, and the Department of History's "brown bag" seminar at Rice University. Further iterations of the manuscript were later presented at institutions including the Jewish Museum Frankfurt, the Vienna Humanities Festival, Southern Methodist University (Dallas), and the Institute for Holocaust, Genocide, and Memory Studies at the University of Massachusetts, Amherst. I am also grateful to the conveners of the DAAD workshop *Entangled Otherings* for the opportunity to present my work at Cambridge University's Faculty of Divinity in July 2024.

1 "Philosemitic Europe"
A Contradiction in Terms?

In German-ruled Europe, observed the Holocaust historian Saul Friedländer, "anti-Jewish policies could unfold to their most extreme levels without the interference of any major countervailing interests." In every country, to be sure, individual efforts or clandestine networks attempted to save Jews marked for murder. While in the East, rescue only marginally reduced the colossal tally of Jewish victims, in Western Europe, non-Jewish helpers mitigated the lethality of the Final Solution. Public silence about the fate of the Jews, however, remained a distinctive feature of the "years of extermination." One of the first scholars to criticize the passivity of the Vatican, Friedländer extended this judgment to all wartime institutions: "not one social group, not one religious community, not one scholarly (...) or professional association in Germany and throughout Europe declared its solidarity with the Jews." The Amsterdam workers' strike of February 25, 1941, offered a rare example of public protest against anti-Jewish brutality. But during ghettoization or the "Holocaust by bullets" in the East, and when deportations to death camps started across Europe, "only very rare gestures of solidarity with the victims occurred on a collective scale."[1] From London, governments-in-exile condemned persecution, promised the return of equal status after the war, and threatened collaborators with retribution. Yet fearful to be seen as defending Jewish interests, they seldom instructed populations to hide or assist endangered Jews.[2] In addition to the numerous accomplices it found east and west of the continent, Nazi Germany could also count on Europe's "moral indifference" to carry out its program of annihilation.[3]

---

[1] Saul Friedländer, *Nazi Germany and the Jews, 1939–1945: The Years of Extermination* (New York: Harper Perennial, 2008), xxi, 426.

[2] The London Poles issued such an order in May 1943 when large amounts of Polish Jews had already been killed. See Antony Polonsky, "Introduction" in Jan Láníček and James Jordan (eds.), *Governments-in-Exile and the Jews during the Second World War* (London: Vallentine Mitchell, 2013), 1–32.

[3] On "moral indifference," see Zygmunt Bauman, *Modernity and the Holocaust* (Ithaca, NY: Cornell University Press, 2002), 18–23.

This deficit of solidarity is this book's point of departure: the baseline against which shifts in the history of Europe and the Jews since the Holocaust must be gauged. Focused on the Western side of the Iron Curtain from 1945 to 1989, and on the European Union since its inception, this study documents the valorization of Jews from the collapse of the Third Reich to the present. Although tabooed in the public domain after the defeat of Nazism, antisemitism immediately resurfaced in the form of latent or "secondary" expressions. But a reversal occurred in mainstream politics and culture. Animus against Jews lost its public permissiveness while qualified tolerance required a thicker veneer of sympathy. On the other end of the spectrum, discourses of defense or esteem migrated from the periphery to the center of public conversation. Judeophobic stereotypes, or the idea of irreducible Jewish otherness, easily found their way into pro-Jewish expression. Yet ranging from mere rejection of prejudice to special deference, new languages of solidarity offered an unprecedented counterpoint to antisemitism. This evolution picked up pace at the end of the Cold War. Half a century after the Holocaust, Hitler's Jewish enemy morphed into archetypal friend in the official rhetoric of European Union leaders. In the words of the historian Enzo Traverso, the memory of the Jewish genocide "made the former pariah people a protected minority."[4]

The postwar period, from this point of view, is nothing short of revolutionary in the history of Europe's "Jewish question" since the Enlightenment. A lucid critic of the emancipation era, Hannah Arendt wrote in the late 1930s that "in a society on the whole hostile to the Jews – and that situation obtained in all [European] countries in which Jews lived, down to the twentieth century – it is possible to assimilate only by assimilating into anti-Semitism also."[5] Equal rights and incorporation, she intimated, required surrender to normative hostility. But if prewar Europe, despite key East/West differences, can plausibly be labelled "against the Jews," European democracies after 1945 made the befriending of Jews a key marker of post-fascism.[6] After 150 years of ambivalent emancipation, it took a genocide to create more hospitable conditions; and readers of this book will discover how valorization also exacted a price on Jews, Muslims, and Palestinians. When applied to the recent past, however, Arendt's penetrating phrase warrants

---

[4] Enzo Traverso, *The End of Jewish Modernity* (London: Pluto Press, 2016), 3.
[5] Hannah Arendt, *Rahel Varnhagen: The Life of a Jewish Woman* (New York: NYRB Classics, 2022), 224.
[6] Götz Aly, *Europe against the Jews: 1880–1945* (New York: Metropolitan Books, 2020).

crucial modifications. In societies committed to tolerance, Jews have gained acceptance without obligatory assimilation into antisemitism. For their good fortune but not without costs, post-Holocaust Europe has extended them a puzzling invitation: to assimilate "into philosemitism also."

Before Guilt: "Love for the Jews" from the Late Nineteenth Century to 1945

The German publicist Wilhelm Marr popularized the word "antisemitism" in 1879, but opponents of "Semites" in Imperial Germany simultaneously invented "philosemitism" to disparage alleged Jew-lovers.[7] The German Liberals first castigated as "philosemites," however, refuted the charge of love. They claimed instead to only reject antisemitism in the name of democratic ideals. Few "valued the Jew for what he had to give, rather than for what he had to give up," the German-Jewish scholar Gershom Scholem pointed out in a notorious essay; most pinned their hopes on conversion and intermarriage to put an end to anti-Jewish hostility.[8] Yet a small network of Protestant and Liberal self-declared "philosemites" attempted to defend Jews, Judaism, or Jewish learning in Imperial and Weimar Germany.[9] Already critical in her wartime writings of a relationship based on non-Jewish "benefactors" and Jewish "protégés," Hannah Arendt pounced on these supposed friends in *The Origins of Totalitarianism* (1951). Such "philosemites," she wrote, showed their true face after Hitler's seizure of power when "they felt as though they had to purge themselves of secret viciousness."[10] The French Jewish journalist Bernard Lazare, Arendt's favorite "conscious pariah," had already cautioned against defenders of Jews during the Dreyfus Affair. "Philosemites," Lazare noted in 1901, "go at length to establish that the

---

[7] Wolfram Kinzig, "Philosemitismus- was ist das? Eine kritische Begriffanalyse" in Irene A. Diekmann and Elke-Vera Kotowski (eds.), *Geliebter Feind, Gehasster Freund: Antisemitismus und Philosemitismus in Geschichte und Gegenwart* (Berlin: Verlag für Berlin-Brandenburg, 2009), 25–60; Marc Grimm, "Die Begriffsgeschichte des Philosemitismus," *Jahrbuch für Antisemitismusforschung* 22 (2013): 244–266.

[8] Gershom Scholem, "Jews and Germans" (1966) in *On Jews and Judaism in Crisis. Selected Essays* (New York: Schocken Books, 1976), 71–92.

[9] Michael Brenner, "'Gott schütze uns vor unseren Freunden' – Zur Ambivalenz des Philosemitismus im Kaiserreich," *Jahrbuch für Antisemitismusforschung* 2 (1993): 174–199; Alan T. Levenson, *Between Philosemitism and Antisemitism: Defense of Jews and Judaism in Germany 1871–1932* (Lincoln, NE: University of Nebraska Press, 2004).

[10] Hannah Arendt, "Pro Paul Tillich" (1942) in Jerome Kohn and Ron Feldman (eds.), *The Jewish Writings: Hannah Arendt* (New York: Schocken Books, 2007), 167–169; *The Origins of Totalitarianism* (San Diego, CA: Harcourt Brace & Company, 1979), 86.

Jew is perfectly similar to the people surrounding him, only to remark on his certain inferiority."[11]

Few advocates of Jews, however, called themselves "philosemites" after the term came into being in the 1880s. In England, "philo-Semitism" entered the *Oxford Literary Dictionary* in 1914. Yet the conservative and Liberal politicians who extolled the Jewish people in the early twentieth century did not need the word to engage in apologetics. Jews formed "the most formidable and the most remarkable race which has ever appeared in the world," wrote Winston Churchill in 1920 – before excluding from his praise "diabolical" Jewish revolutionaries.[12] Churchill had his good and bad Jews, yet he heralded those deserving of his admiration as exceptional contributors to Western civilization. During World War I, English Judeophilia fatefully conflated with pro-Zionism. While British support for "a national home for the Jewish people" in Palestine partly stemmed from imperial calculations, the Balfour Declaration's demotion of indigenous Arabs into "existing non-Jewish communities" also bore the mark of Protestant restorationism. "As you must remember, we had been trained even more in Hebrew history than in the history of our own country," explained David Lloyd George in 1925 to justify the "natural sympathy" for the Zionist cause shared by imperial elites of his generation.[13]

British philo-Zionism nevertheless included hostile views of Jews. As prime minister, Balfour had passed the 1905 Aliens Act restricting Jewish immigration from the Russian Empire. In 1919, he wrote that the settlement of Jews in Palestine would "mitigate the age-long miseries created for Western civilization by the presence in its midst of a Body which it too long regarded as alien and even hostile."[14] The language of racial kinship, however, reversely conveyed appreciation. In his testimony to the Palestine Royal Commission (1936–37), Churchill included Jews into the "higher-grade" race that in the past offered "Red Indians in America" and "Black people in Australia" the benefits of modernity. Jewish fellow civilizers, he intimated, now pursued this noble

---

[11] Cited in Antoine Compagnon, "Antisémitisme ou antimodernisme"? Anatole Leroy-Beaulieu, Bernard Lazare, Léon Bloy" in Ilana Y. Zinguer and Sam W. Bloom (eds.), *L'antisémitisme éclairé. Inclusion and Exclusion: Perspectives on Jews from the Enlightenment to the Dreyfus Affair* (Leiden: Brill, 2003), 423–447.
[12] Winston S. Churchill, "Zionism versus Bolshevism: A Struggle for the Soul of the Jewish People" (1920), cited in Martin Gilbert, *Churchill and the Jews: A Lifelong Friendship* (New York: Henry Holt & Company, 2007), 43.
[13] Lloyd George cited in Eitan Bar Yosef, "Christian Zionism and Victorian Culture," *Israel Studies* 8, no. 2 (Summer 2003): 18–44.
[14] Cited in Mitchell J. Cohen, *Britain's Moment in Palestine. Retrospect and Perspectives, 1917–1948* (London: Routledge, 2014), 12.

goal in Palestine.¹⁵ The British statesman's words were expunged from the record, but the Royal Commission's report distinguished between "resourceful, Western-minded" Jews from "predominantly Asiatic" Arabs. The Labour politician Herbert Morrison, for his part, claimed in 1939 that Jews in Palestine "have proved to be first-class colonizers, to have the real, good, old, Empire building qualities": Interwar British philo-Zionists wavered between the negative racialization of Jews – whether poor Eastern European immigrants or "rich plutocratic" financiers – and the positive racialization of the Zionist project.¹⁶ Contrary to what the Anglo-Jewish historian Cecil Roth argued in 1949, and since then accounts of "admiration and support" for Jews from Cromwell to Churchill, philosemitism in Britain never amounted to a cohesive "movement."¹⁷ More favorable to mythicized Semites or Hebrews than to Judaism or modern Jews, or better disposed toward "first-class colonizers" in Palestine than urban Jews in Europe, this peculiar current of English religious and political thought was above all a subset of Christian, Victorian, and imperialist worldviews.¹⁸ Even pronounced admiration for Jews among educated elites did not turn Judeophilia into a fixed ideology. From its lexical birth to World War II, philosemitism carried instead a wide range of meanings in European politics – in Britain as on the continent.

The word's original antisemitic connotation was not lost on Nazi ideologues. Joseph Goebbels first hijacked the term in 1928. Over eight issues of Der Philosemit, a satirical supplement to his weekly newspaper *Der Angriff*, Hitler's henchman posed as a friend of Jews only to

---

¹⁵ Cited in Michael Makovsky, *Churchill's Promised Land: Zionism and Statecraft* (New Haven: Yale University Press, 2007), 156.
¹⁶ Herbert Morrison (House of Commons, 1938) cited in Paul Kelemen, *The British Left and Zionism: History of a Divorce* (Manchester: Manchester University Press, 2012), 27; James Renton, "The End of the Semites" in James Renton and Ben Gidley (eds.), *Antisemitism and Islamophobia in Europe: A Shared History?* (London: Palgrave Macmillan, 2017), 99–140; Yair Wallach, "The Racial Logic of Palestine's Partition," *Ethnic and Racial Studies* 46, no. 8 (2023): 1576–1598.
¹⁷ Cecil Roth, "Philo-Semitism in England" (1949) in *Essays and Portraits in Anglo-Jewish History* (Philadelphia, PA: The Jewish Society Publication of America, 1962), 10–21. See also William D. Rubinstein and Hilary L. Rubinstein, *Philosemitism: Admiration and Support in the English-Speaking World for Jews, 1840–1939* (Houndmills, Basingstoke, Hampshire: Palgrave Macmillan, 1999); Gertrude Himmelfarb, *Philosemitism in England from Cromwell to Churchill* (New York: Encounter Books, 2011).
¹⁸ On British imperialism and philosemitism, see among others Abigail Green, "The British Empire and the Jews: An Imperialism of Human Rights?" *Past & Present* 199, no. 1 (May 2008): 175–205; Eric Michael Reisenauer, "Anti-Jewish Philosemitism: British and Hebrew Affinity in Ninetieth Century British Antisemitism," *British Scholar* I, no. 1 (September 2008): 79–104; David Feldman, "Jews and the British Empire, c. 1900," *History Workshop Journal* 63, no. 1 (2007): 70–79.

engage in rabid antisemitism.[19] He then devoted his attention to crypto-philosemitism among Nazi elites. In February 1935, Goebbels went so far as to accuse the editor of *Der Stürmer* Julius Streicher of "tendencies towards philosemitism."[20] His attacks on imaginary Jew-lovers intensified during the war. In September 1942, Goebbels lashed out at German "economic and industrial experts" guilty in his mind of "philosemitic intellectual propaganda." By "philosemitism," the chief propagandist meant their recommendation to keep temporarily alive, as slave laborers, 30,000 Jews in Berlin. Such weak resolve, he complained, harmed the struggle against Judeo-Bolshevism.[21] A few months later, Goebbels seethed against the "philosemitic world" pushed to war against the Reich under the sway of international Jewry: a recurrent theme in his speeches until his death by suicide in May 1945.

In Europe, however, the philosemitism against which Nazism rebelled only amounted to a variety of political forces merely opposed to antisemitism. Liberalism, reformist or revolutionary socialism, like interwar antifascism, did not count many demonstrative philosemites in their ranks. Yet even if they did not profess "love" or even friendship, political programs committed to civic equality offered Jews a safety zone of membership and rights. Such inclusion, opined Stefan Zweig, was satisfactory enough. "Everything that is not destructive, uprooting, thoughtless," the Austrian-Jewish writer noted in 1931, deserved the label "philosemitic."[22] What has been later called "anti-antisemitism," of course, did not require rejection of prejudice or a desire to defend Jews as Jews. Political challengers of antisemitism in the interwar era did not see the phenomenon as a central ill of Western modernity, but as a by-product of reactionary conservatism, fascism, or monopoly capitalism. Between 1919 and 1939, however, the European left formed the main line of defense against antisemitism. The victory of "progress" over fascism remained its primary objective. But this prospect also crucially entailed the acceptance of Jews into the ranks of undifferentiated humanity.

Philosemitism meant more than anti-antisemitism for the unofficial network of Catholic churchmen and intellectuals who in the late 1930s

---

[19] Helmut Heiber, *Goebbels* (London: Robert Hale & Company, 1972), 55–56; Christian T. Barth, *Goebbels und die Juden* (Paderborn: Schöningh, 2003), 62.
[20] *Die Tagebücher von Joseph Goebbels* (Munich: K.G. Saur, 2005), Part I (1923–1941), February 16, 1935.
[21] Ibid., Part II (1941–1945), September 30, 1942, and December 15, 1942.
[22] Cited in Alan T. Levenson, "From Recognition to Consensus: The Nature of Philosemitism in Germany, 1871–1932" in Jonathan Karp and Adam Suttcliffe (eds.), *Philosemitism in History* (Cambridge: Cambridge University Press, 2011), 190–210.

took a stance against the Nazi racial state.[23] Emblematic of this current, the French philosopher Jacques Maritain exhorted Christians to show "a lot of love" to Jews to avert imminent catastrophe. "There are in the Europe of today," Maritain presciently stated in February 1938, "those who want extermination and death, and first and foremost the extermination of the Jews – because after all that is really what it comes down to, does it not?" Against the "idiotic apparatus of scientific racism," European Catholicism's foremost thinker countered that "Jews are in no way a biological race," but "a community of mental and moral structures, of ancestral experiences." Maritain nonetheless reintroduced "race" in a positive sense when he warned against "the general massacre of the race of Moses and Jesus." His ominous prediction foreshadowed a Christian philosemitism predicated on imitative alignment with Jewish victimhood. "Never before in the history of the world were the Jews persecuted so universally," explained Maritain, "and never has persecution attacked, as today, both Jews and Christians." The Holocaust as "Passion of Israel," and therefore foundational Judeo-Christian event, is a theme to which Maritain later returned during his wartime exile in the United States.[24]

The Vatican, too, gestured toward Judeo-Christian kinship. "Spiritually, we are all Semites," declared Pius XI in September 1938, after reminding the faithful that "antisemitism is inadmissible." The Holy See's affinities with "Semites," however, did not translate into overt solidarity with persecuted Jews. Issued in March 1937, the encyclical *Mit brennender Sorge* [*With Burning Anxiety*] denounced the "aggressive paganism" of Hitler's regime without any mention of the dire situation of German Jews. Pius XI's "hidden encyclical," written in 1938 but never made public, deplored "the flagrant denial of the elementary rights of Jews." The document nonetheless cautioned against excessive empathy "as long as the unbelief of the Jews and their hostility toward Christianity persist." A month after Hitler's invasion of Poland, Pius XII's Summi Pontificatus once again affirmed the incompatibility of racism with the Catholic faith without a word on antisemitism. At the onset of the German assault on European Jewry, anti-Judaism forced the Church into condescending pity: compassion for an "unfortunate

---

[23] On Catholic anti-racist thought in the 1930s, see John Connelly, *From Enemy to Brother: The Revolution in Catholic Teachings on the Jews 1933–1965* (Cambridge: Cambridge University Press, 2012), 94–146.

[24] Richard Francis Crane, "Jacques Maritain, the Mystery of Israel, and the Holocaust," *The Catholic Historical Review* 95, no. 1 (January 2009): 25–56; Vittorio Possenti, "Maritain and the Jewish Question" in Robert Royal (ed.), *Jacques Maritain and the Jews* (Notre Dame, IN: University of Notre Dame Press, 1994), 104–122.

people condemned to wander the face of the earth forever" mixed with enduring distaste for the obstinate Synagogue.[25] Christian rescuers or sympathizers of Jews in German-occupied Europe took more risks but did not always deviate from this view. For Catholic spiritual resisters in France, antisemitism violated Christian teachings but opposition to Vichy's racial laws did not require special esteem for Jews or Judaism. "It is not necessary to be a philosemite," stated the underground publication Témoignage Chrétien in the spring of 1942, "to condemn without hesitation all forms of antisemitism."[26]

The imminent defeat of Nazi Germany did not popularize the word "philosemitism" in soon liberated Western Europe. In February 1945, the famed French writer André Malraux confided to his fellow resistance comrade Roger Stéphane that "if there is a Jewish question, neutrality is inconceivable. I am a philosemite, let it be known." This remark struck its Jewish recipient as worthy of note yet remained private.[27] As the historian Cecil Roth observed in 1949, "the psychological and political attitude to which I would like to call attention [i.e., philosemitism] has not yet entered the European vocabulary."[28] The word, however, already circulated among surviving German Jews who gave it a distinctive negative meaning: a friendly disposition detrimental to Jews. "Many Germans," Hannah Arendt wrote in 1942, "believe they have done enough if they declare themselves philosemites (…) but that does not prevent such attitudes from being at best politically meaningless, and usually harmful."[29] The exiled thinker, unaware that decades later streets in all major German cities would bear her name, introduced then a critique destined to a long future in the Federal Republic. In a speech delivered during the 1956 "Week of Brotherhood," the novelist and moral figure Heinrich Böll warned against "a pro-Semitism that is as scary to me as antisemitism."[30]

---

[25] Michael R. Marrus, "The Vatican on Racism and Antisemitism, 1938–1939: A New Look at a Might-Have-Been," *Holocaust and Genocide Studies* 7, no. 3 (Winter 1997): 378–395.

[26] See "Antisémites" (April–May 1942) in François and Renée Bédarida, *La résistance spirituelle. Cahiers et courriers clandestins du Témoignage Chrétien* (Paris: Albin Michel, 2001), 154.

[27] Roger Stéphane, *André Malraux: Entretiens et précisions* (Paris: Gallimard, 1984), 114. On Malraux's philosemitism, see Michaël de Saint-Cheron, *Malraux et les Juifs: Histoire d'une fidélité* (Paris: Desclée de Brouwer, 2008).

[28] Roth, *Philo-Semitism in England*, op. cit., 10.

[29] Arendt, "A Way toward the Reconciliation of Peoples" (1942) in *The Jewish Writings*, op. cit., 258–263.

[30] Cited in Stephan Braese, "Verlagerungen: Zur Ökonomie des Philosemitismus in der westdeutschen Nachkriegsliteratur" in Philipp Theisohn and Georg Braungart (eds.), *Philosemitismus: Rhetorik, Poetik, Diskursgeschichte* (Leiden: Wilhelm Fink Verlag, 2017), 345–356.

But from the Adenauer era to the twenty-first century, German-Jewish writers led the charge. Hyperbolic Judenfreundlichkeit (friendliness toward Jews), they claimed, amounted to repressed Judenhass (Jew-hatred), flawed reckoning with Nazi crimes, recreation of Jewish stereotypes, and not least, insufferable theatrics.

Philosemitism in the Age of Guilt: The German Template

In the wake of the so-called Swastika Epidemic, a two-month episode of antisemitic vandalism in 1959–60, the Central Council of Jews in Germany lamented the "intrusive, ostentatious conciliatoriness" of West German citizens eager to sympathize with the few Jews still living in the country. "Genuine humanitarianism" was welcome, declared Jewish representatives, but "fashionable philosemitism" only sought "the applause of simple souls." The anti-Nazi émigré of Jewish origin Norbert Muhlen, however, challenged the reluctance of the Jewish communal leadership to accept non-Jewish solicitude. "Breast-beating do-gooders," Muhlen countered during a visit of his homeland in 1961, only represented a fraction of the country's "moral elite." On the whole, he wrote, the "Jewish trend" (jüdische Konjonktur) "has remained basically healthy." In his mind, a book market "saturated with works on Jewish subjects," the dissemination of a "new, positive image of Judaism," the popularity of Lessing's Nathan the Wise or widespread interest in Anne Frank's diary within the young generation, only demonstrated progress. For the educated classes, Muhlen conceded, Jews "held some of the attraction that (…) the 'noble savage' held for them in previous epochs": Yet among cultural or religious elites, good will toward Jews was palpable in the Bonn Republic.[31]

Jewish intellectuals who unlike Muhlen still resided in West Germany did not share this view. Without using the word philosemitism, Theodor Adorno condemned in 1962 "the mechanical replacement of negative prejudice into a positive one." The philosopher Ernst Bloch was more explicit. "A patronizing way of making amends," he wrote in 1963, "philosemitism implies something like a certain element of antisemitism, that while vanquished, remains immanent." Adorno and Bloch set into motion a long history of German-Jewish distrust. In 1965, the political scientist Eleonore Sterling reflected on penitent West Germans who lavished praise on Jews as symbols of high culture or pitied them as

---

[31] Norbert Muhlen, *The Survivors: A Report on the Jews in Germany Today* (New York: Thomas Y. Cowell, 1962), 150–172.

"Auschwitz Jews." Like antisemitism, Sterling remarked, philosemitism reflected a "mental incapacity to truly respect the 'other'." In 1978, the Viennese-born writer Manès Sperber rejected a solicitude that "humiliates me as would a compliment based upon an absurd misunderstanding (...) I do not ask, I decidedly do not wish, that we be loved in this fashion." Jewish intellectuals in the Federal Republic still found philosemitism repulsive during the last decade of the Cold War. An expression of "German guilt complexes," it imposed on them "a status of being special" and prevented the possibility "to feel free as equals among equals." When after reunification the Holocaust occupied a larger place in Germany's national memory, the publicist Henryk Broder noted that "no matter whether Jews are first to be murdered or afterwards to be memorialized, the objective is followed with persistence, tenacity, and a sense of the gigantic." In 1996, a Jewish weekly offered satirical advice to well-intentioned Germans on how to interact with Jews. Avoid the phrase "Of all people, you as Jew must understand...," the newspaper instructed, before imploring philosemites to stop involving Jews in their personal struggle with guilt. Young German-Jewish writers in the twenty-first century, in turn, resented "the political correctness of philosemitism" masking unresolved nervousness about Jews; or refused the role of model minority assigned to them by the atoning Federal Republic. "I am a German Jew, and I would love to be normal," pleaded a director and playwright in 2020.[32]

This polemical tradition, however, has been less concerned with a central feature of West German philosemitism since the 1952 Reparations Agreement: the recurrently tense yet special relationship binding "the land of perpetrators" to the state of Israel. An alternative definition of

---

[32] Theodor W. Adorno, *Zur Bekämpfung der Antisemitismus heute?* (1962) (Berlin: Suhrkamp, 2024); Ernst Bloch, "The So-Called Jewish Question" (1963) in *Literary Essays* (Stanford, CA: Stanford University Press, 1998), 488–491; Eleonore Sterling, "Judenfreunde – Judenfeinde. Fragwürdiger Philosemitismus in der Bundesrepublik," *Die Zeit*, December 10, 1965, available at: www.zeit.de/1965/50/judenfreunde-judenfeinde; Manès Sperber, untitled essay (1978), in Hans Jürgen Schultz (ed.), *Mein Judentum* (Stuttgart: Kreuz Verlag, 1978), 180–194; Jack Zipes, "The Vicissitudes of Being Jewish in West Germany" in Anson Rabinbach and Jack Zipes (eds.), *Germans and Jews since the Holocaust* (New York: Holmes & Meier, 1986), 27–49; Henryk M. Broder in *Der Spiegel*, April 17, 1995, cited in Robert S. Wistrich, *Demonizing the Other: Antisemitism, Racism and Xenophobia* (London: Routledge, 1999), 362; Wolfgang Benz, "Jewish Existence in Germany from the Perspective of the Non-Jewish Majority: Daily Life between Anti-Semitism and Philo-Semitism" in Leslie Morris and Jack Zipes (eds.), *Unlikely History: The Changing German-Jewish Symbiosis, 1945–2000* (New York: Palgrave, 2002), 101–118; Yascha Mounk, *Stranger in My Own Country: A Jewish Family in Modern Germany* (New York: Farrar, Straus and Giroux, 2014); Max Czollek, *Desintigriert euch!* (Munich: BtB Verlag, 2018); Tobias Ginsburg, "I am a German Jew, and I Would Like to Be Normal," *Haaretz*, May 19, 2020.

philosemitism as guilt-ridden pro-Zionism complicit in the oppression of Palestinians emerged instead from the ranks of the New Left after the 1967 Six-Day War. The Federal Republic's reflexive pro-Israel stance, argued its first challengers, enabled "the German" to devolve to "the Arab" the role of "perpetrator and eternal persecutor of Jews" while absolving the newly democratic nation from sins.[33] The "German catechism" of the twenty-first century, added a recent commentator, not only asserts the uniqueness of the Holocaust at the expense of colonial genocides but also prescribes blind loyalty to Israel and censorship of pro-Palestinian voices: a "redemptive philosemitism" seeking to erase the redemptive antisemitism of the Nazi era.[34]

Jewish left-wing intellectuals, however, have since the days of the Jüdische Gruppe created in Frankfurt in 1980 spoken out against Israeli policies.[35] But until Jewish dissident voices emerged in the early twenty-first century – including that of Israeli transplants in Berlin – the German-Jewish "anti-philosemitic" position traditionally approved of the Federal Republic's special ties to the Jewish state. The "negative symbiosis" between surviving Jews and postwar Germany – participation in the republic but estrangement from the heimat – was always countervailed, for most, by positive identification with Israel. Post-Holocaust German Jews primarily pushed back against a pro-Jewish fascination masquerading as genuine confrontation with the Nazi past. "If someone only likes me because I am Jewish," observed the writer Rafael Seligmann in 2016, "then I know that something makes them do it." The root cause of German philosemitism, he summarized, "is the desperate search for absolution."[36]

Similar suspicion is traceable in the historical scholarship dedicated to philosemitism in the Federal Republic. Focused on the period of Allied occupation (1945–49) and the Adenauer chancellorship (1949–63), Frank Stern's pioneering study portrayed the "metamorphosis of attitudes towards Jews" after the Holocaust as an attempt to "whitewash

---

[33] Friedemann Buttner, "German Perceptions of the Middle East Conflict: Images and Identifications during the 1967 War," *Journal of Palestine Studies* 6, no. 2 (Winter 1977): 66–81.
[34] A. Dirk Moses, "The German Catechism," *Geschichte der Gegenwart* (May 23, 2021), available at: https://geschichtedergegenwart.ch/the-german-catechism/.
[35] Anna Corsten, "Jewish Left-Wing Intellectuals in Postwar Germany: The Case of Micha Brumlik and the Israeli Palestinian Conflict between Antisemitism and Antizionism" in Alessandra Tarquini (ed.), *The European Left and the Jewish Question 1848–1992* (Cham, Switzerland: Palgrave Macmillan 2021), 263–282.
[36] Rafael Seligman in *Deutschlandfunk Kultur* (August 8, 2016), available at: www.deutschlandfunkkultur.de/philosemitismus-einer-zweifelhaften-zuneigung-auf-der-spur-100.html.

the yellow badge." Philosemitic discourse in the early postwar period, the historian showed, relied on stereotypes and distortions. A surrogate for real confrontation with criminality, what passed as friendship traded polite declarations and reparations for a clean historical sheet. Banned as racial pollution under Nazism, Judenfreundlichkeit allowed the Bonn Republic to pass the test of democracy. Compulsory exercises in philosemitism, generalized Stern, are "German therapy for German pain. The Jew became the enemy who now had to be loved."[37] In the German "theater of memory," added the sociologist Y. Michal Bodemann, German Jews during the Cold War, and new arrivals from the former Soviet Union afterwards, have only been "loved" as "bodily presence" guaranteeing the redemption of perpetrators from sin. This approach, no doubt, illuminates the peculiar psychology of German denial and atonement since the 1950s. Yet it systematically reduces philosemitism to a mere stratagem: the tactic of people who have something to hide or to confess.

While this definition has the merit of clarity, it also negates the possibility of pro-Jewish interventions not directly driven by perpetrator guilt. As this book shows, numerous sympathizers of Jews and/or Zionism in the 1950s and 1960s had a "good war" in resistance movements or in victorious Britain. If guilt motivated them, it was only guilt by association. Other factors where at play, including legacies of "colonial humanism" in positive perceptions of the young state of Israel and the first Israeli Jews. Likewise, performances of philosemitism in contemporary Europe extend beyond obligatory atonement or ritualistic contrition. In post-Communist Poland, non-Jewish civic activists have attempted to resurrect the Jewish past to defend liberal pluralism against Catholic nationalism and authoritarian populism – "a redefinition of Polishness through Jewishness."[38] In reunified Germany, the Holocaust "remembrance culture" of the last thirty years has remained tethered to expiation. Its manifestations, however, transcend the rote recitation of Holocaust "catechism" to include a "routine accomplishment of civility" based on positive sentiments toward Jews, Judaism, and Israel.[39] Not just a diktat

---

[37] Frank Stern, *Whitewashing of the Yellow Badge: Antisemitism and Philosemitism in Postwar Germany* (New York: Oxford University Press, 1992); "The Revival of Antisemitism in United Germany: Historical Aspects and Methodological Considerations" in Michael Brown (ed.), *Approaches to Antisemitism: Context and Curriculum* (New York: American Jewish Committee, 1994), 78–94.
[38] Geneviève Zubrzycki, *Resurrecting the Jew: Nationalism, Philosemitism, and Poland's Jewish Revival* (Princeton, NJ: Princeton University Press, 2022).
[39] Irit Dekel, "Philosemitism in Contemporary German Media," *Media, Culture & Society* 44, no. 4 (2020): 746–763.

from the high levels of state, German philosemitism is also anchored in civil society: an invitation to explore its deeper meanings instead of merely expose a maneuver of guilt deflection.

Heritage philosemitism in post-1989 East-Central Europe, to be sure, has created virtual Jewish spaces in which the absence of Jews matters more than their negligeable presence. Although Jewish revivalism by non-Jews in the former Communist bloc also entails critical engagement with the past, it is not immune from fetishization or cultural appropriation. Philosemitism has generated its own nefarious consequences in contemporary Germany. After reunification, many Jews in the Federal Republic still felt like exotic beings not "subject to the ups and downs of mortal men and women." Others still lament today the inability of Germans to understand that Jewish life can exist outside of their narrow field of vision – either Holocaust or Israel.[40] Since the early 2000s, accusations of "imported" antisemitism in Germany have been leveled at Muslims despite police reports showing in 2021 that only 1 percent of perpetrators of antisemitic acts can be designated as Islamic or Islamist. After Angela Merkel announced in August 2015 that "we can manage" the absorption of 800,000 mostly Middle Eastern migrants, Holocaust education programs for refugees have also placed on suspicious Muslims a burden of philosemitic betterment.[41] Even before the Bundestag passed its (nonbinding) anti-BDS resolution in 2019, "antisemitism commissioners" in the Federal Republic have castigated outspoken defenders of Palestinians – including leftist Jews – as arch-violators of German civility – the new "villains of the German state." What has been called "philosemitic McCarthyism" only intensified in the aftermath of October 7, 2023.[42]

Assessing the costs of philosemitism for Jews, Muslims, and Palestinians, as shown in this book, must form an integral part of its study: Investigating "love" requires permanent attention to its oppressiveness. Yet if seen from the long perspective of modern

---

[40] Jeffrey Peck, *Being Jewish in the New Germany* (New Brunswick, NJ: Rutgers University Press, 2005), 14.

[41] Irit Dekel and Esra Özyürek, "The Logic of the Fight against Antisemitism in Germany in Three Cultural Shifts," *Patterns of Prejudice* 56, no. 2–3 (2022): 157–187; Esra Özyürek, *Subcontractors of Guilt: Holocaust Memory and Muslim Belonging in Postwar Germany* (Stanford, CA: Stanford University Press, 2023); Peter Kuras, "The Strange Logic of Germany's Antisemitism Bureaucrats" in *Jewish Currents* (Spring 2023), available at: https://jewishcurrents.org/the-strange-logic-of-germanys-antisemitism-bureaucrats.

[42] "Palestine between German Memory of Politics and (De-) Colonial Thought" (anonymous author), *Journal of Genocide Research* 23, no. 3 (2021): 374–382; Anna-Esther Younes, "Fighting Anti-Semitism in Contemporary Germany," *Islamophobia Studies Journal* 5, no. 2 (2020): 249–266; Susan Neiman, "Historical Reckoning Gone Haywire," in *The New York Review of Books*, October 19, 2023.

European history, the a priori valorization of Jews – dead or alive, figural or real – remains a revolutionary hallmark of the post-Holocaust period. In 1952, Wiedergutmachung – "to make good again" through monetary reparations – inaugurated the age of official philosemitism in West Germany: the Bonn Republic's reintegration into the community of nations through good will and "reconciliation" with Jews. Wiedergutwerdung, however, captures a deeper reparative process not limited to guilty Germans: "to become good again" through the befriending of the Jew "who, in Europe at least, is the most radical incarnation, indeed the epitome, of the stranger."[43] Grand narratives of post-1945 European history now conclude with reflections on Holocaust memory as "the pertinent European reference."[44] Yet even if initially at the periphery of public culture, the reconstruction of European morality through "the Jew" already began in 1945: a civilizational turning point hardly imaginable before the Jewish catastrophe.

Beyond Lachrymosity

To write the history of post-Holocaust Europe as that of "philosemitic Europe," however, requires departure from "the lachrymose conception of Jewish history." Nearly a century ago, Salo W. Baron enjoined students of the Jewish past to not only highlight persecution but also positive features of Jewish–non-Jewish interactions. The Jewish American scholar reiterated this view after World War II. "One should not be surprised," he wrote in 1956, "if historians of the future, would date the beginning of real Jewish emancipation, not with 1787 or 1790 or even 1848, but rather with the first postwar year of 1946." Only eleven years had passed since the liberation of death camps, yet Baron portrayed the post-Holocaust era as the starting point of "real" Jewish inclusion into Western modernity.[45] The "lachrymose conception" nonetheless continued to appeal to European Jewish intellectuals. "What is called Jewish history is but one long contemplation of Jewish misfortune," wrote Albert Memmi in 1962. The Tunis-born Parisian acknowledged "that we may have entered upon a wholly new period of history, one that would see at last the progressive liquidation of that oppression the

---

[43] On "becoming good again" in postwar Germany, see Eike Geisel (1945–1997), *Die Wiedergutwerdung der Deutschen* (Berlin: Edition Tiamat, 2015); Zygmunt Bauman, "Jews and Other Europeans, Old and New," *European Judaism* 42, no. 1 (Spring 2009): 121–133.

[44] Tony Judt, *A History of Europe since 1945* (New York: The Penguin Press, 2005), 803.

[45] Salo W. Baron, "The Modern Age" in Leo W. Scharz (ed.), *Great Ages and Ideas of the Jewish People* (New York: Random House, 1956), 315–484.

Jews have suffered for so long." For the time being, however, Memmi ruled out improvement. Although transplanted North African Jews found a welcoming new home in France, the author of Portrait of the Jew doubted "that the generosity of a few men, feigned or real (...) can change the essential substance of my situation." Before liberation either through revolution or Zionism – and in Memmi's subsequent writings, through Zionism alone – "a tremendous negativity continues to limit, stifle and cut off the life of every Jew."[46] In London, the Trotskyite émigré Isaac Deutscher warned in 1968 against "the impression that antisemitism is a spent force because in this our welfare state people are, on the whole, contented and satisfied." Under the surface, "barbarity is there (...) always ready to surge up." For the fierce critique of post-1967 Israel, the only choice of the diaspora Jew was not Zionism, but to remain an "eternal protester."[47] From Brussels, the Austrian exile and Auschwitz survivor Jean Améry faulted the Left for failing to realize that "the Jew is still worse off than Frantz Fanon's colonized individual." Unlike Memmi and Deutscher, Améry had no escape route: "for each and every Jew, whether he grasps this or not, is abandoned to a catastrophic fate, he is a 'catastrophe Jew'."[48]

The "non-Jewish–Jewish" historian Eric Hobsbawm was among the first European intellectuals to challenge lachrymosity. "A large part of the world," he wrote in 1980, now welcomed Jews "on their merits." Hobsbawm also observed in the West "a striking though not universal recession of anti-semitism." The distinguished professor upped the ante twenty-five years later. "There is no historic precedent," he argued in 2005, "for the triumph of the Aufklärung [Enlightenment] in the post-Holocaust diaspora." A few years before his death, Hobsbawm added that "the Jews, inside and outside Israel, have enormously benefited from the bad conscience of a Western world that had refused Jewish immigration in the 1930s before committing or failing to resist genocide." He nonetheless wondered "how much of that bad conscience, which virtually eliminated anti-semitism in the West for sixty years and produced a golden era for its diaspora, is left today?" His question, however, did not indicate belated conversion to the "eternal antisemitism" thesis. The Marxist historian long critical of Zionism blamed the end

---

[46] Albert Memmi, "Portrait of the Jew" (1962) in Jonathan Judaken and Michael Lejman (eds.), *The Albert Memmi Reader* (Lincoln, NE: The University of Nebraska Press, 2020), 69–96.
[47] Isaac Deutscher, *The Non-Jewish Jew* (1968) (London: Verso, 2017), 48.
[48] Jean Améry, "Virtuous Antisemitism" (1969) in Marlene Gallner (ed.), *Essays in Antisemitism, Anti-Zionism, and the Left* (Bloomington, IN: Indiana University Press, 2021), 34–40.

of the "golden era" on the actions of the Israeli state, not on the rise of "new antisemitism" in the twenty-first century.[49]

Proponents of the term "new Judeophobia," to the contrary, breathed new life into the "lachrymose conception."[50] A glum undercurrent, to be sure, had always been noticeable in ruminations on Jewish existence in post-Holocaust Europe. As late as the 1990s, pessimists predicted "a return to the ghetto" and the "vanishing" of the European Jewish diaspora: The continent was always more "accursed" than "glorious" in accounts of ever-dying Jewish communities.[51] Yet in the early twenty-first century, the discourse of "new antisemitism" intensified these anxieties. "What we are witnessing today," stated Britain's Chief Rabbi Jonathan Sacks in 2004, "is the second great mutation of antisemitism in modern times, from racial antisemitism to religious anti-Zionism."[52] According to this view, the devilish Zionist replaced the demonic Jew: the symbol of evil in the modern world and the embodiment of imperialism, racism, and oppressive whiteness. Under the guise of antiracism, confidently proclaimed the decipherers of "new antisemitism," anti-Zionism became the new "rumor about the Jews." Its propagators were not only pro-Palestinian activists or Muslims in Europe and the global south: The European Left also allegedly reverted to the grammar of antisemitism by turning Israel into a "collective Jew" and the "Zio" into the arch-enemy of human emancipation.[53] For denouncers of "Islamo-Fascism," or liberals alarmed by "new antisemitism" after the year 2000, European Jewish history returned to its tragic path after a short and illusory reprieve.

---

[49] Eric J. Hobsbawm, "Are We Entering a New Era of Anti-Semitism?" in Helen Fein (ed.), *The Persisting Question* (Berlin: Walter de Gruyter, 1987), 374–379; "Benefits of Diaspora" in *The London Review of Books*, October 20, 2005; "Responses to the War in Gaza," *London Review of Books*, January 29, 2009.

[50] The French scholar Pierre-André Taguieff coined the term in *La nouvelle judéophobie* (Paris: Fayard, 2002). For a critical history of "new antisemitism," see Anthony Lerman, *What Happened to Antisemitism? Redefinition and the Myth of the "Collective Jew"* (London: Pluto Press, 2022).

[51] On David Vital's *The Future of the Jews* (1990) and Bernard Wasserstein's *Vanishing Diaspora* (1996), see Michael Brenner, "The Ever-Dying Jewry? Prophets of Doom and the Survival European Jewry" in Gideon Reuveni and David Franklin (eds.), *The Future of the German Jewish Past* (West Lafayette, IN: Purdue University Press, 2021), 76–89; Jehuda Reinharz and Yaacov Shavit, *Glorious, Accursed Europe: An Essay on Jewish Ambivalence* (Boston: Brandeis University Press, 2010).

[52] Cited in Brian Klug, "The Myth of New Antisemitism" in *The Nation*, January 15, 2004, available at: www.thenation.com/article/archive/myth-new-anti-semitism/.

[53] See among others Alvin Rosenfeld (ed.), *Deciphering the New Antisemitism* (Bloomington, IN: Indiana University Press, 2015); Jonathan Judaken, "So What's New? Rethinking the 'New Antisemitism' in a Global Age," *Patterns of Prejudice* 42, nos. 4–5 (2008): 531–560.

The lachrymose conception, however, also found its way into recent studies of philosemitism. A long tradition of German-Jewish criticism had already bestowed upon the term a negative meaning. "The threatening nature of [philosemitism's] benevolence" unsurprisingly remained a dominant theme in a large edited volume on the topic published in Germany in 2009.[54] Scholars across the Atlantic similarly stressed "the intersections between philosemitism and antisemitism" in Anglo-American culture. When they are not "more insidious than transparent antisemitism," charged Phyllis Lassner and Lara Trubowitz, actions and sentiments directed in favor of Jews provide an "opportunity to criticize Jews and Jewish culture for the failure to live up to the ideal other groups have interpreted as Jewish." The phenomenon, according to this view, always manifests itself through instrumentalized fondness for Jews, Judaism, or Jewish culture, as well as overemphasis of imputed Jewish traits. It can also take the form of demonstrative support for the state of Israel, although liberal critics of pro-Israelism in the United States traditionally had in mind the millennialism of evangelical Christians, not normative pro-Zionism in American politics. Behind this excessive attention, critics regularly point out, hostility lives on. Philosemitism always replicates antisemitism by setting Jews apart as radically different people; by borrowing stereotypes from the vocabulary of Jew-hatred, or by splitting Jews, not unlike snobbish antisemitism, into "good" and "bad" categories. A specialist in German-Jewish history delivered the lachrymose coup de grace. "A philo-Semitic society can desire Jews or be repelled by them," wrote Gabriel Motzkin, "but it cannot accept them, because it always has the possibility of being anti-Semitic."[55]

Adding to these deficiencies, argue lachrymose critics of philosemitism, is the contemporary cult of Holocaust memory. The atoning West, contended a prize-winning Harvard professor in 2021, only loves murdered Jews who can "teach us something." With the help of Jewish educators or museum curators, Holocaust remembrance culture in the United States and Europe, or as far as China, has turned Jews into people who "for moral and educational purposes" are supposed to be dead. Reflecting on a "haunted present," Dara Horn only saw around

---

[54] Moshe Zuckermann, "Aspeckte des Philosemitismus" in Irene A. Diekmann and Elke-Vera Kotowski (eds.), *Geliebter Feind, Gehasster Freund: Antisemitismus und Philosemitismus in Geschichte und Gegenwart*, op. cit., 61–72.

[55] Gabriel Motzkin, "Love and Bildung for Hannah Arendt" in Steven Aschheim (ed.), *Hannah Arendt in Jerusalem* (Berkeley, CA: University of California Press, 2001), 291, cited in Ofri Ilany, "Feverish Preference": Philosemitism, Anti-antisemitism, and Their Critics" in Scott Ury and Guy Miron, *Antisemitism and the Politics of History* (Waltham, MA: Brandeis University Press, 2024), 167–186.

her rampant exploitation of Jewish death "to flatter the living."[56] From this perspective, the study of philosemitism only becomes "a new way of thinking about antisemitism and the Jewish Question."[57] After centuries of prejudice, discrimination, and violence, Jews are now purportedly the victims of "love." Although a counternarrative charges that contemporary philosemitism – especially in its radical German form – suppresses above all Palestinian, Muslim, or dissident Jewish voices critical of Israel, here its chief sufferers remain the Jews.

More nuanced commentators have resisted panic. Not "the reverse side of the antisemitic coin," argued Adam Sutcliffe and Jonathan Karp in a landmark volume, positive perceptions of Jews are best comprehended "within their broader intellectual framework."[58] Like Samuel Moyn, who in a book on Holocaust memory in France conceptualized philosemitism as a "cultural code," they approach the phenomenon "without a predetermined assessment."[59] What matters is the "significance and function" of philosemitism – or for Frances Tanzer, how this discourse shaped cultural meaning in the postwar period – not the unmasking of deceitful Judeophiles or the celebration of genuine ones.[60] Maurice Samuels likewise enjoined scholars "to investigate how defense, love, and admiration of Jews and Judaism (…) serve as vehicles for specific political agenda."[61] To investigate philosemitism, proposed Anthony D. Kauders, is not to search for love only to discover "that it is nowhere to be found." It is instead an exploration of "discussed Jews" in politics, culture, and thought.[62] David J. Wertheim, however, views the legitimation of non-Jewish ideas through "the Jew" not as philosemitism

---

[56] Dara Horn, *People Love Dead Jews: Reports from a Haunted Present* (New York: W. W. Norton & Company, 2021).

[57] Phyllis Lassner and Lara Trubowitz (eds.), *Antisemitism and Philosemitism in the Twentieth and Twenty-First Centuries: Representing Jews, Jewishness and Modern Culture* (Newark: University of Delaware Press, 2008), 7–17.

[58] Adam Sutcliffe and Jonathan Karp, *Philosemitism in History* (Cambridge: Cambridge University Press, 2011), 1–26. See also Sutcliffe, "The Unfinished History of Philosemitism," *Jewish Quarterly* 58, no. 1 (2011): 64–68.

[59] Samuel Moyn, "Antisemitism, Philosemitism and the Rise of Holocaust Memory," *Patterns of Prejudice* 43, no. 1 (2009): 1–16; *A Holocaust Controversy: The Treblinka Affair in Postwar France* (Waltham, MA: Brandeis University, 2005).

[60] Frances Tanzer, *Vanishing Vienna: Modernism, Philosemitism and Jews in a Postwar City* (Philadelphia, PA: University of Pennsylvania Press, 2024).

[61] Maurice Samuels, "Philosemitism" in Sol Goldberg, Scott Ury, and Kalman Weiser (eds.), *Key Concepts in the Study of Antisemitism* (London: Palgrave Macmillan, 2019), 201–214.

[62] Anthony D. Kauders, "History as Censure: 'Repression' and 'Philo-Semitism' in Postwar Germany" in *History and Memory* 15, no. 1 (Spring/Summer 2003): 97–12. On Jews as "subjects of conversation," see Jacques Berlinerblau, "On Philo-Semitism," *Program for Jewish Civilization Occasional Papers* (Washington, DC: Georgetown University, 2007).

but allosemitism – the term coined by Zygmunt Bauman to describe the reification of Jewish alterity, whether positive or negative. Yet as seen in Chapter 7, the use of "the Jew" to legitimate democracy, or postnationalism, necessarily entailed valorization. In Germany, wrote the philosopher Jürgen Habermas in 2012, "fatherless" postwar generations learned from Jewish thinkers "magnanimous enough to return to the country that had driven them out (…) how to distinguish the traditions that are worthy of being continued from a corrupt intellectual heritage."[63] After the Holocaust, "the Jew as legitimation" continued as in the past to serve as "evidence for the truth of non-Jewish beliefs": Yet it also revealed the normalization of Jewish alterity in the Western liberal imagination.[64]

This book takes its cue from these critical insights. It nonetheless offers its own definition of philosemitism, a word as deficient as antisemitism but nonetheless reflective of historical experience. Here "love for the Semites" is not the syndrome of people who claim to delight in the Jews' existence, harbor admiration for their achievements, or feel irresistible attraction to Judaism. This study likewise leaves aside imaginary, allegorized, or figural "good Jews" in literature and thought. In the following pages, philosemitism is not (only) a dehumanizing narcissistic projection – or Judenfetisch in the German context.[65] The term connotes instead a befriending process: the emergence of a "Jewish friend" in mainstream European politics and culture, with particular emphasis on Germany and France. Post-Holocaust declarations of amity, of course, have never been devoid of ambiguity. To befriend Jews or Israel in return of absolution – the German philosemitic trade-off since 1949 – always involved "political opportunism and utility."[66] Christian revisions of anti-Judaic teachings, momentous as they were, did not dash hopes of Jewish entry into the Church. In critical theory or politics, the rejection of antisemitism did not require appreciation of Jews as Jews. Anti-antisemites, charged Elad Lapidot, prefer their Jews "delivered of substance."[67] Yet since 1945, and with greater vigor after 1989,

---

[63] Jürgen Habermas, "Jewish Philosophers and Sociologists in the Early Federal Republic: A Recollection" in J. Habermas (ed.), *The Lure of Technocracy* (Cambridge: Polity Press, 2015), 105–118.
[64] David J. Wertheim, "Introduction" in D. Wertheim (ed.), *The Jew as Legitimation: Jewish-Gentile Relations beyond Antisemitism and Philosemitism* (Cham: Palgrave Macmillan, 2017), 1–16.
[65] Deborah Feldman, *Judenfetisch* (Berlin: Luchterhand Literaturverlag, 2023).
[66] Frank Stern, "Antisemitism and Historical Consciousness: German Attitudes towards Jews and Israel," *Patterns of Prejudice* 27, no. 2 (1993): 29–38; Daniel Marwecki, *Absolution? Israel und die deutsche Staatsräson* (Göttingen: Wallstein Verlag, 2024).
[67] Elad Lapidot, "A Critique of Anti-Antisemitism" in *Tablet*, May 19, 2021; *Jews Out of the Question: A Critique of Anti-Anti Semitism* (Albany, NY: State University of New York Press, 2020).

empathetic discussions of Jews in the liberal public sphere have been premised on abhorrence of antisemitism, acknowledgement of guilt and shame, or acceptance of Zionism as just cause, without counterbalancing demands for Jewish "regeneration." Verbesserung or "amelioration," once a prerequisite of Jewish civic incorporation, became instead the burden of liberal Europe: the befriending of Jewishness as "admission ticket" into post-Holocaust morality.

When defined as a priori politics of friendship, philosemitism since 1945 is best comprehended as a spectrum of iterations.[68] On one end stands anti-antisemitism. Opposition to anti-Jewish prejudice, argued Jonathan Judaken, is only a category "for talking about those who have defended Jews or Judaism in contexts of antisemitism." It is distinct from philosemitism, which commonly "implies a love of Jews and Judaism."[69] Yet if anti-antisemitism never promised amity, "opposition to prejudices and stereotypes related to Jews, Judaism, and Jewishness" after 1945 was not mere color-blind universalism: anti-antisemitism, including as "instrument of domination,"[70] constitutes in this book the baseline of European philosemitism. Holocaust memory stands at midpoint of the philosemitic spectrum. In the following pages, the recognition – or sacralization – of the Jewish genocide is a permanent gauge of pro-Jewish friendship. German philosemitism, including the radicalization of "remembrance culture" since the start of the twenty-first century, constitutes a third typology: In Europe, the epicenter of the ever-problematic valorization of Jews after the Shoah remains the former "land of perpetrators."

Entangled with anti-antisemitism, Holocaust memory, and compensatory Judenfreundlichkeit, is philo-Zionism. "The valorization of Jewish Otherness" after the Shoah, wrote Brian Klug, simultaneously led to the "valorization of Israel."[71] For Palestinians and their defenders, Western Europe's support of the Jewish state from 1948 to 1967, and the European Union's continuing acceptance of Zionism's

---

[68] On the "multiple ways to be a philosemite," see Pierre-André Taguieff, "Antisémitisme ou philosémitisme: un problème mal posé," *Cités* 3, no. 87 (2021): 99–112.

[69] Jonathan Judaken, "Between Philosemitism and Antisemitism: The Frankfurt School's Anti-Antisemitism" in Phyllis Lassner and Lara Trubowitz (eds.), *Antisemitism and Philosemitism in the Twentieth and Twenty-First Centuries*, op. cit., 23–46; *Jean-Paul Sartre and the Jewish Question: Anti-Antisemitism and the Politics of the French Intellectual* (Lincoln, NE: University of Nebraska Press, 2006), 20.

[70] Moshe Zuckermann, *"Antisemit!": Ein vorfurf als Herrschaftsintrument* (Vienna: Promedia Verlag, 2010).

[71] Brian Klug, "An Emblematic Embrace: New Europe, The Jewish State, and the Palestinian Question" in Bashir Bashir and Leila Farsakh (eds.), *The Arab and Jewish Question: Geographies of Engagement in Palestine and Beyond* (New York: Columbia University Press, 2020), 47–67.

legitimacy, whitewashed European sins "at the expense of another."[72] The penitent recognition of Jews "as the classical victims of history," famously wrote Edward Said, proceeded with utter indifference for "the victims of the victims."[73] Yet while motivated by guilt, or deflection of responsibility, various modes of positive identification with the Jewish state also made "Israelophilia" a pillar of post-Holocaust philosemitism: a phenomenon whose languages evolved throughout the postwar decades.

Befriending the Jew: From 1945 to the Present

Although volumes on "old" and "new" antisemitism abound, there is to this day not a single synthetic history of philosemitism in postwar Europe. Completed prior to October 7, 2023 – philosemitism "after Gaza," to quote Pankaj Mishra, will require separate discussion -- this granular account of the continent's change of heart after the Holocaust treads in uncharted territory. This book, however, begins with the resurgence and reinvention of antisemitism in Western Europe in the aftermath of World War II (Chapter 2). To understand why anti-antisemitism became a distinctive philosophical, theological, and political project, requires attention to the resilience of Judeophobia in the late 1940s and 1950s. In Marshall Plan Europe, however, a new moratorium on public antisemitism demarcated democracy from fascism. Although unrepentant Nazis, former pro-German collaborators, or traditionalist Catholics transgressed the taboo, the delegitimation of antisemitism in the public arena forced Judeophobia to take cover behind favorable views of Jews: Tactical philosemitism in occupied Germany and the early Federal Republic is a case in point.

Chapter 3 documents the mutation of the most preeminent form of non-Jewish defense of Jews since the late nineteenth century. From mere disapproval of prejudice, anti-antisemitism evolved in 1945 into a singular struggle against Jew-hatred. Leftist parties in liberated Western Europe continued to oppose antisemitism in the name of universal anti-racism. But in Britain and France, anti-antisemite pioneers such as the Labour MP Richard Crossman, the Anglican scholar James Parkes, and above all the philosopher Jean-Paul Sartre, reframed antisemitism as a special ill – the problem of "contaminated" non-Jewish society.

---

[72] Ussama Makdisi, "Atonement at the Expense of Another" in *New Fascism Syllabus* (2021), available at: https://newfascismsyllabus.com/opinions/the-catechism-debate/atonement-at-the-expense-of-another/.

[73] Edward Said, *The Question of Palestine* (New York: Viking Press, 1992), xxi.

From London, George Orwell offered the first postwar critique of this view. To single out the Jew as "a species of animals different from ourselves," he wrote against Sartre's typification of the "Jew" and the "antisemite" in Réflexions sur la question juive (1946), could only "make antisemitism more prevalent that it was before." The Parisian thinker's decisive contribution to "philosemitic Europe," however, was to turn the "war on antisemitism" into a politics of pro-Jewish solidarity – a progressive stance also accepting of Zionism until 1967 and beyond.

Chapter 4 situates philosemitism within the discourse of postwar humanism. Despite a burgeoning revolt against the Western conception of "man" in French and anti-colonial philosophy, "everyday humanism" remained omnipresent in early postwar culture. How did this postfascist humanist consensus affect perceptions of the Holocaust, Jewish refugees, and Israel during the first two decades of Western European democracy? Until the late 1950s, the humanist reprobation of Nazi inhumanity universalized the Holocaust as the catastrophe of mankind. Sympathetic observers of the new state of Israel went further. The Jewish homeland, for its admirers, not only rescued but also fulfilled the promise of European humanism.

Chapter 5 reconstructs the tortuous path of "Judeo-Christian Europe" from 1945 to the Vatican's Nostra Aetate declaration of 1965. Contrary to Cold War America, where Judeo-Christian affinities accelerated the mutation of Jews into "white folks," the concept was met with fierce resistance in postwar Europe. The founding fathers of European integration, for their part, did not invoke "Judeo-Christian values" to advocate unity: The phrase only gained popularity with the rise of post-1989 anti-immigrant populism. Yet for a network of Catholic and Protestant churchmen, the tragedy of the Holocaust required epochal rapprochement with Judaism. In French catholic intellectual circles, "Judeo-Christian Europe" also meant the Judeo-Christianization of the Holocaust: an appropriation of the crime which also elevated the Jew to the rank of proximate friend.

Chapter 6 follows "the long 1960s" in Western Europe. Although the decade began with a transnational "Swastika Epidemic," it was a pivotal moment for philosemitism in the postwar period. The passing of the first hate-speech laws, the decline of antisemitism in public opinion polls, and the entry of the Holocaust into public culture reflected this new climate. Students who in 1967–68 imagined themselves as "long-hair ersatz Jews" in West Germany, or chanted "We are all German Jews" in Paris, admittedly distorted the meaning of the Holocaust. In the Federal Republic, the New Left also rebelled against the official philosemitism of the "fascistoid" Bonn Republic or the pro-Israel exultations of the

Springer press. But "the year of the barricades" had long-lasting consequences for European philosemitism. Although one outcome of the student movement in West Germany was ultra-leftism, another one was memory activism. In France, critical interrogations of the Vichy past soon followed the May events: The path to erinnerungskultur [remembrance culture] and devoir de mémoire [duty of memory] began in 1968.

The development of Jewish studies and Holocaust research in academia during the 1970s and 1980s, or fascination with the "Jewish sign" in postmodern philosophy, were other legacies of 1968 in higher education and thought. But as shown in Chapter 7, another "1968" informed liberal visions of cosmopolitan Europe during the last decade of the Cold War. Deprived of the "privilege of working" after the Prague Spring, and established in France since 1975, the Czech émigré novelist Milan Kundera almost single-handedly prompted the nostalgic rediscovery of Mitteleuropa in the West. His influential essay, "The Tragedy of Central Europe" (1983), romanticized Central European Jewish intellectuals as symbols of lost but retrievable supranational Europe. Advocates of the European Union, however, grounded cosmopolitanism on the memory of the Shoah – the birth certificate of a new Europe allegedly triumphant over nationalism, antisemitism, and racism. Competing memories of communist oppression impeded the export of Holocaust remembrance across the former Iron Curtain. Yet post-Communist countries developed their own forms of Shoah memorialization, even if "to control the way in which the Holocaust is remembered, understood, and interpreted." At the start of the twenty-first century, noted Tony Judt, the commemoration of murdered Jews had become "our contemporary European entry ticket."[74]

Islamophobic and anti-immigrant parties in the European Union also found benefits in philosemitism. Postwar Europe had until then resisted Judeo-Christian civilizationalism, but Islamophobia – coupled with Palestinophobia – precipitated this conversion. The antisemites of yesterday, joined by culturally progressive "Enlightenment fundamentalists," yearned for a Jewish–Christian alliance against "Islamo-fascism" and Muslim immigrants. Muscular Israel now symbolized Western resistance against Islam: For illiberal philosemites, the Jewish state showed weak liberal Europe the path to its survival. In Germany, "remembrance culture" hardened into a key symbol of national identity during the long Angela Merkel chancellorship (2005–21). In the Federal Republic, the nationalization of Holocaust

---

[74] Jelena Subotić, *Yellow Star, Red Star: Holocaust Remembrance after Communism* (Ithaca, NY: Cornell University Press, 2019), 206; Tony Judt, *Past Imperfect*, op. cit., 803.

memory translated into permanent alert against "imported" antisemitism, shielded the Holocaust from comparability, affirmed Germany's commitment to Israel's security in the name of "reason of state," and demarcated "redeemed Germans" from dangerous challengers of national memory culture.

Since the start of the twenty-first century, what has been called "reactionary philosemitism" has been subjected to radical critique. "State philosemitism," argued decolonial writers, drives a wedge between good "white" Jews on one hand, and bad racialized groups on the other, Muslims chiefly among them. It is violent when the cult of the Holocaust erases the suffering of others. And it is oppression when the governance of anti-antisemitism polices or stifles pro-Palestinian voices. "Shoot Sartre!," proposed the French-Algerian spokesperson of the Parti des Indigènes de la République Houria Bouteldja. By this she meant the enduring legacy of the philosopher's deceased in 1980: a progressive politics devoid of categorical rejection of Zionism and complicit in the weaponization of antisemitism against minorities of color.[75]

As the enumeration of the book's main topics indicates, "Philosemitic Europe" is a contested concept whose expressions have constantly evolved. The "Jewish question," we are recurrently warned, always "returns" through the form of hostility. Yet after 1945, the "Jewish question," or the problem of Jewish difference and incorporation in European societies, lost its hegemonic antisemitic connotation. It became instead foregrounded in the language of philosemitism writ large. Europe, as suggested in the book's conclusion, may have entered the post-philosemitic age. Yet while counterintuitive or implausible to many, the phrase can nonetheless be rid of quotation marks: Philosemitic Europe is not a love story, but the history of Europe from the Holocaust to the present.

---

[75] Houria Bouteldja, *Whites, Jews, and Us: Towards a Politics of Revolutionary Love* (South Pasadena, CA: Semiotext(e), 2016); Alana Lentin, *Why Race Still Matters* (Cambridge: Polity Press, 2020); Steven Friedman, *Good Jew, Bad Jew: Racism, Anti-Semitism, and the Assault on Meaning* (Johannesburg: Wits University Press, 2023).

2 From Antisemitism to Tactical Philosemitism (1945–1960)

"Do not flaunt your rights; that would be going too far (...) Act so that the good French people of France who hoped to never see you again forget that you exist." In his recommendations to a fictitious young Jewish friend published as a short book in February 1945, the French-Jewish lawyer André Weil-Curiel used irony to describe an inhospitable climate. Your first duty as a Jew, the disillusioned jurist advised his imaginary interlocutor, "was to not draw attention to yourself." French society, he explained, expected discretion from Jewish survivors. Invisibility was the price to pay to "once again live without hurdles in the land of your forefathers": The main obstacle to reintegration was not discrimination but indifference to the fate of the Jews during the German occupation.[1]

Like Weil-Curiel, the French-Jewish novelist Albert Cohen spent the war in London before returning to Paris after the Liberation. His thoughts on the afterlife of antisemitism after Nazism, however, were more somber. "I know that the old wish for 'death to the Jews'," Cohen observed in September 1945, "still awaits me on the walls of all capitals." The future best-selling author of *Belle du Seigneur* [*Her Lover*, 1968] and recipient of the French Academy Prize did not view the defeat of the Third Reich as a Zero Hour of Judeophilia. "Death to the Jews" painted on walls, or graffiti in the Parisian subway mocking the return of Holocaust survivors as "Hitler's revenge," revealed inveterate hatred. Cohen wrote these lines in an essay dedicated to his first encounter with antisemitism during his youth in Marseille, where at the age of ten he endured the mockery of a Jew-baiting peddler and a surrounding crowd. His boyhood dream, he explained, was to one day be able to recount this traumatic experience in writing. The aspiring young novelist imagined a cathartic scenario: His tale of shame would elicit remorse in his former tormentors and forgiveness in the adult writer. Both would then reconcile, "forever kind to each other." The fifty-year-old man

---

[1] André Weil-Curiel, *Règles de savoir-vivre à l'usage d'un jeune Juif de mes amis* [*Good Manners Advice for a Young Jewish Friend*] (Paris: Éditions du Myrthe, 1945).

of letters fulfilled his childhood wish in September 1945 in the pages of *Esprit*. Yet by then he had abandoned hope for common ground. "I know that these men and women," he wrote, "will not cry after reading me and will not like me more than in the past." Despite the return of democracy, Cohen believed, prejudice was here to stay.[2]

Jewish-American observers of liberated Europe shared a similar sentiment. "The world-wide dissemination of the poisonous virus of antisemitism," predicted the historian Koppel Pinson in April 1945, "will remain to plague the victorious United Nations for many years to come."[3] Three years later, however, the European correspondents of the American Jewish Year Book (AJYB) offered encouraging insights. Published under the auspices of the American Jewish Committee, the AJYB monitored the rebuilding of Jewish life after the Holocaust. This yearly report relied on a network of French, British, German, Austrian, Italian, Dutch, and Belgian contributors spread across European capitals. In 1948, they found Jewish communities in formerly German-occupied countries in Western Europe "relatively stabilized. The pre-war political status of the Jews was re-established. Jewish civic rights were restored, and individual and institutional life returned to normal to a considerable extent." The AJYB also praised the economic recovery of Jews, which exceeded "the pace towards readjustment of general populations." The observers of Jewish reconstruction recognized that "anti-Jewish sentiment [...] persisted in all areas and strata of society." Yet three years after the Holocaust, "hardly any overt or organized anti-Semitism has taken root in Western Europe."[4] This assessment did not include Allied-occupied Germany and Austria where public opinion polls revealed high levels of hostility. The AJYB likewise addressed antisemitic tumult in Britain in a separate section. But since 1945 its correspondents described a consistent trend. In Western European countries freed from German occupation, as in victorious Britain, antisemitism lost its public respectability. The French Catholic writer Georges Bernanos acknowledged in his own way this new code of conduct. Himself not immune from anti-Jewish feelings before the war, Bernanos blamed Nazism for giving mild despisal of Jews a bad name.

---

[2] Albert Cohen, "Jour de mes dix ans: Fragments," *Esprit* 114 (1945): 77–87.
[3] Koppel S. Pinson, "Antisemitism in the Post-War World," *Jewish Social Studies* 7, no. 2 (April 1945): 99–118.
[4] *American Jewish Year Book* (hereafter AJYB), Volume 50 (1948–1949), 329. On postwar Jewish reconstruction, see David Weinberg, *Recovering a Voice: West European Jewish Communities after the Holocaust* (Oxford: The Littman Library of Jewish Civilization, 2015).

Hitler, he wrote in May 1944, had forever "dishonored" antisemitism. In June 1945, the British diplomat and man of letters Harold Nicolson expressed a similar sentiment. While he still disliked Jews, he now also "loathed" antisemitism. In Vienna, "The Nazis have ruined everything – including antisemitism" was another iteration of this view. The defeat of the Third Reich, as Albert Cohen noted, was not the defeat of Judeophobia. At a minimum, however, Hitler's fall deprived "moderate" antisemites from the free rein they enjoyed prior to 1945.[5]

Other monitors of Jewish life were justifiably more preoccupied with the situation of Holocaust survivors in East-Central Europe. In Soviet-controlled areas, wrote the Swiss francophone philosopher Denis de Rougemont in September 1946, the "hellish fire" of antisemitism continued to burn "even in provinces unaware of a Jewish problem since the Middle Age."[6] Freshly returned from six years of exile in the United States, the proponent of European federalism was reacting to the recent Kielce pogrom of July 4, 1946, the most publicized outbreak of anti-Jewish violence in Poland since the end of the war. Until the summer of 1946, criminal acts against Jews in the Western Soviet Union, Hungary, and Czechoslovakia had passed unnoticed outside the region. In Poland during the same period, homicides occurred in Białystok, Krakow, Lublin, Łódź, and Rzeszów.[7] But the shocking murder in Kielce of forty-two Holocaust survivors accused of blood libel made international headlines. It also awakened De Rougemont, the author of *Love in the Western World* (1939) and a dreamer of European unity, to the "rage of antisemitism" across the Iron Curtain. The atrocities perpetrated in Kielce, similarly wrote in July 1946 the French Catholic thinker and ambassador to the Vatican Jacques Maritain, unleashed an "unprecedented fury of humiliation and cruelty."[8] From 1945 to 1953, and from destalinization

---

[5] Georges Bernanos, *Le Chemin de la Croix des Dames* (Paris: Gallimard, 1948); Harold Nicolson, *Diaries and Letter, Volume 2, 1939–1945* (London: Collins, 1967), 469; Lisa Silverman, "Rethinking Jews, Antisemitism, and Jewish Difference in Postwar Germany" in Gideon Reuveni and Diana Franklin (eds.), *The Future of the German Jewish Past* (West Lafayette, IN: Purdue University Press, 2021), 135–146.
[6] Albert Cohen, "Jour de mes dix ans: Fragments," op. cit.; Denis de Rougemont, *Rencontres Internationales de Genève, Tome I: L'esprit européen* (Neuchâtel: Les Editions de la Baconnière, 1946), 176.
[7] Péter Apor et al., "Post-World War II Anti-Semitic Pogroms in East and East Central Europe: Collective Violence and Popular Culture," *European Review of History: Revue européenne d'histoire* 26, no. 6 (2019): 913–927; Joanna Tokarska-Bakir, "Postwar Violence against Jews in Central and Eastern Europe" in Kata Bohus et al. (eds.), *Our Courage: Jews in Europe 1945–48* (Oldenbourg: De Gruyter, 2021), 64–81; Jan T. Gross, *Fear: Antisemitism in Poland after Auschwitz: An Essay in Historical Interpretation* (Princeton, NJ: Princeton University Press, 2006).
[8] Maritain cited in Michael R. Marrus, "The Ambassador and the Pope: Pius XII, Jacques Maritain, and the Jews," *Commonweal* 131, no. 18 (October 22, 2004): 14–18.

to the end of the Cold War, the level of both official and grassroot antisemitism in Soviet satellite countries – a topic beyond the purview of this chapter – varied according to national cases. But the steady emigration of many remaining East-Central European Jews turned discrimination or scapegoating across the Iron Curtain into a distinctive "antisemitism without Jews."[9] Anti-Jewish hostility in the Communist bloc until 1989, and as discussed in the last part of this book, heritage philosemitism in East-Central Europe after 1989, shared a common feature: Both took place in the background of Jewish absence.

"Antisemitism without Jews," however, also applied to occupied Germany and Austria where the near entirety of the prewar Jewish population was driven out or murdered during the Third Reich era. The meager trickle of Jewish "remigrants" in both countries during the first postwar years never reestablished sizeable Jewish communities. Approximately 282,000 Jews had emigrated from Nazi Germany by September 1939 and 117,000 from annexed Austria. Only a few thousand returned to their native countries. Allied-occupied Germany, however, hosted close to a quarter million Jewish displaced persons between 1945 and 1948, a number superior to the approximately 100,000 Jewish survivors who transited through Austria at the same time. In both countries, the unexpected presence of Yiddish-speaking survivors encouraged the portrayal of Holocaust refugees as "black-marketeering," "parasitic," or "criminal": In Jewish-populated American occupation zones, antisemitism did not operate "without Jews."

The number of Holocaust survivors in West Germany, of course, dwindled to approximately 30,000 after the departure of most displaced persons (DPs) to Israel and North America by 1950. Yet "secondary antisemitism," the mechanism of guilt repression and self-victimization identified in the early 1950s by the Frankfurt School critical theorists, remained predicated on the fantasy of Jewish omnipresence. The haunting image of the surviving Jew, a group experiment conducted in 1950 and 1951 revealed, impeded the repression of the Nazi past by reminding Germans of their crimes. Through psychological inversion, observed Theodor Adorno, Germans turned the victims of the Holocaust into persecutors of an innocent nation. "It was not the SS people who were brutal, who tortured the Jews," Adorno remarked, "but the Jews who supposedly forced the Germans to acknowledge the crimes of the SS." Despite the murder or emigration of most German Jews, subliminal anger directed at "Jewish power" turned Jewish absence into a

---

[9] The Hungarian émigré Paul Lendvai popularized the term in 1971: *Anti-Semitism Without Jews: Communist Eastern Europe* (New York: Doubleday, 1971).

tormenting presence.[10] "Can something be perceived to be present if it is no longer there?," wondered the German Jewish philosopher Ernst Bloch in 1963. "Doubtless," he answered, "the Jews are perceived in this way, even though the country has been nearly emptied of them."[11] Similar guilt-defensiveness was apparent in antagonistic comments about Jewish returnees in Austria: opportunists who abandoned their country after 1938 and lived in luxury abroad while the nation suffered.[12]

"Antisemitism without Jews" in East-Central Europe and "secondary antisemitism" in West Germany or Austria, however, were not the only mutated forms of Judeophobia after 1945. In the Western half of the continent, "antisemitism without antisemites" best describes the transformation of anti-Jewish animus in the wake of the Holocaust.[13] Awareness of Nazi atrocities against the Jews, as André Weil-Curiel and Albert Cohen noticed in liberated France, did not eliminate resentment. But after the figure of the Jewish enemy took center stage in Nazi-ruled Europe, the revival of democracy on the Western part of the continent was premised on the prohibition of fascist or Nazi ideology. In what became Marshall Plan Europe, a moratorium on public expressions of antisemitism demarcated the old from the new: For the first time in European history, overt animus against Jews became off-limits in public discourse. Antisemitism, in the words of the French philosopher Maurice Blanchot, became then "bereft of antisemitism": a sentiment no longer identifiable in political programs and ideologies but private, latent, or unconscious.[14] The following overview of "antisemitism without antisemites" in Western Europe from 1945 to 1960 reveals the simultaneous return of prejudice and the delegitimation of antisemitism in politics and culture. Loss of public respectability, however, forced the redirection of negative perceptions of Jews toward positive representations: For non-Jews with a lingering Jewish problem, philosemitism now offered an alternative channel of expression.

---

[10] Lars Rensmann, "Guilt, Resentment and Post-Holocaust Democracy: The Frankfurt School's Analysis of 'Secondary Antisemitism' in the *Group Experiment* and Beyond," *Antisemitism Studies* 1, no. 1 (Spring 2017): 4–37.
[11] Ernst Bloch, "Die sogenannte Judenfrage" [The So-Called Jewish Question, 1963] in *Literary Essays* (Stanford, CA: Stanford University Press, 1998), 488–491.
[12] Elizabeth Anthony, *The Compromise of Return: Viennese Jews after the Holocaust* (Detroit: Wayne State University Press, 2021), 157–158.
[13] On the origins and uses of this phrase, see Bernd Marin, *Antisemitismus ohne Antisemiten: Studien zur Vorurteildynamik* (Vienna: Campus Verlag, 2000); Keith Kahn-Harris, *Strange Hate: Antisemitism, Racism, and the Limits of Diversity* (London: Repeater, 2019), 55–63.
[14] Cited in Emmanuel Levinas, *Du Sacré au Saint* (Paris: Les Editions de Minuit, 1977), 48–49.

Resurgence and Disrepute: Antisemitism in Republican France

"I do not stand with those who deny the existence of antisemitism in France," the Catholic novelist and essayist François Mauriac wrote in October 1945. "The mail I receive at Le Figaro," he added, "is a daily proof of its vigor."[15] Omnipresent in collaborationist newspapers under the Vichy regime, antisemitic propaganda finally ceased at the Liberation.[16] Yet Mauriac still saw around him large pockets of hostility. French Jews persecuted under Vichy, however, swiftly recovered their status of citizen. The road to civic reintegration began in colonial Algeria. On October 20, 1943, the French National Liberation Committee based in Algiers reinstated the Crémieux Decree abrogated in October 1940. Although long in the making, this decision allowed 140,000 native Algerian Jews to recuperate French citizenship. In metropolitan France, the Ordinance of August 9, 1944 reestablished the civil rights of 225,000 Jews who survived the occupation in hiding or returned eight months later from death camps (only 3 percent of the 76,000 French and foreign Jews deported from March 1942 to August 1944 came back). The program of national reconstruction drafted by the leaders of the resistance in March 1944 had promised "absolute equality of all citizens before the law." Like other blueprints for the restoration of the republic, it did not single out Jews from other victims. The August 9 Ordinance was a noticeable exception. All acts "that establish or apply any discrimination whatsoever founded on the quality of *being Jewish*" were abolished even before the full liberation of the French territory.[17] The restoration of Republican legality also entailed affirmative measures to protect Jews against defamation. Reinstated on August 9, 1944, the Marchandeau Law issued in April 1939 but repealed by the Vichy regime prohibited "insult against a group of persons belonging by their origin to a particular race or religion." Jews were not explicitly named, but the law's original purpose was to defend them against antisemitic libel. After the German occupation, public offenders of Jews could still take cover behind the 1881 law on the freedom of the press. The reinstatement of the Marchandeau Law

---

[15] Cited in Anne Grynberg, "Des signes de résurgence de l'antisémitisme dans la France de l'après-guerre" in Anne Grynberg and Catherine Nicault (eds.), *Survivre à la Shoah. Exemples français. Les Cahiers de la Shoah 5* (Paris: Les Belles Lettres, 2001), 171–224.
[16] François Azouvi, "La délégitimation de l'antisémitisme au lendemain de la Seconde Guerre mondiale" *Archives Juives* 2, no. 49 (2016): 15–25.
[17] Patrick Weil, "The Return of Jews in the Nationality or in the Territory of France (1943–1973)" in David Bankier (ed.), *The Jews Are Coming Back*, op. cit., 58–71; Maud S. Mandel, *In the Aftermath of Genocide: Armenians and Jews in Twentieth-Century France* (Durham: Duke University Press, 2003), 52–55.

nonetheless signaled that the age of permissive antisemitic incitement had come to a close.[18]

Despite the legal safeguards enacted after the Liberation, however, anti-Jewish agitation flared up among inhabitants of Jewish-owned apartments confiscated during the war. In Paris alone, 25,000 Jewish families (approximately 100,000 people) had been evicted from their places of residence. The Ordinance of November 14, 1944, opened a legal avenue for the restitution of Jewish flats or businesses placed under the trusteeship of non-Jewish administrators. But until a more favorable law was passed on April 21, 1945, Jewish claimants were not entitled to recover apartments occupied by war widows and in certain cases had to repay the full amount of the purchase price to the new possessors. They were also met with the resistance of new tenants and owners, among them war-displaced French refugees accommodated in empty Jewish apartments. It took for instance a year and a half of legal wrangling for the family of the future lawyer and Holocaust historian Serge Klarsfeld to recover its apartment on the western outskirts of Paris. "Our predecessors," recalled Klarsfeld, "had dirtied the walls and teared the wallpaper to make sure that we would not benefit from their investment."[19]

Organized in a dozen of associations, defenders of "property rights" couched their grievances in a language unadulterated by the demise of the Vichy regime. "What an injustice to expel a Frenchman in favor of a foreign Jew who wants to reclaim his pre-war lodging," exclaimed one of them.[20] Returning Jews, wrote the Jewish writer of Russian origin Nina Gourfinkel, reclaimed "their homes, their stores, and even, what impudence, their accounts. Then the provisional owners felt a bitter regret: 'Why didn't they all perish in the ovens!'"[21] Gourfinkel failed to add that in virtually all cases, tribunals vindicated Jewish claimants. But the short-lived anti-restitution movement exemplified the persistence of prejudice within parts of the French population. A survey conducted in 1946 showed that for 37 percent of respondents, Jews could not be considered "Frenchmen like all others."[22]

---

[18] Emmanuel Debono, *Le racisme dans le prétoire: Antisémitisme, racisme et xénophobie devant la justice* (Paris: Presses Universitaires de France, 2019), 31–64.
[19] Beate and Serge Klarsfeld, *Mémoires* (Paris: Flammarion, 2015), 82.
[20] Shannon L. Fogg, *Stealing Home: Looting, Restitution, and Reconstructing Jewish Lives in France, 1942–1947* (Oxford: Oxford University Press, 2017), 68; Leora Auslander, "Coming Home? Jews in Postwar Paris," *Journal of Contemporary History* 40, no. 2 (2005): 237–259.
[21] Gourfinkel cited in Maud S. Mandel, *In the Aftermath of Genocide: Armenians and Jews in Twentieth-Century France* (Durham: Duke University Press, 2003), 58.
[22] Florent Le Blot, "La solitude des juifs spoliés confrontés au problème de la récupération de leurs biens après l'Occupation," *Archives Juives* 2, no. 49 (2016): 26–41.

In 1946, the AJYB correspondent in Paris nonetheless commended France for "the absence of antisemitism as a political force."[23] Far-right ideology, however, slowly reemerged on the margins of mainstream politics. Although temporarily blacklisted or imprisoned, veterans of the wartime "antisemitism of the pen" all resumed literary or journalistic activities in the early 1950s.[24] Other fascist sympathizers during the war, such as the literary critique Maurice Bardèche, mutated into Holocaust deniers. "We have all become Jews," lamented Brasillach's brother-in-law in his pamphlet *Nuremberg ou la terre promise* [*Nuremberg or the Promised Land*] published in 1948. Foreboding a theme dear to future Holocaust revisionists, Bardèche denounced a Jewish monopoly on the memory of World War II.[25] The former pro-German collaborationist was condemned in March 1952 to a year of incarceration for "apology of war crimes" but only spent two weeks in prison. Wartime enforcers of antisemitic policies, from higher echelon officials to police officers, were more forcefully prosecuted. Although low-level bureaucrats of the Commissariat-General on Jewish Affairs generally escaped justice, the purge of collaborators in France did not bypass the persecutors of Jews. Yet leniency rapidly mitigated retribution. Xavier Vallat, the head of the Commissariat from March 1941 to May 1942, was condemned to ten years in prison in 1947, released in 1949, authorized to sign books for his supporters in 1953, and amnestied in 1954.[26] French Jews, from then on, had to live in a society in which one of the key enablers of the Final Solution in the country roamed free.

The reappearance of Vichy-era antisemites did not however impede the rebuilding of the French-Jewish community. Approximately 300,000 Jews, 60 percent of them still of Eastern European origin, securely lived in France at the start of the 1950s. The revival and development of cultural and religious institutions progressed apace.[27] For the intellectual review *Esprit*, the time had arrived to declare antisemitism a foreign phenomenon. The essayist Jean-Marie Domenach saw

[23] *AJYB*, Volume 48 (1946–1947), 291; Volume 49 (1947–1948), 324.
[24] Joseph Algazy, *La tentation néo-fasciste en France 1944–1965* (Paris: Fayard, 1984), 66–67. See also Richard C. Vinen, "The End of an Ideology? Right-Wing Antisemitism in France, 1944–1970," *The Historical Journal* 37, no. 2 (June 1994): 365–388.
[25] Valérie Igounnet, "Les premières voix françaises du négationisme" (1945–1953), *Archives Juives* 2, no. 49 (2016): 56–68.
[26] Laurent Joly, *Xavier Vallat (1891–1972): Du nationalisme chrétien à l'antisémitisme d'Etat* (Paris: Grasset, 2001).
[27] Laura Hobson Faure, *"A Jewish Marshall Plan": The American Jewish Presence in Post-Holocaust France* (Bloomington, IN: Indiana University Press, 2022); David Weinberg, "'The Revival of French Jewry' in Post-Holocaust France: Challenges and Opportunities" in Seán Hand and Steven T. Katz (eds.), *Post-Holocaust France and the Jews* (New York: New York University Press, 2015), 26–37.

Jew-hatred in full display in New York during the trial of Julius and Ethel Rosenberg in March 1951, a *cause célèbre* equated in France to the Dreyfus Affair. While in the United States cautious Jewish-American leaders refused to "inject the false issue of antisemitism" in public discussions of the Rosenberg trial, the couple executed in 1953 was portrayed by its French defenders as "scapegoats for American antisemitism."[28] Hate of Jews, added Domenach, simultaneously flared in Prague with the show trial in November 1952 of the Jewish-born Rudolf Slánský and thirteen other defendants (ten of them also Jewish) accused of conspiracy against the state. Obscenities still appeared in the far-right press, but the fertile ground of antisemitism was now McCarthyite America and Stalinist Eastern Europe, "where Jews are simultaneously accused of the same crime."[29] Searching for a "third way" between Atlanticism and Communism, Cold War intellectuals such as Domenach viewed the two superpowers as equal persecutors of Jewish citizens. Paling in comparison, French antisemitism only amounted to a shameful but largely contained illness.

The rabbi and archivist Isaac Schneerson, founder in 1943 of the clandestine Center of Contemporary Jewish Documentation, did not share this optimism. In 1947, Schneerson coordinated in Paris the first meeting of Jewish historical commissions from eleven different European countries. Like his colleagues at the time, Schneerson was confident that antisemitism would no longer affect Jewish life in Western Europe. The pioneering chronicler of the Final Solution changed his mind in 1955. "Ten years after the splendid victory," he observed, "antisemitism, under its neo-Nazi guise or otherwise, has reappeared in public life."[30] The Institute of Jewish Affairs of the World Jewish Congress (WJC) concurred. "The period of relative fear, when the anti-Semites did not dare to profess themselves such, is now over and wide liberty prevails in this respect," reported its Parisian representative in 1956."[31] Pierre Poujade, the leader of a shopkeeper, artisan, and lower-middle class protest movement, was in the mid 1950s the most vocal transgressor of the antisemitic taboo in France. Ten years on from the Vichy regime, the populist demagogue publicly challenged

---

[28] Lori Clune, *Executing the Rosenbergs: Death and Diplomacy in a Cold War World* (Oxford: Oxford University Press, 2016), 47.
[29] Jean-Marie Domenach, "L'antisémitisme reste logique," *Esprit*, January 1953, 148–149.
[30] Isaac Schneerson, "Avant-propos" in J. M. Machover (ed.), *Dix ans après la chute de Hitler* (Paris: Editions du Centre, 1957), 7–9.
[31] *European Jewry Ten Years after the War: An Account of the Development and Present Status of the Decimated Jewish Communities of Europe* (New York: Institute of Jewish Affairs, 1956), 216.

Pierre Mendès-France's right to lead the French nation because of his Jewish origins. Predicated on anti-taxation, anti-urbanization, and antimodernization, Poujadism was unevenly contaminated by antisemitism. This ephemeral electoral rebellion nonetheless revealed how Judeophobic rhetoric easily crept into the politics of resentment. Public expressions of antisemitism, however, remained both rare and off-limit. For the Jewish intellectual Wladimir Rabi, author in 1962 of the first comprehensive study of the postwar Jewish community, the problem of antisemitism in France was not its "sporadic manifestations" but its dormant "virtualities."[32]

"Jew-Consciousness": Belgium

In Belgium, where half of the 65,000 Jews who resided in the country in 1940 perished in Auschwitz and other camps, all the anti-Jewish measures in force during the occupation were abrogated after Allied troops liberated Brussels on September 4, 1944. The AJYB praised Belgian authorities for their efforts to "abolish antisemitism from the country" but added a note of caution: "The general population in Belgium, as in all other countries of Nazi occupation, has not been immune from infection with the anti-Semitic virus, which is now showing its effect even after liberation."[33] Progress was nonetheless noticed. Antisemitism, reported the AJYB in 1947, was "despised by the population at large." Yet anti-Jewish statements remained traceable in the press "under the cover of xenophobia (...) and the "situation has not progressed favorably during the past year." Régine Orfinger-Karlin, the AJYB correspondent in Brussels, warned that "Jew-consciousness, practically unknown before the war, now exists."[34] Of particular concern was "xenophobia (...) heightened by the influx of foreign Jews on Belgian soil, since the recent immigrants had to compete with returning Belgian war veterans for jobs and business opportunities."[35]

Antisemitism in Belgium intersected with the "alien problem" revived after the war with the influx of Eastern European refugees and displaced persons from Germany. Like the vast majority of the approximately 25,000 Jews deported from Belgium, most of the 30,000 Jewish survivors who came out of hiding as well as the approximately 1,300

---
[32] Wladimir Rabi, *Anatomie du judaïsme français* (Paris: Les Editions de Minuit, 1962), 208.
[33] *AJYB*, Volume 47 (1945–1946), 381–382.
[34] *AJYB*, Volume 49 (1947–1948), 329.
[35] *AJYB*, Volume 50 (1949–1949), 330.

returnees from extermination camps were foreign nationals of predominantly Polish and German origin: Less than 5 percent of the Jews present in Belgium at the end of the war were citizens of the country. Jewish refugees trickling in from Germany added to this tally. In 1947, government figures placed at 4,500 the number of such "transients." As in the 1930s, "aliens" and "Jews" remained interchangeable in anti-foreigner rhetoric. On April 30, 1946, the Flemish social Christian newspaper *Het Volk* hoped that "one can go through with a wide broom" to rid Belgium of black-marketeering "aliens," a euphemism for Jews. Others blamed "aliens, especially the Jews" for their "brutal" capitalist exploitation of the Belgian middle class.[36]

Prejudice also played a part in the exclusion of Holocaust survivors from the categories of war victims entitled to official status and material compensation. The majority of surviving Jews in Belgium (or their spouses or children if deceased) did not receive the status of "political prisoners" defined, in a law enacted in March 1947, as persons arrested for acts or resistance. Jewish survivors unable to show proof of anti-German activities prior to their deportation were consequently denied pensions. The inferior position of Jews in the hierarchy of patriotic martyrs was already evident in the debates preceding the passing of the law. Arrested during the war by the Gestapo and imprisoned for three years, the Resistance leader Camille Joset balked at comparison between underground fighters and Jewish victims of Nazism. "You don't have to be anti-semitic to be troubled if someone wrongly suspects you of having been arrested as a Jew," Joset declared in April 1946. Members of the powerful Christian Social Party likewise belittled the suffering of "racial deportees" not involved in "patriotic activities." As one of them contended, Jews only arrested for "racial motives and others interned for different reasons, such as sellers on the black market" were not equals to heroic "political prisoners."[37]

In France, a law passed on August 6, 1948 separated the *déportés résistants* – active resistance fighters sent to concentration camps – from "political deportees and internees," a category including the victims of the Final Solution. Until 1970, French resisters deported to Buchenwald, Dachau or Ravensbrück received higher pensions than the rare Jews who came back from Auschwitz. But in the French Republic, Jewish survivors were nonetheless incorporated into the highly symbolic community of

---

[36] Frank Caesteker, "The Reintegration of Belgian Survivors into Belgian Society, 1943–1947" in Bankier (ed.), *The Jews Are Coming Back*, op. cit., 72–107.
[37] Pieter Lagrou, *The Legacy of Nazi Occupation: Patriotic Memory and National Recovery in Western Europe, 1945–1965* (Cambridge: Cambridge University Press, 1999), 220–223.

déportés. In Belgium, Holocaust victims unable to secure the status of "political prisoner" after the war only obtained official recognition, if still alive, at the start of the twenty-first century.[38]

Discrimination in compensation was not, however, indicative of pervasive antisemitism. At the start of the 1950s, the approximately 40,000 Jews residing in Belgium and divided between Brussels and Antwerp experienced difficulties in acquiring citizenship. Yet according to the AJYB, "there was scarcely any manifestation of anti-Semitism" in the country. Derogatory cartoons occasionally appeared in Flemish periodicals but the Orthodox community of Antwerp resumed its activities in the diamond trade without hostility. "In the main," reported Régine Orfinger-Karlin in 1952, "the Jewish community lives as a well-respected neighbor of the very large Catholic community."[39] The WJC reached a similar conclusion. "Antisemitism in Belgium," confirmed the New York–based organization in 1955, "manifests itself sporadically and in mild forms."[40] The position of the Jewish population in Belgium, estimated at about 40,000, was "good and improving," noted the AJYB in 1957.

Exiled from Vienna to Brussels, the Auschwitz survivor Jean Améry was not troubled by antisemitism in his host country when after twenty years of silence he reflected on his wartime ordeal. "My neighbor greets me in a friendly fashion, Bonjour Monsieur; I doff my hat, Bonjour Madame," Améry wrote in *At the Mind's Limit*, published in 1964. "But Madame and Monsieur," he added, "are separated by interstellar distances." The problem of the "Catastrophe Jew," as Améry defined himself, was not hostility from non-Jews but an unbridgeable gap between him and the surrounding society. A Jew without "positive determinants," Améry resolved himself to "get along without trust in the world."[41] The marginalization of antisemitism in postwar democracy, he intimated, offered meager alleviation of trauma.

The Dutch Paradox

In the liberated Netherlands, the number of Jews declined from 140,000 on the eve of the war to approximately 30,000 in 1945. Out

---

[38] Maxime Steinberg and Joël Kotek, "Turning a Blind Eye: Aspects of Holocaust Memory in Belgium" in Roni Stauber (ed.), *Collaboration with the Nazis: Public Discourse after the Holocaust* (London: Routledge, 2011), 91–109; see also *La Belgique docile. Les autorités belges et la persécution des juifs en Belgique pendant la Seconde Guerre Mondiale* (Bruxelles: Centre d'études et de documentation Guerre et Sociétés Contemporaines, 2007), 1025–1026.
[39] *American Jewish Yearbook*, Volume 53 (1952), 289–290; Volume 54 (1953), 267.
[40] *European Jewry Ten Years after the War*, op. cit., 249.
[41] Jean Améry, *At the Mind's Limit* (Bloomington, IN: Indiana University Press, 1980), 94–95.

of the 104,000 Jewish deportees to Auschwitz, Sobibor, and Bergen Belsen, only 5,200 survived.[42] The tragedy of Dutch Jews did not however elicit visible empathy in the months following the liberation. In May 1945, returning Holocaust survivors received a colder reception than forced laborers liberated earlier from Germany. Suspicious Dutch citizens alleged that Jews had fled the country to spend the war in safety. Others claimed that stashes of hidden bank notes awaited them upon their return. In tramways or shops, Jews were occasionally told that "they have forgotten to gas you." In Amsterdam, some survivors found their homes looted or boarded up and forced to spend months in rudimentary centers.[43] All anti-Jewish measures were annulled in September 1944, and in May 1945 the first synagogue service held in Amsterdam attracted many non-Jews who came to sympathize with the aggrieved Jewish community. Yet in the summer of 1945, the situation was worrying enough to warrant the creation of a study group, composed of intellectuals from Amsterdam, on "antisemitic attitudes in the Netherlands." The AJYB reported unprecedented animosity in the wake of the German surrender: "For the first time in the history of the Netherlands, open attacks against Jews appeared in the press, indicating that anti-Semitism has become prevalent among some sections of the population."[44]

These hostile attitudes did not however translate into political agitation. There was "nothing in the way of organized antisemitism and no trace of antisemitism in government policy" in a country traditionally tolerant toward its Jewish population.[45] Abel Hertzberg, a Jewish lawyer and survivor of Bergen Belsen, found antisemitism "very widespread" in 1945 but took comfort in the rise of "very strong countercurrents."[46] Nonetheless, the popularity of stereotypes such as Jewish "ungratefulness" revealed the fragile position of Jews in Dutch society. In July 1945, the resistance newspaper *De Patriot* enjoined Jews to "refrain from excessive behavior" and "think constantly how grateful they ought to be." They had indeed the "noble, principled and consistently Christian

---

[42] Ido de Haan, "The Holocaust in the Netherlands: National Differences in a Western European Context," *Ab Imperio*, no. 2 (2019): 83–93.
[43] Dieke Honduis, *Return: Holocaust Survivors and Dutch Antisemitism* (Westport, CT: Praeger, 2003); Evelien Gans, "The 'Jew' as Dubious Victim" in Evelien Gans and Remco Emsel (eds.), *The Holocaust, Israel and 'the Jew': Histories of Antisemitism in Postwar Dutch Society* (Amsterdam: Amsterdam University Press, 2016), 61–81.
[44] *American Jewish Yearbook*, Volume 47 (1945–1946), 383.
[45] Ibid., Volume 48 (1946–1947), 296.
[46] Conny Kristel, "Revolution and Reconstruction: Dutch Jewry after the Holocaust" in *The Jews Are Coming Back*, op. cit., 136–147, here p. 139.

feeling of the Dutch population to thank for."[47] Many Dutch citizens helped 28, 000 hunted Jews find places of hiding and others looked after their possessions. But approximately 8,000 Jews were victims of denunciations and passive forms of antisemitism hindered greater rescue. Few in the Netherlands questioned the myth of a Dutch nation united against German anti-Jewish operations. In 1945, the social-democrat Hilda Verwey-Jonker was a rare politician claiming that the population behaved "utterly miserably" toward their persecuted countrymen.[48] The AJYB, for its part, relativized the extent of Dutch rescue efforts. "While many Netherlands citizens of other faiths showed great solidarity with their Jewish compatriots," reported the American publication in 1946, "this did not occur on as large a scale as in France and Belgium."[49]

Amsterdam Jews, however, dutifully met the challenge of "gratefulness." Despite financial hardships, the Jewish community raised funds for a Monument of Jewish Gratitude inaugurated in 1950. The memorial paid tribute to Dutch "love," "protection," and "resistance" during the Holocaust. This polite manifestation of Jewish solidarity with Dutch suffering ("Mourning with You" is one of the monument's inscriptions) did not signify harmonious reintegration: Sharpened by the war, a chasm separated the small Jewish community from the rest of society. Between 1945 and 1953, approximately 5,000 Dutch Jews emigrated to Western countries or Israel. The "Dutch paradox," a phrase coined at the start of the 1950s, connoted the inability of a resurgent Jewish community to envision a future in the Netherlands.[50] Unequal in their quest for restitution and official recognition, Jews experienced isolation at a time of greater national unity. The weakening "pillarization" of Dutch society, which until the war divided Catholic, Protestant, and working-class socialist constituencies, allowed for greater national homogeneity: The "spirit of resistance" now captured the essence of the Dutch nation. Unification under the banner of anti-German heroism, however, ostracized "passive" Holocaust victims from national remembrance until the beginning of the 1960s.[51]

[47] *De Patriot*, July 2, 1945, cited in Deborah Dwork and Robert-Jan van Pekt, "The Netherlands" in David Wyman (ed.), *The World Reacts to the Holocaust* (Baltimore, MD: The Johns Hopkins University Press, 1996), 45–80.
[48] Evelien Gans, "The 'Jew' as Dubious Victim," op. cit., 68; Ido de Haan, "The Memory of the Rescue of Jews in the Netherlands, 1945 to the Present" in Natalia Aleksiun et al. (eds.), *The Rescue Turn* (Detroit, MI: Wayne University Press, 2024), 21–64.
[49] *American Jewish Yearbook*, Volume 48 (1946–1947), 296.
[50] Philo Bregstein, "Le paradoxe néerlandais" in Léon Poliakov (ed.), *Histoire de l'antisémitisme 1945–1993* (Paris: Seuil, 1994), 97–120; Kristel, *Revolution and Reconstruction*, op. cit., 136.
[51] Ido de Haan, "The Postwar Jewish Community and the Memory of the Persecution in the Netherlands" in Chaya Brasz and Yosef Kaplan (eds.), *Dutch Jews as Perceived by Themselves and Others* (Leiden: Brill, 2000), 404–435; Evelien Gans, "Disowning

In 1947, the publication of Anne Frank's diary passed relatively unnoticed until its international success propagated the image of Dutch neighborly help during the Holocaust. The young girl's journal, perceived by its first readers as a shocking violation of childhood innocence, did not however promote interest in the situation of Holocaust survivors in the Netherlands. But its growing popularity coincided with a steady decline of antisemitism in the Netherlands. From 1950 to 1955, the AJYB correspondent in Amsterdam struggled to find "anything that could be described as outright discrimination or anti-Semitism." In 1955, the WJC offered a more balanced assessment: "The Dutch people now became Jew-conscious. Though unable to speak of concrete antisemitism, one can say that the Jew as such is more conspicuous than in the past."[52] Awareness of Jewish difference, however, also paved the way for new attitudes at the start of the 1960s. As Dutch society embraced cultural progressivism, attention to psychic trauma consecrated Jewish victimhood as a yardstick for human suffering and injustice.[53] This outcome, foreboding greater sympathy for Jews and the state of Israel in the 1960s and 1970s, was not easily predictable during the first postwar decade, when the wedge drawn between Jews and Dutch society during the German occupation still separated both sides.

Italy: "Persecution of Love"?

Approximately 47,000 Jews lived in Italy before Mussolini's regime enacted its first racial law on November 17, 1938. An estimated 30,000 Jews were still in the country after its complete liberation from German occupation in April 1945; around 8,000 Jews perished in Auschwitz and other camps after the German invaders began deportations in the fall of 1943. Less than 1,000 Jewish survivors returned home. Only completed in 1947, the annulment process of the 1938 racial laws was frustratingly long. But at the Liberation, hostile acts against Jews were exceptionally rare.[54] "Anti-Semitism has not taken root among the Italian

---

Responsibility: The Stereotype of the Passive Jew as a Legitimizing Factor in Dutch Remembrance of the Shoah" in David J. Wertheim (ed.), *The Jew as Legitimation: Jewish-Gentile Relations beyond Antisemitism and Philosemitism* (Cham: Palgrave Macmillan, 2017), 173–193.

[52] *European Jewry Ten Years after the War*, op. cit., 222.

[53] Ido de Haan, "Prominent Jews: The Absence and Presence of Jews in Postwar Netherlands," *Historein* 18, no. 2 (2019), available at: https://doi.org/10.12681/historein.14636.

[54] Guri Schwartz, *After Mussolini: Jewish Life in Post-Fascist Italy* (London: Vallentine Mitchell, 2012), 3–13; Ilaria Pavan, *Persecution, Indifference and Amnesia: The Restitution of Jewish Rights in Postwar Italy* (Jerusalem: Yad Vashem, 2006).

people," reported the AJYB in 1945.⁵⁵ The approximately 50,000 Jewish displaced persons who entered Italy on their way to Palestine between 1945 and 1948 were generally met with sympathy, even if impoverished Sicilians envied "the abundance of luxury goods like American cigarettes and chocolate" availed to Jewish refugees.⁵⁶ Antisemitism, however, did not entirely fade from view. German-language newspapers in the Alto Adige, formerly South Tyrol, indulged in anti-Jewish attacks. In Rome, a neofascist mob rioted in the Jewish quarter on April 16, 1948.⁵⁷ But antagonism toward Jews also expressed itself in milder forms. The experiences of Jewish university professors banned in 1938 and reemployed after the war is a case in point. Some resentful academics, miraculously redeemed from prior allegiance to Fascism, attached the stigma of "usurpers" to reappointed Jewish scholars.⁵⁸

For the Jewish litterateur Giacomo Denebedetti, however, the most worrying issue at the time of liberation was not antisemitism but a counterintuitive "persecution of love." While he lauded the sympathy shown to surviving Jews in the territories freed of German occupation, Debenedetti feared that these "generous attempts to recompense Jews" for their suffering might once again serve to distinguish "the Jewish race from the human race." It would be better, he added, if sympathy was "diluted into an enduring, continuous solidarity, capable of steadily averting evil."⁵⁹ Debenedetti's contempt for this "surplus of love" epitomized the embrace of the resistance ethos among postwar Jewish elites. The participation of many Italian Jews in the anti-German struggle facilitated the absorption of the Jewish experience within the national antifascist struggle. For Jews especially, the *Resistanza* carried a promise of democratic and social renewal after seven years of exclusion and persecution. Even Jewish intellectuals who did not take part in armed resistance, such as the rabbi and journalist Dante Lattes, dutifully integrated the Holocaust into an acceptable antifascist narrative.

---

[55] *AJYB*, Volume 1947 (1945–46), 389.
[56] Cinzia Villani, "We Have Crossed Many Borders": Arrivals, Presence and Perceptions of Jewish Displaced Persons in Italy (1945–1948)" in Sabine Aschauer-Smolik and Mario Steidel (eds.), *Tamid Kadima – Immer vorwärts: Der jüdische Exodus aus Europa 1945–1948* (Innsbruck: StudienVerlag, 2010), 261–281.
[57] *AJYB*, Volume 50 (1948–1949), 351.
[58] Giorgio Israel, "Redeemed Intellectuals and Italian Jews," *Telos* 139 (Summer 2007): 85–108; Roberto Finzi, "Da perseguitati a "usurpatori": per una storia della reintegrazione dei docent ebrei nelle università italiane" in Michele Sarfatti (ed.), *Il ritorno alla vita: vicende e diritti degli ebrei in Italia dopo la seconda guerra mondiale* (Milan: Fondazione Centro di Documentazione Ebraica Contemporanea, 1998), 95–114.
[59] Giacomo Debenedetti, *October 16, 1943: Eight Jews* (1944) (Notre Dame, IN: University of Notre Dame Press, 2001), 79–87.

"Six million dead," claimed Lattes, were the Jewish "contribution to the struggle against fascism."[60]

For the Italian Communist Party and the Christian Democracy, however, the Resistance had more instrumental purposes. Like in France, Communists claimed ownership of the anti-German armed struggle to mobilize a wide working-class electorate. Christian Democrats, for their part, turned the legacy of the Resistance into a symbol of postwar Italian unity. Neither party was interested in confronting the deep impregnation of Italian society with fascism. The refusal of Italian political elites to confront the country's recent past was made evident on June 22, 1946, with the passing of an amnesty law covering most fascist crimes. The "second risorgimento" hoped for by Italian Jews dissolved into a "good Italian" myth according to which the nation resisted fascism in spirit if not in deeds, despite more than two decades of mass support for Mussolini.[61] The Liberal philosopher Benedetto Croce had already set the tone in October 1944: Fascism was a "moral and intellectual illness" yet a parenthesis in the healthy course of Italian history. Although tens of thousands of Italians assisted the German occupation apparatus in roundups and expropriation, the murder of approximately 8,000 Italian Jews could safely be blamed on German actions.[62] Italian Jews supported this interpretation. In 1946, the Jewish journalist and lawyer Eucardio Momigliano called the Fascist regime "tragic and grotesque" but lauded the Italian character allegedly impervious to Jew-hatred.[63]

The eagerness of the Italian Jewish community to find its place in the self-proclaimed antifascist nation did not prevent the occasional airing of derogatory views on Holocaust survivors. A former partisan and future president of the Italian senate, the Liberal party member

---

[60] Cited in Manuela Consonni, *L'eclisse dell'antifascismo: Resistenza, questione ebraica e cultura politica in Italia dal 1943 al 1989* (Bari: Gius. Laterza & Figli, 2015), 22. On Italian Jews and antifascism, see Luca La Rovere, "Fascismo, "questione ebraica" e antisemitismo nella stampa socialista. Un'analisi di lungo period: 1922–1967" in Mario Toscano (ed.), *Ebraismo, sionismo e antisemitismo nella stampa socialista italiana* (Venice: Marsilio Editori, 2015), 95–161.

[61] Claudio Fogu, "Italiani brava gente: The Legacy of Fascist Historical Culture on Italian Politics of Memory," in Richard Ned Lebow, Wulf Kansteiner, and Claudio Fogu (eds.), *The Politics of Memory in Postwar Europe* (Durham: Duke University Press, 2006), 147–176; Guri Schwarz, "On Myth Making and Nation Building: The Genesis of the 'Myth of the Good Italian' 1943–1947," *Telos* 164 (Fall 2013): 11–43.

[62] For a discussion of Italian complicity in the Holocaust, see Simon Levis Sullam, *The Italian Executioners: The Genocide of the Jews in Italy* (Princeton, NJ: Princeton University Press, 2018).

[63] Robert S. C. Gordon, *The Holocaust in Italian Culture, 1944–2010* (Stanford, CA: Stanford University Press, 2012), 50.

Cesare Merzagora, drew in December 1945 and January 1946 a long list of warnings to Jewish survivors repatriated from German extermination camps. "Jews who return should control themselves. Italy has changed in many ways," urged Merzagora. The inhumane treatment inflicted to Jews provoked "a general sense of solidarity with the persecuted, but it did not eliminate all the questions concerning the Jews themselves."[64] Benedetto Croce encouraged Jews to refuse particular "preferences and privileges." The Neapolitan thinker, who in 1938 refused to sign fascist forms attesting to his non-Jewish ancestry, recalled "shivering with horror" while Jews in Italy were persecuted. But it was now time for them to abandon the "surviving traits of a barbaric and primitive religiosity." Hitler, by "making his own" the Jewish idea of the chosen people, had fully demonstrated its dangerous potential.[65]

Catholic publications, for their part, did not enforce a strict moratorium on anti-Judaism. The influential Jesuit journal *La Civiltà Cattolica* reined in overt attacks on Jews after 1945 but justified some of the measures taken "in defense of Christian society" during the Mussolini era. The *Enciclopedia Cattolica* published between 1948 and 1954 declared "racism and antisemitism" contrary to the "dictates of catholic morality." Yet while it urged Catholics to embrace converted Jews and show "love" to those still unbaptized, Jesuit writers still considered "antisemitism legitimate in the field of ideas" to protect "the religious-moral and social heritage of Christianity." By "antisemitism," the *Enciclopedia* meant theological opposition to Judaism, not racist discrimination.[66] But even if the election of Angelo Roncalli (John XXIII) to the papacy in

---

[64] Guri Schwartz, *After Mussolini*, op. cit., 8–9; Roberto Finzi, "Tre scritti postbellici sugli ebrei di Benedetto Croce, Cesare Merzagora, Adolfo Omodeo" *Studi storici* 1, no. 47 (January–March 2006): 81–108; Adriana Goldstaub, "Appunti per uno studio sui pregiudizi antiebraici nei primi anni del dopoguerra (1945-1955)" in *Il ritorno alla vita*, op. cit., 139–150.

[65] Benedetto Croce was not the only Western European intellectual to draw similarities between Aryan supremacy and Jewish chosenness. In 1947, the French poet and future member of the Académie Française Pierre Emmanuel considered Jews and Nazis "identical in their pride [...] claiming to be the sole bearers of the Revelation." See Pierre Emmanuel, *Qui est cet homme* (1947) published in English as *The Universal Singular* (London: Grey Walls Press, 1950), 166–167.

[66] Elena Mazzini, "Transforming Antisemitism: The Civiltà Cattolica after the Shoa" in James Bernauer and Robert A. Maryks (eds.), *"The Tragic Couple": Encounters between Jews and Jesuits* (Leiden: Brill, 2014), 233–245; "Presence of Antisemitism in the Catholic World: The Case of the Enciclopedia Cattolica" (1948-1954) *Quest: Issues in Contemporary Jewish History*, no. 1 (April 2010): 106–120. See also Manuela Consonni, "The Church and the Memory of the Shoah: The Catholic Press in Italy, 1945-1947" in Eli Lederhendler (ed.), *Jews, Catholics, and the Burden of History: Studies in Contemporary Jewry XXI* (Oxford: Oxford University Press, 2005), 21–35.

1958 marked a turning point in Jewish–Christian relations, the revision of the Church's anti-Judaic teachings, soon carried out during the Second Vatican Council (1962–65), did not elicit ecclesiastical enthusiasm.[67] The Catholic hierarchy's resistance to reform, however, did not affect the lives of the approximately 33,000 Jews who lived in Italy in the mid- to-late 1950s. A joke on Jewish love for money heard in a radio broadcast or caricatures of orthodox Jews with protruded noses in a comic book signaled, to be sure, the persistence of stereotyping. But the Italian Jewish community, reported the AJYB in 1956, had "happily relatively little to do" regarding the protection of its members from antisemitism. Neofascist antisemitic agitation occurred in Rome in May 1958 and will again flare-up in 1960, yet "anti-Semitism in Italy did not exist on any significant scale."[68]

Britain: Riots and Snobbery

Divided between an old-established elite, East-European immigrants, and recent refugees from Nazism, approximately 450,000 Jews lived in Britain at the start of the 1950s.[69] Between 1940 and 1945, the struggle against Nazi Germany generated both pro-Jewish sentiment and Judeophobia on the home front. On December 17, 1942, the members of the House of Commons solemnly rose "in sympathy with the Jewish people and in protest against Nazi infamy."[70] But although Oswald Mosley's British Union of Fascists was proscribed in 1940, anti-Jewish stereotypes such as "refuspies," black-marketers, profiteers, or draft-dodgers circulated during the war. Writing in 1942, George Orwell gave a measure of this phenomenon: "One is constantly coming on pockets of it, non-violent, but pronounced enough to be disquieting."[71] Dislike of excessive Jewish visibility survived the war. In 1945, the publisher and writer Eduard Hulton, whose magazine *Picture Post* denounced Nazi persecutions in the 1930s, urged Jews to "self-discipline" so as not to provoke further antagonism. Anti-Jewish attitudes recorded by the Mass

---

[67] Elena Mazzini, *L'antiebraismo cattolico dopo la Shoah: Tradizioni e culture nell'Italia del secondo dopoguerra (1945–1974)* (Rome: Viella, 2012).
[68] AJYB, Volume 57 (1956), 349; Volume 58 (1957), 267; Volume 60 (1959), 183.
[69] Geoffrey Alderman, *British Jewry since Emancipation* (Buckingham: The University of Buckingham Press, 2014), 323.
[70] William D. Rubinstein and Hillary L. Rubinstein, *Philosemitism: Admiration and Support in the English-Speaking World for Jews, 1840–1839* (New York: St. Martin's Press, 1999), 96.
[71] Anthony Julius, *Trials of the Diaspora: A History of Anti-Semitism in England* (New York: Oxford University Press, 2010), 327.

Observation social research project between 1945 and 1947 confirmed the popularity of such stereotypes.[72]

For the Jewish Central Information Office, established in 1934 by the German-Jewish refugee Alfred Wiener, a more pressing issue was the "anti-Jewish campaign for the revival of fascism."[73] The release from prison of dozens of Mosley's henchmen at the end of the war encouraged antisemitic agitation. No longer "kept down by a truly Christian culture," lamented the Jewish historian Lewis Namier in 1946, British antisemitism was on the rise.[74] Mosley himself started a new political party, the Union Movement, in 1947. But not all Jewish observers believed that the reemergence of British fascism constituted a serious threat. "Not in a few Jew-baiter associations," argued the German-Jewish exile Herbert Friedenthal, "lies the danger of antisemitism in Britain but in that unmistakable differentiation between Jewish citizens and British citizens." The main form of anti-Jewish prejudice in England, he wrote in May 1947, was the "subtle distinction between Jews and Gentiles": The minor antisemitism still ingrained in British society.[75]

In the first days of August 1947, however, growing tensions in Mandate Palestine led to physical violence against Jews. After the hanging of two British sergeants by the Irgun in retaliation for the execution of three of its fighters, angry crowds in economically depressed Liverpool, Manchester, and Glasgow beat up Jews, damaged synagogues and torn down shops. Other attacks occurred in London, Bristol, and Hull. These events, reported the AJC correspondent in London, "shook the assurance of many who had been confident that overt manifestations of anti-Semitism were alien to England."[76] A month after the riots, however, Mass Observation found that the disturbances did not have any "pronounced lasting effect" on public opinion. The research conducted by the sociologist James H. Robb in Bethnal Green between 1947 and

---

[72] Simon Garfield, *Our Hidden Lives: The Remarkable Diaries of Post-War Britain* (London: Ebury Press, 2005), 132, 244, 257; Keith Kahn-Harris, *Strange Hate: Antisemitism, Racism, and the Limits of Diversity*, op. cit., 55–57.
[73] Jewish Central Information Office, *Organized Anti-Semitism in Great Britain 1942–1946*, May 1946.
[74] Lewis B. Namier, "The Jewish Question," *The Manchester Guardian*, March 8, 1946, reprinted in *Facing East* (London: Hamish Hamilton, 1947), 142–150.
[75] Herbert Friedenthal cited in Tony Kushner, "Comparing Antisemitisms: A Useful Exercise?" in Michael Brenner, Rainer Liedtke, and David Rechter (eds.), *Two Nations: British and German Jews in Comparative Perspective* (Tübingen: Mohr Siebeck, 1999), 91–11.
[76] *AJYB*, Volume 50 (1948–1949), 285. See also Tony Kushner, "Anti-Semitism and Austerity: The August 1947 Riots in Britain" in Panikos Panay (ed.), *Racial Violence in Britain in the Nineteenth and Twentieth Centuries* (London and New York: Leicester University Press, 1996), pp. 150–170.

1949 yielded more ambivalent results. In this working-class London borough, "only one inhabitant [...] in eight is completely tolerant, but more than half of the remainder have to be openly invited to express their anti-Semitism before they will do it." In 1949, fifty-five assaults against Jews were registered in metropolitan London.[77]

Antisemitic snobbery among British educated elites was more polite. In 1945, Eton College discretely curtailed the admission of "too many boys who, though themselves British subjects, were alien in outlook and difficult to assimilate into the intimate life of college." In 1952, the conservative writer Evelyn Waugh's candid remark epitomized this "mild" form of enduring prejudice: "I am afraid I must admit to a shade of anti-Jew feeling. Not anti-Semite."[78] Replete with unpleasant portrayals of Jews, the era of Chesterbelloc literature (1900–36) had drawn to a close. Yet negative connotations of Jews resurfaced in a few early postwar literary works.[79] Ambiguous Jewish characters also appeared in cinema. David Lean's movie adaptation of Dickens's *Oliver Twist* (1948), featuring Alec Guiness, exaggerated the facial features of Fagin the Jew. In March 1949, Jewish refugees in Berlin staged a protest after the movie was released in the British occupation sector. They saw in Lean's rendition of Fagin disturbing similarities with Veit Harlan's *Jud Süss*. In 1954, a new cinematographic adaptation of George du Maurier's novel *Trilby* (1894) popularized once again the manipulative and allusively "Jewish" character Svengali.[80]

At the start of the 1950s, however, the Board of Deputies of British Jews held the view that antisemitism in Britain was on the decline. A survey undertaken by Mass Observation in 1951 indeed revealed that in Liverpool, the London working-class district of Whitechapel and the residential London suburb of Golders Green, 54 percent of respondents "had nothing against the Jews" while 14 percent declared themselves "pro-Jewish."[81] With Mosley now dividing his time between Ireland and Paris, only a few "notorious antisemites survived," observed

---

[77] James H. Robb, *Working Class Anti-Semite: A Psychological Study in a London Borough* (London: Tavistock Publications, 1954); *AJYB*, Volume 52 (1951), 241.
[78] Julius, *Trials of the Diaspora*, op. cit., 36; Evelyn Waugh cited in Ritchie Robertson, "The Representation of Jews in British and German Literature" in M. Brenner et al. (eds.), *Two Nations: British and German Jews* (Tübingen: Mohr Siebeck, 1999), 411–441.
[79] Julius, *Trials of the Diaspora*, op. cit., 322.
[80] Frank Stern, *The Whitewashing of the Yellow Badge: Antisemitism and Philosemitism in Postwar Germany* (Oxford: Pergamon Press, 1992), 356–357; Margaret Stetz, "The Hate That Dared Not Speak Its Name: Svengali, Anti-Semitism and Post-War British Heritage Cinema." *Journal of European Popular Culture* 3, no. 2 (2012): 155–167.
[81] Sydney Salomon, *Anti-Semitism and Fascism in Post-War Britain* (London: The Woburn Press, 1950); *AJYB*, Volume 53 (1952), 269.

the Jewish historian Barnet Litvinoff in 1955. "Moribund" in 1956, fascist antisemitism no longer posed a serious threat.[82] British Jews in the late 1950s continued to be occasionally banned from suburban golf clubs, but in 1958 racist animus was directed toward Black immigrants during violent riots in Nottingham and London's Notting Hill. In the third edition of his celebrated *The History of Jews in England*, the Jewish scholar Cecil Roth exuded optimism. The old "alembic of English tolerance," argued Roth, continued to work its magic after 1945: A tolerant country had embraced its long-established Jews and "newer arrivals as well."[83] By 1960, British Jews had secured their place in "white" society, although acts of neo-Nazi vandalism in the coming years would once again undermine the safety of the Jewish community.

Austria: Antisemitism in a Victim Nation

Annexed to the Third Reich in March 1938, Austria regarded itself as a victim of German expansionism. It did so with Allied encouragement. Intended to stimulate acts of resistance against Nazism, the Moscow Declaration of 1943 consecrated the Alpine nation as the "first country to fall a victim to Hitlerite aggression." The document also stipulated that Austria had "a responsibility, which she cannot evade, for participation in the war on the side of Hitlerite Germany." The founding fathers of the Second Austrian Republic preferred however to interpret the Declaration as a certificate of antifascism rather than a demand for self-examination. Austrian antisemitism was therefore as "null and void" as Hitler's annexation of the country to the Reich. The first elected chancellor Leopold Figl, a member of the conservative Austrian People's Party and former Dachau prisoner, assuaged all doubts in June 1947. While "certain Austrians" initially succumbed to Nazi anti-Jewish propaganda, compassion for persecuted Jews had "completely obliterated antisemitism in Austria. I do not believe that the question will ever again have the slightest significance."[84]

After the large wave of emigration in 1938–39 and the death of 65,000 Jews during the Holocaust, Vienna's prewar Jewish population of 180,000 dwindled to approximately 4,000 Jews who reappeared in the badly damaged city in April 1945. Jewish survivors who returned

---

[82] *AJYB*, Volume 56 (1955), 311.
[83] Cecil Roth, *A History of the Jews in England* (Oxford: Clarendon Press, 1964), 270.
[84] Leopold Figl cited in Martin Reisigl and Ruth Wodak, *Discourse and Discrimination: Rhetorics of Racism and Antisemitism* (London: Routledge, 2001), 91.

from concentration camps encountered hostile reception. "There were no kind words," remembered Gertrude Schneider of Vienna. "Instead, there was the typical exclamation, 'you people always come back' and with that we had to be satisfied."[85] A small number of exiled Jews returned from Shanghai, Palestine, the United States, or Britain, and a few Eastern European survivors settled in Vienna. In 1949, 8,038 Jews were registered with the Jewish community.[86]

The reassurances coming from Austria's leaders contrasted with the testimonies of Jews. "All of us look with dread on the present and the future, which is practically without hope," reported representatives of the Vienna Jewish Community in March 1946. Were it not for the protection of the four-powers allied occupation, "not one of the 4,000 Jews would be able to appear in the streets." Vienna, they claimed, was "as before the center of the ugliest and most treacherous antisemitism." Short-term application deadlines and bureaucratic hurdles impeded the restitution of 60,000 Jewish apartments reallocated to non-Jews during the war. "Among Jews now living in public asylums," reported the AJYB in the spring of 1946, "are many whose homes are still occupied by former Nazis."[87]

Although not opposed to restitution, Leopold Figl was not inclined to give dispossessed Jews special consideration. There was "no difference between citizens," Figl told members of the Anglo-American Commission visiting Vienna in February 1946. As he explained, "we only want to be Austrians, equals, irrespective of religion." Karl Renner, the first president of the Second Republic, did not favor the full restitution of Jewish economic assets. "I do not think that Austria in its present mood," he confided in early 1946, "would allow Jews once again to build up these family monopolies."[88] Several restitution laws, however, gradually improved conditions for the small number of Jews still in the country, while Wehrmacht veterans and amnestied Nazis also received help. But Austria's position was that the "first victim of Hitlerite aggression" did not need to pay special attention to

---

[85] Gertrude Schneider, *Exile and Destruction: The Fate of Austrian Jews, 1938–1945* (Westport, CT: Praeger, 1995), 159; Elizabeth Anthony, *The Compromise of Return. Viennese Jews after the Holocaust* (Detroit: Wayne State University Press, 2021), 43–83.

[86] Evelyn Adunka, *Die vierte Gemeinde: Die Wiener Juden in der Zeit von 1945 bis heute* (Berlin: Philo, 2000), 18; Gerhard Botz, "Dynamics of Persecution in Austria, 1938–45" in Robert S. Wistrich (ed.), *Austrians and Jews in the Twentieth Century: From Franz Joseph to Waldheim* (New York: Palgrave, 2001), 199–216.

[87] *AJYB*, Volume 47 (1946–1947), 316–321, here p. 319.

[88] "Kein unterschied unter den Staatsbürgen" in *Wiener Zeitung*, February 2, 1946; Robert Knight, "'Neutrality', Not Sympathy: Jews in Postwar Austria" in Robert Wistrich (ed.), *Austrian and Jews in the Twentieth Century*, op. cit., 220–233.

the compensation of Jewish victims or their heirs around the world. Restitution laws were passed, commissions were set up, but many loopholes remained to advantage spoliators. Under Allied pressure, however, the Austrian government deprived hundreds of thousands of former Nazi party members of the right to vote and imposed on them hard penalties. Between 1945 and 1955, People's Courts launched legal proceedings against 137,000 individuals and convicted to death forty-three war criminals. Yet denazification, largely abandoned after 1948, did not prevent instances of dog-whistling antisemitism in local newspapers.[89]

Anti-Jewish antagonism was also palpable within the citizenry. As surveys conducted in 1946 in the American occupation zone revealed, nearly half of the Austrian population opposed the return of Jews who had survived the war in emigration. According to the Mauthausen survivor and Nazi hunter Simon Wiesenthal, cinema audiences reacted to newsreels showing the return of Austrian Jews from Shanghai with "raucous laughter [...] and exhortations to Gas'em."[90] Hostility was also rife even in areas where Jews hardly ever lived. In the summer of 1945, the young writer Ingeborg Bachmann described how her romance with a British army officer of Jewish origin shocked her neighbors in the southern province of Carinthia. "Going out with the Jew" was frowned upon yet Bachmann defiantly confronted her neighbors: "I'd walk up and down through Vellach and through Hermagor ten times over with him, even if everyone gets in a stew about it, especially then."[91]

Between 1945 and 1951, the transit in Austria of approximately 100,000 Jewish displaced persons exacerbated these negative attitudes. Contrary to the ethnic German "expellees" who simultaneously flooded the occupied country, Jewish refugees from Hungary, Romania, Czechoslovakia, or Poland had no intention to settle permanently in Austria.[92] To remove any doubts, Karl Renner had already made clear in 1946 that after the devastation of the war his government would not allow "a new Jewish community to come here from Eastern Europe and

---

[89] Evelyn Adunka, "Antisemitismus in der Zweiten Republik: Ein Überblick anhand einiger ausgewählter Beispiele" in Heinz P. Wassermann (ed.), *Antisemitismus in Österreich nach 1945* (Innsbruck: StudienVerlag, 2002), 12–65.
[90] Heidemarie Uhl, "From Victim Myth to Co-Responsibility: Nazi Rule, World War Two, and The Holocaust in Austrian Memory" in Lebow et al. (eds.), *The Politics of Memory in Postwar Europe*, op. cit., 40–73.
[91] Ingeborg Bachmann, *War Diary* (London: Seagull Books, 2011), 16.
[92] Tara Zahra, "Prisoners of the Postwar: Expellees, Refugees, and Citizenship in Postwar Austria," *Austria History Yearbook* 41 (2010): 191–215.

establish itself while our own people need work." Jewish displaced persons were stigmatized as profiteers enjoying a privileged life in the spa towns of Bad Gastein or Bad Ischl, both located in the American occupation zone. In May 1948, 34 percent of the Viennese population and at least 43 percent of the inhabitants of Linz and Salzburg viewed Jewish refugees as "parasites."[93]

Hostility toward Holocaust refugees did not only stem from the harsh economic conditions plaguing the war-torn country. Narratives of victimization also stultified empathy. In 1945, Austria's two leading political parties – the socialists and conservative Catholics – had already crafted their own tales of suffering at the hands of Austro-Fascists between 1934 and 1938 or the Nazis following the Anschluss. Numerous socialists and catholic leaders had been deported to Dachau or Mauthausen while others, like the future Jewish socialist Prime Minister Bruno Kreisky, went into political exile. Both parties cultivated an image of victimized Austrian patriots, a self-identification leaving little room for the distinctive suffering of Jews. In addition, socialists and Catholics competed for the votes of 550,000 former Nazi party members, most of them amnestied by 1948. About 1.3 million demobilized Wehrmacht soldiers and prisoners of war who returned from Yugoslavia and the Soviet Union were also figured in these calculations. In 1955, the Catholic right wooed this constituency by commemorating fallen Wehrmacht veterans as Austrian martyrs. Like the Federal Republic of Germany, the Austrian Second Republic absorbed former Nazis and ex-soldiers within its democratic system. That alone was not conducive to the critical examination of Austria's role in the Holocaust, despite condemnations of antisemitism from the country's political leadership.[94]

After ten years of four-powers occupation, however, hostile rhetoric against Jews was significantly more muted than in the immediate postwar period. As the AJYB reported in 1955, there were "no overt manifestations of antisemitism" in the newly independent country.

---

[93] Thomas Albrich, "Fremd und jüdisch: Die ost-Europäischen Überlebenden des Holocaust – erste Projektionziele des Nachgriegsantisemitismus" in Heinz P. Wasserman (ed.), *Antisemitismus in Österreich nach 1945* (Innsbruck: StudienVerlag, 2002), 66–96; Michael John, "Dislocation, Trauma, and Selective Memory: Austria 1945–50. Recollections of Jewish Displaced Persons," *Holocaust Studies* 3, no. 19 (2013): 73–104; Robert Knight, "National Construction Work and Hierarchies of Empathy in Postwar Austria," *Journal of Contemporary History* 49, no. 3 (2014): 491–513.

[94] Peter Pirker, "The Victim Myth Revisited: The Politics of History in Austria Up until the Waldheim Affair" in Günter Bishof, Mark Landry, and Christian Karner (eds.), *Myths in Austrian History: Construction and Deconstruction* (New Orleans: University of New Orleans Press, 2020), 153–174.

Several public scandals would later contradict this assessment. But as the country gained membership into the democratic West, the last remaining Jews in Austria were less preoccupied with hostility or discrimination than with "the indifference of the general public [...] to the terrible experience of the Anschluss period."[95] After a decade of democracy, the main obstacle to normalization was no longer the endemic antisemitism of the immediate postwar years, but an Austrian identity premised on victimhood, Cold War neutrality, and amnesia.

Antisemitism after Nazism: West Germany

On September 20, 1945, soon after the establishment of the Allied Control Council in defeated Germany, all Nazi laws were abolished and the citizenship of approximately 15,000 German Jews still in the country restored. The immense shadow of Nazism, however, continued to affect attitudes toward surviving Jews. "The German people in their majority are still anti-Jewish," editorialized the Berlin Jewish community magazine *Der Weg* in February 1947, "and even the newly appointed officials hesitate to extend a helping hand to the Jews." In 1949, the first US High Commissioner for Germany John McCloy famously stated that the Federal Republic's stance toward its Jewish citizens would serve as the "real touchstone" of its democratic progress. But the multiple public opinion polls carried out since 1945 in the three Western occupation zones did not indicate improvement. In 1947, 75 percent of interviewees agreed that Jews "belonged to a different race" and nearly as many Germans opposed intermarriage. In the American zone of occupation where most Jewish refugees resided, 18 percent of respondents were found "fanatically antisemitic," 21 percent were merely "antisemites," and 22 percent self-identified as "racists." In Bavaria especially, antagonism against "criminal" Jewish displaced persons or "DPs" was particularly rife.[96] The presence until 1948 of approximately 250,000 predominantly Polish Jewish refugees did not inspire compassion but resentment.

---

[95] *AJYB*, Volume 57 (1956), 406.

[96] Anna J. Merritt and Richard J. Merritt, *Public Opinion in Occupied Germany: The OMGUS Surveys, 1945–1949* (Urbana, IL: University of Illinois Press, 1970); Elisabeth Noelle and Erich Peter Neumann, *The Germans: Public Opinion Polls 1947–1966* (Allensbach: Verlag für Demoskopie, 1967); Werner Bergmann and Rainer Erb, *Antisemitismus in der Bundesrepublik Deutschland. Ergebnisse der empirischen Forschung von 1946–1989* (Leske + Budrich: Opladen, 1991). On hostility towards Jewish DPs, see Atina Grossmann, *Jews, Germans, and Allies: Close Encounters in Occupied Germany* (Princeton, NJ: Princeton University Press, 2007), 173–174.

The DPs were held responsible for food shortages and black marketing at the expense of starving Germans and millions of "expellees" driven out of East-Central Europe. Through commemorational practices, religious observance but also demographic vitality, Jewish refugees remarkably normalized their lives in the charnel house of Nazism. For many Germans, however, the spectacle of Jewish survival remained an unnerving reminder of guilt.

As Theodor Adorno observed in a group essay published in 1955, a mirror effect between vanquished Germans and surviving Jews transformed German antisemitism into a defense mechanism against "guilt and remembrance." Less concerned with Jewish racial pollution than with deflection of accountability, a permissible "secondary antisemitism" had since 1945 replaced the tabooed racism of the Third Reich era.[97] After Nazism dreamed of a world without Jews, defeated Germans uncomfortably coped with (few) living Jews in their midst. To be sure, Adorno's investigation also found citizens who wished for pacified relations with Nazism's existential enemies. But as Hannah Arendt had also argued in her notorious report on the aftermath of Nazi rule in Germany (1950), most of the public exhibited a "deep-rooted, stubborn, and at times vicious refusal to face and come to terms with what really happened."[98] If Arendt mentioned Jews at all, however, it was to commend the population of Berlin for its "frank and detailed recital of what happened to Berlin's Jews at the beginning of the war." Arendt otherwise explained the German "flight from reality" as the result of years of totalitarian rule rather than a reaction to the haunting presence of survivors in the country. In distinct but complementary ways, however, Arendt and Adorno illuminated the mechanism of willful ignorance within the West German citizenry.

Yet antisemitism in occupied Germany did not solely manifest itself through evasion of responsibility. Although derogatory comments against Jews were now deemed unacceptable public behavior, blue-collar and white-collar workers, members of the clergy, academics, and government officials continued to propagate negative images of Jews.[99] Verbal or physical assaults on Jewish DPs, as well as the desecration of 200 Jewish cemeteries between 1945 and 1950 alone, also proved that primary antisemitism enjoyed a healthy afterlife after Nazism. This was

---

[97] Theodor Adorno, "Guilt and Defense" (1955) in Jeffrey K. Olick and Andrew J. Perrin (eds.), *Guilt and Defense: On the Legacies of National Socialism in Postwar Germany* (Cambridge, MA: Harvard University Press, 2010), 51–185.
[98] Hannah Arendt, "The Aftermath of Nazi Rule: Report from Germany" in *Commentary* 10 (October 1950), 342–353.
[99] Frank Stern, *The Whitewashing of the Yellow Badge*, op. cit., 158–263.

also true of anti-Jewish rhetoric, tamped down yet never absent from public discourse. In November 1949, the nationalist Bundestag member Wolfgang Hedler wondered aloud "whether the means for gassing the Jews was the best way, about this one can be of different minds. Perhaps there would have been better ways of ridding ourselves of their kind." A tribunal in Kiel, including two judges who were also former NSDAP members, acquitted the politician. Only after a media campaign was this decision reversed in July 1951.[100]

The birth of the Federal Republic in September 1949 nonetheless imposed a new code of conduct. "After everything that took place in the National Socialist period," declared its first chancellor Konrad Adenauer in September 1949, "we consider it unworthy and incredible per se that there should still be individuals in Germany who persecute and despise Jews because they are Jews." Adenauer reduced German antisemitism to the condemnable actions of mere "individuals," but his reprobation of Jew-hatred legitimated the democratic nature of the Bonn republic. Adenauer, however, ruled out collective guilt in his landmark speech to the Bundestag on September 27,1951. Horrendous crimes were perpetrated by Nazis in the name of Germans, declared Cologne's former mayor, but "they [Germans] did not participate in them." The early years of the Federal Republic were nevertheless marked by state-sanctioned efforts to improve relations with Jews domestically and on the international stage. Although hate speech was only criminalized in 1960, legal sanctions were already in place in the 1950s to prosecute acts of antisemitism, even if penalties were generally mild. The process of restitution and reparations to Holocaust survivors and the state of Israel, finalized in the Luxemburg Agreement of 1952, also indicated Bonn's goodwill. Yet according to surveys, only 11 percent of West Germans approved of the agreement. Pollsters also found that 37 percent of the public wished to see the remaining 30,000 Jews leave the country while a third of the population still held Hitler in high esteem. Other inquiries revealed than more than half of the German adult population claimed to have never witnessed or heard of Nazi crimes. Thirty percent of respondents believed that "the figure of five million Jewish victims" was vastly inflated. While only one-sixth overtly expressed antisemitism, many others preferred not to display anti-Jewish attitudes openly.[101]

---

[100] On the Hedler affair, see Norbert Frei, *Adenauer's Germany and the Nazi Past* (New York: Columbia University Press, 2002), 237–250.

[101] Jeffrey Herf, *Divided Memory: The Nazi Past in the Two Germanies* (Cambridge, MA: Harvard University Press, 1997), 267–234; Jeffrey K. Olick, *The Sins of the Fathers: Germany, Memory, Method* (Chicago, IL: University of Chicago Press, 2016), 138–160; Samuel Salzborn, "Anti-Jewish Guilt Deflection and National Self-Victimization" in

Rapprochement with Jews, the German-Jewish émigré Kurt Grossmann observed in 1954, was not "a problem which electrifies the sentiments and minds of the Germans."[102]

Other observers noted in 1955 that while overt expressions of anti-Jewish prejudice were infrequent, "there was much evidence of latent anti-Semitism simmering below the surface in Western Germany, at times to boil over in scarcely disguised fashion."[103] Throughout the 1950s, numerous scandals and court cases demonstrated the permanence of vocal antisemitism, while more diffuse antagonism lurked behind a wall of silence on German crimes against the Jews. "A kind of invisible curtain," reported the AJYB in 1957, "still existed between the few and isolated Jewish inhabitants of postwar Germany and their gentile neighbors."[104] Bonn's polite pronouncements, elite protests, or student demonstrations against former Nazis in universities or public service counterbalanced outspoken fanatics of the Third Reich or violators of the antisemitic taboo. But these laudable efforts did not prevent a Judeophobic upsurge in public opinion polls toward the end of the decade. In 1957, three different surveys showed that 30 percent of respondents shared "clearly antisemitic" views. Among self-declared "indifferent" interviewees were many citizens who likely preferred to keep their opinion private.[105] "A large percentage of university students" also openly declared their dislike of Jews. Neo-Nazism, while electorally weak, made headlines. The "Swastika Epidemic" of 1959–60, which started with the words *Juden raus* daubed on a synagogue in Cologne, will mark the culmination of anti-Jewish vandalism in the early postwar period.

From Antisemitism to Tactical Philosemitism

In France, Belgium, the Netherlands, and Britain, anti-Jewish resentment surfaced at the end of the war and then declined at the start of the 1950s. Despite foreign admiration for the country's friendliness, some Italian Jews remained painfully aware of their "latent otherness." While mostly confined to neofascist circles or traditionalist catholic publications, antisemitic stereotypes in Italy occasionally appeared in the media,

---

Lars Rensmann and Julius H. Schoeps (eds.), *Politics and Resentment: Antisemitism and Counter-Cosmopolitanism in the European Union* (Leiden: Brill, 2011), 397–423.

[102] Kurt R. Grossmann, "The Germans and the Jews" in *European Jewish Yearbook: Jewish Life in Europe, 1953–1954* (Frankfurt am Main: Union Druckerei u. Verlagsanstalt, 1954), 148.
[103] *AJYB*, Volume 56 (1955), 366.
[104] *AJYB*, Volume 58 (1957), 290.
[105] *AJYB*, Volume 59 (1958), 294.

cinema, or even among antifascist intellectuals otherwise known for their solidarity with Jewish suffering. In 1960, the communist Salvatore Quasimodo, author in 1956 of the humanist poem *Auschwitz* and winner of the 1959 Nobel Prize in Literature, wrote of the Jews' "financial power" and portrayed them as a "race which has never been able to feel tied to a country or a society."[106] In Austria and West Germany, secondary antisemitism substituted itself to primary *Judenhass*. Yet everywhere, vocal antisemitism underwent delegitimation in the public realm. Disrepute, however, did not seal off all possibilities to circumvent the taboo. What the French-Jewish philosopher Robert Misrahi called in 1969 "mechanistic philosemitism" was one of these escape routes. After the war, observed Jean-Paul Sartre's disciple, antisemitism expressed itself through benevolent exculpation of Jews. Their "avariciousness," for instance, could be blamed on the Church's prohibition of usury which in the Middle Age turned Jews into moneylenders. Jewish "cunningness" and "bellicosity," while still assumed to be real, were forgiven as unfortunate results of a long history of persecution. The illegitimacy of overt anti-Jewish expression, argued Misrahi, forced the antisemite "who claims not to be one" into a difficult role: "If too hastily critical of Jews, his mask falls off; if too quickly forgiving, he is unmasked again."[107]

The migration of negative stereotypes toward pro-Jewish expression was also apparent in early postwar cinema. Prior to 1960, the presence of Jewish characters in Western European films was rare or allusive. While the history of the Holocaust on screen started immediately after the war, most national cinemas began to substantially address the topic in the 1970s. Two films, both released in 1948, nonetheless illustrate how antisemitic themes found a niche in cultural artefacts sympathetic to Jews. In Austria, Georg Wilhelm Pabst's *Der Prozess* (*The Trial*, 1948) told the story of Hungarian Jews unjustly accused of the ritual murder of a young Christian girl in 1882. Rounded up by superstitious villagers, the Jewish inhabitants of the town are put to trial. At great risk to his life, an idealist non-Jewish lawyer sets out to prove the Jews' innocence. His passionate defense of Jewish villagers exposed the irrationality of antisemitism. The director of two films commissioned by Joseph

---

[106] Giacomo Lichtner, "The Latent Sense of Otherness: Old and New Anti-Semitisms in Postwar Italy" *Modern Italy* 4, no. 23 (2018): 461–472; Paola Bertilotti, "Anatomie d'une crise: Les épisodes antisémites de l'hiver 1959–1960 en Italie" *Laboratoire italien* 11 (2011), available at: http://journals.openedition.org/laboratoireitalien/576; AJYB (63), 1962, 325.

[107] Robert Misrahi, "L'antisémitisme latent" in Patrice de Comarond and Claude Duchet (eds.), *Racisme et Société* (Paris: François Maspero, 1969), 219–231.

Goebbels in 1941 and 1943, Pabst now used cinema to condemn anti-Jewish prejudice. For this effort, he received the Best Director award at the 1948 Venice Film Festival. Yet for some critics, his philosemitism was hard to distinguish from antisemitism, since the film accentuated supposed Jewish traits and featured repulsive faces reminiscent of Nazi propaganda. Viewers of *Der Prozess*, in other words, were invited to identify with persecuted Jews through the recreation of Jewish difference. The gendered "semitic gaze" in German cinema before 1949 fulfilled a similar function. In the few high-circulation films that indirectly addressed Jewish topics, close-ups on "beautiful Jewesses," highlighting dark eyes, sadness, and a morally untainted Jewish gaze, attempted to overcome the visual antisemitism of the Nazi era through a philosemitism impregnated with racialization.[108]

In Italy, *L'ebreo errante* (*The Wandering Jew*, 1948) showcased similar ambiguity. Directed by Goffredo Alessandrini, a filmmaker who had already enjoyed a successful career under Fascism, the movie featured Vittorio Gassman in the role of Matteo Blumenthal, a Parisian Jew during the German occupation. A temporal flashback at the start of the film reveals that in an earlier period Matteo was a wealthy Jew in ancient Jerusalem who had mocked Jesus on his way to the cross. For this he was condemned to wander eternally. Nearly two thousand years later in wartime Paris, Matteo is a rich Jewish banker who could easily buy his way out of deportation. He nonetheless choses to share the fate of fellow Jews and follows them to a concentration camp. There he leads an escape of prisoners in the company of his female lover Cortese. When Matteo realizes that all remaining Jews in the camp will be murdered unless he returns, the fugitive turns himself in. The film ends in troubling manner: Only after being machine-gunned by the Germans can Blumenthal finally break the curse of the wandering Jew. His martyrdom both encouraged viewers to feel sympathy and interpret the Holocaust as expiation for the Jews' refusal to embrace Christ. The seventh most popular Italian film for the year 1947–48, *L'ebreo errante* seamlessly blended philosemitism with anti-Judaism.[109]

---

[108] Lisa Silvermann, "Absent Jews and Invisible Antisemitism in Postwar Vienna: Der Prozess and The Third Man," *Journal of Contemporary History* 52, no. 2 (2017): 211–228; Frank Stern, "The 'Semitic' Gaze from the Screen: German and Austrian Cinematic Discourse between Antisemitism and Philosemitism" in *Central European University Jewish Studies Yearbook, IV, 2004–2005*, 159–170, available at: https://jewishstudies.ceu.edu/sites/jewishstudies.ceu.edu/files/attachment/basicpage/72/11stern.pdf.

[109] Millicent Marcus, *Italian Film in the Shadow of Auschwitz* (Toronto: University of Toronto Press, 2007), 30–32; Emiliano Perra, *Conflicts of Memory: The Reception of Holocaust Films and TV Programmes in Italy, 1945 to the Present* (Bern: Peter Lang, 2010), 33–38.

In the immediate postwar period, however, the main form of migration from antisemitism to philosemitism was strategic compensation. Works of Dutch literature challenging the heroic myth of rescue illustrated this phenomenon. In various novels published in the 1940s and the early 1950s, non-Jewish characters feeling shame for wartime inaction romantically longed for Jewish female survivors.[110] At the level of social interactions, however, the principal site of this transmutation was occupied Germany. In 1945, recalled the German-Jewish exiled historian Peter Gay, the 15,000 German Jews in the country were suddenly treated "with a kind of dirty courtesy, with conspicuous admiration for everything that Jews said, did, or believed." Jews, he added, mocked the "rediscovered love for everything Jewish (...) as 'white antisemitism'."[111] *Judenfreundlichkeit* (friendliness toward Jews), a punishable crime under the 1935 Nuremberg Laws, was now motivated by opportunism. In September 1945, the literary scholar and diarist of distant Jewish origin Victor Klemperer was visited by the son of a non-Jewish friend, who requested "an attestation that he had been favorably disposed towards the Jews despite his swastika."[112] Klemperer had converted to Protestantism in 1912 and viewed himself as a "German and a communist, nothing more." He nevertheless fulfilled the role of refereeing Jew by helping the young man obtain a *Persilschein*, a "clean bill of health" and precious certificate of good behavior. At the height of denazification, quipped the satirical right-wing writer Ernst von Salomon in his autobiographical novel *Der Fragebogen* (*The Questionnaire*, 1951), "everyone had his own rescued Jew."[113]

The opportunistic revalorization of Jews during the Allied occupation stemmed from a reverse balance of power: professed friendliness or admiration for things Jewish helped vanquished Germans meet their occupiers' expectations. Before foreign visitors noticed a strange "philosemitic fashion" within cultural and intellectual circles at the start of the 1960s, the mutation of German antisemitism into tactical philosemitism during the Allied occupation had already reshaped formerly negative Jewish traits into positive attributes. The Jews' financial abilities were now an asset for economic reconstruction.

---

[110] Ido de Haan, "The Memory of the Rescue of Jews in the Netherlands, 1945 to the Present," op. cit.
[111] Cited in Arvi Sepp, "Zwischen allen Stühlen: Reflections on Judaism in Germany in Victor Klemperer's Post-Holocaust Diaries," *Humanities* 8, no. 168 (2019): 1–13.
[112] Ibid.
[113] Cited in Ido de Haan, "Paths of Normalization after the Persecution of Jews: The Netherlands, France, and West Germany in the 1950s" in Richard Bessel and Dirk Schumann (eds.), *Life after Death* (Cambridge: Cambridge University Press, 2003), 65–92.

Their cosmopolitanism made them perfect mediators with Allied officials. Their "intellectualism" benefited the revival of German culture and science after Nazism. This rhetoric, however, was not always used as strategic ploy. The new democratic Germany, declared the socialist leader Kurt Schumacher in September 1949, should be built with the help of the "Jewish intellect and the Jewish economic potential." Contrary to Konrad Adenauer's wish to let bygones be bygones, Schumacher told the Bundestag that the "dishonor" of Nazi crimes will weigh on the nation "for an unforeseeable long time to come": His stereotypical praise for intellectual or economic Jews was also a rare plea for historical reckoning.[114] In the mid 1960s, however, German-Jewish intellectuals resented the philosemitic portrayal of Jews as bearers of culture or gifted economic actors, a *Judenidolatrie* (idolization of Jews) whose seeds were already planted during the years of Allied occupation.[115] German–Jewish distaste for the idea of "Jewish contribution to German culture," a laudatory phrase perceived as an attempt to turn the murder of Jews into a German loss, will persist over the next decades.

In occupied Austria (1945–55), the reclamation of [Jewish] modernism in the visual arts helped the country project an image of democracy and Europeanism. Although Viennese Jewish artists and writers had emigrated or perished during the Holocaust, the revival of coffeehouses and cabaret culture likewise turned Jewish absence into coded presence in a city now almost without Jews.[116] At the level of personal relations, non-Jewish attitudes toward returning Austrian Jews could take the form of sympathy and acceptance. The Viennese Jewish remigrant Erich Lessing, who spent the war in exile in Palestine, found in 1947 "subterranean" antisemitism in his native city but characterized his left-wing circle of friends as "philosemitic." Yet the writer of Jewish origin Friedrich Torberg, who also resettled in Vienna after the war, felt like a token Jew or "Jud vom Dienst," although he never used this protected status to challenge the country's history of antisemitism.[117] In Austria, as opposed

[114] Cited in Herf, *Divided Memory*, op. cit., 273.
[115] The German-Jewish political scientist Eleonore Sterling coined the word *Judenidolatrie* in "Judenfreunde: Fragwürdiger Philosemitismus in der Bundesrepublik," *Die Zeit*, December 12, 1965.
[116] In her study of philosemitism in postwar Austria, Frances Tanzer shows how cultural artifacts "that were previously deemed racially and culturally inferior, became emblematic of 'authentic' Austrian culture." See Frances Tanzer, *Vanishing Vienna: Modernism, Philosemitism and Jews in a Postwar City* (Philadelphia, PA: University of Pennsylvania Press, 2024).
[117] Elizabeth Anthony, *The Compromise of Return*, op. cit., 231; Malachi Haim Hacohen, *Jacob & Esau: Jewish European History between Nation and Empire* (Cambridge: Cambridge University Press, 2019), 560.

to West Germany, compensatory or whitewashing philosemitism was not a necessity. In order to redefine Viennese culture after fascism, to be sure, Austrian elites imagined Jewish remigrant artists or humorists as embodiments of untainted liberal culture preserved in exile. Yet by definition, the "first victim of Hitlerite aggression" did not owe any *idolatrie* to its dead Jews or few remaining Jewish citizens.

In Italy, the foreign ministry went at length to convince the Western Allies of the nation's impeccable philosemitic record. A report issue in the spring and autumn of 1946 in anticipation of the Paris Peace Treaty conveniently simplified the history of anti-Jewish persecution in Italy since the late 1930s. Mussolini's "racial policy," stated the ministry, was an aberration at odds with the Italian devotion to "liberty, equality, and tolerance." Yet Giorgio Almirante, the former supporter of Mussolini's racial doctrine and founder in 1946 of the neofascist Italian Social Movement, cautiously abjured antisemitism at the end of the war.[118] In *Eight Jews* (1944), the first work of Holocaust literature to appear in Italy, the Jewish writer Giacomo Debenedetti commented with irony on the miraculous popularity of philosemitism among former functionaries of the Mussolini regime: "What was the most conspicuous feature of Fascism? Its calling card, so to speak? Its fingerprint? There you go! Persecution of Jews. Therefore, what is the most characteristic indication of anti-Fascism? Protection of Jews." The most "incontrovertible" proof of democratic morality, the Fascist characters in *Eight Jews* quickly realized, was to "show sympathy for Jews."[119]

Tactical or compensatory friendliness, however, was not unique to post-fascist Italy, post-Nazi Germany or postwar Austria. In France, the Catholic writer Georges Bernanos did not abandon his life-long admiration for the anti-Dreyfus journalist Edouard Drumont, "a man of libraries, a man of learning (…) defenseless against the mob." But to speak favorably of Drumont in 1949 required accompanying homage to "the heroes of the Warsaw Ghetto."[120] Exiled in Paris since 1941, the Romanian philosopher Emil Cioran best showcased the mechanism of philosemitic compensation. In 1936, the thinker of French expression born in 1911 had famously lashed out at Romanian democracy for "defending Jews and Judeo-Romanian capitalism."

---

[118] Guri Schwarz, "On Myth Making and Nation Building," op. cit.; Antonio Carioti, "La lunga ambiguità: Neofascismo e antisemitismo nell'Italia repubblicana" in Marcello Flores et al., *Storia della Shoah in Italia: Vicende, memorie, rappresentazioni*, Volume 2 (Turin: UTET, 2010), 267–286.

[119] Debenedetti, *Eight Jews*, op. cit., 66, 83.

[120] Georges Bernanos, "L'honneur est ce qui nous rassemble" (1949) in *Français, si vous saviez* (Paris: Gallimard, 1995), 323–328.

In his essay *Un peuple de solitaires* [*A People of Solitaries*], published in 1956, Cioran reckoned with past antisemitism and flirtation with the fascist Iron Guard movement. "If at twenty I loved [the Jews] to the point of regretting not being one of them," he admitted, "later on, unable to forgive them for having played a leading role in the course of history, I found myself loathing them with the fury of love turned to hate." His self-critical essay now valorized Jews to an extreme by heralding their superiority over the rest of mankind. "Man," he announced, is only a "Jew who did not fulfill himself." Such dubious compliment paid to a people "exceptional in its destiny" resurrected a radical antisemitic distinction between humanity and Jews, now under the veneer of philosemitism. For the postwar Cioran, Jews were neither "mere mortals [nor] an ordinary variety of the human type": a mark of esteem still leaving wide open the possibility of contempt.[121] Yet if Cioran's remorseful writings exemplified strategic compensation, post-Holocaust philosemitism is not reducible to mere opportunism or tactics. As seen in Chapter 3, anti-antisemitism did not require special deference or "love" for the Jews. The "war on antisemitism," whose post-Holocaust roots we now explore, nonetheless became after 1945 a singular marker of philosemitism in European democracies.

---

[121] Andrei Oisteanu, *Inventing the Jew: Antisemitic Stereotypes in Romanian and other Central-East European Cultures* (Lincoln, NE: University of Nebraska Press, 2009), 229, 437; Sylvère Lotringer, "L'éloge fait aux Juifs," *Pardès* 38, no. 1 (2005): 99–115; Alexandra Laignel-Lavastine, *Cioran, Eliade, Ionesco: L'oubli du fascisme* (Paris: Presses universitaires de France, 2002).

3 Genesis of a Struggle
Anti-antisemitism (1945–1948)

"For us Jews," wrote the French essayist Wladimir Rabi in September 1945, "the fight against antisemitism belongs to the past. We believe that it behooves the non-Jews, and the non-Jews alone, to lead this struggle."[1] Throughout the 1930s, the predominantly Jewish members of the LICA (the International League Against Antisemitism, created in 1928) countered the antisemitic far-right in the name of "humanism (…), the irreducible refusal to admit the inequality of human races." In 1942, Jewish resisters close to the Communist party founded the clandestine National Movement Against Racism (MNCR), the precursor of the left-wing antiracist association MRAP. After the liberation, the two organizations united forces to erase the "profound traces left by German propaganda" in the country.[2] Anti-defamation efforts, argued Rabi, were admirable but futile. After the dark years of Vichy collaborationism, a "secret wound" separated Jews from the rest of the population. Feeling "terribly isolated," the Vilna-born publicist left activism to others. Jews had done what they could: The containment of antisemitism was now the responsibility of "the non-Jews, and the non-Jews alone."

The Italian Jewish writer Giacomo Debenedetti viewed the problem differently. The antifascist literary critic was more worried about the danger of philosemitism than the threat of antisemitism. To be "gratuitously loved, undeservedly loved, that is, wrongly loved," he warned in September 1944, would be worse than bigotry. After years of persecution, the Jews' only demand was to recover "the right to not have special rights. Special, meaning racial." Debenedetti not only rejected demonstrative solicitude. He also claimed that among "the liberties that constitute Liberties is the liberty to be anti-Semitic." What he benignly called

---

[1] Wladimir Rabi, "Etat du judaïsme français," *Esprit*, no. 114 (September 1945): 480–490.
[2] Ralph Schor, *L'antisémitisme en France dans l'entre-deux-guerres* (Brussels: Editions Complexes, 1992), 212–213; Emmanuel Debono, *Aux origines de l'antiracisme: La LICA, 1927–1940* (Paris: Éditions du CNRS, 2012); Johannes Heuman, "Comme les Juifs sous l'Occupation": La mémoire de la Shoah dans la lutte antiraciste en France," *Archives Juives* 2, no. 51 (2018): 39–58.

"an anti-Semitism of free men" was in his mind a blessing in disguise. After years of persecutions, "Liberal anti-Semitism" offered Italian Jews an opportunity "to speak out in the open." While Rabi enjoined his coreligionists to leave the fight against antisemitism to non-Jews, Debenedetti found disputation "revitalizing, regenerating for the Jewish people."[3]

Rebuilders of Jewish communities in Western Europe navigated between these two positions. Cautious distance from society in West Germany and Austria, retreat into communal affairs in the Netherlands, faith in the protective Republic in France, alignment with the antifascist consensus in Italy, and quiet interventionism in Britain (although Jewish ex-servicemen favored more muscular tactics): In the immediate aftermath of the Holocaust, Jewish communal leaders responded in multiple ways to manifestations of hostility.[4] Vigilance against antisemitism, however, soon became one the main functions of Jewish representative institutions. In France and Britain, the only two countries with still sizeable Jewish populations in Western Europe, the Conseil Représentatif des Institutions Juives de France (CRIF) and the Board of Deputies of British Jews took over the years an outspoken stance against defamation in the press or the political arena.[5] Smaller federative bodies remained behind the stage of politics until the late twentieth century but likewise rang the alarm on antisemitism. Jewish communal institutions in democratic Europe evolved from confessional entities to watchdog organizations: The moratorium on public antisemitism enforced after 1945 legitimized in return bolder Jewish militancy.

The containment of antisemitism, however, did not only rest on Jewish shoulders. The American historian Koppel S. Pinson, a scholar of German antisemitism and editor of *Jewish Social Studies*, acknowledged

---

[3] Giacomo Debenedetti, *October 16, 1943 and Eight Jews* (Notre Dame, IN: University of Notre Dame Press, 2001), 83–87.

[4] Dan Diner, "Jews in Germany after the Holocaust: An Interpretation" in Michael Brenner (ed.), *A History of Jews in Germany since 1945: Politics, Culture, and Society* (Bloomington, IN: Indiana University Press, 2018), 26–139; Suzanne Cohen Weisz, *Jewish Life in Austria and Germany after 1945: Identity and Communal Reconstruction* (Budapest: Central European University Press, 2016); Sarah K. Cardaun, *Countering Contemporary Antisemitism in Britain: Government and Civil Society Responses between Universalism and Particularism* (Leiden: Brill, 2015); Evelien Gans, "Jewish Responses to Post-Liberation Antisemitism" in Remco Emsel and Evelien Gans (eds.), *The Holocaust, Israel and "the Jew": Histories of Antisemitism in Postwar Dutch Society* (Amsterdam: Amsterdam University Press, 2017), 127–149; Muriel Pichon, *Les Français juifs: Récit d'un désenchantement* (Toulouse: Presses du Midi, 2009); Guri Schwarz, "On Myth Making and Nation Building: The Genesis of the 'Myth of the Good Italian' 1943–1947" *Telos* 164 (Fall 2013): 11–43.

[5] Samuel Ghiles-Meilhac, *Le CRIF: De la résistance à la tentation du lobby* (Paris: Robert Laffont, 2011); Raphael Langham, *250 Years of Convention and Contention: A History of the Board of Deputies of British Jews, 1760–2010* (London: Vallentine Mitchell, 2010).

at the end of the war the primary role of non-Jews in this regard. "There is a greater awareness (...)," observed Pinson, "that antisemitism is not so much a problem for the Jew to solve as it is for the non-Jewish world." The historian Salo W. Baron similarly stated that "the Jews themselves can do relatively little about combatting antisemitic propaganda."[6] The West European transition from Nazism, fascism, or pro-Axis collaborationism toward democracy fortunately required the rejection of overt prejudice in mainstream politics. Although the delegitimization of antisemitism forced the recoding of Judeophobia, democratic Europe also pushed anti-Jewish animosity beyond the pale of public permissiveness.

Moderate conservatives, Liberals and above all the antifascist left, to be sure, had already disapproved of antisemitism before the war. But what began to change in 1945 is not only the vigor of this reprobation but also the position of antisemitism in relation to other forms of racial prejudice. "Of all the various group tensions, that known as Anti-Semitism concerns the whole world and calls for special treatment," declared the Catholic, Protestant, and Jewish participants in an emergency meeting convened in Switzerland in August 1947. The Seelisberg conference was only a first step toward a new relationship between Christians and Jews after the Holocaust, but its concluding report revealed a new approach toward antisemitism. Since "an attack on Jewry" was an assault on "our ordered human society," it was "advisable to deal with anti-Semitism as a special case requiring special treatment."[7] On the eve of decolonization, the Seelisberg ecumenical forum did not specify whether European colonial domination also counted as assault against "human society." In the aftermath of the Holocaust, intimated the first protagonists of the Christian Jewish dialogue, the containment of Jew-hatred was particularly urgent: The moral purification of postwar European societies required special attention to the antisemitic disease. This viewpoint was still minoritarian both within the Church and secular society. It was nonetheless indicative of a new political, theological, and philosophical commitment: In 1945, anti-antisemitism began to mutate into a singular crusade against the scourge. Never disentangled from the question of Zionism, the writings of first-generation "anti-antisemites" illuminate the genesis of this struggle.

---

[6] Koppel S. Pinson, "Antisemitism in the Post-War World," *Jewish Social Studies* 7, no. 2 (April 1945): 99–118; see also Salo Baron's foreword in Koppel S. Pinson (ed.), *Essays on Antisemitism* (New York: Conference on Jewish Relations, 1946), viii.

[7] Christian Rutishauser, "The 1947 Seelisberg Conference: The Foundation of the Jewish-Christian Dialogue," *Studies in Christian-Jewish Relation* 2, no. 2 (2007): 34–53.

"Rationally Anti-antisemitic"

"We were pro-Jew in 1939 as part of antifascism," reflected the British socialist Richard Crossman in 1946; "now most of us are not emotionally pro-Jew, but only rationally 'anti-antisemitic' which is a very different thing."[8] The thirty-eight-year-old Labour MP for Coventry did not only use rare terminology. He also implied that to be "anti-antisemitic" after Nazism required a departure from humanist antifascism. Whether liberals or communist fellow-travelers, however, antifascist intellectuals in the 1930s took an unbending stand against racial persecution in the Third Reich. Admittedly, the distinguished European writers committed to the "defense of culture" prior to 1939 understood Nazism as an onslaught on civilization more than a longing for a world purified of Jews. In antifascist eyes, Hitler's ideology remained above all a reactionary attack against freedom and progress, or the product of monopoly capitalism in the view of economic Marxism.[9] Antifascism, however, did not blind his followers to the realities of Jewish victimhood. "We, who boast that we are fighting for humanity and human dignity against barbarism," wrote the exiled Thomas Mann in the last months of the war, "must ask ourselves if we are doing everything in our power to allay this indescribable suffering, which debases all humanity."[10] As Crossman himself acknowledged, it was through antifascism that he initially felt "emotionally pro-Jew." But after the war, the former Oxford don strayed from the universalism of the left in favor of "rational" anti-antisemitism: a search for unique remedies to the special problem of Jew-hatred.

Although Crossman was initially skeptical of Zionism, the realization of Jewish statehood in Palestine became his preferred solution to antisemitism. Appointed by Foreign Secretary Ernest Bevin to the Anglo-American Committee of Inquiry in November 1945, the Labour politician did not begin his mission with high appreciation for the Zionist movement.[11] "Any Gentile, who is compelled to study Zionism for weeks on end, reached a point where he feels inclined to bang on the table and walk out of the room," he pointed out in his recollections. But after encountering Holocaust survivors in Vienna and Jewish displaced persons in occupied Germany, Crossman took stock of the destruction

---

[8] Richard Crossman, *Palestine Mission: A Personal Record* (New York and London: Harper & Brothers Publishers, 1947), 19.
[9] Enzo Traverso, *Fire and Blood: The European Civil War: 1914–1945* (London: Verso, 2016), 272–273.
[10] Thomas Mann, "The Fall of the European Jews" in J. J. Lynx (ed.), *The Future of the Jews: A Symposium* (London: Lyndsay Drummond, 1945), 13–16.
[11] The Anglo-American Commission of Inquiry was created in November 1945 to study the situation of Jewish refugees in Europe and consider their resettlement in Palestine.

of Jewish life in East-Central Europe. Until late 1945, he still maintained that "it is the anti-Semites and racists who want to clear the Jews out of Europe and place them together in Palestine." In September 1946, however, the "rationally anti-antisemitic" socialist pleaded for the relocation of East-Central European Holocaust survivors out of the continent: "In Poland, Hungary and Rumania, the Jews have the bare choice of either ceasing living as Jews or of leaving Europe ... this nation must emigrate." Crossman generalized this diagnosis to the whole continent: "The Jew who wanted to be a Jew, separate from the rest of the nation, must leave Europe; those who remain must accept assimilation."[12] In agreement with the Committee's report issued in April 1946, Crossman advocated the admission of 100,000 Holocaust refugees in Mandate Palestine while urging other countries, including Britain and the United States, to also open their gates. Within weeks, however, Crossman and his Labour acolyte Michael Foot supported the establishment of a "Judean state" in partitioned Palestine.[13] The price exacted on the native Arab population appeared tolerable. "Looking at the position of the Palestinian Arab," he observed during his short visit of Mandate Palestine in March 1946, "I had to admit that no western colonist in any other country had done so little harm, or disturbed so little the life of the indigenous people."[14]

Jewish statehood, however, appealed to Crossman for another reason. A "Jewish commonwealth," he still believed immediately after the war, "will neither solve the Jewish problem nor reduce anti-Semitism." But on this topic too, Crossman quickly changed his mind. The fulfillment of Zionist goals, he told Jewish audiences in the United States in November 1946, was necessary to salvage Western democracy from antisemitic contamination. His anti-antisemitism derived from pragmatic calculus: Regardless of the claims of Palestine's Arab population, less Jews in Europe meant less antisemitism on the continent. "Unless we British Socialists could accomplish the right relationship to the Jewish problem," Crossman declared in New York, "our whole democracy might be corrupted by the seed of antisemitism." As he told a Manhattan audience, "every Gentile has the virus of anti-Semitism in his veins." Awareness of the disease was the first step to recovery: "then you can make the rational compensations that are necessary in this life of Jew and Gentile." As Crossman candidly acknowledged, his pro-Zionist

---

[12] Richard Crossman, *Palestine Mission: A Personal Record*, op. cit., 65, 19, 95, 202, 204.
[13] Richard Crossman and Michael Foot, *A Palestine Munich?* (London: Victor Gollancz, 1946), 31.
[14] Cited in Paul Kelemen, *The British Left and Zionism: History of a Divorce* (Manchester: Manchester University Press, 2012), 115–116.

Labour faction did not oppose Ernest Bevin's "policy of injustice (...) because we like the Jews." Crossman's concern was for "our own Gentile democracy": A potent "antisemitic virus" jeopardized its existence. This metaphor equated antisemitism to an infectious disease, yet immunity was within reach. Support for a Jewish state, Crossman avowed, helped "conquer [antisemitism] in ourselves."[15] The Labour MP, to be sure, admitted partiality. "If I were an Arab," he recognized, "I would fight Zionism with all my powers."[16] But Crossman was an Englishman worried of the negative effect of antisemitism on the democratic West. For the future editor of the liberal anti-communist manifesto *The God That Failed* (1949), the fate of Western liberalism hinged upon the robustness of its anti-antisemitism: "The test of a democracy in the modern world is how it manages the Jewish problem. It is a very simple test of freedom."[17]

In his pro-Zionist writings, Crossman abundantly referred to the existence of a "Jewish problem" begging for solution. "This is the very centre of the Jewish problem, in a world of nation-states the Jew is in a false position," he wrote in *Palestine Mission*.[18] This "problem" differed from the one propagated by Judeophobes after Nazism: black-marketeering (in occupied Germany and Austria), overrepresentation in commerce or the professions, "ghetto mentality," or as the French playwright Gabriel Marcel lamented after the liberation of Paris, the tendency of Jews to "encroach" on society.[19] Crossman's "Jewish problem," to the contrary, referred to the disadvantageous position of Jewish survivors in East-Central Europe: The Anglo-American Committee of Inquiry, to which he belonged from November 1945 to April 1946, was precisely established to investigate "Jewish problems in Palestine and Europe" – a formulation also used by sympathizers of Zionism.

Evocations of a "Jewish problem," however, inevitably echoed century-old debates over Europe's "Jewish question." Popularized in the mid nineteenth century amid a broad "age of questions," the expression referred to the problem of Jewish incorporation in modern European societies.[20] Bourgeois liberalism and Marxism alike traditionally offered integrationist solutions. Both advocated assimilation in the nation-state

---

[15] Richard Crossman, *An Englishman Looks at Palestine* (New York: United Palestine Appeal, 1947), 5.
[16] Richard Crossman, "The Riddle of Palestine" in *MacLean's* (Canada), April 1, 1947.
[17] *An Englishman Looks at Palestine*, op. cit., 5.
[18] *Palestine Mission: A Personal Record*, op. cit., 65.
[19] Gabriel Marcel, "Lendemain de persécution" in *Témoignage chrétien*, October 21, 1944; François Azouvi, *Le mythe du grand silence: Auschwitz, les Français, la mémoire* (Paris: Gallimard, 2015), 38–42.
[20] Holly Case, *The Age of Questions* (Princeton, NJ: Princeton University Press, 2018).

or the working class to remedy oppression or prejudice. Political antisemitism, to the contrary, transformed the "Jewish question" into a rallying cry against Jews to reverse the process of emancipation. Nazi racial warfare, lastly, sought cosmic redemption from Jews and Judaism. The last grand theorists of the "Jewish question," Hitler's henchmen used the slogan to justify genocide: The "Final Solution to the Jewish Question" indeed left an indelible taint on the expression. In January 1946, however, the exiled Hannah Arendt still accepted the validity of the term. As she wrote to her former mentor Karl Jaspers, "I have refused to abandon the Jewish question as the focal point of my historical and political thinking." But other German-speaking Jewish thinkers soon discredited the phrase. The philosopher Ernst Bloch argued in 1963 that whoever speaks of the Jewish Question" "verges upon, and perpetuates, an anti-Semitic way of framing the problem." The Austrian-born writer Jean Améry likewise abhorred the notion. For the Auschwitz survivor, the "Jewish question" remained "the anti-Semites' preserve, their ignominy, their sickness."[21]

In 1945, however, anti-antisemite defenders of Jews seized upon the catchphrase. Reopening the "Jewish question," of course, risked reviving the language of extermination. Jean-Paul Sartre drafted his *Réflexions sur la question juive* in the fall of 1944, only a few months after Vichy's Commissariat-General for Jewish Questions ceased its infamous activities. Discredited over time, the slogan nonetheless offered Sartre a point of entry into the problem of antisemitism. In 1948, the Hungarian democratic political thinker István Bibó probed the depth of antisemitism in his country through a similar lens. The communist take-over soon sidelined Bibó but his "Jewish Question in Hungary" turned the table on the phrase's antisemitic connotation.[22] With Sartre in France and Bibó in Hungary, the "question" underwent epochal rehabilitation: Synonymous with the permanence of antisemitism in European societies, it became a crucible for postwar morality. As the French protestant leader Charles Westphal wrote in 1947, it was now "the question

---

[21] Lotte Kohler and Hans Saner (eds.), *Hannah Arendt Karl Jaspers Correspondence* (New York: Harcourt, 1992), 31; Ernst Bloch, "The So-Called Jewish Question" (1963) in *Literary Essays* (Stanford, CA: Stanford University Press, 1998), 488–491; Jean Améry, "On the Impossible Obligation to Be a Jew" (1966) in Marlene Gallner (ed.), *Essays in Antisemitism, Anti-Zionism, and the Left* (Bloomington, IN: Indiana University Press, 2021), 9–26.

[22] István Bibó, "The Jewish Question in Hungary after 1944" (1948) in *Democracy, Revolution, Self-Determination: Selected Writings* (New York: Columbia University Press, 1991), 155–322; Ferenc Fehér, "István Bibó and the Jewish Question in Hungary: Notes on the Margin of a Classical Essay," in *New German Critique* 3, no. (21) (1980): 3–46.

among all questions."²³ Jewish observers favorably looked upon this phenomenon. "It requires more personality in a Gentile to take a dispassionate or a truly Christian interest in the Jewish question," wrote the British historian Lewis Namier in 1946, "that for a Jew to be disturbed about it."²⁴ How to approach the "question" nonetheless divided opponents of antisemitism. At the end of World War II, new anti-antisemites reopened the Jewish question to declare war on Judeophobia. Old ones, however, immediately announced its closure.

Closing the "Jewish Question": The European Left, 1945–1948

"There is no Jewish question," opined Herbert Kohlich, an editor of the Viennese socialist newspaper *Arbeiter-Zeitung*, in March 1946. After Nazism categorized Jews as racial outsiders, Austrian Social-Democrats championed their civic and legal rights in the newborn Second Republic. Yet the "martyrdom endured by the Jews," added Kohlich, did not justify any "special treatment": Giving Jews any other status than "Austrian citizens of the Jewish faith" would amount to "racism in reverse." Jewish victims, in any case, "only amounted to a sixth or seventh of the thirty-four million victims of National-Socialism." Oscar Pollak, the newspaper's Jewish editor-in-chief, reminded his colleague that "promoting empathy is the responsibility of each individual socialist." But Kohlich's article only stirred up minor controversy. Like their Christian conservative coalition partners, Austrian socialists disapproved of special relief and restitution policies for the miniscule community of Jewish survivors in Vienna. After the country was recognized by the Allies in 1943 as the "first victim of Hitlerite aggression," the ruling political parties made a point of claiming that all citizens had suffered equally. As the governmental mouthpiece *Wiener Zeitung* editorialized in January 1946, justice commanded "equality between all confessions."²⁵

---

[23] Cited in Patrick Cabanel, "Le Protestantisme français face à la Shoah et l'antisémitisme, de 1945 à nos jours," *Revue d'Histoire de la Shoah*, no. 192 (2010): 47–77.
[24] Lewis Namier, "Anti-Semitism" in *Facing East: Essays on German, the Balkans and Russia in the Twentieth Century* (London: Hamish Hamilton, 1947), 129–141.
[25] Herbert Kohlich, "Eine jüdische Frage?" in *Arbeiter-Zeitung*, March 27, 1946; Richard Mitten, "Jews and Other Victims: The 'Jewish Question' and Discourses of Victimhood in Postwar Austria," in Günter Bischof (ed.), *Austria in the European Union* (New Brunswick, NJ: Transaction, 2002), 223–270; Thomas Albricht, "'Es gibt keine jüdische Frage': Zur Aufrechterhaltung des österreichischen Opfermythos" in Rolf Steiniger (ed.), *Der Umgang mit dem Holocaust: Europa–USA–Israel* (Vienna: Böhlau Verlag, 1994), 147–166. See also "Für Gleichheit der Konfessionen" in *Wiener Zeitung*, January 6, 1946.

The Jewish publicist Artur Rosenberg, however, countered that a "Jewish question" was alive and well in postwar Austria. Enduring antisemitism, difficulties in restitution, and denial of co-responsibility for the persecution of Jews since 1938 were its unmistakable features. Abolishing the Jewish question, agreed Rosenberg, was "an ideal to be aspired to." Yet for the time being, its erasure only encouraged evasion of guilt.[26] A Viennese Jew long distanced from his Jewish roots, the socialist writer and returning exile Hans Weigel inveighed against Rosenberg's "racially defined" attitude. Throughout his political career, the *konfessionslos* (nondenominational) Jew and future socialist prime minister Bruno Kreisky would similarly object to the existence of a "Jewish question."[27] The dissenting Rosenberg drew another conclusion. The relegation of the "Jewish question" to the past, he argued before his emigration to France in the summer of 1946, first required the acknowledgment of its existence.

Whereas in Vienna socialists marginalized the "Jewish question" in favor of pan-Austrian victimhood, in occupied Germany the Social Democratic Party (SPD) did not steer clear from the phrase. Although the expression was still redolent of Nazism, the SPD leader Kurt Schumacher reversed its meaning: The "Jewish question" conveyed in his eyes the "injustice committed against the Jews" as well as a duty of "moral and material reparation."[28] Banned under Hitler, the SPD opposed the idea of collective guilt and did not place Jews above other victims. An outspoken anti-Nazi, Schumacher himself spent more than ten years in various concentration camps. In June 1947, however, he enjoined socialists to "for once talk about the Jews in Germany and in the world." The party, he declared, recognized that the "Third Reich attempted to exterminate Jewry in Europe. The German people are obligated to reparations and compensation." The statement squarely blamed the Jewish genocide on the Nazi dictatorship but was nonetheless a rare admission of responsibility. Before the Federal Republic's official policy of "reconciliation" with the Jewish world initiated during Konrad Adenauer's chancellorship (1949–63), Schumacher urged an honest examination of the Nazi past. "The average member of the cabinet does not think much

---

[26] Artur Rosenberg, "Land ohne Juden?" in *Neues Österreich*, March 26, 1946, 1–2.
[27] Wolfgang Straub, "'Farewell to the Jews': Hans Weigel, Social Democracy and the 'Jewish Question' in Post-1945 Austria'," *Austrian Studies* 24 (2016): 156–170; Robert S. Wistrich, "The Kreisky Phenomenon: A Reassessment" in Robert S. Wistrich (ed.), *Austrians and Jews in the Twentieth Century: From Franz Joseph to Waldheim* (New York: St. Martin's Press, 1992), 234–225.
[28] Rolf Vogel, *Der deutsch-israelische Dialog: Dokumentation eines erregenden Kapitels deutscher Außenpolitik* (Munich: Saur Verlag, 1987), 43.

about the Jewish question and is generally cool and passive about it," he lamented in November 1950. Contrary to ruling Christian Democrats, he reminded, the SPD had been since 1945 the only German political party "dedicated to the Jewish question."[29]

Socialist parties elsewhere similarly turned the antisemitic "Jewish question" into an issue of persecution and injustice. Because of its negative connotation, however, the phrase itself was absent from their vocabulary. In March 1946, the Labour-friendly *Manchester Guardian* featured a lengthy essay on the "Jewish Question" penned by the pro-Zionist historian Lewis Namier.[30] Yet the Labour party, like its counterparts on the continent, now avoided the term. Socialists showed instead sympathy for the "Jewish problem" of statelessness after the Holocaust. Even Foreign Secretary Ernest Bevin, an opponent to large-scale Jewish immigration to Palestine, declared in November 1945 that the "Jewish problem is a great human one."[31] Although the Attlee government refused to lift restrictions on the number of Jews allowed to settle in Palestine, most Labour backbenchers continued as before the war to support Zionism. In France, socialist politicians facilitated the covert embarkation of Jewish refugees from Mediterranean seaports to Palestine. From 1945 to 1948, the social-democratic solution to the "Jewish problem" coincided with the "solution to the Jewish question" in Palestine, a formulation still in use in Zionist pamphlets circulated in 1945.[32]

East and West of the Iron Curtain, Communists returned to old Marxist ideas on the "Jewish question" and antisemitism: Both were bound to fade away with the advent of a classless and just society. In Soviet-occupied East Germany, the new leaders of the self-proclaimed antifascist nation aggressively suppressed the "question." Although Jewish survivors received recognition as indistinct "victims of fascism," the leadership of the ruling Socialist Unity Party of Germany (SED) deflected attention from the particular fate of the Jews. In Soviet-controlled Europe, Marxist ideologues briefly resurrected the "Jewish

---

[29] On Schumacher and the "Jewish Question," see Jeffrey Herf, *Divided Memories: The Nazi Past in the Two Germanies* (Cambridge, MA: Harvard University Press, 1997), 241–253 and 276; Jay Howard Geller, *Jews in Post-Holocaust Germany, 1945–1953* (Cambridge: Cambridge University Press, 2005), 126–133.
[30] Lewis Namier, "The Jewish Question," *The Manchester Guardian*, March 8, 1946, reprinted in *Facing East*, op. cit., 142–150.
[31] Raphael Langham, "The Bevin Enigma: What Motivated Ernest Bevin's Opposition to the Establishment of a Jewish State in Palestine," in *Jewish Historical Studies* 44 (2012): 165–178.
[32] American Zionist Council, *The Jewish Case: The Place of Palestine in the Solution to the Jewish Question* (New York: American Zionist Council, 1945).

question" to give it proper burial. "The capitalist activities of the Jews and the hatred of Jews are correlated," wrote the Hungarian historian of Jewish origin Erik Molnár in 1946. Socialism, he prophesized, will eliminate the root cause of antisemitism. "An artificial creation of politically motivated demagoguery," the "Jewish question" stood on the brink of extinction. Longing for assimilation and equality, Jewish communists in East-Central Europe similarly yearned for the question's disappearance.[33]

The French PCF and Italian PCI, the two largest communist parties in Western Europe in 1945, did not think differently. Yet contrary to Eastern European ideologues, they refrained from speculating on a "question" reminiscent of Nazism: Accelerated Jewish integration in the party, the working class, and the nation was their antifascist response to the Final Solution. In the immediate postwar period, this proposition still appealed to Eastern European Jewish immigrants in France or Jewish intellectuals in Italy. "At this time," wrote the Jewish communist Emilio Sereni in July 1946, "the cause of Judaism is bound, more than ever, with the worldwide cause of defending democracy and peace." For the young writer Amos Luzzatto, "applied communism" remained the "single possible answer to anti-Semitism."[34]

In 1946, however, the Belgian Trotskyist of Jewish origin Ernest Mandel attempted to rejuvenate Marxist thought on the "Jewish question" – as his mentor Abraham Léon had done before his deportation to Auschwitz in 1944.[35] The "Jewish tragedy," claimed Mandel in reference to the Holocaust, "pushed to the point of paroxysm the barbarity of imperialism's customary methods of our time." Like Hannah Arendt in *The Origins of Totalitarianism* (1951), Mandel related the Nazi program of extermination to the history of European imperial violence.

---

[33] Erik Molnár, "The Jewish Question in Hungary" (July 1946) cited in Yehuda Don, "The Economic Effect of Antisemitic Discrimination: Hungarian Anti-Jewish Legislation, 1938–1944" *Jewish Social Studies* 48, no. 1 (Winter 1986): 63–82; Holly Case, *The Age of Questions*, op. cit., 118. On Eastern European Jewish communists after the Holocaust, see Marci Shore, *Caviar and Ashes: A Warsaw Generation Life and Death in Marxism, 1918–1968* (New Haven: Yale University Press, 2009); Heda Kovaly, *Under a Cruel Star: A Life in Prague 1941–1968* (New York: Holmes and Meier, 1997).

[34] Michel Dreyfus, *L'antisémitisme à gauche: Histoire d'un paradoxe, de 1830 à nos jours*, 41–42; Sereni cited in Andrea Guison, "The Italian Communist Party and the 'Israel Question' during the First Years of the Cold War: Towards a Historical Semantics of Communist Anti-Zionism" in Alessandra Tarquini (ed.), *The European Left and the Jewish Question, 1848–1992* (Cham: Palgrave Macmillan, 2021), 229–242. On Amos Luzzatto, see Matteo Di Figlia, *Israele e la sinistra: Gli ebrei nel dibattito publicco italiano dal 1945 a oggi* (Rome: Donzelli Editore, 2012), 44–46.

[35] Ernest Mandel, *The Jewish Question since World War II* (1946), available at: www.marxists.org/archive/mandel/1946/07/jews.htm.

The genocide of the Jews, in his mind, also showed humanity the "mirror of the future," a new age of colonial and nuclear terror. "The perspective of the disappearance of the Jews from the earth," wrote the Jewish revolutionary, "is part of the perspective of the destruction of the human species." The conceptualization of Auschwitz as blueprint for Hiroshima or Cold War Armageddon departed from Marxist economic interpretations of Nazism. Mandel's solution to the "Jewish question," however, stayed within orthodox bounds. "The Jewish masses," he proclaimed, "will owe their final emancipation to a devoted struggle to the cause of socialism." Contrary to the Frankfurt School's psychoanalytical take on Marxist philosophy, classical Marxism after the Holocaust had little new to say on the nature and function of antisemitism in society.[36]

In liberated Western Europe, some of the first "querists" – non-Jewish writers who opened the question anew – came instead from the ranks of the Christian church. Martinus Slotemaker de Bruine, a Dutch Reformed pastor who during the Holocaust pleaded with Reichskommissar Arthur Seyss-Inquart to stop the deportations of Jews, penned his *Het joodse vraagstuk* [*The Jewish Question*, 1946] out of self-declared compassion. De Bruine's concern was for the "Jewish human being, that very particular and peculiar form of life that arouses so much estrangement and strong affective reactions." Yet by his own admission, his essay was not "typical philosemitic writing." In fact, "anyone who wishes so could even hear antisemitic tones in it." While Jews had "cultural talent," they also displayed "egocentric attitudes" and a "hardly concealed sense of superiority." The Protestant leader did not advocate the conversion of Jews to Christianity, but he advised them to disappear into Dutch society: The precondition of acceptance remained as in the past a drastic change of Jewish behavior or better, full assimilation. This goal required difficult negotiations: "many exchanges of views will still have to be conducted (...) before the mentality of the ghetto can finally be overcome."[37] Post-Holocaust Christian writers on the "Jewish question," as the Dutch clergyman demonstrated, still liberally blamed Jews for antisemitism. In England, however, the Anglican pioneer of Christian-Jewish dialogue James Parkes had since the 1930s followed a different path. The "Jewish question," he countered, was synonymous with the question of Christian anti-Judaism in the West.

---

[36] Enzo Traverso, *The Jewish Question: History of a Marxist Debate* (Leiden: Brill, 2018), 202–207; Philip Spencer, "European Marxism and the Question of Antisemitism," *European Societies* 14, no. 2 (2012): 275–294.
[37] Martinus Cornelis Slotemaker de Bruine, *Het Joodse Vraagstuk* (Nijkerk: G.F. Callenbach, 1946), 14, 5, 139, 195.

"Enemy of the People": James Parkes's Anti-antisemitism

In *The Conflict of the Church and Synagogue: The Origins of Antisemitism*, first published in 1934, Parkes challenged a core tenet of Christian doctrine. Responsibility for antisemitism, wrote the Anglican scholar, did not rest on the Jews' rejection of Christ but upon theological representations of the Jew "as a being perpetually betraying God and ultimately abandoned by Him." After the outbreak of World War II, Parkes reiterated this position in his pamphlet *The Jewish Question*, written to sway the wartime British public away from anti-Jewish prejudice.[38] Parkes's exculpation of Jews for their victimization was even more trenchant in his *Emergence of the Jewish Problem 1878–1939* published in 1946. The hatred of Jews, he explained, functioned as a "political weapon deliberately invented (...) for ends which have nothing to do with the Jewish people or the Jewish religion."[39]

This interpretation, of course, was not new to Jewish theorists of antisemitism. On the eve of the war, Hannah Arendt had already observed that as opposed to earlier periods, in the twentieth century "the foundations of antisemitism are found in developments that have very little to do with Jews."[40] But coming from a clergyman, such discharge of Jews from culpability departed from the "philosemitic antisemitism" still rife in European Christian discourse: a condemnation of anti-Jewish bigotry or violence which also blamed its victims for the phenomenon. The idea of the Jews' responsibility for their otherwise contemptable persecution had not disappeared at the end of the war, least among churchmen or writers still convinced that Jewish suffering was the consequence of deicide. The provocative Parkes claimed, to the contrary, that antisemitism was exclusively "a problem of the Gentile" independent of Jewish actions.[41] The Anglican reverend reversed the classic terms of Jewish emancipation: The burden of *verbesserung* or "regeneration," once the obligation imposed on Jews for their acceptance in modern European societies, now exclusively fell on the non-Jews.

Parkes's acquittal of Jews for the hatred surrounding them reflected a new direction in post-Holocaust theories of antisemitism: a shift from the "Jewish question" to the "antisemite question" peculiar to the

---

[38] James Parkes, *The Jewish Question*, Oxford Pamphlets on World Affairs, no. 45 (Oxford: Clarendon Press, 1941).
[39] James Parkes, *The Emergence of the Jewish Problem 1878–1939* (London: Oxford University Press, 1946), 195.
[40] Hannah Arendt, "Antisemitism" (1938) in Jerome Kohn and Ron H. Feldman (eds.), *The Jewish Writings: Hannah Arendt* (New York: Schocken Books, 2007), 46–124.
[41] James Parkes, *A Problem for the Gentiles* (London: Peace News, 1945).

Christian West. Parke's focus on the Gentile's deficiencies, however, did not leave Jews without faults. In *An Enemy of the People: Antisemitism* (1945), a book published in England and the United States and distributed in occupied Germany to promote denazification, Parkes stressed again that "the onslaught on the Jews" did not result from "actual Jewish conduct." But in a chapter dedicated to the "Psychological and Sociological Problems of Jewry," Parkes validated some of the stereotypes he sought to discredit. The Jews' "contempt for the non-Jew" or their "lower business morality," he claimed, were "disabilities a minority must suffer from." Such unattractive Jewish traits, he predicted, will fortunately disappear with the full acceptance of Jews in Christian society.[42] The Austrian-born Jewish émigré psychologist Marie Jahoda, however, doubted Parkes's benevolence. "The *lapsis mentis* of Dr. Parkes," she charged in 1947, "offers additional sad evidence (quite unneeded) of the ubiquity of anti-Semitism."[43] Jahoda harshly judged a clergyman who according to his Jewish admirers "also spoke as a Jew."[44] Yet Parkes inadvertently gave credence to Jahoda's criticism. "If I were asked what proportion of the population were at least slightly unbalanced on the subject of the Jews," he speculated, "I would say: about 95 per cent, including (...) all the people who have made a deep study of the Jewish question."[45]

Parkes's lapses proved again that anti-antisemitism did not preclude negative or ambiguous views of Jews. The Anglican scholar nevertheless declared an all-out crusade against the scourge. He described the struggle in epic language: "The giant [of anti-semitism] is as dangerous an enemy (...) as any that we shall meet." The Holocaust, however, played little role in Parkes's call to arms. Published in 1945, *An Enemy of the People* enjoined the Christian public to act against prejudice without evoking more than in passing the Jewish tragedy.[46] Antisemitism was above all a danger because of its corruptive effect on Christian society. The crushing of the "giant" was above all self-purification: "For our own sakes, we must clear him from our path." Parkes's secondary goal was

---

[42] James Parkes, *An Enemy of the People: Antisemitism* (Harmondsworth: Penguin, 1945), 11, 96, 101, 145.
[43] *Commentary*, January 1, 1947, 97–99.
[44] Haim Chertok, *He Also Spoke as a Jew: The Life of The Reverend James Parkes* (London: Vallentine Mitchell, 2006).
[45] Parkes, *An Enemy of the People*, 138.
[46] On Parkes's response to the Holocaust, see Dan Stone, "The Domestication of Violence: Forging a Collective Memory of the Holocaust in Britain, 1945–6" *Patterns of Prejudice* 33, no. 2 (1999): 13–29; Tony Kushner, "James Parkes and the Holocaust" in John K. Roth et al., *Remembering for the Future: The Holocaust in an Age of Genocide* (New York: Palgrave, 2001), 1501–1512.

the protection of the Jews. The behemoth, he urged, "we must slay also for the sake of the victims, for the sake of the Jews."

One means of eradication, Parkes argued, was the education of Christians in schools and churches. But a more immediate form of action was support for Jewish statehood. "In southern Syria," admitted the Church of England reverend, "conditions exist in which two rights confront each other, both valid." Yet if a "Jewish commonwealth were to be established, the situation of the Jews in Europe is not difficult of solution. For there is a home to which those who do not wish to remain in Europe are able to go." Parkes's Zionism was pragmatic, not biblical. "The making of Palestine (or part of it) into a Jewish Commonwealth," he claimed, "would not be destroying an Arab country; it would be diminishing the area of Syria."[47] The benefit far outweighed the cost. Like the Labour MP Richard Crossman, Parkes envisioned the defeat of the "enemy of the people" through the emigration of many Jews to Palestine. The country is "not empty," recognized Parkes, "and the resulting conflict of interest is one which will need the most serious attention." But group settlement in Palestine was still preferable to Jewish "infiltration in the world's great cities," the traditional "breeding grounds for antisemitism." With or without Arab acceptance, Palestine was enrolled into Europe's battle against its antisemitic self.[48]

Parkes's ruminations on the "Jewish question," in sum, encapsulated the key tenets of the new anti-antisemitic cause. "The present general neurosis about the Jews" was not the result of Jewish actions but the exclusive "problem of the Gentile"; the persistence of anti-Jewish prejudice hindered the reconstruction of healthy societies; distinct from antifascism or progressive politics, anti-antisemitism sought to expunge the "virus" from the body of the citizenry; support for a Jewish state in Palestine became part and parcel of the struggle. Other anti-antisemitic writers, however, ascribed an additional purpose to the "Jewish question": to serve as blueprint for new ideas of rights.

Personhood and the "Jewish Question"

In *Intorno alla questione ebraica* [*On the Jewish Question*], published in 1942, Ernesto Orrei, a law professor at the University of Rome, courageously protested Mussolini's racial laws in effect since 1938. This was a risky attempt. To deflect censorship, the legal scholar disguised his

---

[47] Parkes, *An Enemy of the People*, 134, 137.
[48] Parkes, *The Emergence of the Jewish Problem*, op. cit., 233.

criticism of the Fascist regime behind the writings of historical figures known for their defense of Jews. The early nineteenth-century Prussian reformer Wilhelm von Humboldt, who pledged to "labor ceaselessly with all my strengths (...) to give Jews full civil rights," was one of his decoys.[49] True to form, Orrei also argued in favor of the "reconstitution" of a Jewish state integrated in the international order. Such resurgence, he claimed, would finally disprove the antisemitic claim of "Jewish ethnic inferiority."[50]

Yet Orrei's "examination of the Jewish question," reissued in 1947, pleaded above all for the "full recognition of the rights of the personality."[51] Since the interwar period, Catholic intellectuals in Western and Central Europe championed the "rights of the human person" against the "rights of Man" dear to secular liberalism. "The concept of, and devotion to, the rights of the human person," wrote the French philosopher Jacques Maritain from the United States in 1942, "is the most significant political improvement of modern times."[52] At war's midpoint, Pope Pius XII similarly called for the restoration "to the human person [of] the dignity given to him by God from the very beginning." In his notorious 1942 Christmas address, however, the pontiff made only one oblique reference to the ongoing annihilation of European Jews. Through the dignity of the human person, Pius XII claimed a Christian stake in postwar human rights politics without reference to antisemitism. Orrei, to the contrary, derived the "principle of personhood" from his sympathetic discussion of the "Jewish question." The persecution of the Jews revealed to him the urgency of a "progressive law" grounded on the sacred "rights of the personality."[53] The Jesuit periodical *La Civiltà Cattolica* rightly recognized in Orrei's essay "a defense of the Jewish cause based on respect for personality, humanity, and civil tolerance." But the Vatican's unofficial mouthpiece also protested Orrei's excessive philosemitism. Charity and justice for the Jews, the Catholic public was reminded, did not preclude "a prudent and moderate defense" against them.[54]

---

[49] Ernesto Orrei, *La questione ebraica: Lineamenti di storia e di dottrina* (Roma: Le edizioni del lavoro, 1947), 247. On Orrei, see Michele Sarfatti, *Jews in Mussolini's Italy: From Equality to Persecution* (Madison, WI: The University of Wisconsin Press, 2006), 156; Giuseppe Acerbi, *Le leggi antiebraiche e razziali italiane ed il ceto dei giuristi* (Milan: Giuffrè Editore, 2011), 181–182.
[50] Orrei, *La questione ebraica*, 243.
[51] Orrei, *La questione ebraica*, 230.
[52] Maritain cited by Samuel Moyn, *Christian Human Rights* (Philadelphia, PA: University of Pennsylvania Press, 2015), 123.
[53] Orrei, *La questione ebraica*, 246.
[54] Elena Mazzini, "Transforming Anti-Semitism: The Civiltà Cattolica after the Shoah (1945–1965)" in James Bernauer and Robert A. Maryks (eds.), *"The Tragic Couple": Encounters between Jews and Jesuits* (Leiden: Brill, 2014), 233–245. News of Orrei's

The French Left-Catholic philosopher Emmanuel Mounier similarly referred to the "Jewish question" to highlight the idea of personhood. In 1936, his influential "Personalist Manifesto" had affirmed the absolute value of the human person without any reference to Judaism. Influenced by Catholicism, personalism reacted against the "tyranical reality" of bourgeois liberalism, fascism, and communism. Against decadent individualism and mass politics, Mounier and his "non-conformist" followers idealized the human person grounded in community.[55] In September 1945, however, Mounier added a Jewish dimension to his personalist philosophy. Modern Jews, explained the founder of the review *Esprit*, traditionally faced the choice of assimilation or retreat into the ghetto. Yet because of "persecution and the rising force of Zionism," he noticed, many Jews now refused the dilemma of emancipation. Mounier drew inspiration from the Jewish poet and writer Henri Hertz, who in *Esprit* rejected integrationism in favor of dual belonging to France and a "Jewish nation."[56] Discovering through Hertz the idea of diaspora nationalism, Mounier marveled at the fluidity of Jewish identity. The "Jewish paradoxe," he wrote, was "a model for the new world": the emancipation of the human person from the "univocal nationalism of the Jacobins and the Maurassists," from French republicanism and its far-right enemies. In the same vein, the *Esprit* essayist François Bondy praised the Jews' "plurality of bonds," a model for "open society (...) and the full development of the personality."[57] Mounier waxed even more lyrical: A "force for the future," Jewishness heralded the age of "entangled belongings" and supranational "European patriotism."

Against appearances, however, the personalist thinker was not a prophet of cosmopolitan Europe. The Jews' simultaneous belonging to a "temporal Jewish community" and to a "French, Russian or English community" reminded him instead of medieval Christendom. "Was not the Christian medieval lord," Mounier asked, "already bound to different loyalties: to his overlord, to the King of overlords, and to the head of his Church?" The hybridity of Jewish identity, ultimately, only validated older forms of Christian bonds. Mounier nevertheless assigned a positive purpose to Jewishness: to serve as a template for more "complex"

---

death in 1952 caused "profound sorrow" among Italian Jews. They hailed his *On the Jewish Question* as "an open defense of Judaism and a fierce criticism of Fascist brutalities." See *American Jewish Yearbook*, Volume 53 (1952), 302–307.

[55] Emmanuel Mounier, *Manifeste au service du personnalisme* (1936).
[56] Emmanuel Mounier, "Les juifs parlent aux nations," *Esprit* 114, no. 10 (September 1, 1945): 457–459; in the same issue, see Henri Hertz, "Etre ou ne pas être Juif," 509–514.
[57] François Bondy, "Le Judaïsme et la catastrophe européenne" in Esprit 114 (10), op. cit., 491–505.

identities in the postwar era. The personalist philosopher, to be sure, did not forget the Jews' "errors, deficiencies, faults, some at times more irritating than others." Fortunately, these defects were correctible: "What history did, history can undo." His remarks nevertheless valorized the function of Jewishness in postwar society. They also disrupted the "strange silence" which, to his dismay, surrounded the issue of Jewish victims in liberated France.[58] Since the fall of 1944, however, the rising star of the French intelligentsia had already set out to give the "Jewish question" unprecedented publicity.

Sartre's Philosemitism

"It is not up to the Jews first of all to form a militant league against antisemitism," wrote Jean-Paul Sartre in his *Réflexions sur la question juive* [thereafter *Réflexions*], "it is up to us."[59] In his well-known essay, the existentialist philosopher famously reframed antisemitism as a problem for non-Jews. Like James Parkes, who across the Channel defined Jew-hatred as a "problem for Gentiles," Sartre notoriously posited that "antisemitism is not a Jewish problem, it is our problem." Parkes, however, remained throughout his life a dissident voice within the Anglican church. The French philosopher's growing prestige, to the contrary, lent to the "non-Jewish problem" incomparable visibility. Although the first edition of *Réflexions* was brought out in 1946 by a little known company (the famed Gallimard publishing house reprinted it in 1954), Sartre's towering position within the French intelligentsia gave particular resonance to his plea: "We must be very blind indeed not to see that [antisemitism] is our concern to the highest degree."[60]

That "not a word" was being said about Jewish victims in liberated France is what prompted Sartre to start writing *Réflexions* in the fall of 1944. The essay's philosophical origins, however, harkened back to his prewar thought. The forty-year-old philosopher approached the "Jewish question" through existentialist phenomenology and the ethics of intellectual commitment.[61] In *Réflexions*, the Jewish problem becomes the

---

[58] Renée Poznanski, "The *Jewish Question* versus the Jewish Problem: Sartre amid a Strange Silence" in Manuela Consonni and Vivian Liska (eds.), *Sartre, Jews, and the Other: Rethinking Antisemitism, Race, and Gender* (Berlin: De Gruyter Oldenburg, 2020), 75–89.

[59] Jean-Paul Sartre, *Antisemite and Jew: An Exploration of the Etiology of Hate* [hereafter: AAJ] (New York: Schocken Books, 1995).

[60] Ibid., 152.

[61] On the philosophical origins of *Réflexions*, see Jonathan Judaken's *Jean-Paul Sartre and the Jewish Question: Anti-Antisemitism and the Politics of the French Intellectual* (Lincoln, NE: University of Nebraska Press, 2006), chapters 1–3; and *Critical Theories of Anti-Semitism* (New York: Columbia University Press, 2024), 21–44.

problem of the antisemite, a displacement of responsibility greeted with emotion by his first Jewish readers. During the German occupation, the French Jewish philosopher Vladimir Jankélévitch had already remarked that "antisemitism succeeds at creating a question that does not exist, and yet exists on its own in the mythology of the executioners."[62] While also drawing the "Portrait of the Jew," *Réflexions* similarly examined the phenomenon of Jew-hatred from the aggressor's perspective. Yet Sartre's "Jewish question" was not just the lethal fantasy of executioners. Because antisemitism made "hangmen of all of us," the Parisian celebrity recognized the syndrome as a central pathology of modernity.

Exiled in the United States, the mainstays of the Frankfurt School of critical theory had already diagnosed a similar ill. "A malady so deeply rooted in civilization," wrote Theodor Adorno and Max Horkheimer in 1943, antisemitism was a "deeply imprinted schema, a ritual of civilization itself."[63] Their sociopsychological critique, however, was a German Jewish response to the catastrophe unfolding in Europe. "Jews have been made what the Nazis always pretended they were, the focal point of world history," finally realized Horkheimer in 1944.[64] Like Hannah Arendt, the Frankfurt School émigrés reacted to the genocide by deciphering the function of Jew-hatred in Europe and the United States. Adorno and Horkheimer's *Dialectic of Enlightenment* (1944 and 1947), Adorno's *The Authoritarian Personality* (1950), and Arendt's *The Origins of Totalitarianism* (1951) revitalized critical theories of antisemitism after the Holocaust.

These seminal works nonetheless continued a distinctively Jewish project. From the start of the 1920s to World War II, critical theories of antisemitism in Europe chiefly emanated from German-Jewish thinkers.[65] Some of the explanatory schemes of antisemitism popularized

---

[62] Vladimir Jankélévitch, "Existe-t-il une question juive?" (1943) in *L'esprit de résistance: Textes inédits, 1943–1983* (Paris: Albin Michel), 126. Unnoticed by Sartre's commentators, this text published clandestinely in 1943 already addressed some of *Réflexions*' main themes.

[63] See Thesis II of "Elements of Antisemitism" in Theodor W. Adorno and Marx Horkheimer, *Dialectic of Enlightenment* (London: Verso 2016), 366–367.

[64] Jack Jacobs, *The Frankfurt School, Jewish Lives and Antisemitism* (New York: Cambridge University Press, 2015), 75; Lars Rensmann, *The Politics of Unreason. The Frankfurt School and the Origins of Modern Antisemitism* (Albany, NY: State University of New York Press, 2017), 18–21.

[65] Franzeska Krah, "Ein Ungeheuer, das wenigstens theoretisch besiegt sein muss," in *Pioniere der Antisemitismusforschung in Deutschland* (Frankfurt: Campus Verlag), 2016; Hans-Joachim Hahn and Olaf Kistenmacher (eds.), *Beschreibungsversuche der Judenfeindschaft: Zur Geschichte der Antisemitismusforschung vor 1944* (Berlin: De Gruyter Oldenbourg, 2015); Birgit Erdle and Werner Konitzer (eds.), *Theorien über Judenhass – eine denkgeschichte: Kommentierte Quellenedition (1781–1931)* (Frankfurt: Campus Verlag, 2015).

after 1945 had indeed already been hammered out during the Weimar Republic. Arnold Zweig, a great admirer of Sigmund Freud, presciently attributed to antisemitism a psychoanalytical function. "As long as we know about the antisemitic affect," he wrote in 1927, "it has been used as a means to something else."[66] In 1929, Norbert Elias offered a sociological diagnosis of German antisemitism. Ahead of Hannah Arendt's writings on the subject, Elias traced the roots of the phenomenon to the "changing social position of the Jews." Four years before the Nazi seizure of power, he also introduced an idea dear to the existentialist Sartre. In the face of antisemitic violence, argued Elias, "a clear understanding of one's own position is preferable in any case to self-deception."[67] In 1936, the Swedish historian of Jewish origin Hugo Valentin offered an interpretation destined to greater popularity after 1945. "For it is not Jews who are hated," Valentin wrote, "but an imaginary image of them (...) and the Jews actual 'faults' play a very unimportant part in the matter."[68]

Jewish scholars of antisemitism in the United States joined the fray. Two seminal collective volumes published in New York in 1942 searched for the historical, sociological, psychological, and religious origins of Jew-hatred.[69] Non-Jewish thinkers such as the American sociologist Talcott Parsons also took part in this movement.[70] But the main contributors to the "Anti-Semitism Project" and the "Studies in Prejudice" conducted under the auspices of the Frankfurt School were Jews, most of them born in Central Europe: *antisemitismusforschung* (research on antisemitism) remained as in the past a Jewish intellectual project. Combining various academic disciplines, its protagonists strove

---

[66] Bart Philipsen and Georgi Verbeeck, "Caliban in the Weimar Republic, Arnold Zweig and Antisemitism" in Nadia Lie and Theo D'haen (eds.), *Constellation Caliban. Figurations of a Character* (Amsterdam: Rodopi B.V., 1997), 163–184.
[67] Norbert Elias, "On the Sociology of German Anti-Semitism" *Journal of Classical Sociology* 2, no. 1 (2001): 219–225. See also Danny Trom, "Elias on Antisemitism: Zionism or Sociology," *Annales. Histoire, Sciences Sociales* (English edition) 71, no. 2 (June 2016): 249–289.
[68] Cited in Jonathan Judaken, "Anti-Semitism (Historiography) in Sol Goldberg et al. (eds.), *Key Concepts in the Study of Antisemitism* (Cham: Palgrave Macmillan, 2021), 25–38.
[69] Isaque Graeber and Steuart Henderson Britt (eds.), *The Jew in the Gentile World* (New York: The Macmillan Company, 1942); Koppel S. Pinson and Salo W. Baron (eds.), *Essays on Antisemitism* (New York: Conference on Jewish Relations, 1942); on this volume, see Elisabeth Gallas, "Theoriebildung und Abwehrkampf während der Katastrophe. Essays on Antisemitism, New York 1942" in Hans-Joachim Hahn, Olaf Kistenmacher (eds.), *Beschreibungsversuche der Judenfeindschaft*, op. cit., 403–425.
[70] Jonathan Judaken, "Talcott Parsons's 'The Sociology of Modern Anti-Semitism': Anti-antisemitism, Ambivalent Liberalism, and the Sociological Imagination" in Marcel Stoezler (ed.), *Antisemitism and the Constitution of Sociology* (Lincoln, NE: University of Nebraska Press, 2014), 249–273.

toward a post-antisemitic age. "Our aim," wrote Max Horkheimer, "is not merely to describe prejudice but to explain it in order to help in its eradication."[71]

Sartre's *Réflexions* indicated the arrival of a new campaigner: the non-Jewish, anti-antisemite, "committed" intellectual. To be sure, his "exploration of the etiology of hate" unknowingly echoed the "Jewish" Frankfurt School. Adorno and Horkheimer uniquely tried to understand "the mental energy harnessed by antisemitism" through a critical reappraisal of the Enlightenment. But in addition to arguing that "society itself can only be understood through antisemitism," they also defined hatred of Jews as "the bad conscience of the parasite"; or stressed its "largely projective character": Sartre's analysis of antisemitism included similar ideas.[72] Without equivalent in Europe or in the United States, however, *Réflexions* was the first non-Jewish philosophical intervention on behalf of post-Holocaust Jews. This fact is often eluded by faultfinding readers of Sartre more concerned with the essay's numerous shortcomings. But one of its first French Jewish commentators did not miss this crucial dimension. Published in *Esprit* in 1947, Wladimir Rabi's review of *Réflexions* was revealingly entitled "Portrait of a Philosemite." The phrase was not derogatory. Although he drew attention to Sartre's ignorance of the concrete reality of Jewishness, Rabi nonetheless recognized the philosemitic distinctiveness of his intervention: not just opposition to antisemitism but also a radical project of solidarity with Jews. Although eminent commentators of Sartre's opus only designate the French thinker as "anti-antisemite," the intensity of this solidarity, and the risk-taking involved, inaugurated a new form of pro-Jewish intervention: not devotion to Jews or Judaism, but a state of emergency on behalf of the Jew.

Admittedly, the investigation of the antisemitic psyche offered Sartre a convenient platform to showcase fashionable existentialist ideas: "fear of the human condition," "inauthenticity," and "bad faith" found in the figure of the (French) antisemite an ideal testing ground. But *Réflexions* above all proclaimed the absolute criminality of antisemitism, a violence "that affects us all directly."[73] This diagnosis led Sartre to conclude that "we must fight for the Jews no more and no less than for

---

[71] Cited in Jacobs, *The Frankfurt School, Jewish Lives and Antisemitism*, op. cit., 107.
[72] Nicolas Weill, "L'antisémitisme selon Sartre et selon l'École de Frankfurt: esquisse d'une comparaison" in Indrid Galster (ed.), *Sartre et les Juifs* (Paris: La Découverte, 2005), 201–210.
[73] Frédéric Worms, "Antisemitism as Existential Crime" in Manuela Consonni and Vivian Liska (eds.), *Sartre, Jews, and the Other: Rethinking Antisemitism, Race, and Gender* (Berlin: De Gruyter Oldenburg, 2020), 24–34.

ourselves" [AAJ 151]. This injunction potentially revived the difference between "Jews" and "ourselves," the very premise of antisemitism. Yet with Sartre, the universalist, humanist, and antifascist defense of the Jews escalated, as the philosopher later explained, into a "declaration of war against antisemites."[74] Although he admitted that "Sartre's theory (…) can be disappointing," the French-Jewish thinker Emmanuel Levinas immediately recognized its powerful novelty. "The most striking figure of Sartre's fight," the Vilna-born philosopher observed, "resides less than in his victory than the new weapons he deploys. They are wholly new."[75] Levinas's remarks highlighted the unique contribution of Sartre's essay. Despite its deficiencies, *Réflexions* transformed the meaning of anti-antisemitism after 1945. A new politics of solidarity with Jews, Sartre's "declaration of war" was also the first philosemitic manifesto of the postwar era.

Anti-antisemitism: Template for Anti-racism

Already the subject of voluminous scholarship, the portrayal of the antisemite and the Jew in *Réflexions* does not need lengthy recapitulation. Escaping freedom, dreading responsibility and truth, and projecting his inadequacies on the figure of her enemy, the antisemite creates the Jew to give her life meaning. Although superficially acquainted with Jews, Judaism or Jewish history, Sartre redefined the meaning of antisemitism: a "passion" and not an "opinion," a "sadistic attraction," a refusal of "oneself and of truth," a "fear of the human condition." As Sartrean scholars have shown, however, the existentialist philosopher immediately applied these concepts to other forms of racism. "Replace the Jew with the Black, the anti-Semite with the supporter of slavery," Sartre stated in 1948, "and there would be nothing essential to be cut from my book."[76] During the Algerian War (1954–62), Sartre departed from existentialist

---

[74] Sartre cited in Elad Lapidot, *Jews Out of the Question: A Critique of Anti-Anti Semitism* (Albany, NY: State University of New York Press, 2020), 82. On the "War against Antisemitism," see Gil Anidjar, "Antisemitism and Its Critics" in James Renton and Ben Gidley (eds.), *Antisemitism and Islamophobia in Europe: A Shared History?* (London: Palgrave Macmillan, 2017), 187–214.

[75] Emmanuel Levinas, "Existentialism and Anti-Semitism" (1947) reprinted in *October* 87 (Winter 1999): 27–31.

[76] Cited in Jonathan Judaken, "Sartre on Racism: From Existential Phenomenology to Globalization and the 'New Racism'" in J. Judaken (ed.), *Race after Sartre: Antiracism, Africana Existentialism, Postcolonialism* (Albany, NY: State University of New York Press, 2008), 23–53; see also Judaken, "Sartre's Multidirectional Anti-Racism" in Manuela Consonni and Vivian Liska (eds.), *Sartre, Jews, and the Other*, op. cit., 107–130.

phenomenology to portray colonial racism as a system of domination based on capitalist exploitation. French rule in Algeria, in his mind, offered "the most legible example of the colonial system."[77] But ten years after *Réflexions*, his support for Algerian nationalism replicated his unitary struggle "for the Jews" and "for ourselves." Sartre's goal was to "deliver both the Algerians and the French from colonial tyranny": In *Réflexions*, France's foremost public intellectual had already inscribed the "Jewish question" at the center of his struggle against racial oppression.[78] "The writer's duty is to take side against all injustices wherever they come from," Sartre proclaimed in 1947. But the philosophical foundation of his antiracism remained anti-antisemitism. The "Jewish question" propelled him to the "Negro question," the French colonial question, the attendant "question" of torture in French Algeria, and to solidarity with Third World liberation movements.[79]

Sartre's "Jewish question," however, did not lead him to the question of Palestine. His anti-antisemitism bore little resemblance to that of Richard Crossman or James Parkes, but he shared with them a positive opinion of Zionism. In *Réflexions*, the existentialist Sartre famously encouraged Jews to authenticity in order to overcome the antisemite's aggression. Jewish self-acceptance, he acknowledged, was perfectly attainable in the diaspora, whether as "Jews in France" or integrated French Jews. The choice of authenticity, however, could also legitimately lead Jews to create "a Jewish nation possessing its own soil and autonomy" [AAJ 139]. In his first writings on Zionism (1945–48), Sartre, like most members of the European left, never considered Jewish self-determination from the standpoint of Palestine's native inhabitants. "It is the task of the non-Jews to help the Jews, and the Palestinian [e.g., Zionist] cause," he declared in February 1948. He reiterated this point one month before the establishment of the State of Israel. "We cannot dissociate ourselves from the cause of the Hebrews," he wrote in April 1948.[80] Sartre provided no indication that Zionism might threaten the Arab majority in Mandate Palestine. If Jewish nationhood was at all harmful, it was "to the Jews who wish

---

[77] Jean-Paul Sartre, "Colonialism Is a System" (1956) in *Colonialism and Neocolonialism* (New York: Routledge, 2001), 30–47.
[78] Ethan Katz, "Sartre's Algerian Jewish Question" in *Sartre, Jews, and the Other*, op. cit., 63–74.
[79] On the "question" of torture in Algeria, see Sartre's preface to Henri Alleg, *La question* (Paris: Editions de Minuit, 1958).
[80] Judaken, *Jean-Paul Sartre and the Jewish Question*, 188; see also Farouk Mardam-Bey, "Sartre, Israël et les Arabes: la 'détermination affective'" *Matériaux pour l'histoire du temps present* 4, no. 96 (2009): 38–41; "French Intellectuals and the Palestine Question," *Journal of Palestine Studies* XLIII, no. 3 (Spring 2014): 26–39.

to remain in their original fatherland" [AAJ 139]. Sartre indeed worried that the establishment of a Jewish state would give Jew-haters "another proof that the Jew is out of place in the French community." Irrespective of its consequences, self-determination in Palestine offered Jews a pathway to authenticity and freedom: Both antisemitism and Zionism provided Sartre with a test case for existentialist liberation. But his refusal to apply to Israel the anti-colonial and antiracist lens he used to illuminate other forms of oppression will soon disappoint his admirers in the Arab world.

Sartre's assault on what he termed the "politics of assimilation" added another philosemitic dimension to *Réflexions*.[81] The democrat humanist who "saves [the Jew] as man and annihilates him as a Jew" becomes in Sartre's opus the antisemite's partner in crime. Until he dissolved it through revolution, Sartre ascribed value to Jewish difference. Like all other forms of racism, Sartre posited, the otherness of the Jew originates in a mental construct. But after its migration from the antisemite's mind to the heart of society, Jewishness not only becomes social reality. It also forms the basis of "concrete liberalism": the valorization of human difference against the cult of abstract human nature. "Arabs and Negroes," clarified Sartre, were also "concrete persons" deserving as Arabs and Blacks of recognition and respect. Yet against a liberalism unable to recognize Jewish singularity, Sartre's "Jew as Jew" typified positive difference: "It is with his character, his customs, his tastes, his religion if he has one, his name and his physical traits that we must accept him"[82] [AAJ 147].

The last pages of *Réflexions*, however, have notoriously exposed the Jew-friendly intellectual to the charge of inconsistency. "The authentic Jew," Sartre wrote, "renounces (…) an assimilation that is today impossible," but the socialist revolution will remove all obstacles for the assimilation of "his sons." For all its value, Jewish difference suddenly seemed destined to temporary existence. In 1947, the sympathetic Wladimir Rabi stressed the ironic similarity between Sartre and the assimilationist "democrat" vilified in the essay.[83] Late twentieth-century multiculturalists, for their part, have pounced on Sartre's

---

[81] On this aspect of Réflexions, see Maurice Samuels, *The Right to Difference: French Universalism and the Jew* (Chicago, IL: University of Chicago Press, 2016), 139–161; Sarah Hammerschlag, *The Figural Jew: Politics and Identity in Postwar French Thought* (Chicago, IL: University of Chicago Press, 2010), 68–92.
[82] Tony Kushner, *The Holocaust and the Liberal Imagination: A Social and Political History* (London: Wiley-Blackwell, 1995).
[83] Wladimir Rabi, "Sartre, Portrait d'un philosémite," *Esprit* 138, n.o. 10 (October 1947): 532–546.

"concrete liberalism." Contradicted by the return of assimilationism in the last section of *Réflexions*, Sartre's ephemeral pluralism was only a "second-best solution to the problem of anti-Semitism." The French intellectual uniquely illuminated the psychology of antisemitism, but his misleading celebration of human diversity only killed Jews "softly." Despite the novelty of his position, Sartre allegedly offered an all too banal leftist solution to the Jewish question.[84]

Réflexions, in its closing argument, indeed returned to Marxist universalism. In a society based on "mutual bonds of solidarity," antisemitism and Jewishness will no longer have reason to exist. Yet contrary to Karl Marx's *On the Jewish Question* (1843), Sartre's most urgent problem was not bourgeois capitalism but the lethal threat of antisemitism. "The anti-Semite is in the very depths of his heart a criminal," he solemnly wrote, "what he wishes, what he prepares, is the death of the Jew" [AAJ 49]. Because of its arch-criminality, antisemitism obligated non-Jews to stand shoulder to shoulder with Jewish difference, not just to compassion for persecuted Jews. The utopian and hasty last pages of *Réflexions* obscured this innovation: To the language of *pity*, Sartre opposed the language of *solidarity*. The French thinker who famously defined the public intellectual as "someone who gets involved in matters which are none of his business" perfectly fulfilled this role: The "business" of antisemitism was now central to the ethics of intellectual commitment.

"We Are All Bound to the Jew"

Sartre professed solidarity with Jewishness, gestured toward valorization of Jewish difference ("concrete liberalism") but notoriously struggled to explain what Jewish difference meant. In *Réflexions*, Jews are only defined as an "abstract historical community ... for it keeps a memory of nothing but a long martyrdom, that is, of a long passivity" [AAJ 66, 67]. In the wake of the Holocaust, the only Jewish difference that jumped to Sartre's eye was the "situation" created by the antisemite: the Jew as "the stranger, the intruder, the unassimilated at the very heart of our society" [AAJ 83]. Sartre's first critics charged that such a definition of the Jew gave the antisemite the upper

---

[84] See Michael Walzer's preface to *Anti-Semite and Jew*, op. cit., xviii–xviv; Max Silverman, "'Killing Me Softly': Sartre's Racial Ambivalence in Réflexions sur la question juive" in Phyllis Lassner and Lara Trubowitz (eds.), *Antisemitism and Philosemitism in the Twentieth and Twenty First Century: Representing Jews, Jewishness in Modern Culture* (Newark, DE: University of Delaware Press, 2008), 47–62; On the return of assimilationism "through the back door" in *Réflexions*, see Maurice Samuels, *The Right to Difference*, op. cit.

hand: If reduced to a "situation," Jewishness does not exist independently of the racist gaze. Although sympathetic of Sartre's intervention, Emmanuel Levinas refused to "fixate the Jewish fate according to antisemitism." Contrary to Sartre's empty Jewishness, "being Jewish" was for Levinas an ontological and metaphysical "fact."[85] While grateful for the "philosemite" Sartre, Wladimir Rabi condemned his disregard of Jewish subjectivity. In *Réflexions*, he noted, Jews are downgraded to mere "objects of Sartre's generosity."[86] Alongside his supposed silence on the Holocaust or his unconscious recycling of antisemitic clichés, Sartre's inability to grasp the "facticity" of Jewish existence has since ranked among the most damning accusations leveled against *Réflexions*.[87] This controversial aspect of his thought has also prompted scholars to criticize the "disfiguration" of the Jew and Judaism in his anti-antisemitic intervention – and by extension in post-Holocaust anti-antisemitic thought.[88]

This indictment overlooks the radicality of Sartre's position. When he defined the Jewish condition as that of the "unassimilated at the very heart of our society," the philosopher admittedly naturalized the antisemitic fantasy of Jewish difference. After Hitler's war against the "eternal Jew," however, Sartre rescued the strangeness of the Jew from abjection. In distant New York, Hannah Arendt attempted similar revalorization. Contrary to upstart Jewish "parvenus" only relishing "the permission to ape the Gentiles," she argued in 1944, the Jewish pariah "tried to make the emancipation of the Jews that which it really should have been – an admission of the Jews as Jews to the ranks of humanity."[89] Arendt's celebration of the Jewish pariah, however, was above all a critique of Jewish emancipation. Sartre, for his part, turned the tables on the negative image of the wandering Jew. While not an ode to Jewish rootlessness, *Réflexions* already announced a fascination for Jewish nomadism peculiar to French postmodern thought.[90]

---

[85] Emmanuel Lévinas, "Existentialisme et Humanisme" (1947) in *Etre Juif: Suivi d'une lettre à Maurice Blanchot* (first published in 1947) (Paris: Payot & Rivages, 2015), 50. Levinas's reading of *Réflexions* has been the subject of numerous publications. A recent commentary is Brunot Chaouat, "Being and Jewishness: Levinas Reader of Sartre" in *Sartre, Jews, and the Other*, op. cit., 90–106.
[86] Rabi, "Sartre, Portrait d'un philosémite," op. cit.
[87] Francis Kaplan, "Sur des lectures étonnantes de Sartre" in Galster (ed.), *Sartre et les juifs*, op. cit., 89–99.
[88] Elad Lapidot, *Jews Out of the Question: A Critique of Anti-Anti-Semitism*, op. cit.; "Disfigured Friends," *Jewish Studies Quarterly* 2, no. 27 (2020): 109–129.
[89] Hannah Arendt, "The Jew as Pariah: The Hidden Tradition," *Jewish Social Studies* 6, no. 2 (April 1944): 99–122.
[90] Sarah Hammerschlag, *The Figural Jew: Politics and Identity in Postwar French Thought* (Chicago, IL: University of Chicago Press, 2010), 68–92.

As his early comments on Zionism revealed, however, Sartre was equally supportive of rooted Jews. Although he hoped that one day the "Jewish problem finds its definitive solution in a humanity without borders," as he wrote in June 1949, the creation of the state of Israel was for him "one of the most important events of our times."[91] In addition to the national Jew, Sartre's philosemitism encompassed the assimilated French *israélite* as well as the hyphenated Jew. His sympathy came at a price. Conversion to Christianity, as the German-Jewish writer Heinrich Heine recognized in the 1820s, was once the Jews' "admission ticket to European culture." With Sartre, self-consciousness became their entry-ticket to freedom. But as he approvingly noted, Jewish self-awareness was already on the rise. "The suffering the Jews have undergone during the past few years has done much to open their eyes," Sartre observed, "and it seems to me even probable that there are more authentic Jews than authentic Christians" [AAJ 138].

If according to Sartre minority Jews were more "authentic" than majority Christians – a philosemitic tribute to the Jewish choice of freedom – Jewishness in *Réflexions* is not merely an antisemitic projection. Antisemitic persecution also creates the Jew as a real social subject conscious of her otherness: The awakening of many assimilated Jewish readers to a Jewish identity rescued from vilification exemplified the regenerative power of Sartre's thought.[92] The Jewish turn to self-acceptance warranted a new pattern of non-Jewish intervention: The novelty of Sartre's anti-antisemitism was not only opposition to prejudice but political solidarity with all forms of conscious Jewishness. "I mistrust 'anti-antisemitism' if it is based on 'a spirit of tolerance' and 'broad ideas'," the philosopher had already stated in 1939.[93] "What must be done," he explained in *Réflexions*, "is to point out to each one that the fate of the Jews is *his* fate" [AAJ 153]. When Sartre also proclaimed that "we are all bound to the Jew, because anti-Semitism leads straight to national-socialism" [AAJ 151], he arguably only saw in the Jewish fate a signal of looming danger for the rest of society. "We are all bound to the Jew," however, were exceptional words in post-Holocaust Europe: In Paris, the star philosopher turned the "Jewish question" into a platform for friendship between left intellectuals and Jews, with crucial consequences for pro-

---

[91] See "Naissance d'Israel," June 7, 1949, in Michel Contat and Michel Rybalka (eds.), *Les Écrits de Sartre: Chronologie, bibliographie commentée* (Paris: Gallimard, 1970), 212.
[92] Eyal Lapidot offers this counterreading in "Decolonizing Anti-Semitism Studies," *Judaica: Neue Digitale Folge* 3 (2022): 1–7.
[93] *Les Écrits de Sartre*, op. cit., 167–168. This interview features a rare use of the word "anti-antisemitism" prior to 1945.

gressive philosemitism and philo-Zionism after 1945. The export of Parisian existentialism beyond the borders of France soon propagated Sartre's "Jewish question" internationally.[94] In London, however, the democratic socialist George Orwell failed to understand why Sartre's "cerebration" should be taken seriously. Commissioned in October 1948 to review the English edition of *Réflexions*, Orwell did not hide his intentions: "I think Sartre is a bag of wind and I am going to give him a good boot."[95]

George Orwell: Reflections on Anti-antisemitism

The plain-spoken English writer delivered his main attack on what he believed to be Sartre's main claim: "[The Jew] is wrong, at this stage of history, if he tries to assimilate himself, and we are wrong if we try to ignore his racial origin. He should be accepted into the national community, not as an ordinary Englishman, Frenchman (...) but as a Jew." Orwell found such view "dangerously close to antisemitism."[96] In February 1939, he already contended that the best strategy against prejudice was to "remind people that Jews are human beings before they are Jews." Nearly ten years later, Orwell faulted Sartre for allegedly claiming that the Jew, "of whichever variety, is not just another human being." The French philosopher, of course, did not invalidate Jewish humanity. The Sartrean Jew was both a "man" without a predetermined essence and an antisemitic creation. Such speculations, however, had more appeal on the Seine's left bank than by the Thames. While Sartre turned the Jew into an exemplar figure of alterity, Orwell clung to humanist sameness. To single out the Jew as "a species of animals different from ourselves," he feared, could only "make antisemitism more prevalent that it was before."

Orwell's scathing review featured other fusillades. One of Sartre's shortcomings, the English writer charged, was his failure to relate antisemitism to "colour prejudice." Orwell's pique was not without merits. Although in *Black Orpheus* (1948) the French intellectual used Jewish otherness to explore Black alterity, his Judeocentric *Réflexions* did not engage in comparative racism. More damning for Orwell was Sartre's

---

[94] On the global reception of French existentialism, see Alfred Betschart and Juliane Werner, *Sartre and the International Impact of Existentialism* (London: Palgrave Macmillan, 2020).
[95] George Orwell, "To Fredric Warburg" (October 22, 1948) in Peter Davidson (ed.), *The Complete Works of George Orwell* (London: Secker & Warburg, 1998), Volume 18, 457. Hereafter CWGO.
[96] *The Observer* (November 7, 1948), in *CGWO*, Volume 18, 464–465.

inability to explain why antisemites "pick on Jews rather than some other victim." *Réflexions*, in fairness, answered this question: The antisemite's obsession with the Jew resulted from an existential choice. But as Orwell pointed out, Sartre kept silent on the historical and sociological factors accounting for enmity. "Little discussion of the subject, and no factual evidence worth mentioning," concluded the English empiricist.

Orwell's dismissal of Sartre, however, was not meant to trivialize antisemitism. The outbreak of World War II indeed marked a turning point in his thoughts about Jews. The man of letters who until the mid 1930s sprinkled his writings with unflattering depictions of Jews now took anti-Jewish prejudice seriously.[97] Antagonism against Jews and "refuspies" on the home front alerted him in turn to the irrationality of British antisemitism: "The Jews are supposed to dodge military service, to be the worst offenders on the Black Market etc. etc. I have heard this kind of talk even from country people who had probably never seen a Jew in their lives."[98] Hostility also blinded the war-battered British public to the tragedy unfolding in Nazi-ruled Europe. "People dislike the Jews so much," Orwell wrote in 1943, "that they do not want to remember their suffering." The wartime diarist and publicist commented several times on Hitler's intention to "kill off every Jew in Europe."[99] But Orwell did not reflect at length on the event. What prompted his interest in antisemitism was less the destruction of European Jews than prejudice in Britain. "Why are so many people," he wondered in January 1944, "still ready to believe that the Jews "smell," or that (…) they are responsible for slumps, revolutions, and venereal disease? The whole subject needs cold-blooded investigation."[100]

Published in the United States in April 1945, Orwell's essay "Anti-Semitism in Britain" attempted to answer these questions.[101] Like James Parkes, Orwell considered antisemitism "a neurosis … at bottom quite irrational." He also ventured into psychology when he remarked that "the Jew is evidently a scapegoat, though for what he is a scapegoat

---

[97] David Walton, "George Orwell and Anti-Semitism," *Patterns of Prejudice* 16, no. 1 (1982): 19–34.
[98] Cited in Anthony Julius, *Trials of the Diaspora: A History of Anti-Semitism in England* (Oxford: Oxford University Press, 2010), 327.
[99] On Orwell and the Holocaust, see John Newsinger, "Orwell, Anti-Semitism and the Holocaust" in John Rodden (ed.), *The Cambridge Companion to George Orwell* (Cambridge: Cambridge University Press, 2007), 112–25.
[100] *The Observer*, January 30, 1944 in CGWO, Volume 16 (1943–1944), 84–85.
[101] "Anti-Semitism in Britain," *Contemporary Jewish Record*, April 1945, in CGWO, Volume 17 (2007), 64–70.

we do not yet know." By his own admission, Orwell did not have any "hard-and-fast theory" to offer. His observations of British public opinion nonetheless allowed him to show that "one of the marks of antisemitism is an ability to believe stories that are not possibly true." Irrational claims, Orwell pointed out, did not prevent the antisemite to think of himself "as a rational being." Here Orwell unknowingly concurred with Sartre, who had debunked the illusion of antisemitic rationality. Yet for the Englishman, hatred for Jews was not a projective phenomenon but "part of the larger problem of nationalism which has not yet been fully examined." Belief in the superiority of "a single nation or other unit" inevitably entailed scapegoating or exclusion. More originally, Orwell also defined nationalism as a system of lies. "Every nationalist," he wrote a few months later in his "Notes on Nationalism," "is capable of the most flagrant dishonesty, but he is also (…) unshakably certain of being in the right."[102] The disease of nationalism, he concluded, spawned the lie of antisemitism: This was Orwell's overall slim contribution to the anti-antisemitic genre.

Anti-Semitism in Britain is noteworthy for an opposite reason: The essay offered the first critique of the postwar *anti-antisemitic* position. The fight against antisemitism, Orwell first charged, did not require automatic support for the establishment of a Jewish state. Unlike James Parkes, Richard Crossman, and Sartre, Orwell disliked Zionism. His reservations derived from his aversion to narrow nationalism, the violence of Jewish terrorism in Palestine, and anti-colonialist feelings inherited from youthful years spent in imperial Burma.[103] Immersed in the dystopian world of Stalinism, Orwell never espoused the cause of Palestine's Arabs. He nonetheless broke ranks with the British Left intelligentsia over its "incongruous" support of Zionism. The shocking persecution of Jews, he wrote, did not obligate "enlightened people to accept the Jewish case as proved and avoid examining the claims of the Arabs." This position "might be correct on its own merits," Orwell conceded to his Jewish-American readers. But what grated on him was uncritical groupthink. Contrary to Labour party intellectuals, Orwell considered Zionism part of the "disease" of nationalism. His premature death in 1950 prevented him from expressing an opinion on Arab nationalist regimes. But in April 1945, Zionist Jews seemed to him "merely antisemites turned upside down, just as many Indians and Negroes display the normal colour prejudice in an inverted form."

---

[102] "Notes on Nationalism" (*Polemic*, October 1945) in CWGO, Volume 17, 141–157.
[103] Giora Goodman, "George Orwell and the Palestine Question," *The European Legacy: Toward New Paradigms* 20, no. 4 (2015): 321–333.

Orwell counterbalanced his objections to Zionism with empathy for Holocaust refugees. "Hundreds of thousands of homeless Jews," he wrote in November 1946, "are now trying desperately to get to Palestine. No doubt many of them will ultimately succeed, but other will fail. (...) How about inviting, say, 100,000 Jewish refugees to settle in this country?"[104] Orwell argued that Jewish immigrants could help remedy labor shortages and the low British birth rate: The novelist may have privately struggled with his own Jewish problem but fear of Jewish invasion did not haunt his thoughts. Solidarity with stateless Jews was also detectable in Orwell's crowning achievement. In *Nineteen Eighty-Four* (1949), the main protagonist Winston Smith opens up to the possibility of dissidence after watching a propaganda film in which a "ship of refugees" is "bombed somewhere in the Mediterranean." (Orwell drafted his novel between 1946 and 1947, at the height of the British blockade against Jewish illegal immigration to Palestine.) The cinema audience, Winston noticed, gleefully laughed at drowning refugees, including a "Jewess" clinging to her child: This episode awakens the diligent Ministry of Truth employee to the dehumanizing power of the Party. As Winston's transformative experience illustrates, the drama of Jewish refugees at sea led Orwell to antitotalitarian politics, not philo-Zionism.[105]

Orwell's reflections on anti-antisemitism also tackled the issue of hypocrisy and truth. "What vitiates nearly all that is written about antisemitism," he wrote, "is the assumption in the writer's mind that he himself is immune to it." This was both a personal admission and an invitation to collective humility. "We are all of us good democrats, anti-Fascist, anti-imperialist, contemptuous of class distinctions, impervious to colour prejudice, and so on and so forth," Orwell wrote of sympathizers of the Left in March 1948.[106] Against these comforting certainties, the author of *Nineteen Eighty-Four* cautioned against doublethink: the simultaneous rejection of antisemitism and secret attraction to it. Antagonism to Jews "comes more naturally to people of Conservative tendency," he acknowledged in his "Notes on Nationalism," but the left, including its pro-Zionist component, was not impervious to it. The student of antisemitism, he advised, should start "with the one place where he could get hold of some reliable evidence – that is, in his own mind."

---

[104] *As I Please*, November 15, 1946 in CGWO, Volume 18, 482.
[105] On refugees and statelessness in Orwell's writings, see Lyndsey Stonebridge, *Placeless People: Writing, Rights, and Refugees* (Oxford: Oxford University Press, 2018), 73–95.
[106] *Writers and Leviathan* (1948), available at: https://orwell.ru/library/articles/leviathan/english/e_wal.

Although published in April 1945, *Anti-Semitism in Britain* already challenged postwar critical theory. Instead of drawing the "portrait of the antisemite" or delineating the contours of the "authoritarian personality," Orwell urged self-reflexivity. Without it, he wrote in his devastating review of Sartre's opus, "books on antisemitism tend to be mere exercises in casting motes out of other people's eyes." Turning the syndrome into "a disgraceful aberration, almost a crime," he added, will only help people "claim to be immune from it." But this position forced him back to a banal explanation of antisemitism: a deplorable "nationalistic prejudice" only solvable through the eradication of "the larger disease of nationalism." This diagnosis enabled Orwell to charge that "modern civilization," predicated on the belief that "whole races or nations are mysteriously good or mysteriously evil," is tainted with antisemitism. Yet reduced to a nationalist "lunacy," antisemitism was not different from other forms of racial prejudice. "Disliking Jews isn't intrinsically worse than disliking Negroes or Americans or any other block of people," Orwell wrote in October 1948. The gravely ill author, however, initiated a debate he would not live to join: Should anti-antisemitism be part of antiracist politics or independent of it?

Futures of Anti-antisemitism

This explosive question was still premature in the immediate postwar period: The main theorists of antisemitism after the Holocaust did not disaggregate Jew-hatred from other racialized ideologies. Sartre's *Réflexions* singled out the Jew from other victims of oppression yet his anti-antisemitism turned the "Jewish question" into a template for other antiracist struggles. Modern antisemitism received separate treatment in Hannah Arendt's *The Origins of Totalitarianism*, but she studied the phenomenon in relation to imperialism and "the decline of the rights of Man." The Frankfurt School mainstays realized during the Holocaust that "society itself can only be understood through antisemitism," yet Theodor Adorno and Max Horkheimer conceptualized anti-Jewish aggression as the key indicator of universal barbarism. Anti-antisemitism and antiracism also remained close bedfellows at the level of grassroot activism. The history of antiracist politics in post-Liberation France exemplifies this proximity. Despite its predominantly Jewish membership, the "Antiracist Alliance" formed in Paris in 1946 broadened the fight against antisemitism to include the defense of racialized people in metropolitan France and the colonies. The issue of anti-communism split the organization in 1949, but the French Left, like its counterparts in Western Europe, continued to subsume antisemitism under the general concept of racism.[107]

The antiracist anti-colonial thinkers of the 1940s and 1950s similarly believed that antisemitism originated from the division of humankind into superior and inferior racial groups. During visits in prewar Poland and Nazi Germany, the African-American intellectual W. E. B. Du Bois had already brought the "Jewish problem" in relation with other atrocities. "There has been no tragedy in modern times," he wrote in 1936, "equal in its awful effects to the fight on the Jew in Germany. It is an attack on civilization, comparable only to such horrors as the Spanish Inquisition and the African slave trade."[108] After the war, Du Bois related the Final Solution to a "racial philosophy" peculiar to Britain and America. His visit of the Warsaw Ghetto in 1949 prodded him, however, to revise his earlier views on the "problem of the color line" in the twentieth century. In front of the monument dedicated to the Jewish ghetto fighters, the civil rights activist garnered "not so much clearer understanding of the Jewish problem in the world as a real and more complete understanding of the Negro problem." In interaction with the Holocaust, American racism appeared less "separate and unique (...) no longer a matter of color and physical and racial characteristics." Racial hatred, Du Bois wrote, now reached "all sorts of people and caused endless evil to all men."[109]

In *Discourse on Colonialism* (1955), Aimé Césaire also unified antisemitism and colonial racism. Nazi terror, claimed the Afro-Caribbean poet, resulted from the import of "European colonialist procedures" until then reserved to subaltern subjects beyond the color line. In *Black Skin, White Masks* (1952), however, the Martinique-born philosopher Frantz Fanon distinguished the form of anti-Jewish persecution from anti-Black racism. The white Jew, observed Fanon, his only "disliked from the moment he

---

[107] Johannes Heuman, "From Jewish Resistance to Intercultural Solidarity: Antiracism and Identity Politics in Immediate Postwar France" in Magdalena Dziaczkowska and Adele Valeria Messina (eds.), *Jews in Dialogue: Jewish Responses to the Challenges of Multicultural Contemporaneity* (Leiden: Brill, 2020), 141–162; Jim House, "Anti-racism in France (1898–1962): Modernity and Beyond" in Floya Anthias and Cathie Llyod (eds.), *Rethinking Anti-Racisms: From Theory to Practice* (London: Routledge, 2002), 111–127.

[108] Cited in Eve Darian-Smith, "Re-Reading Du Bois: The Global Dimensions of the US Civil Rights Struggle," *The Journal of Global History* 7, no. 3 (2012): 483–505; see also B. Sevitch, "W.E.B. Du Bois and Jews: A Lifetime of Opposing Antisemitism," *Journal of African American History* 87 (2002): 323–337. On Du Bois and Holocaust Memory, see Michael Rothberg, *Multidirectional Memory: Remembering the Holocaust in the Age of Decolonization* (Stanford, CA: Stanford University Press, 2009), 111–134.

[109] W. E. B. Du Bois, "The Negro and the Warsaw Ghetto" (1952) in Eric J. Sundquist (ed.), *The Oxford W.E.B. Du Bois Reader* (New York: Oxford University Press, 1996), 469–473.

is tracked down. But in my case (...) I am the slave not of the "idea" that others have of me but of my own appearance." This distinction reappears in other parts of Fanon's classic essay. "The Jew is attacked in his religious identity, in his history, in his race, in his relations with his ancestors," he wrote, "but it is in his corporeality that the Negro is attacked." The anticolonial intellectual nonetheless conjoined both forms of aggression. The antisemite, he notoriously proclaimed, "is inevitably anti-Negro."[110]

The unproblematic association of antisemitism and racism, and therefore of anti-antisemitism and antiracism, was not bound to last. In anticolonial thought and politics, or in the Black Power movement in the United States, "racism" no longer referred to European racial theories – and their lethal implementation during the Holocaust – but to systemic white domination.[111] Already apparent at the height of decolonization, the denunciation of Zionism as racist oppression by the Palestinian liberation movement, Third World states, the Soviet Union, and the anti-imperialist Left, likewise splintered ecumenical antiracism. A pivotal moment in the history of this separation was the acrimonious adoption of the United Nations Convention on the Elimination of All Forms of Racial Discrimination (1965), which under Soviet leadership elevated apartheid to the rank of emblematic racism but did not think the same of antisemitism.[112] Alleging both neglect of antisemitism and unfair criticism of Israel, Jewish international organizations withdrew then into separatist human rights politics, especially through campaigns in support of Soviet Jews. After the passing of the United Nations resolution "Zionism is Racism" in November 1975, anti-antisemitism entered a new phase: For an emerging network of watchdog organizations, the main danger no longer came from fringe neo-Nazism or Holocaust revisionism but from what they now viewed as the "new antisemitism" of the anti-Zionist left.[113] A decade later, a leading theorist of "new Judeophobia" lamented

---

[110] Aimé Césaire, *Discourse on Colonialism* (New York: Monthly Review Press, 1972), 3. See also Rothberg, *Multidirectional Memory*, op. cit., 66–110. Frantz Fanon, *Black Mask, White Skin* (London: Pluto Press, 2008), 125, 92. See also Bryan Cheyette, "Postcolonialism and the Study of Anti-Semitism," *The American Historical Review* 123, no. 4 (October 2018): 1234–1245.

[111] David Feldman, "Antisemitism, Racism, and Anti-Racism" in *History Workshop* online (October 8, 2024), available at: www.historyworkshop.org.uk/anti-racism/antisemitism-racism-and-anti-racism/.

[112] On these debates, see James Loeffler, *Rootless Cosmopolitans: Jews and Human Rights in the Twentieth Century* (New Haven: Yale University Press, 2018), 248–256; Nathan Kurz, *Jewish Internationalism and Human Rights after the Holocaust* (Cambridge: Cambridge University Press, 2021), 112–137.

[113] Abba Eban, "Zionism and the UN," *The New York Times*, November 3, 1975, cited by Esther Romeyn, "(Anti) 'New Antisemitism' as a Transnational Field of Racial Governance," *Patterns of Prejudice* 54, no. 1–2: 199–214.

this fracture. "The antiracist ideologization of humanism, an apparatus that remained unitary until the defeat of the Axis powers, has since evolved in the direction of a differentiation into two opposing camps," diagnosed the French scholar Pierre-André Taguieff in 1987.[114]

This splintering of antiracist politics, and the standoff between Holocaust and anti-colonial memory within the antiracist movement, were still distant prospects in the early postwar period. For the time being, antisemitism and racism preserved their proximity because anti-antisemitism, anti-colonialism, and antiracism remained politically compatible. This bond stemmed from the enduring appeal of unitary humanism in the aftermath of World War II, despite philosophical or anti-colonial assaults on the Western humanist tradition. During the first two post-Holocaust decades, philosemitism not only consisted in the delegitimization of antisemitism, or for zealous anti-antisemites, in all-out war against Jew-hatred. As shown in Chapter 4, philosemitism also meant the reintegration of the Jew into "the family of man": a humanization conducive to positive perceptions of the state of Israel and the first Israeli Jews.

---

[114] Pierre-André Taguieff, *The Force of Prejudice: On Racism and Its Doubles (1987)* (Minneapolis, MN: University of Minneapolis Press, 2001), 232.

4 From Humanism to Israelophilia (1945–1967)

In his *Letter on Humanism* penned in November 1946, Martin Heidegger famously questioned the necessity to "retain the word humanism" in the postwar vocabulary. A corruption of thought by metaphysics, argued the German thinker, the man-centered Western intellectual tradition was also the culprit of destructive modernity. His intricate *Letter* debunked the tenets of philosophical humanism yet also offered an intriguing sociological observation. Although "-isms have for a long time now been suspect," Heidegger remarked with humanism in mind, "the market of public opinion continually demands new ones. We are always ready to supply the demand." The discourse of Man, lamented the philosopher of Being, was alive and well in the aftermath of World War II.[1]

Heidegger's assessment was not off the mark. In France especially, the liberation from German occupation was accompanied by an explosion of humanist rhetoric. "Existentialism is a humanism," proclaimed Jean-Paul Sartre in October 1945. The Marxist philosopher Henri Lefebvre, for his part, retrieved humanism from Karl Marx's early writings. Under the influence of Jacques Maritain, Christian humanists championed the sacredness of the person against secular individualism. Interest for the "human" in France, however, was not limited to high-brow philosophy: A dozen of books published in 1945 and 1946 alone contained the words "l'homme" or "l'humanisme" in their titles. "Our country," wrote the novelist and essayist François Mauriac in March 1945, "is the most humanist par excellence ... our moralists carried to perfection that science of man which is valid for all, Christians and unbelievers alike."[2]

Contrary to the boastful Mauriac, however, proponents of humanism in liberated France pointed instead to a crisis of man after Nazism. One of twenty-three international thinkers tasked by UNESCO to help

---

[1] Martin Heidegger, "Letter on Humanism" in David Farrell Krell (ed.), *Basic Writings* (London: Harper Perennial, 2008), 213–266.
[2] Michael Kelly, "Humanism and Unity," *History of European Ideas* 20, no. 4–6 (1995): 923–928; François Mauriac cited in Tony Judt, *Past Imperfect: French Intellectuals, 1944–1956* (New York: New York University Press, 2011), 262.

the new organization advance the "common welfare of mankind," the novelist and art theorist André Malraux compared "bloodstained and ravaged" Europe to the "face of the Man that she had hoped to bring to the world." But after rejecting blind faith in human mastery and progress, the French intellectual announced that "there is a humanism possible to the European man."[3] The "man" in question remained the victim of Nazism more than colonial oppression. "Torture has meant for us more than physical pain," Malraux declared, even if the last-hour resister never personally suffered at the hands of the Gestapo. A decade before counterinsurgency methods in Algeria spurred anti-colonial activism in France, Malraux used the metaphor of torture to illuminate the degradation of the "European man" and signal the start of his recovery.

Malraux's reflections validated Heidegger's observation: Despite a burgeoning revolt against Western humanism in French philosophy, "man" remained omnipresent in early postwar culture.[4] The German thinker banned from Freiburg University eluded, however, the reason behind this popularity: The terror inflicted on Europe by nearly six years of German rule. In countries occupied by the Third Reich, resistance movements not only fought for national liberation but also placed "man" at the forefront of their cause. That one of the first clandestine organizations in wartime France was founded by staff members of Paris's *Musée de l'Homme* (Museum of Mankind) was not incidental. In France and across German-ruled Western Europe, intellectual resisters of different political background dreamed of moral and social renewal to rehabilitate man from fascism.[5] Albert Camus, who joined the underground network *Combat* in 1943 as a journalist, was one of them. "I continue to believe that this world has no ultimate meaning," wrote Camus in July 1944, "but I know that something in it has meaning and that is man, because he is the only creature to insist on having one."[6]

Dramatized by the resistance humanism of the war years, the figure of man made a spectacular come back in 1945. In philosophy, literature, and the arts, this return took the form of a solemn reassessment of the category "human." Some of the first memoirs of concentration

---

[3] André Malraux, "Man and Artistic Culture" in David Hardman and Stephen Spender (eds.), *Reflections on Our Age: Lectures Delivered at the Opening Session of UNESCO at the Sorbonne* (New York: Columbia University Press, 1949), 84–100.

[4] On the roots of "anti-humanism" in French philosophy, see Stefanos Geroulanos, *An Atheism That Is Not Humanism Emerges in French Thought* (Stanford, CA: Stanford University Press, 2010).

[5] On "resistance humanism," see James D. Wilkinson, *The Intellectual Resistance in Europe* (Cambridge, MA: Harvard University Press, 1981); Alya Aglan, *Le temps de la résistance* (Paris: Actes Sud, 2008), 225–253; Jeroen Dewulf, *Spirit of the Resistance: Dutch Clandestine Literature during the Nazi Occupation* (Rochester, NY: Camden House, 2010).

[6] Albert Camus, *Lettres à un ami allemand* (Lausanne: Marguerat, 1946), 72–73.

camps contributed to this reexamination. Viktor Frankl's *Man's Search for Meaning* (1946), David Rousset's *L'univers concentrationaire* (1946), and Robert Antelme's *L'espèce humaine* (1947), three texts emblematic of this genre, documented the process of human degradation in Nazi camps. Yet they simultaneously rescued man from the abyss. Frankl's testimony was first entitled in German "Nonetheless Say Yes to Life" before the Viennese Jewish psychiatrist and Auschwitz survivor became an international sensation. Even a handful of prisoners able to "keep their inner liberty," wrote Frankl, was proof that "man's inner strength may raise him above his outward fate." The former French resisters and internees David Rousset and Robert Antelme likewise salvaged man's irreducible consciousness from the horrors of concentration camps. "The more our condition as men is contested by the SS," wrote Antelme, "the more likely our chances to be confirmed as such." Rousset, for his part, detailed the "total disaggregation of the individual" in the Nazi camp system. He nonetheless discovered in Buchenwald "the power and the beauty of the fact of living itself (…) even through the worst crises or the most serious setbacks."[7]

In *If This Is a Man* [*Survival in Auschwitz*], first published and barely noticed in 1947, Primo Levi famously questioned the possibility of human sovereignty within the universe of the camp. His Hobbesian tale of survival in Auschwitz, where the Italian Jewish prisoner descended "into the arena as a beast against beasts," illuminated the drowning of man more than the preservation of human essence. In various writings published between 1946 and 1950, the French poet and Mauthausen survivor Jean Cayrol used the allegory of Lazarus rising from the dead to distinguish returnees from concentration camps, solitary and beyond repair, from the rest of humanity. In the United States, Hannah Arendt portrayed Nazi terror as an attempt to create "human beings superfluous," the starting point of posthumanist interpretations of concentration camps. But as Frankl, Rousset, Antelme, and other humanist camp memoirs demonstrated immediately after the war, the *lager* (camp) symbolized both the *destruction* and the *reconquest* of humanity.[8] These two images, about which more below, were also projected on Holocaust refugees and the first Israeli Jews.

---

[7] Viktor Frankl, *Man's Search for Meaning* (New York: Washington Square Press, 1988), 89; Robert Antelme, *L'espèce humaine* (Paris: Gallimard, 1978), 107; David Rousset, *L'univers concentrationnaire* (Paris: Les Editions de Minuit, 1965), 109, 184.

[8] Amos Goldberg, "If This Is a Man: The Image of Man in Autobiographical and Historical Writing during and after the Holocaust," *Yad Vashem Studies* 33 (2005): 381–429; Dan Stone, "The Holocaust and 'The Human'" in *The Holocaust, Fascism and Memory: Essays in the History of Ideas* (Houndmills, Basingstoke, Hampshire: Palgrave Macmillan, 2013), 49–63.

Although Western humanism came under attack in French thought, humanism retained its popular appeal throughout the 1950s. The success of the travelling photographic exhibition *The Family of Man* is a case in point. First shown at the New York Museum of Modern Art in 1955, its purpose, according to its curator Edward Steichen, was to highlight "the essential oneness of mankind throughout the world." Although French, British, and Dutch so-called police actions or emergencies had since 1945 brought back colonial warfare in the emerging Third World, large crowds from Rome to Stockholm marveled at unitary mankind, depicted in 503 images from 68 countries. That same year, Aimé Césaire's *Discourse on Colonialism* lashed out at a "pseudo-humanism that for too long has diminished the rights of man (…), is incomplete and biased and, all things considered, sordidly racist." In *The Wretched of the Earth* (1961), Franz Fanon called for "tabula rasa" on a humanism which had only achieved "a succession of negations of man, and an avalanche of murders."[9] Yet in postwar Europe, humanism not only survived World War II unscathed: With *The Family of Man*, the most widely seen exhibition in the history of photography, it also gained a place of choice in the cultural Cold War.[10]

How did this post-fascist humanist consensus affect perceptions of the Holocaust, Jewish refugees, and Israel during the first two decades of Western European democracy? Until the late 1950s, the humanist reprobation of Nazi inhumanity universalized the Holocaust as the catastrophe of mankind, thereby reintegrating the Jew into the family of man. Sympathetic observers of the new state of Israel went further. The Jewish homeland, in their eyes, not only rescued but fulfilled the promise of European humanism. Democracy reinstated the Jew as Man: From 1948 to 1967, Israelophilia heralded the Jew as symbol of the human.

Humanism and Genocide

Through various iterations, humanism became in 1945 the prime language of European "recivilization" after the moral collapse of war.[11]

---

[9] Aimé Césaire, *Discourse on Colonialism* (New York: Monthly Review Press, 2000), 37; Frantz Fanon, *The Wretched of the Earth* (London: Penguin, 2001), 252.

[10] Eric J. Sandeen, "The Show You See with Your Heart: The Family of Man on Tour in the Cold War Period" in Jean Back and Viktoria Schmidt Linsenhoff (eds.), *The Family of Man, 1955–2001* (Marburg: Jonas Verlag, 2004), 101–121; Ariella Azoulay, "The Family of Man: A Visual Declaration of Human Rights" in Thomas Keenan and Tirdad Zolghadr (eds.), *The Human Snapshot* (Berlin: Sternberg Press, 2013), 19–48.

[11] Paul Betts, *Ruin and Renewal: Civilizing Europe after the Second World War* (New York: Basic Books, 2020).

Despite the persistence of European imperial rule at the end of World War II, the idea of man as bearer of values or dignity helped demarcate recovered democracy from dictatorship. Exorcizing fascism also entailed the rehumanization of Jews after Nazism. "Victors' justice" at the Nuremberg Trial (1945–46), to be sure, did not separate the planned murder of Jews from other crimes. But thanks to documentary evidence on death squads, ghettoization, and the Final Solution, the prosecution of "crimes against humanity" showcased in return the incontrovertible humanity of Jewish victims.[12]

The return of humanism after barbarism, however, did not guarantee particular attention to the Jewish catastrophe. The first international discussions on the rehabilitation of humanistic culture confirmed this pattern. Convened in Paris in late 1946, UNESCO's inaugural conference ignored the recent extermination of European Jews. The new organization only resolved to conduct a perfunctory study of the "social and psychological problems of Nazism."[13] Attended by a plethora of European thinkers, the forum *Rencontres internationales de Genève* dedicated in September 1946 to the revival of the "European spirit" – two other meetings took place in 1949 and 1951 – was equally silent on the subject. The German philosopher Karl Jaspers was the only participant to devote a few lines to Jews when he referred to biblical Judaism as "one of the fundamental forces in the history of the West." In earlier lectures delivered at Heidelberg, however, Jaspers called upon fellow Germans to "answer for the acts of the regime you tolerated." Passivity when "to our ineradicable shame and disgrace, the synagogues (...) went up in flames throughout Germany," he wrote, "made all of us guilty in front of God."[14] Jaspers's plea for moral purification laid out the foundations of a culture of guilt shunned by most Germans but later conducive to deeper confrontation with the Nazi past. His lecture in Geneva, however, did not include any mention of German crimes against the Jews. Even for the courageous advocate of "guilt consciousness," the reconstitution of humanist Europe could proceed without explicit engagement with the genocide. The young Swiss-Jewish literary critic Jean Starobinski took notice of this omission. "It seems that these six million dead Jews have been quickly forgotten," he told the

---

[12] On the place of the Holocaust at the Nuremberg Trial, see David Bankier and Dan Michman (eds.), *Holocaust and Justice:. Representation and Historiography of the Holocaust in Post-War Trials* (Yad Vashem: Jerusalem, 2010), 11–113.
[13] See proceedings at https://unesdoc.unesco.org/ark:/48223/pf0000114580/PDF/114580 engo.pdf.multi.
[14] Karl Jaspers, *The Question of German Guilt* (New York: Fordham University Press, 2000), 65.

attendees in Geneva, "and the European spirit, in its abstract generality, appears as unbothered as in the past."[15]

Also present in Geneva, the French philosopher Maurice Merleau-Ponty had recently reflected on his own blindness. Prior to his discovery of "German antisemitism," Merleau-Ponty observed in October 1945, "we did not think there were Jews or Germans but only men, or even consciousnesses." The French thinker, however, still yearned for a society "in which past traumas have been wiped out" and essential identities left behind. Simone de Beauvoir admitted to a similar mindset. Before 1945, the famed intellectual only saw "men" in her Jewish friends and acquaintances. "I was right to refuse essentialism," she remarked, "but the universalism to which I subscribed took me far away from reality."[16] De Beauvoir ultimately recognized the validity of Jewishness after the Holocaust, a discovery which in the late 1940s translated into pro-Israel sympathies and silence on indigenous Palestinians. Yet like Merleau-Ponty, she entered the postwar period unprepared to grasp the distinctiveness of the category "Jew." This propensity was characteristic of intellectual antifascism in general. Contrary to Soviet-controlled Eastern Europe, antifascism in Western Europe did not require obligatory alignment with communism. To be intellectually "antifascist" after 1945 meant revolting against the wreckage wrought by Nazi terror on the human condition. Such antifascism consecrated Jews as victims of inhumanity, yet their tragedy remained only one piece in the greater puzzle of Nazi criminality.

Both published in 1946, the first systematic studies of Nazi concentration camps exemplified this approach. In *L'univers concentrationnaire*, the former Neuengamme and Buchenwald prisoner David Rousset acknowledged that separate "camps for Jews and Poles" functioned as sites of "widespread destruction and industrialized torture." He also labeled Auschwitz-Birkenau, where nearly 1 million Jews perished, the "largest city of death." The only difference between extermination camps and "normal" concentration camps, he observed, was one of "degree not kind."[17] In *Der SS-Staat*, the left-Catholic German writer Eugen Kogon, a survivor of six years of internment at Buchenwald, similarly described the galaxy of Nazi concentration camps as a "super state ... a

---

[15] Jean Starobinski, *L'esprit européen: Rencontres internationales de Genève* (Neuchatel: Editions de la Baconnière, 1947), 296.

[16] Maurice Merleau-Ponty, *La guerre a eu lieu* (1945), cited in Samuel Moyn, "Intellectuals and Nazism" in Dan Stone (ed.), *Oxford Handbook to Postwar European History* (New York: Oxford University Press), 671–691; Simone de Beauvoir, *La force de l'âge* (Paris: Gallimard, 1963), 191.

[17] David Rousset, *L'univers concentrationnaire*, op. cit., 50.

system of terror unparalleled in the history of civilized nations." Kogon's meticulous analysis empathized with the ordeal of Jews. The anti-Nazi German author even hinted at the uniqueness of the Final Solution when he avowed that "it is impossible to present here anything like an exhaustive picture of the Jewish mass tragedy."[18] But like Rousset, Kogon blended "extermination" and "concentration" camps into a singular system of terror encompassing forced laborers, political, and racial deportees from all corners of Europe.

Shown at the Cannes Festival in 1956, Alain Resnais's documentary film *Nuit et Brouillard (Night and Fog)* gave cinematographic form to this mode of thought. A humanist meditation on concentration camps with only one occurrence of the word "Jew" in the screenplay, *Nuit et Brouillard* was nonetheless filmed in Auschwitz-Birkenau and Majdanek. It also included images of Dutch prisoners with yellow stars at the Westerbrok transit camp, of Hungarian Jews arriving at Auschwitz, as well as photographs of the Vel d'Hiv – the Parisian cycling stadium where French authorities interned Jews in July 1942. In charge of the commentary, the former Mauthausen prisoner Jean Cayrol disregarded these Jewish signs in favor of a general reflection on human dignity. "Under its hygienic pretext," he wrote of prisoners stripped of their clothes before disinfection, "nakedness (...) surrenders to the camp a man already humiliated." Indeed, viewers of *Nuit et Brouillard* did not learn any facts about the racial war waged between 1939 and 1945 against European Jews. "At the end," wrote Cayrol in the screenplay, "all deportees resemble each other." The film, as Alain Resnais himself acknowledged, was not about the Final Solution but the *peste concentrationnaire* ("the plague of concentration camps") – and its resurgence in the form of colonial violence in French Algeria.

Until Claude Lanzmann's *Shoah* supplanted it in 1985, however, *Nuit et Brouillard* remained for three decades the most popular documentary representation of the Jewish genocide on screen. Slow pans across the abandoned remnants of Auschwitz, unsettling archival footage, or the actor Michel Bouquet's haunting narration, were suggestive enough to code *Nuit et Brouillard* as a Holocaust film. Resnais's "meditation on the most important phenomenon of the twentieth century," commented the film-maker François Truffaut in 1956, was about "the human being in ourselves, who has to open wide his eyes and at his turn, to wonder." *Nuit et Brouillard* did not separate Jews from other targets of Nazi terror, and as Truffaut intimated, saw "human beings" before Jews. Yet its evocative aesthetics nonetheless showed the genocide without talking

---

[18] Eugen Kogon, *Der SS-Staat (1946)*, translated in English in 1950 as *The Theory and Practice of Hell* (New York: Berkley Books, 1998), 175.

about it. This humanist perspective, of course, potentially exempted viewers from ever thinking about the Jewish fate. Yet for all its ambiguities, *Nuit et Brouillard* soon offered student or artsy audiences in Britain, the Netherlands, and above all West and East Germany, a first encounter with a universal "Holocaust," at midpoint between silence and Judeocentric remembrance.[19]

The humanist lens, however, did not always magnify the drama of mankind at the expense of Jewish experiences. Between 1946 and 1948, Jewish refugees from Eastern Europe elicited distinctive pro-Jewish sentiment in France and Italy, where Holocaust survivors passed through on their way to British-ruled Palestine. Approximately 200,000 Jewish displaced persons also lived in occupied Germany during the same period, but the "DPs" did not inspire broad compassion in the chaotic aftermath of the war. As opposed to the United States, where the situation of Jewish refugees in occupied Germany was monitored in the press, the displaced persons did not make headlines on the rebuilding continent. In Britain, suspicion of Zionist ploys to alter the demography of Palestine, as well as acts of Jewish terrorism in the country still under mandate, did not endear Jewish DPs to public opinion. The transit of Holocaust survivors through Mediterranean ports, however, left a different impression. From 1946 to 1948, an estimated 15,000 to 20,000 Jews entered the French territory before illegally embarking to Palestine. Between 50,000 and 70,000 Jewish border-crossers also arrived in Italy as part of the *Brichah* (Flight), the Zionist code name for the secretive immigration of Jews.[20] Although brief, this experience inspired long-lasting empathy for "humanity at sea."[21]

Humanitarian Philosemitism

Returning to his home country after his liberation from Auschwitz, Primo Levi was struck to discover young Jews "travelling with us towards Italy at

---

[19] Ewout van der Knaap (ed.), *Uncovering the Holocaust: The International Reception of Night and Fog* (London: Wallflower Press, 2006); Sylvie Lindenperg, *Night and Fog: A Film in History* (Minneapolis, MN: University of Minnesota Press, 2014).

[20] Constance Pâris de la Bollardière and Simon Perego, "Les migrations juives d'Europe centrale et orientale en France au lendemain de la Shoah," *Archives Juives* 54, no. 1 (2021): 4–24; Chiara Renzo, "Our Hopes Are Not Lost Yet": The Jewish Displaced Persons in Italy: Relief, Rehabilitation and Self-Understanding" *Quest: Issues in Contemporary Jewish History*, no. 12 (December 2017), available at: www.questcdecjournal.it/our-hopes-are-not-lost-yet-the-jewish-displaced-persons-in-italy-relief-rehabilitation-and-self-understanding-1943-1948/.

[21] Itamar Mann, *Humanity at Sea: Maritime Migration and the Foundations of International Law* (Cambridge: Cambridge University Press, 2016).

the end of our train (...) coming from all the countries of Eastern Europe. They felt immensely free and strong, lords of the world and of their destinies."[22] When in the summer of 1945 Jewish refugees who passed themselves off as "Austrians" crossed the Brenner Pass into Italy, members of the national unity government demanded firm action. The former resistance leader and prime minister Ferrucio Parri, however, extended hospitality. "The Italian Government considers right and proper to give help to the Jews forced to leave other countries because of racial persecution," declared Parri in November 1945. He trusted that "immigrants can find in our country at least the spirit of freedom and human solidarity that animates the Italian people in their Risorgimento."[23]

Jewish displaced persons reached almost all Italian regions including the Cinecittà DP Camp in the vicinity of Rome. Yet few Italians took notice of their presence until the forty-five days standoff between British authorities and Jews in the Ligurian port of La Spezia (April–May 1946). Intent of blocking two ships from illegally sailing to Palestine, the British Navy sealed the bay off with heavy weaponry. Under the captainship of the secret agent Yehuda Arazi, Jewish refugees responded with a hunger strike and threats of collective suicide. Their steadfastness impressed Italian observers. "The Daughters of Israel, marked by the fire of Teutonic barbarians, invoke the Promised Land," editorialized *Il Corriere della Sera*. Admiring of their tenacity, *Avanti!* offered them the full "solidarity of Italian socialists."[24]

While the return of Italian Jewish survivors of concentration camps did not generate particular interest, the events at La Spezia stirred up popular emotion. On May 8, 1946, a large crowd of well-wishers bid farewell to 1,014 Jewish immigrants after the British agreed to issue entry certificates. A few months later, neighbors of the Cinecittà DP camp, including a carabinieri chief convinced that Palestine was "somewhere in Africa" and a mayor who located it in "faraway Asia," greeted Jewish refugees with shouts of "Viva la Palestina Ebraica!"[25] The standoff at La Spezia solidified a positive perception of Jewish refugees as symbols of antifascist resistance. As in the case of the *Enzo Sereni*, an illegal ship

---

[22] Primo Levi, *The Reawakening* (New York: Touchstone, 1995), 205.
[23] Cited in Cinzia Villani, *Infrangere le frontiere: l'arrivo in Italia delle displaced persons ebree 1945–1948*. PhD thesis, University of Trento (2010), 102.
[24] *Il Corriere della Sera*, April 7, 1946, cited in Susanna Kokkonen, *The Jewish Refugees in Postwar Italy: 1945–1951* (Saarbrücken: Lambert Academic Publishing, 2011), 88. *L'Avanti!*, April 13, 1946, cited in Mario Toscano, *La "Porta di Sion": L'Italia e l'immigrazione clandestina ebraica in Palestina (1945–1948)* (Bologna: Mulino, 1990), 86–87.
[25] Mario Rossi, "Italy: Viva la Palestina Ebraica!" in *Commentary*, July 1947, available at: www.commentary.org/articles/mario-rossi/italy-viva-la-palestina-ebraica/.

who left the small port of Vado Ligure in January 1946, former partisans offered discrete assistance to Jews en route for Palestine.

The idealization of the *Brichah* as continuation of the Italian antifascist struggle popularized Zionism within the Left. On June 30, 1946, the communist mouthpiece *Unità* denounced "the repression of the independence movement of the Jews in Palestine [...] who are fighting for the liberation of the country from British oppression." In keeping with Soviet strategy in the Middle East, Italian communists veered toward anti-Zionism after 1948. Until then, however, the PCI heralded Jewish refugees as freedom fighters against fascism and British imperialism. *Avanti!*, for its part, portrayed the Jews' dream to "rebuild their homeland" as "sacrosanct." A recurring feature of this discourse was the scant attention paid to the country's indigenous Arab population. "Martyred" Jews, learned the readers of the socialist newspaper in mid July 1946, sailed across the Mediterranean to redeem Palestine from the grip of feudal *effendis* and heartless British imperialism, with only benefits for Arab masses. Contrary to their European counterparts, Italian Socialists remained committed to "unity of action" with the Communist Party. Yet emotional support for the cause of Jewish refugees in the pages of *Avanti!* already announced the special relationship soon to bind "humanist socialism" – as social democracy branded itself during the Cold War – and the young state of Israel.[26]

In France, the *Exodus* saga drew even larger sympathy. Clandestinely brought from Germany, 4,500 Jewish refugees set sail from the port of Sète on July 11, 1947. Their goal was to run the British blockade of Palestine and advertise the plight of Jews in search of a homeland. In a show of force, Royal Navy sailors boarded *Exodus 1947* and diverted it to Haifa. On July 20, the refugees were put on board three deportation vessels and sent back to Port-de-Bouc near Marseille. The French state offered permanent asylum. "In this painful case," declared the government's spokesman and future socialist president François Mitterrand, "France intends to adopt an attitude of humanity": The event was a decisive moment in Mitterrand's life-long friendliness with Israel.[27] The majority of Jewish passengers, however, refused to disembark.

---

[26] Matteo Di Figlia, *Israele e la sinistra: Gli ebrei nel dibattito pubblico italiano dal 1945 a oggi* (Roma: Donzelli Editore, 2012), 19–20; Claudio Brillanti, *Le sinistre italiane e il conflitto arabo-israelo-palestinese* (Roma: Sapienza Università Editrice, 2018), 19–26; Alessandra Tarquini, *La sinistra italiana e gli ebrei: Socialismo, sionismo e antisemitismo dal 1882 al 1992* (Bologna: Mulino, 2019), 89–90.

[27] Cited in Frédérique Schillo, "La décision française dans l'affaire de l'Exodus: Retour sur un malentendu historique," *Relations Internationales* 142, no. 2 (2010): 37–51; Jean-Pierre Filiu, *Mitterrand et la Palestine* (Paris: Fayard, 2005), 17.

For more than a month, a large press corps reported on their deplorable situation. In the socialist newspaper *Le Populaire*, the former Popular Front leader Léon Blum described a "moral and physical suffering surpassing all human limits ... a red iron on a bleeding wound." French communists contributed their own imagery. *L'Humanité* compared the ships in Port-de-Bouc to a "floating Auschwitz, the only way to depict the hell in which the passengers of *Exodus 47* live."[28] Under a glare of negative publicity, the Exodus passengers were returned to displaced persons camps in northern Germany. The episode ended in a British fiasco and a propaganda victory for Zionism.

The travails of Jewish refugees, pointed out Simone de Beauvoir in October 1947, "has nothing to do with pity, it is a matter of justice." As the famed feminist wrote in her autobiography (1963), "the niceties of English democracy were meaningless for these men crammed in camps, wandering on boats, despaired."[29] De Beauvoir's comments revealed the effect of the Exodus saga on prominent French intellectuals: the identification of Jews stranded at sea as exemplar victims of injustice. The pro-Zionist French League for a Free Palestine, to which her companion Jean-Paul Sartre lent his name, rallied prestigious members of the intelligentsia to the cause of Exodus, including Emmanuel Mounier, Maurice Merleau-Ponty, Paul Claudel, and Raymond Aron. Artists and writers also entered the fray. The painter Henri Matisse, the Communist poet Louis Aragon, and the former resister Vercors, among others, added their names to an anti-British poster distributed in Paris. In the pages of *Esprit*, the Catholic priest and Jewish convert Alexandre Glasberg drew a dire conclusion. The British abuse of Jews, he wrote, proved that Hitler continued to live "in ourselves."[30] David Rousset, for his part, saw in Holocaust refugees "the pathetic witnesses of our own bankruptcy." For the early French critic of the Soviet Gulag, British internment camps in Cyprus, packed with Jews diverted from their journey to Palestine, demonstrated the perpetuation of barbarity after Nazism. Even after the defeat of the Third Reich, the Jew remained "the first sacrificed victim of the concentration camp world (*le monde concentrationnaire*)."[31] The former Buchenwald internee later demanded reciprocity when he

---

[28] David Lazar, *L'opinion française et la naissance de l'état d'Israël 1945–1949* (Paris: Calmann-Lévy, 1972), 86–95; Laurence Coulon, *L'opinion française, Israel et le conflit israelo-arabe* (Paris: Honoré Champion, 2009), 36–40.

[29] Denis Charbit, "Les raisons d'une fidélité: Simone de Beauvoir. Israël et les Juifs," *Simone de Beauvoir Studies* 17 (2000–2001): 48–63.

[30] Alexandre Glasberg, "La leçon sociale de l'affaire Exodus," *Esprit* 138, no. 10 (October 1947): 500–523.

[31] David Rousset, "Préface" in François-Jean Armorin (ed.), *Des juifs quittent l'Europe* (Paris: La Jeune Parque, 1948), 8–13.

sought the involvement of Holocaust survivors in his campaign against Soviet labor camps. Yet in the aftermath of the Exodus affair, Jewish refugees trapped in "prison-ships" or deported to Cyprus symbolized in his eyes the banalization of political terror after 1945.

Humanitarian philosemitism was expectedly less visible in Britain where the press routinely compared the clandestine immigration of Jews to an enterprise of "nationalist fanatics." The pro-Labour *Manchester Guardian* was an exception: "It is against the ghostly background of Buchenwald, Auschwitz and a dozen of other places whose name have acquired an indelible significance of horror that the present condition of Jewish displaced persons must be studied."[32] Some British soldiers who took part in disembarking operations at Hamburg docks felt sympathy: "We were told that these Jews had a way of sneaking up to you and cutting you with razor blades. What we saw were poor bewildered people clutching a few belongings moving towards the train."[33] But in August 1947, reports on the hanging of two British sergeants at the hands of Irgun terrorists in Palestine elicited far greater outrage than the "prison ships" anchored in Port-de-Bouc.

In Belgium and the Netherlands, the press occasionally discussed the situation of Jewish displaced persons but mainly as potential manpower for industrial reconstruction. The Dutch Protestant weekly *De Spiegel*, however, compared the "Exodus stunt" to the methods of Joseph Goebbels.[34] In Austria, newspapers only sparingly reported on the Exodus story through brief communiqués issued by Viennese Jews.[35] In Germany, the press covered the event but news of 4,000 Jewish refugees returning to the country elicited mixed reactions. Not a single town offered hospitality. Newspaper headlines, however, alerted their readers to the mistreatment of Jews by British troops in Hamburg, and in one case featured a front-page photograph of two Exodus passengers with the caption "once again behind bars."[36]

---

[32] Antero Holmila, *Reporting the Holocaust in the British, Swedish and Finnish Press, 1945–1950* (London: Palgrave Macmillan, 2011), 137–118 and 141; Daphne Baram, *Disenchantment: The Guardian and Israel* (London: Guardian Books, 2004), 74–76.

[33] Peter Absolon, "The Exodus Affair: Hamburg 1947," *The Journal of Holocaust Education* 6, no. 3 (Winter 1997): 65–79.

[34] Marlou Schrover and Tycho Walaardt, "Displaced Persons, Returnees and 'Unsuitables': The Dutch Selection of DPs (1945–1951)," *Continuity and Change* 33, no. 3 (2018): 413–440; *De Spiegel*, October 4, 1947, cited in Remco Remsel and Evelien Gans, *The Holocaust, Israel and the 'Jew'*, 99.

[35] See, for instance, *Wiener Kurier*, "Wiener Juden gegen Behandlung der "Exodus"-Flüchtlinge," September 5, 1947.

[36] *Lübecker Nachrichten*, "Exodus-Juden in Lübeck," September 10, 1947. On reactions to the Exodus affair in Germany, see the online archive *Post-War Europe: Refugees, Exiles and Resettlement 1945–1950* (The National Archive of the UK and The Wiener Library, London).

In Bavaria, a public opinion poll conducted by American authorities revealed that most businessmen, journalists, university professors, and students supported Jewish refugees against the British. For some respondents, the Exodus affair presented an opportunity to minor down German guilt through philosemitic expression. "One cannot blame us for the concentration camps and at the same time block the road to freedom for these oppressed people," an outraged student told American interviewers.[37]

Empathy and exculpation similarly overlapped in Italy. Before its Americanization through Leon Uris's novel (1958) and Otto Preminger's film adaptation (1960) – both riddled with grotesque anti-Arab racism – the Exodus story inspired Duilio Coletti's *Il grido della terra* (*The Earth Cries Out*, 1948), a melodramatic film on Jewish immigrants who sailed from southern Italy to Palestine. Coletti, who had worked as a film director under Mussolini, gave in the movie a symbolic role to the Genoese ship captain who led Jews to their destination. "This journey," declares the seafarer at the end of the screenplay, "has great meaning for me ... I feel like a Good Samaritan rather than a sailor." Through the character of the benevolent captain, a brave helper of stateless Jews, *Il grido della terra* reinforced the myth of "good Italians" innately allergic to both Fascism and antisemitism.[38]

Sympathy for "humanity at sea," however, had a more important consequence for philosemitism in Western Europe: the legitimation of Zionism as moral imperative, irrespective of its effect on Palestine's native population. The Exodus Affair indeed elicited a harmless vision of Jewish self-determination while magnifying the humanity of its protagonists. In France, Albert Camus's reaction to the predicament of Holocaust refugees epitomized the appeal of humanitarian Zionism among writers moved by "all those who have trembled, day after day, for years, who are nowhere at home, and were told about orange orchards and lakes where nobody would spit on their face."[39] Such empathy, in Camus's case, was also the result of a unique intellectual trajectory.

---

[37] Frank Stern, *The Whitewashing of the Yellow Badge: Antisemitism and Philosemitism in Postwar Germany* (New York: Oxford University Press, 1992), 155–157.

[38] Asher Salah, "The Earth Cries Out, Aliya Bet and the War of Independence from an Italian Perspective" in *In Response to an Italian Captain: Aliya Bet from Italy, 1945–1948* (Tel Aviv: Eretz Israel Museum, 2016), 82–94; Millicent Marcus, *Italian Film in the Shadow of Auschwitz* (Toronto: University of Toronto Press, 2007), 32–33; Emiliano Perra, *Conflicts of Memory: The Reception of Holocaust Films and TV Programs in Italy, 1945 to the Present* (Oxford: Peter Lang, 2010), 46–48.

[39] Albert Camus, "Persécutés-Persécuteurs" (1948) in Albert Camus (ed.), *Oeuvres complètes*, III (Paris: Gallimard, 2006), 383–385.

Jews as Moral Rebels: Camus's Philosemitism

Contrary to Jean-Paul Sartre, the French Algerian writer born in 1913 did not devote particular attention to the "Jewish question" after the liberation of France. In May 1945, the *Combat* essayist addressed the situation of liberated French concentration camp survivors still awaiting repatriation from Dachau. Although Camus quoted a prisoner reporting that "everyday Jews are dying and once dead they are piled in a corner of the camp," his article mainly drew attention to "the thousands of [non-Jewish] political deportees ... the guardians of honor and the witnesses of courage."[40] Until May 1947, Camus's journalistic writings only indirectly touched on Jews or antisemitism. As one entry in his private *Carnets* suggests, Camus may have exercised self-censorship. "What seals my mouth," he wrote to himself, "is the fact that I was never deported. But I know which scream I stifle when I say this."[41] After reading David Rousset's second account of internment at Buchenwald (*Les jours de notre mort*, 1947), Camus admitted his inability to speak in the place of all survivors of concentration camps, Jews and non-Jews alike.

In Camus's most famous novel, allusions to the Holocaust remained allegorical. *The Plague*, published in 1947, could indeed be read on multiple levels. The best-selling chronicle of a bubonic plague in Oran was simultaneously a factual description of an epidemic, a reflection on the human condition, a call to act against the absurd, and a thinly disguised account of life in German-occupied France. The novel, which since sold millions of copies in France and across the world, also metaphorically evoked the Holocaust. "Men and women (...) flung into death-pits indiscriminately," or "a vague odor [of burned corpses] coming from the East" were some of the suggestive images conjuring up the Jewish catastrophe. Yet the victims of the plague remained unnamed, the word Jew is not spelled out and extermination is only referred to as "the scandal." To see the Holocaust in *The Plague* would have required special attention for persecuted Jews and a desire to decode the story accordingly, both lacking in the late 1940s. What was hard to miss, however, was Camus's commitment to solidarity. "But now that I have seen what I have seen," tells the journalist Raymond Rambert to Docteur Rieux after visiting devastated Oran, "I know that I am from here, whether I want it or not. This business concerns all of us (*cette histoire est notre histoire*)." As Camus pointed out to the literary theorist Roland Barthes, "compared to *The Stranger*,

---

[40] Actuelles I, "La Chair" in *Combat*, May 17, 1945.
[41] "Je sais quel cri j'étouffe lorsque que je dis ceci." Albert Camus, "Cahier V, September 1945–April 1948," in Albert Camus (ed.), *Œuvres complètes, II* (Paris: Gallimard, 2006), 1107.

The Plague marks the transition (...) from an attitude of solitary revolt to the recognition of a community whose struggle we must share."[42]

"Community" did not of course specifically mean Jews. In Camus's journalistic essays ranging from the late 1930s to his accidental death in 1960, exploited Arab Algerian workers and famished Kabylian peasants, Spanish Republicans, East-German demonstrators, Algerian and Tunisian nationalists sentenced to death, French anti-torture activists, or Hungarian insurrectionists in 1956, were all "communities" warranting solidarity. His "shared struggle" with Arab Algerians, however, was limited to equal rights without self-determination. And although *The Plague* takes place in Oran, Arabs are absent from the novel, an erasure famously compared by postcolonial critics to an "artistic Final Solution" of the Arab question.[43] The weak spot in Camus's ethics of solidarity remained the issue of Algerian independence, even if in May 1945 Camus wrote that the "era of Western imperialism has passed." Nonetheless, as Camus explained, *The Plague* reflected his evolution from the individual experience of the absurd toward "solidarity and participation" in times of oppression.

Revealingly, Camus launched at the same time a blistering attack against French racism and antisemitism. "It is impossible to accept without revolt," he wrote in *Combat* in May 1947, the reappearance of a "stupid and criminal disease." Unwavering support for the French army in the press, despite massacres perpetrated by troops in colonial Madagascar, was one symptom of racist contamination. In Algeria, the use of torture to obtain "spontaneous confessions" from insurgents also proved that "in these instances, we are doing what we reproached the Germans of doing." Yet the popularity of certain antisemitic stereotypes in France was another indication of racist contagion: "You will invariably come across a Frenchman who (...) thinks that Jews exaggerate [their suffering] and that they are wrong to stick together." Camus equated unsavory but nonviolent antisemitism with colonial brutality. "Spectacular or not," he argued, "these signs of racism reveal what is most abject and senseless in the heart of men."[44]

The pied-noir moralist, however, soon singled out what in his mind constituted the unique feature of antisemitism in postwar democracy: not discrimination or the infliction of harm, but the disappearance of the

---

[42] Albert Camus, "Letter to Roland Barthes on *The Plague*" in Albert Camus (ed.), *Lyrical and Critical Essays* (New York: Vintage Books, 1970), 339.

[43] Conor Cruise O'Brien, *Albert Camus: Of Europe and Africa* (New York: Viking Press, 1970), 48.

[44] "La contagion" (*Combat*, May 10, 1947) in Albert Camus, Œuvres complètes, II, op. cit., 429–431.

"persecuted" from public sight. "Our society is fed up with persecuted people and does everything to not see them," Camus wrote in his preface to Jacques Méry's *Laissez passer mon peuple* (*Let My People Go*, 1947). This journalistic reportage followed 600 Jewish immigrants aboard the *Ben Hecht*, the illegal vessel which left Port-de-Bouc to Palestine on March 1, 1947. Their journey and imprisonment in Cyprus, observed Camus, challenged the conscience of "those who will turn their head away and those who will change the subject." In this "Odyssey, in which Ithaca is surrounded by barbed-wire and Ulysses beaten," wrote the admirative prefacer, the journalist Jacques Méry "listened, on the most beautiful of all seas, throughout long nights, to the song of the persecuted." Here Camus's love for the Mediterranean reinforced his sympathy for Jewish refugees without consideration of Palestine's native inhabitants. "After years of unspeakable martyrdom," Holocaust survivors on the high seas forced the question of responsibility on Great Powers until now content to simply look away.

Another reason accounted for Camus's attraction for the *Ben Hecht* passengers. Already at work since 1946 on *L'homme révolté* (*The Rebel*, 1951), Camus saw in them a symbol of moral rebellion against humiliation. Contrary to doctrinaire revolutionaries, "the survivors of the ovens" did not seek absolute justice or absolute freedom. The people "who had enough of mass graves" only wanted a place where it would no longer be "spat upon." In this idyllic Arab-free vision, a "land of orchards and lakes" awaited Jews who only longed for "the right to have a burial place." Camus briefly counterbalanced this lyricism with a question: "Mind you, what if the persecuted learned the lesson and became, one day, the persecutors?"[45] Yet he did not dwell long on this thought: The Holocaust refugee validated his notorious distinction between ethical rebellion and violent revolution. Perhaps not aware that the *Ben Hecht* was sponsored by American Revisionist Zionists committed to Jewish supremacy over the whole territory of mandatory Palestine, Camus identified with "the people which is the symbol of persecution": moral rebels who said no to injustice without blind pursuit of power or utopia. Present at a rally organized in Paris in May 1948 to salute the birth of the state of Israel, the towering writer swiftly evolved from humanitarian Zionist to fervent Israelophile.[46] Journalists, intellectuals, and politicians who saw in Jewish statehood the fulfilment of European humanism felt similar admiration.

---

[45] See: Vincent Grégoire, "Le thème de l'holocauste dans les écrits de Camus," *The French Review* 80 (2007): 117–136.
[46] Maurice Szafran, *Les juifs dans la politique française: De 1945 à nos jours* (Paris: Flammarion, 1990), 83.

Humane Israel

"On one hand, there where the disunited Arab states (...) whose troops, because they did not know why they fought, fought poorly; on the other, there was this extraordinary Jewish people (...) showing to this soil the passionate love of men who see a house built, a tree grow, and a garden flourish out of their own hands." This is how the French novelist and journalist Joseph Kessel, who from mid May to mid June 1948 covered the War of Palestine for the high-circulation newspaper *France-Soir*, summarized the conflict: against "enemies barely awakened from the Middle Ages" stood "men who in this world only have their labor and the culture of the spirit."[47] A former Free French aviator, the writer of Russian-Jewish origin and coauthor of the *Chant des partisans* (the moving anthem of the French resistance) also compared Jewish troops to heroic *maquisards*, the underground fighters who resisted German occupiers. Echoing his earlier enthusiasm for Jewish settlers in Palestine (*Terre d'amour*, 1927), Kessel's articles stood out in their mystical admiration for "a newborn people and yet a thousand-year-old." Although French reports on the war between Jews and Arabs before May 15, 1948, and the interstate military conflict afterwards, were predominantly sympathetic to the Jewish side, Kessel's exaltation remained exceptional. Even the pro-Zionist Arthur Koestler, whose articles written from Palestine for the *Manchester Guardian* (June–November 1948) also appeared in *Le Figaro* and numerous European newspapers, refrained from such fervor. The Central European Jewish émigré, to be sure, offered his own orientalist clichés. "Holy Jihad and Arabian Knights on one side: the Bible with the Maccabeans on the other," he wrote from Tel Aviv on June 16, 1948.[48] But his misgivings about "native Jewish Tarzans" contrasted with Kessel's euphoria. Koestler instead rationalized the emergence of Jewish statehood as the inexorable march of modernity. Zionists, he wrote a year later, "did not dispossess, or victimize or exploit [Palestine's] native owners, but substituted themselves for the former by virtue of a historic fatality." Better coordinated than their "primitive adversaries," victorious Jewish soldiers were only "the relatively decent human executors of the amoral workings of history."[49]

---

[47] Joseph Kessel, *Terre d'amour et de feu. Israël 1926–1961* (Paris: Tallandier, 2018), 117, 180, 362; Lucille Cairns, *Francophone Jewish Writers: Imagining Israel* (Liverpool: Liverpool University Press, 2015), 24–29.

[48] Arthur Koestler, "Israel: First Impressions. Fervor, Faith and Bitterness" in *The Manchester Guardian*, June 16, 1948.

[49] Arthur Koestler, *Promise and Fulfillment: Palestine 1917–1949* (New York: Macmillan, 1949), 29; Susie Linfield, *The Lions' Den: Zionism and the Left from Hannah Arendt to Noam Chomsky* (New Haven: Yale University Press, 2019), 80–109.

Other British correspondents present in Palestine before May 15, 1948, like *The Observer* Clare Hollingsworth, focused instead on Jewish "actions" in Deir Yassin, Haifa, and Tiberias, "a calculated execution of a policy of terror learned (...) from the Germans." Her reports did not signify solidarity with Palestinians but confirmed that adulation for Zionist humanism had no place in British coverage of the events. In the Italian media, including the Catholic Press, the establishment of the state of Israel was met with limited interest or reservations. But writers from the Left, such as the socialist journalist Paolo Vittorelli, cast a positive light on Jewish statehood, portrayed as a just struggle for freedom and emancipation through socialist Jewish-Arab coexistence. In Germany, media coverage of the events in Palestine was resolutely pro-Zionist. This had less to do with philosemitism than with the journalists entrusted with the reporting. Lacking resources to send their own correspondents, newspapers relied on Jewish writers of German or Austrian origin who did not hide their sympathies. In France, the Catholic newspapers *Témoignage Chrétien* and *La Croix* were the only discordant voices within a press generally supportive of the Jewish homeland.[50] Yet whether favorable to the Jewish side or, more infrequently, sympathetic to Arabs, press coverage of the 1948 events did not captivate Western European readers. Neither the success of Jewish forces against Arab armies nor the flight and expulsion of most Palestinians from their land – an issue only discussed in detail after the "problem of refugees" became a *fait accompli* – preoccupied societies more concerned with economic reconstruction and the intensification of the Cold War.

At the start of the 1950s, however, intellectuals fascinated with the new state recognized in Israel a positive symbol of Western humanism. "Israel remains a living witness to the triumph of human idealism (...) over the allegedly inexorable laws of historical evolution," wrote the British Jewish political philosopher Isaiah Berlin in 1953, "and this seems to me to be to the eternal credit of the entire human race."[51] The Oxford

---

[50] James Rodgers, *Headlines from the Holy Land: Reporting the Israeli-Palestinian Conflict* (London: Palgrave Macmillan, 2015), 8–39; Mario Toscano, "14 maggio 1948: La fine di un pellegrinaggio bimillenario" in Mario Toscano (ed.), *L'Italia racconta Israele 1948–2018* (Viella: Rome, 2018), loc. 195-1009 (Kindle edition); Elena Mazzini, "Terra Santa, Luoghi Santi, tali restano integralmente per il Cristianesimo: Lo Stato di Israele nella stampa cattolica italiana (1948–1967)," in M. Simoni and A. Marzano (eds.), *Roma e Gerusalemme*, op. cit., pp. 97–116; Gilad Margalit, "Israel through the Eyes of the West German Press 1947–1967," *Jahrbuch für antisemitismusforschung* 11 (2002): 235–248; Jacques Droz, *La création de l'Etat d'Israël vu par la presse française* (Paris: La Documentation Française, 1993).

[51] Isaiah Berlin, "The Origins of Israel" (1953) in Henry Hardy (ed.), *The Power of Ideas* (Princeton, NJ: Princeton University Press, 2002), 173–196.

professor did not ponder whether the "the last State built on the humane and liberal foundations heralded by the great French revolution and the European revolutions of 1848" also came at a human cost. In Berlin's reflections on the birth of Israel, Arabs only make one brief appearance as "neighbors" of the new state who yearn for the Jews' extermination. The scholar knighted in 1957 greeted instead the establishment of a state for a people with "too much history and too little geography." Israel, in his eyes, also revolutionized Jewish life in the diaspora. To become Israeli, assimilate in another country or remain in "a betwixt-and-between condition," Berlin marveled, "is now a purely individual problem which each Jew is free to solve as he chooses (...) as an individual human being."[52] Both anglophile and attached to Israel, Berlin saw in diaspora Zionism a welcome alternative to single-loyalty nationalism: a chance for Jews everywhere in the West to realize themselves "in as many directions as freely, variously and richly as they can."[53]

Berlin's praise for the "human idealism" of Jewish statehood was a Jewish intellectual response to the creation of Israel. In the 1950s, however, the projection of humanness on the Jewish state occurred within a larger Israelophile current. Like Cold War liberals in the United States, Western European socialists formed the backbone of progressive philo-Zionism between 1948 and 1967. The forty-year-old Margaret Thatcher, to be sure, lauded the new country for its supposed anti-welfarism. "They don't pay people for being idle in Israel," she reported after her first visit in 1965.[54] But social democrats set the tone of admirative discourse. Israel, in their eyes, epitomized socialism "at a human scale." Their romanticization of Jewish settlers in Palestine, part and parcel of a vision of empire as disseminator of modernity, nonetheless predated the year 1948. From the mid 1920s to the outbreak of World War II, European socialist parties heralded Labor Zionism as their outpost in the non-Western world and considered the Jewish colonization of the land a benign infringement beneficial to backward Arab natives oppressed by "feudal" effendis.[55]

---

[52] Isaiah Berlin, "Jewish Slavery and Emancipation" (1951) in *The Power of Ideas*, op. cit., 196–226.
[53] Arie M. Dubnov, *Isaiah Berlin: The Journey of a Jewish Liberal* (New York: Palgrave Macmillan, 2012), 196–200; Malachi Haim Hacohen, "The Strange Fact That the State of Israel Exists": The Cold War Liberals between Cosmopolitanism and Nationalism," *Jewish Social Studies* 15, no. 2 (Winter 2009): 37–81.
[54] Cited in Eliza Filby, *God & Mrs Thatcher: The Battle for Britain's Soul* (London: Biteback Publishing, 2015), 252.
[55] Paul Kelemen, "In the Name of Socialism: Zionism and European Social Democracy in the Inter-War Years," *International Review of Social History* 41, no. 3 (December 1996): 331–350.

This rhetoric evolved after World War II. Like most members of the Labour party's intelligentsia, the pro-Zionist MP Richard Crossman believed in 1947 that "the establishment of a Jewish national home in Palestine is an important part of the Socialist creed." But the Jewish "socialist Commonwealth, intensely democratic, intensely collectivist" was no longer an exotic oasis of utopian socialism: It now inspired the welfarist New Jerusalem which Clement Attlee's government pledged to build in England.[56] Sam Watson, the Labour party's leader who visited Israel in 1950, acknowledged this kinship. "It is a fact that on all economic and social problems," reported Watson in the pages of the left-Labour mouthpiece *Tribune*, "we are attempting to carry out the same policy." The 1 million inhabitants of Israel, he also reported, are "progressive, democratic, and Socialistic."[57] Not all social democrats, to be sure, enthused about Zionism. In West Germany, the SPD initially reacted with reserve to the creation of Israel before changing course. Although supportive of Jewish self-determination, Italian socialists harbored less enthusiasm for Israel than the far more sympathetic SFIO in France. But a dominant representation of the Jewish state imposed itself within the noncommunist left after 1948: the country where socialism revealed its human face.

Created in 1951, the umbrella organization of socialist parties known as the Socialist International officialized this admiration. In March 1955, its secretary Julius Braunthal marveled at "socialist Israel, which has succeeded in the realization of splendid social, economic, and cultural aspirations in the face of difficulties such as scarcely any socialist party in the world has ever encountered." The Histadrut trade union, he added, "is a labour organization without parallel in the world (...) a powerful rock on which the magnificent edifice of Socialism in Israel is built."[58] Dedicated to the exclusion of Arab workers from "Hebrew Labor" in the 1920s and 1930s, the sectarian Histadrut only agreed to full Arab membership in 1960: By then the approximately 200,000 Palestinian residents of Israel placed under military rule until 1966 no longer challenged Jewish hegemony in the labor market.[59] The kibbutz

---

[56] Richard Crossman, *Palestine Mission: A Personal Record* (New York and London: Harper & Brothers Publishers, 1947), 91, 177. See also Paul Kelemen, *The British Left and Zionism: History of a Divorce* (Manchester: Manchester University Press, 2017), 115–177.

[57] James R. Vaughn, "'Keep Left for Israel': *Tribune*, Zionism and the Middle East, 1937–1967," *Contemporary British History* 27, no. 1 (2013): 1–21.

[58] Socialist International Archives, Folder 672 (International Institute of Social History, Amsterdam); see also Julius Braunthal, *History of the International, Volume 3, 1943–1968* (Boulder, CO: Westview Press, 1980), 354–355.

[59] Arnon Degani, "On the Frontier of Integration: The Histadrut and the Palestinian Arab Citizens of Israel," *Middle Eastern Studies* 56, no. 3 (2020): 412–426.

movement, for its part, took over the land of destroyed Palestinian villages and agricultural fields abandoned after 1948. That the Histadrut and Israel's vaunted collectivist farms were also instruments of dispossession did not dent their reputation in socialist eyes. Even young Marxist idealists in search of an authentic communist experience felt drawn to the Jewish state. Born in 1933, the radical Italian philosopher Antonio Negri became later in life a theorist of capitalist globalization and a fierce critique of Israel. In 1954, however, Negri discovered in Kibbutz Nahshonim "practices of Communism that were as radical as they were elementary. The utopia was real. Its reality had bite." Negri already sensed then "the guilt of the expropriator who always gives a vulgar coloring to the figure of the colonizer." But as the Italian intellectual ideologically close to the Red Brigades stunningly avowed, "Israel was my luck, my chance – and my symbol."[60]

The 1956 Suez crisis further reinforced Israel's humanness in West European eyes. The "Nazification" of Gamal Abdel Nasser following Egypt's nationalization of the Suez Canal in July 1956 affixed to the new country the image of democratic enclave in a totalitarian Middle East. The British conservative Prime Minister Anthony Eden, to be sure, equated the Egyptian leader to Hitler without effusive pro-Zionism. "Nasser's plans and intentions," argued Winston Churchill's successor, were akin to the Führer's "acts of aggression" on the eve of World War II.[61] In France, however, the socialist head of government Guy Mollet dubbed Nasser a "would-be Hitler" while lavishing praise on the Jewish state. A day after Israeli forces entered the Sinai Peninsula, Mollet extolled Israel's "attachment to the rights of man and the fundamental principles of democracy – principles whose price the Israelis, more than any other people perhaps, know the exact cost."[62] Together with the Labour party's leader Hugh Gaitskell, the Welch socialist politician Aneurin Bevan mounted a vigorous campaign against the French–British–Israeli military expedition. Yet Bevan also detected in the Egyptian regime's "basic fascist tendencies." Arab socialism, in the mind of Labourites favorable to Zionism, paled in comparison to its Israeli counterpart. "There is a socialist state growing up in the Middle East," the trade unionist Sam Watson had already announced in 1955, "and that socialist state contains within itself some of the finest creative

[60] Antonio Negri, *Pipeline: Letters from Prison* (Cambridge: Polity Press, 2014), 34–43.
[61] Lindsay Frederick Brau, "Suez Reconsidered: Anthony Eden's Orientalism and the Suez Crisis," *The Historian* 65, no. 3 (Spring 2003): 531–535.
[62] Statement by Guy Mollet on the Suez Crisis (October 30, 1956), available at: www.cvce.eu/en/obj/statement_by_guy_mollet_on_the_suez_crisis_30_october_1956-en-83519932-30fa-4562-8b7d-6615c4c14257.html.

impulses mankind has ever seen.⁶³ The Socialist International spokesman Julius Braunthal shared a similar view. "The cause of socialism in Israel," argued the Austrian-born émigré in Britain in August 1956, "is the cause of democratic socialism all over the world."⁶⁴

Anti-colonialism, of course, had already began to steer parts of the European Left away from its earlier support or acceptance of Zionism. Yet in France, the Suez crisis invigorated the pro-Israel feelings of socialists still wedded to the idea of French rule in Algeria. In Britain, the Labour party's opposition to the tripartite invasion of Egypt did not undermine its predominant pro-Zionist orientation. And in both countries, the portrayal of Nasser as "Hitler of the Nile" valorized the humane reputation of Israel in public opinion.⁶⁵ "The survival and freedom of the State of Israel," wrote Albert Camus in 1958, "may well dash the dreams of Nasser or other slave-owning kings." Camus also sympathized with the "misery of Arab peoples" yet for the 1957 recipient of the Nobel Prize in literature, solidarity with "exemplary Israel" remained the moral obligation of "us, Europeans, who are still accountable for the martyrdom of millions of Jews."⁶⁶

Numerous Christian Democrats, anti-communist conservatives and far-right "antisemitic Zionists" impressed with Israel's military strength also spoke favorably of the Jewish state in the wake of the Suez crisis.⁶⁷ But until 1967, the idealization of Israel in the political arena primarily remained the hallmark of the reformist Left. Key figures of European socialism between 1948 and the Six-Day War – the French François Mitterrand, the Italian Pietro Nenni, the British Harold Wilson, the Dutch Willem Drees, or the Belgian Camille Huysmans – harbored lifelong sympathy for Israel. Born in 1913, Willy Brandt had taken "a skeptical view of Zionist ideas" in his youth, favoring then the "social and cultural integration" of Jews in Germany. Yet the "Israelis' will to succeed and their remarkable ability to make the desert bloom," which he first discovered during a visit in 1960, left a deep impression on the West Berlin mayor and future chancellor. "Israel's arduous first thirty years of

---

⁶³ David Feldman, "Zionism and the Labour Party" in Larissa Allwork and Rachel Pistol (eds.), *The Jews, The Holocaust, and The Public: The Legacies of David Cesarani* (London: Palgrave Macmillan, 2019), 45–72.

⁶⁴ Archives of the Socialist International, Folder 672 (Institute of Social History, Amsterdam).

⁶⁵ Jane Owen, "The Polls and Newspaper Appraisal of the Suez Crisis," *Public Opinion Quarterly* 21 (Fall 1957): 350–354.

⁶⁶ Albert Camus, "La gauche française contre Israël?" (February 21, 1957), in *Oeuvres Complètes* IV (1957–1959), 555. See also www.dailymotion.com/video/xe5tmi.

⁶⁷ Pierre Birnbaum, "The French Radical Right: From Anti-Semitic Zionism to Anti-Semitic Anti-Zionism," *The Journal of Israeli History* 25, no. 1 (2006): 161–174.

existence need not to be recounted here," Brandt later wrote in his autobiography, "but I was never indifferent to its fate."[68]

Eyewitnesses of Humanity

Israelophilia was also a literary phenomenon. Throughout the 1950s, glowing reports from the country propagated positive representations of the Jewish state. In the United States, this trend started immediately after Israel's proclamation of independence. Between 1948 and 1950, observed the Jewish American anthropologist Raphael Patai in 1951, "the average frequency of the new publications on Israel in the English language alone was one book every two weeks (...) not counting pamphlets, mimeographed publications, reports, yearbooks, memoranda, directories, musical publications, business publications and documents."[69] This frantic pace was never matched in Western Europe but books on the Israeli experience also found a readership on the continent and Britain. In West Germany, laudatory accounts of Israel compensated for Nazi crimes – an issue discussed in this chapter's final section. Yet in the Federal Republic as in other West European countries, pro-Israel books published in the 1950s emanated in part from Jewish authors sympathetic to Zionism or who had become Israeli citizens. The writings of Arthur Koestler, Jon and David Kimche, Norman Bentwich, Harry Sacher, and Abba Eban in Britain; Elian Finbert, André Néher, André Chouraqui, David Catarivas, Pierre Paraf, or Paul Giniewski in France; Martin Buber and numerous writers of German or Austrian origin in the Federal Republic, all vehiculated an attractive image of Israel. Some of these publications were also translated into Italian and Dutch, alongside books initially published in English in the United States. David Ben-Gurion's *Rebirth and Destiny*, for instance, first appeared in New York in 1954 before its translation in various European languages.[70]

---

[68] Willy Brandt, *People and Politics: The Years 1960–1975* (London: William Collins Sons & Co, 1978), 451–452.

[69] Raphael Patai, "Literature on Israel 1948–1950," *The Jewish Quarterly Review* 41, no. 4 (April 1951): 425–438.

[70] See among others (in abridged format): Arthur Koestler, *Promise and Fulfillment*, op. cit., 1949; Norman Bentwich, *Israel* (1952), *Israel and Her Neighbours* (1955) and *Israel Resurgent* (1962); Jon Kimche, *Seven Fallen Pillars* (1950); Jon and David Kimche, *The Secret Roads* (1954); Harry Sacher, *Israel: The Establishment of a State* (1952); Abba Eban, *Voice of Israel* (1958). French-Jewish authors include: David Catarivas, *Israël* (1955); André Néher and Jos Milbauer, *Israël* (1955); André Chouraqui, *L'Etat d'Israël* (1955); Elian Finbert, *Pionniers d'Israël* (1956); Paul Giniewski, *Quand Israël combat* (1957); Pierre Paraf, *L'état d'Israël dans le monde* (1958). German and Austrian Jews who reported from Israel include Martin Buber, *Israel und Palästina: Zur Geschichte einer Idee* (1950); Walter A. Berendsohn, *Aufbauarbeit in Israel* (1953); Moshe Ya'akov

Israelophile travel writing, of course, was not an exclusive Jewish phenomenon. The state of Israel indeed rapidly attracted the attention of visiting European journalists, politicians, trade unionists, intellectuals, artists, and Christian personalities. One theme common to these apologetic writings was "the birth of a new race," as the French journalist Henri Amouroux already observed in 1950. The Jews he encountered in Israel no longer resembled "the Jews of Warsaw who docilely obeyed the orders of the SS"; or "Parisian Jews" convinced that the Legion of Honor protected them against persecution. The new race, wrote Amouroux, was "hardened, proud and stubborn." Laborers in kibbutzim, the journalist added without fear of antisemitic innuendos, were proof that "this people could resist the old temptation of money."[71] The French novelist Georges Duhamel, for his part, detected changes in Jewish anatomy. Israelis, he discovered, "have clear eyes, blond hair, a short nose and a thin and mobile mouth." Transplantation to Palestine, concluded the man of letter also trained in medicine, "can modify the structure of an organism."[72]

Another characteristic of travel reports from Israel, especially when published in the early 1950s, was their unreformed colonial and/or orientalist language. "Crossing the Mandelbaum Gate in Jerusalem to reach Israel from Jordan," noted the French Catholic journalist André Frossard, meant "leaving contemplation and pleasant idleness" for the world of "organizing realism." The former member of the French resistance also informed his readers that "while the Jew plants, the Arab idly leans against the wall."[73] One of the founders of the *Amitié Judéo-Chrétienne de France*, the Catholic intellectual Jacques Madaule likewise opposed "immobile" Islam to Jewish vitality. The state of Israel, argued the visitor of the country in 1951, realized in Palestine "what colonial powers achieved or should have achieved in other parts of the world."[74] The idea of Zionism as exemplary colonial project was also conveyed to British readers. "Israel," marveled in 1952 the Arabist and diplomat Gerald de Gaury, "is an unequalled example

---

Ben-Gavriel (Eugen Hoeflich) *Israel, Wiedergeburt eines Staates* (1957); Herbert Weichmann, *Das Werden eines neuen Staates – Eindrücke von einer Reise* (1957); Burghard Freudenfeld, *Israel: Experiment einer nationalen Wiedergeburt* (1959); Theodor Friedrich Meysels, *Israël* (1959); Paul Vogel, *Israel will leben: ein Reisebericht* (1959); Arno Ullman, *Israel: Abenteuer einer neuen Heimat* (1961); Walter A. Berendsohn, *Das Volk der Bibel im Land der Väter: Der junge Staat Israel* (1962); Jacob M. Landau (ed.), *Israel* (1963); Simon Sachs, *Der grüne Traum, Jugend in Israel* (1966).

[71] Henri Amouroux, *Israël ... Israël!* (Paris: Editions Daumat, 1951), 177 and 44.
[72] Georges Duhamel, *Israël, clef de l'Orient* (Paris: Mercure de France, 1952), 17.
[73] André Frossard, *Voyage au pays de Jésus* (Paris: Fayard, 1955), 141–142.
[74] Jacques Madaule, *Le retour d'Israël* (Paris: Desclée de Brouwer, 1951), 79–80.

of the possibility of man to overcome the seemingly impossible in colonization."[75] The British poet and novelist Stephen Spender, who toured Israel in 1952 to write a book on immigrant children, praised the Jewish colonization of Palestine as a model for global demography. "With a little of the zeal of Israel," Spender wrote, "people could be shifted out of crowded areas into empty ones (...) Israel shows that it would be possible to make willingly those shifts in population which would solve many problems."[76] One of the first official German guests of the Jewish state, the CDU economist, and parliamentarian Franz Böhm likewise projected colonial fantasies on the state's "astonishing civilizing efforts." At the height of decolonization, admiration for the "civilizing potency of world Jewry" was not only a way for Germans to distance themselves from Nazism: It also assigned to Israel the role of rescuer of the European colonial idea.[77]

French visitors, for their part, fixated on Palestine's *mise en valeur* (development and improvement) under Israeli rule. Borrowed from the lexicon of French colonial humanism, the phrase described here the modern transformation of a land recently in the hands of "feudal Arab lords oppressing without qualms a miserable population."[78] Elian Finbert's *Pionniers d'Israël* (1956), soon translated into German, English, Italian, and Dutch, made ample use of this image. "I crisscrossed the country in a jeep, by foot, hitch-hiking, and explored it as I would explore any other virgin land," wrote the French traveler. Israel's valleys, he observed, "now look Californian, Umbrian, Australian (...) and increasingly lose resemblance with their physical reality of lore, that of the Levant."[79] The Third Republic's civilizing mission, and until its dissolution in 1958, the Fourth Republic French Union, aimed to bring progress in Indochina and Africa: Jewish *mise en valeur* was now carrying out this task in the Middle East. The renowned theatre and cinema actor Jean-Louis Barrault, however, drew other similarities between the Jewish state and French Republicanism. A guest of the country for two

---

[75] Gerald de Gaury, *The New State of Israel* (London: Derek Verschoyle, 1952), 13. Like de Gaury, other British writers on Israel in the 1950s were former imperial civil servants or government officials in Mandatory Palestine. See L. F. Rushbrook Williams, *The State of Israel* (London: Faber and Faber, 1957); D. R. Elston, *No Alternative: Israel Observed* (London: Hutchinson & Co., 1960).
[76] Stephen Spender, *Learning Laughter* (London: Weidenfeld and Nicholson, 1952), 2–3.
[77] Martin Braach-Maksvytis, "Germany, Palestine, and the (Post) Colonial Imagination" in Volker Langbehn and Mohammad Salama (eds.), *German Colonialism: Race, The Holocaust, and Postwar Germany* (New York: Columbia University Press, 2011), 274–313.
[78] Georges Duhamel, *Israël, clef de l'Orient*, op. cit., 82.
[79] Finbert, *Pionniers d'Israël*, op. cit., 143 and 123.

weeks in 1960, Barrault waxed lyrical about a "nation-in-arms" identical to the one victorious in 1792 "at the battle of Valmy." One of the "noblest events in the history of our civilization," the creation of Israel appeared in his eyes as the *levée en masse* of concentration camp survivors and indomitable fighters.[80]

Barrault's portrayal of Israelis as modern-day French revolutionaries posited historical resemblance between the two countries. In the United States too, sympathy for Israel during the early Cold War era was premised on historical sameness. Otto Preminger's film *Exodus* (1960), for instance, drew absurd but effective parallels between the American Revolution and the Zionist struggle against British rule in Palestine. Throughout the Truman, Eisenhower, and Kennedy presidencies, the "Americanization of Israel" swayed a public until then indifferent to Zionism toward identification with the Jewish state. Protestants celebrated a common biblical heritage while journalists, publicists, and entertainers, stressed similarities between rugged frontiersmen and Jewish settlers; or between the American melting pot and the Israeli ingathering of exiles. The budding special relationship between the United States and Israel derived from geopolitical calculations: It was also grounded on perceived cultural or "Judeo-Christian" kinship.[81]

Yet while "Our American Israel" was imagined as a replica of the United States, European Israelophiles heralded the uniqueness of Israeli society. After a second tour of the country in 1958, the French essayist Henri Amouroux explained to his readers why he would emigrate to Israel had he been Jewish. A country "at a human scale, where everything depends on man and his willpower," Israel was "one of the most extraordinary adventures of the modern world."[82] For André Malraux too, Israel was "a nation unlike the old nations of Europe." The French intellectual had wondered a decade earlier if the "European man" could ever recover from the destruction of war. One unmistakable site of this resurrection was the Jewish state, "the symbol of a metamorphosis which transformed a community of intellectuals and traders into a nation of peasant soldiers."[83] The British artist and photo-reporter Richard Lannoy summarized the function of Israel for the European conscience.

---

[80] Jean-Louis Barrault, *Journal de bord* (Paris: Julliard, 1961), 150.
[81] On the "Americanization of Israel" during the early Cold War, see Michelle Mart, *Eye on Israel: How Americans Came to View Israel as an Ally* (Albany, NY: State University of New York Press, 2006); Amy Kaplan, *Our American Israel: The Story of an Entangled Alliance* (Cambridge, MA: Harvard University Press, 2018).
[82] Henri Amouroux, *J'ai vu vivre Israël* (Paris: Fayard, 1958), 275–279.
[83] See André Malraux's preface to Izis Bidermanas's photographic reportage: *Israël* (Lausanne: Editions Clairefontaine, 1955), 7–11.

The country "may be deciphered any way you chose," the visitor wrote in 1958, yet it remained "the test of everyone's humanity."[84]

Humanism's Other

Enthusiasm for humane Israel, however, went hand in hand with the erasure of the Palestinian trace: Not a single Arab interlocutor appears in a large multilingual corpus of travelogues published during the fifteen years that followed the War of Palestine.[85] The Dutch biblical scholar Theodoor Vriezen, who toured Israel for several weeks in April and May 1950, stopped like other tourists in Nazareth (the Arab Christian town was spared depopulation in 1948) but did not converse with its inhabitants. Although he criticized "Jewish travelogues" for not showing "compassion, and especially respect, for Arabs," the Dutch visitor wrote out Palestinians from his account: The drawing featured on the cover of his book featured an empty land redeemed from desolation at the hands of Israeli farmers, an image also used in some of the first airline advertisements of flights to Israel.[86]

Committed to "record all that I could, as accurately as possible, in a factual way," the British Gerald de Gaury avoided "the controversial politics of the past and that aftermath of the war, the Arab refugee problem."[87] In his sympathetic report on the state's tenth anniversary, the Italian historian and former antifascist partisan Angelo Del Boca interviewed a wide range of Israelis but limited himself to an endnote on "Arab Palestinians," the "seven hundred thousand Arabs who left the country during the war of 1948–1949."[88] The future critic of Italian

---

[84] Richard Lannoy, *Israel* (London: Thames and Hudson, 1958), 22.
[85] In addition to the British and French titles cited above, see for Italy and the Netherlands: Alda Diena, *Israele è la mia pianta: Appunti in un viaggio in Israele* [*Israel Is My Plant: Notes on a Trip to Israel*] (Turin: Rosada, 1958); Angelo del Boca, *Israele Anno Dieci* [*Israel Year Ten*] (Turin: Lattes, 1958); Giorgio Roletto, *Israele* (Milan: Dott. A. Giuffrè, 1960); Giovanni Russo, *L'atomo et la Bibbia: viaggio in Israele* [*The Atom and The Bible: A Journey to Israel*] (Milano: Bompiani, 1963); Theodoor C. Vriezen, *Palestina en Israel* (Wageningen: H. Veenman, 1951); J. H. Grolle, *Een voolk opweeg naar huis* [*A People Returns Home*] (The Hague: J.N. Voorhoeve, 1953); Bertus Aafjes, *Vorstin onder de Landschappen: een reis door het Heilige Land* [*Princess among the Landscapes: A Journey through the Holy Land*] (Amsterdam: Mollenhoff, 1954); C. F. van Dam, *Israël, een staat in wording* [*Israel, A State in the Making*] (Amsterdam: Broekman & De Meris, 1957); R. A. Levisson, *Herboren Land: Israël* [*A Land Reborn: Israel*] (Amsterdam: Querido, 1957); Martinus A. Beek, *Israël: Land, Volk, Cultuur* (Baarn: Wereldvenster, 1962); H. van Praag, *Het verschinjsel Israel* [*The Israel Phenomenon*] (Amsterdam: Moussault's, 1965). West German travel literature is discussed in a separate section.
[86] Theodoor C. Vriezen, *Palestina en Israel*, op. cit., 247.
[87] Gerald De Gaury, *The New State of Israel*, op. cit., 11.
[88] Angelo Del Boca, *Israele Anno Dieci*, op. cit., 161.

colonial crimes in Ethiopia and the Horn of Africa also dedicated several pages to "second-class citizens" in Israel. But this phrase referred to Jewish immigrants from Arab lands, not the remnants of Palestine's indigenous population still under military rule. "I do not believe," remarked a British traveler in 1950, "that anything written on Israel must be United Jewish Appeal propaganda or antisemitic pamphlet."[89] Yet the first European eyewitnesses of Israeli society did not dwell on the price exacted by the establishment of the state on Arab natives. "Israel proves in the final analysis that the world constitutes itself out of will and imagination. It proves the dominance of the spirit over matter," observed the German writer and former anti-Nazi exile Wolfgang Cordan in 1954. Such veneration for Israel's humanness left little space for the humanity of the defeated.[90]

The absence of Palestinians from Israel-friendly travelogues enabled their authors to vehiculate a one-sided interpretation of the "Arab-Israeli conflict": a struggle whose point of origin was the Arab invasion of the new state on May 15, 1948. The depopulation of the country, in these narratives, resulted from the foolishness of Arab leaders who encouraged temporary evacuation and promised imminent victory. The Israeli refusal to readmit Arab "absentees" stemmed from justifiable fears of fifth columnists. When acknowledged, the expulsion of Palestinian peasants and townspeople, or the systematic destruction of conquered villages, was rationalized by the brutality of war. The takeover of abandoned homes and fields to resettle Jews from Europe or Arab countries was not spoliation but necessitated by "immigrants crowding by their thousands into a land desperately short of housing."[91] Israel's official version of its War of Independence found indeed a large echo in this literature. The atrocities committed in "Deriakim" (Deir Yassin) in March 1948, admitted Jacques Madaule in 1951, forced the panicked inhabitants of Palestine's interior into flight but "coastal Arabs," he assured, "undoubtedly" abandoned their homes voluntarily.[92] "A miracle took place," noted the French journalist David Catarivas in 1955. The wonder in question was the mass departure of Arabs from Palestine despite the "supplications of Jewish communal leaders."[93] The rubble of Arab Palestine, wrote the British journalist Roy Elston, symbolized "the wanton absurdity of a war forced upon a simple people by [Arab] leaders (...) who cared very little

---

[89] Mark Milkes, *Land and Honey: Israel Explored* (London: Allan Wingate, 1950), 12.
[90] Wolfgang Cordan, *Israel und die Araber: Versuch einer Anschauung* (Frankfurt: Büchergilde Gutenberg, 1954), 144.
[91] Woodrow Wyatt, *The Jews at Home* (London: A Tribune Pamphlet, 1951), 3.
[92] Jacques Madaule, *Le Retour d'Israël*, op. cit., 57–58.
[93] David Catarivas, *Israël*, op. cit., 111.

for what happened to the unfortunate Arabs of Palestine."[94] Generally, however, sympathetic reports from Israel did not go into such details. The exodus of Palestinians from the land was not the concern of writers who, like Elian Finbert, extolled the "Israeli man, overloaded with history, conscious of his past and of his future."[95] The opening sentence of J. H. Grolle's *A People Returns Home* (1953) was not a lamentation but the start of an extraordinary journey: "Palestine no longer exists."[96]

The Dutch Reformed churchman acknowledged the erasure of Arab Palestine but felt compassion for the refugees he observed in East Jerusalem and Jordan, whose "tent camps (...) could not be habited by animals." Like other pro-Israeli authors, he blamed the persistence of the "refugee problem" on Arab governments unwilling to solve the crisis but recognized the suffering of Palestinians placed under the care of the United Nations Relief and Works Agency (UNWRA). "A mass of misery and destitution," wrote the British Zionist leader Harry Sacher in 1952, the refugees of 1948 only dodged famine thanks to the "philanthropy of the U.N. (...) and happily the worst anticipations of pestilence were avoided."[97] The humanitarianization of Palestinians, however, contrasted with the humanization of Israelis. Compared to refugees "poor and miserable in every way," remarked J. H. Grolle, the Jewish nation was "upright, a people moved by the human spirit, alive!"[98] This contrast was also apparent at the level of visual representation. In the 1950s, photographs of refugee camps produced by UNWRA staff in Gaza, Jordan, or Lebanon reinforced the humanitarian identity of displaced Palestinians. The camera lens of Western photo-reporters lured to the Jewish state, on the other hand, searched for the human among Israeli Jews.

Visual Israelophilia

"The art of photography," wrote in 1955 the curator of *The Family of Man* exhibit Edward Steichen, "is a dynamic process of giving form to ideas and explaining *man to man*." Reaching peak popularity in the 1950s, the humanist photography genre, in the words of Henri Cartier-Bresson, had one overarching subject: "mankind: man and his life, so brief, so frail, so threatened." Using black and white film, other illustrious French photographers such as Robert Doisneau, Brassaï, and Willy

---

[94] D. R. Elston, *No Alternative*, op. cit., 83.
[95] Elian Finbert, *Pionniers d'Israël*, op. cit., 239.
[96] J. H. Grolle, *Een volk op weg naar huis*, op. cit., 5.
[97] Harry Sacher, *Israel: The Establishment of a State*, op. cit., 150.
[98] J. H. Grolle, *Een volk op weg naar huis*, op. cit., 8, 10.

Ronis, captured the spontaneity of human emotions in the simplicity of everyday scenes. Against the depersonalization of the individual in totalitarian ideologies, they highlighted the singular humanity of common people. From Robert Capa's iconic *The Fallen Soldier* (1936), featuring the death of a Spanish Republican combatant, to the unicity of mankind celebrated in *The Family of Man* (1955), humanist photography set out to recover human dignity in the wake of fascism.[99]

Since its appearance in ethnographic books in the 1930s, however, this photographic genre also recorded fragments of Jewish life. In 1935, the American Joint Jewish Distribution Committee commissioned the Russian-born photographer Roman Vishniac to document Jewish communities in East-Central Europe. For three years, Vishniac's Leica camera captured the faces of rabbis, pupils, shopkeepers, and peddlers – the last visual record of a Yiddish-speaking world on the verge of destruction. In 1947, Vishniac also portrayed Holocaust survivors in the displaced persons camps of occupied Germany.[100] Jewish photographers who after 1933 emigrated from Germany and Austria to Palestine, for their part, concentrated on *chalutzim* (pioneers) and children in the Yishuv. Even before 1948, Zionist photography advertised the New Jew through modernist images of vibrant youth and pioneerism.[101]

The creation in New York of the Magnum Photos agency (1947) accelerated the circulation of such photographs. The famous cooperative covered events across the globe but two of its original founders, the Jewish émigrés and war photographers Robert Capa and David Seymour, visited Israel several times between 1948 and 1954. Magnum's task, stated its French cofounder Henri Cartier-Bresson in 1952, was to "evoke a situation, a truth" and capture "the poetry of life's reality." The agency's executive editor John Morris likewise singled out the distinctive talent of Magnum's photo-reporters. Committed to bear witness to the world "in terms of people rather than propaganda of statistics," they offered

---

[99] On humanist photography, see the exhibit catalogue *La photographie humaniste, 1945–1968* (Paris: Bibliothèque Nationale de France, 2006); Peter Hamilton, "Representing the Social: France and Frenchness in Post-War Humanist Photography" in Stuart Hall (ed.), *Representations: Cultural Representations and Signifying Practices* (London: SAGE Publications, 1997), 75–150.

[100] Roman Vishniac, *A Vanished World* (New York: Farrar, Straus, and Giroux, 1986); Hildegard Frübis, "Europe as Transit: Jewish Displaced Persons Camps and the Photographs of Roman Vishniac" in Barbara Lange et al. (eds.), *Rethinking Postwar Europe: Artistic Production and Discourses on Art in the Late 1940s and 1950s* (Vienna: Böhlau Verlag, 2020), 141–153.

[101] Ulrike Pilarczyk, "Chalutzim: Zionist Photography in Germany and Palestine in the 1930s: A Comparative Analysis of Images," *Leo Baeck Institute Year Book* 64, no. 1 (2019): 91–114; Rona Sela, *Photography in Palestine/The Land of Israel in the 1930s and 1940s* (Tel Aviv: Hakibbutz Hameukhad, 2000).

"a peculiarly human point of view."[102] Published in *Life* magazine and other media outlets, Capa's and Seymour's portraits of male and female soldiers, laborers, and new immigrants to the state, highlighted the humanness of everyday Israelis. The photographers of Jewish origin Tim Gidal and Jerry Cooke also joined the fray: Between 1948 and 1950, several photobooks on a state "in which one million Jews (...) can wrestle with their own destiny," already found their place on American coffee tables.[103] In September 1951, *Life* magazine featured a photo-reportage on "The Forgotten Arab Refugees, friendless exiles of Israel" in south Lebanon. These images of "sullen, bitter, and hopeless" people in Saida and Ein El Hilweh countervailed favorable coverage of Israel in the US media. Yet humanitarian photography did not match the humanist vibrancy of John Phillips's portraits of Israeli Jews published in *Life* in 1949; or Capa's close-up photographs of Jewish immigrants displayed in the same magazine in May 1951 and in other media until 1954, the year of his accidental death.[104] The young Swiss photographer Jean Mohr, to be sure, documented UNWRA camps as early as 1949 and visited them throughout his life. But only decades later did his photographs of Palestinian refugees, neither "helpless and miserable-looking" nor "terrorist," receive humanist consecration.[105] In the 1950s, however, Israelis remained a subject of choice for "concerned" photographers dedicated to "truth, commitment, and engagement." In the United States, their visual production appeared in magazines, books, and advertisements well into the 1960s.[106]

Similar images circulated in Western Europe. Through its Parisian office, Magnum sold photo essays on the continent and in Britain.

---

[102] Cited in Nadya Bair, *The Decisive Network: Magnum Photos and the Postwar Image Market* (Oakland, CA: University of California Press, 2020), 213.

[103] I. F. Stone, *This Is Israel* (New York: Boni and Gaer, 1948); Irwin Shaw and Robert Capa, *Report on Israel* (New York: Simon and Schuster, 1950). See also *Palestine, Land of Israel* (Chicago, IL: Ziff Davis, 1948) and *Palestine* (Cleveland: The World Publishing Co., 1948), with photographs by the German-born Herbert Sonnenfeld and the Swede Anna Riwkin-Brock.

[104] See in *Life* magazine: *The Forgotten Arab Refugees*, September 17, 1951 (photographs by James Bell); *The New Israel*, July 19, 1949 (John Phillips); *Israel Faces the Facts of Life*, May 14, 1951 (Robert Capa); Andrew L. Mendelsohn and C. Zoe Smith, "Vision of a New State: Israel as Mythologized by Robert Capa," *Journalism Studies* 7, no. 2 (2006): 187–211. On Magnum's coverage of Israel in the 1950s and beyond, see *Israel 50 Years: As Seen by Magnum Photographers* (New York: Aperture, 1998). For photographs of Israel by Agence France-Presse (AFP), see Xavier Baron, *Israël 1948* (Paris: Hoëbeke, 2008).

[105] Edward W. Said, *After the Last Sky: Palestinian Lives* (New York: Columbia University Press, 1986).

[106] Cornell Capa (Robert Capa's brother) coined the phrase "concerned photographer" in 1954: *The Concerned Photographer* (New York: Grossman Publishers, 1967). On Israel and American photography in the 1950s and 1960s, see Bair, *The Decisive Network*, op. cit., 85–89.

European newspapers also independently relied on photo-reporters based in Israel.[107] As in the United States, however, coffee-table photobooks opened another channel of pro-Zionist humanist expression. Willem Van de Poll's *Daybreak of a Nation*, a collection of photographs published in 1952, was the first volume of this kind in Western Europe. After covering the Netherlands under German occupation and the Dutch Indies on the eve of decolonization, the photographer travelled to Israel in 1949 to document "the daybreak of this old new state." Faithful to the humanist format, Van de Poll portrayed the arrival of Holocaust survivors in Haifa and the faces of Jewish immigrants from all corners of the world. Van de Poll later continued his journey to Jordan, where he took numerous photographs of Palestinian refugees. Yet his photobook on Israel, dedicated "to the memory of those who were destined not to witness it," did not include any of these pictures. It instead staged Jewish survival in the background of Arab absence. One of his photographs features an immigrant from Europe with a concentration camp tattoo on his left arm, holding a child in front of an abandoned Arab house. "A young father and his son on his arm," says the caption, "gazes at the dilapidated remains of the strife-ridden house. How many ruins and how much rubbles have these eyes surveyed already?" The homes left by the "departed Arab population must be cleared (...) and made habitable as soon as possible," the caption also explained, as "a new future of young life is going to rise and flourish."[108]

Another emblematic photographic essay on Israel was the book authored in 1955 by Izraels Bidermanas (known as Izis), a Lithuanian Jew settled in France since the 1930s and a prominent practitioner of humanist photography.[109] Translated into English in 1958, the volume featured various types of Israeli Jews: shoemakers in the streets of Tel Aviv, shepherds in the Galilee, soldiers, and watchmen on the border, dancing children. Yet the "most beautiful photograph of the book," pointed out its prefacer André Malraux, did not show flourishing deserts or vigorous laborers. It featured instead a beggar "reminiscent of Job, immersed in a Prophet's sleep," likely of Yemeni origin, sitting at the doorstep of a condemned Arab house in the city of Ramla (al-Ramla), from which Palestinians were expelled on July 13, 1948. An erudite specialist in ancient art, Malraux only saw in the condemned Arab door a decontex-

---

[107] See for Italy and Germany: Dario Migliucci, "Photographic Portrayal of Israel in the Italian Leftwing Press, 1947–1967," *Israel Affairs* 25, no. 4 (2019): 660–674; Gilad Margalit, "Israel through the Eyes of the West German Press 1947–1967," op. cit.
[108] Willem de Poll, *Daybreak for a Nation* (Meppel: J.A. Boon and Zoon, 1952); see also the catalog *Willem van de Poll 1895–1970* (The Hague: Nationaal Archief, 2005).
[109] Izis Bidermanas, *Israël* (Lausanne: Editions Clairefontaine, 1955).

tualized "Chaldean arch" while the old Jewish beggar evoked the biblical prophetic tradition. The book also contained images of schoolchildren on a hill near Jerusalem planting the Forest of Martyrs "whose six million trees will grow in memory of Hitler's victims." Close-up photographs of an elderly man watching the scene, and of a young girl preparing to plant a tree, encouraged Malraux to muse over the meaning of the Jewish face (*visage* in French). In 1947, the dramatist and visual artist Antonin Artaud had famously stressed the distinction between the plasticity of *face* and the expressiveness of *visage*. "Which means that the human face [*le visage humain*]," wrote Artaud, "has not yet found its face and that it behooves the painter to give it one."[110] Malraux ascribed an identical function to humanist photography: The camera revealed the human *visage* of Israeli Jews. "Although its ruins have all been destroyed," he observed, "the Jewish people still bears on its face [*visage*] the oldest history of the world." Izis, however, also cast his gaze on several Palestinian figures. Yet they consistently appear as fleeting or faceless ghosts, such as a lone Arab woman shepherding a few goats amid the Arab ruins of Lod-Lydda or another one hastily walking in Ramla-al-Ramla.

Such distance between the humanist camera and the Arab subject remained a typical feature of Israelophile photography between 1948 and 1967. Except for Bedouins or Druze enlisted in the Israeli army, occasional children, or exoticized "sons of the desert," close-ups of Palestinians are conspicuously absent from this visual production – a trend only reversed in left-wing photojournalism at the start of the 1970s. In the 1950s and 1960s, however, the Israeli *visage* not only dignified the Jewish face dishonored in antisemitic propaganda: It also magnified the humanity of Zionism in democratic Europe.

The Humanization of Germans

In the Federal Republic of Germany, travelogues and photobooks on Israel similarly forged a mythologized image of the newly established country. Between 1953 and 1955, the first official German guests of the Israeli government, including the Protestant pastor Hermann Maas, the Hamburg journalist Erich Lüth, and the CDU politician Franz Böhm, published enthusiastic accounts of their travels.[111] In search of

---

[110] Antonin Artaud, "Le visage humain" in *Portraits et dessins pat Antonin Artaud* (Paris: Galerie Pierre, 1947).
[111] Hermann Maas, *Und will Rachels Kinder wieder bringen in das Land: Reiseeindrücke aus dem heutigen Israel* (Heilbronn: Eugen Salzer Verlag, 1955); Erich Lüth, *Ein Deutscher sieht Israel* (Hamburg: Gesellschaft für Christlich-Jüdische Zusammenarbeit, 1955); Franz and Marietta Böhm, *Eine Reise nach Israel* (Düsseldorf: Kalima Druck, 1955).

an "experience-based theology" connecting the Bible with the reality of Jewish statehood, Protestant churchmen followed suit at the end of the 1950s. Reflecting on his first visit of the country in 1959, the West Berlin theologian Friedrich-Wilhelm Marquardt compared this experience to a "second baptism."[112] Socialist party leaders also embarked to Tel Aviv. In March 1957, the SPD chairman Erich Ollenhauer inaugurated an oft-repeated ritual: a tour of kibbutzim and Israeli cities punctuated by friendly meetings with David Ben-Gurion and Labor party or Histadrut representatives. The SPD politician Carlo Schmid, the West Berlin mayor Willy Brandt, and members of the trade unions federation, soon walked on Ollenhauer's footsteps.[113] Journalists, independent publicists, and members of Societies for Christian-Jewish Cooperation, likewise flocked to the country from the late 1950s to 1967. The titles given to their books give a measure of their enthusiasm: *Israel State of Hope, Homeland of the Homeless, The Desert Rejoices in the Land of David, Encounters with Israel, Le-Chaim to Life, Schalom Israel*, and so on.[114] In 1967, the psychoanalysts Alexander and Margarete Mitscherlisch famously identified in German society an "inability to mourn" the Nazi past. Yet even before the establishment of diplomatic relations between Bonn and Jerusalem in 1965, German travelers to Israel already displayed an uncanny ability to love.

Such "sentimental advertisement," countered Theodor Adorno in 1962, did little to reduce the latent antisemitism still pervasive in the Federal Republic.[115] To combat Judeophobia, argued the Frankfurt

---

[112] Cited in Gerhard Gronauer, *Der Staat Israel im westdeutschen Protestantismus: Wahrnehmungen in Kirche und Publizistik von 1948 bis 1972* (Göttingen: Vandenhoeck & Ruprecht, 2013), 131.

[113] On the first visits of German socialists in Israel, see Shlomo Shafir, *An Outstretched Hand: German Social Democrats, Jews and Israel 1945-1967 (Hebrew)* (Tel Aviv: Zmora Bitan, 1986), chapters 7 and 8; Martin W. Kloke, *Israel und die deutsche Linke: zur Geschichte eines schwieriegen Verhältnisses* (Frankfurt am Main: Haag + Herchen, 1990), 49–52.

[114] Kurt Schubert and Rolf Vogel, *Israel, Staat der Hoffnung* (Stuttgart: Schwabenverlag, 1957); Petrus Huigens, *Begegnungen in Israel* (Kassel: Schneider & Weber, 1962); Rudolf Weckerling, *Le -Chaim zum Leben: eine Reise nach Israel* (Berlin: K. Vogt, 1962); Wolfgang Dietrich, *Begegnung mit Israel* (Hanover: Verlag "Die Zusammenarbeit", 1962); Ilse Wilm, *Schalom Israel: Tagebuch einer Reise ins Heilige Land* (Bielefeld: Ludwig Bechauf Verlag, 1963); Dagmar Nick, *Einladung nach Israel* (Munich: A. Langen, 1963); Wolfgang Kahle, *Bericht aus Israel: Ein Tag mit Zahava* (Hamburg: C. Wegner, 1964); Erich Rüttel, *Israel: Heimat der Heimatlosen* (Stuttgart: Courier, 1965); Rudolf Braunburg, *Tau über die Wüste* (Hamburg: Baken Verlag, 1966); Alfred Burgsmüller, *Die Wüste jubelt in Davids Land: Junge Menschen erleben das heutige Israel* (Stuttgart: Quell Verlag, 1966); Arnold Scholz, *Israel, Land der Hoffnung* (Berlin: Arani-Verlags, 1966).

[115] Theodor W. Adorno, *Zur Bekämpfung des Antisemitismus heute?* (1962) (Berlin: Suhrkamp, 2024).

School philosopher, the critical study of ingrained anti-Jewish stereotypes was far more effective than "images of water plants and children in kibbutzim." Adorno alluded to the loveable Jew marketed to the public through cultural Israelophilia. Produced in 1955 and 1959, two influential documentary films conveyed to their viewers what authors of travelogues similarly observed: The moral and physical improvement of Jews resettled in Palestine. No longer the hideous or parasitic hucksters depicted in Nazi propaganda, the redeemers of "deserts" also embodied European culture away from the continent. "Isn't it Europa?," marvels the narrator of *Paradies und Feuerofen* [*Paradise and Fire Oven*, 1959] as images of the Israeli Philharmonic Orchestra appear on the screen.[116] In this film prized in 1959 at the Berlin Festival, German-born citizens of Israel are presented as the emissaries of the humanistic "other Germany" transplanted across the Mediterranean. Conservatives, for their part, re-Germanized the victims of Nazism through the lens of militarism. The expression "Prussians of the Middle East" coined at the time of the Suez crisis, or *Bild* magazine's portrayal of Moshe Dayan as "Israel's Rommel" in the wake of the 1967 Arab–Israeli war, resurrected a tabooed German nationalism through Israel's military might. The Viennese psychologist Friedrich Hacker, one of the first analysts of this phenomenon, concluded in 1973 that through identification with Israel, the Germans' "self-esteem and pride in their own past is salvaged and justified at least fragmentarily."[117]

Israelophilia, however, was also part and parcel of a discourse of guilt. The publicist Erich Lüth set the tone in 1955. Because "the Jewish question (...) remains the central problem of our spiritual being," he wrote, "Israel is the country that we must look for with our soul." The initiator of the *Peace with Israel* movement in August 1951, Lüth stood among the first advocates of a special relationship between the two countries. The Reparations Agreement signed between the Federal Republic and Israel in September 1952, in his mind, was only a "first step" toward deeper engagement.[118] Contrary to Konrad Adenauer's government, Lüth did not view the payment of monetary reparations

---

[116] Tobias Ebbrecht-Hartmann, "Projected Encounters: Rolf Vogel and the Beginnings of Cinematic Relations between Germany and Israel," *Leo Baeck Institute Year Book* 63 (2018): 11–33.

[117] Friedrich Hacker, *Terror: Mythos, Realität, Analyse* (1973) is cited in Friedemann Buttner, "German Perceptions of the Middle East Conflict: Images and Identifications during the 1967 War," *Journal of Palestine Studies* 6, no. 2 (Winter 1977): 66–81.

[118] Erich Lüth, "Wir müssen sagen, who wir stehen!" in *Wider den Antisemitismus* (Berlin: Kongress für Kuturelle Freiheit, 1952), 17–23.

as a final settlement of debt. "For us Germans," he wrote in his travelogue, "the salvation of Israel in the present and the future is a crucial admonition for our own transformation." The Left Catholic intellectual Walter Dirks similarly pleaded in 1957 for a "solidarity of destiny" between Germans and Israelis. In 1960, Lüth enjoined again his compatriots to "love the ancient country of the new Israel ... a fate from which one cannot escape."[119]

This language also permeated the writings of Protestant churchmen, mostly former members of the anti-Nazi Confessing Church, who travelled to Israel in the late 1950s. The existence of the Jewish state, Helmut Gollwitzer told a Berlin audience in 1958, should affect Germans "more deeply than the existence of any other country." The Lutheran theologian and future sympathizer of the 1968 student movement cautioned against "setting a blind philosemitism in the place of blind antisemitism." Yet the depth of German guilt required a special bond with the survivors of Nazism. "Every German who travels [to Israel] should be clear," declared Gollwitzer in 1958, "every Jew who lives today lives not because of us, but in spite of us ... in spite of me!" In 1959, the West Berlin student pastor Rudolf Weckerling advised his co-travelers to the Holy Land that "the heaviest baggage you are carrying with you is our guilt to the Jews." Testifying at the Eichmann Trial in May 1961, the Protestant provost Helmut Grüber, imprisoned in Dachau during the war, refused to talk about his own travails. The only non-Jewish German invited to the proceedings instead told the court that he only wanted to bear witness to "the suffering of my Jewish friends." The settlement of German protestants in the communal Christian village of Nes Ammim founded in 1960 in northern Israel, or the tours of the country organized by the Evangelical Church in Germany (EKD) from the late 1950s to 1967, shared the same goal: the earning of absolution from Jews as precondition for German redemption.[120]

---

[119] See Walter Dirks's preface to Elian Finbert, *Pionere der Hoffnung: Israel Abendteuer und Wagnis* (Düsseldorf: Karl Rauch Verlag, 1957), 7–13; A. D. Arielli, *Israel: Introduction by Erich Lüth* (Munich: Wilhelm Andermann Verlag, 1960), 49.

[120] Helmut Gollwitzer, *Israel-Und Wir* (Berlin: Lettner Verlag, 1958), 16–17. See also W. Travis McMaken, "Shalom, Shalom, Shalom Israel!" Jews and Judaism in Helmut Gollwitzer's Life and Theology," *Studies in Christian-Jewish Relations* 10, no. 1 (2005), available at: https://doi.org/10.6017/scjr.v10i1.8657; Rudolf Weckerling is cited in Gerhard Gronauer, *Der Staat Israel im westdeutschen Protestantismus*, op. cit., 131; Helmut Grüber, *Zeige pro Israel* (Berlin: Käthe Vogt Verlag, 1963); Gert van Klinken, "Settlers in a Strange Land: Dutch, Swiss, American, and German Protestants in Nes Ammim (Israel), 1952–1964" in David J. Wertheim (ed.), *The Jew as Legitimation: Jewish-Gentile Relations beyond Antisemitism and Philosemitism* (Cham: Palgrave Macmillan, 2017), 223–240.

In Jerusalem to report on the Eichmann Trial for *The New Yorker*, Hannah Arendt wrote in April 1961 to her husband Heinrich Blücher that the city was swamped "with Germans who are so philosemitic, enough to make one's stomach turn." When next to her a sobbing journalist uttered the words "it is we Germans who did this," she felt as if she were "in a theater."[121] The vast majority of citizens polled on this question, however, did not feel guilty for the Holocaust. Public opinion surveys conducted during or in the wake of the Eichmann Trial returned unambiguous results: West Germans still blamed the fanatical "inner core" of the bygone Nazi regime for the annihilation of European Jews.[122] Conservatives like Franz-Joseph Strauss, the former Wehrmacht officer on the Eastern front twice appointed defense minister between 1956 and 1969, nonetheless acknowledged that "millions of Jews were murdered as a result of German criminality and with German weapons." In 1958, the Bavarian politician compensated for these actions by authorizing covert military aid to Israel. His goal, however, was to quickly "leave the past behind us."[123] During the Konrad Adenauer era (1949–63) and under his successor Ludwig Erhard (1963–66), reparations, reconciliation, and the establishment of diplomatic or military relations with Israel, traded German good will for a clean historical sheet.

Yet in the wake of the Eichmann Trial, a network of Protestant leaders, several Christian Democrat figures, and above all, pro-Israel socialists, harbored a different attitude: Their warm feelings for the state of the victims derived from the indelible stigma of being German after the Holocaust. "The horrendous crimes (…) against millions of Jewish people cannot be extinguished by any good will, any reparation, any recompense," declared Willy Brandt in 1961."[124] A special bond with Israel, however, could humble Germans into guilt. "Pictures of the past," the president of the Bundestag Eugen Gerstenmeier declared after his tour of Yad Vashem in December 1962, "are sufficient in themselves to silence us Germans, and this silence is the silence of shame and the poignant fellow-feeling of countless numbers of my people in thinking

---

[121] Lotte Köhler (ed.), *Hannah Arendt/Heinrich Blücher: Briefe 1936–1968* (Munich: Piper, 1996), 519.

[122] Werner Bergmann and Rainer Erb, *Antisemitismus in der Bundesrepublik Deutschland: Ergebnisse der empirischen Forschung von 1946–1989* (Leske + Budrich: Opladen, 1991), 233–246.

[123] Daniel Marwecki, *Germany and Israel: Whitewashing and State-Building* (New York: Oxford University Press, 2020), 74–76. On German military aid to Israel, see also Daniel Marwecki, *Absolution: Israel und die deutsche Staatsräson* (Göttingen: Wallstein Verlag, 2024).

[124] Hannfried von Hindenburg, *Demonstrating Reconciliation: State and Society in West German Foreign Policy toward Israel, 1952–1965* (New York: Berghahn Books, 2007), 44.

of the people of Israel."[125] In the absence of official Holocaust memory in the Federal Republic, Israel became in the 1960s the stage of German expiation. From 1959 to 1965, 40,000 young Germans visited the Jewish state where they worked in kibbutzim and participated in meetings with Israeli youth. The development of airline travel also encouraged an increasing number of tourists to visit the country. On the eve of the 1967 June War, German public opinion overwhelmingly favored Israel over Arab countries. Such bias, however, did not correlate with acknowledgment of guilt. Support for Jews presented in the media as facing potential extermination (in May 1967, Israel's request of 20,000 gas masks from Bonn reinforced this perception) instead whitewashed the stain of Nazism: The former gassers of Jews now publicly stood on the side of their rescuers. For the minority of West Germans who belatedly shared in Karl Jaspers's "consciousness of guilt," however, solidarity with Israel meant more than compensation for past crimes. The anti-imperialist and pro-Palestinian 1967 student movement, of course, soon assailed the official philosemitism of the Federal Republic. For guilt-ridden older Germans, however, the path of re-humanization passed through a special relationship with the state of Israel. Nonintervention in the Middle East remained the proper course of action, the Grand Coalition's foreign minister Willy Brandt stated on June 7, 1967. But cautious diplomacy, he made clear, neither meant "moral indifference" nor "neutrality of the hearts."[126]

The Apogee of Humanist Philo-Zionism

The emergence of pro-Israel sentiment in Western Europe from 1948 to 1967 did not of course occur without opposition: Israelophilia ran parallel to negative views of Zionism. In the late 1940s, the French orientalist Louis Massignon and the English scholar Arnold Toynbee portrayed the creation of the Jewish state as an act of historical injustice. Although less vociferous than their Stalinist Eastern European counterparts, French and Italian communists turned against Israel in the early 1950s. Following the Suez crisis of 1956, anti-colonial intellectuals began to raise the "question of Palestine" to oppose the positive image of Israel within parts of the Left. Theorists of colonialism in the 1950s,

---

[125] See Rolf Vogel's collection of documents, *The German Path to Israel* (Chester Springs, PA: Dufour Editions, 1969), 144. On Gerstenmeier's visit, see also Jenny Hestermann, *Inszenierte Versöhnung: Reisediplomatie und die deutsch-israelischen Beziehungen von 1957 bis 1984* (Frankfurt am Main: Campus Verlag, 2016), 77–88.
[126] Cited in Carole Fink, *West Germany and Israel: Foreign Relations, Domestic Politics, and the Cold War 1956–1974* (Cambridge: Cambridge University Press, 2019), 253.

including Aimé Césaire and Franz Fanon, did not, however, openly side with Palestinians. But in 1958 the French philosopher Paul Ricoeur questioned the "debt of guilt" paid to Jews at the expense of an innocent native population. Ricoeur accepted the existence of Israel as a fact yet by facilitating its establishment, he argued, Europe and the United States contracted a similar debt to Palestinians.[127] A decade later, the French Marxist sociologist Maxime Rodinson theorized the anti-colonial critique of Israel in *Israël, fait colonial?* [*Israel, A Colonial Fact?*], an essay published in *Les Temps Modernes* in May–June 1967. By the mid 1960s, a more sober tone was even noticeable in books otherwise admirative of Israel. In their travelogues, the British David Pryce-Jones, the Italian Giovanni Russo or the Austrian journalist Bruno Frei all claimed to separate "utopia" from reality.[128] The glorification of "humane Israel," it appeared, was now a matter of the past.

In the weeks preceding the 1967 Arab–Israeli War, however, fears of Israel's destruction elicited a wave of sympathy across Western Europe. Military experts doubted the likelihood of Nasser's victory, but public opinions predominantly sided with Israel. In June 1967, 58% of positive attitudes were recorded in France, 55% in Britain, 56% in Denmark, and 62% in the Netherlands (outlier Italians remained indifferent to the conflict): These percentages increased in the immediate aftermath of the war. Most West Germans and Austrians likewise indicated pro-Israel bias. In these two countries, the press also fervently espoused the Israeli cause.[129] Surveys of French attitudes are a case in point: Between June 8 and June 13, only 2 percent of the population expressed sympathies for the Arab side. In October 1967, 44 percent of the French declared themselves "more strongly anti-Arab than anti-Jewish."[130] Five years after the country's defeat in Algeria, pro-Israel attitudes in France did not only reveal sympathy for "David against Goliath." They also stemmed from what Edward Said later called the "transference" of antisemitism toward Arabophobia: a first step toward the entanglement of philosemitism and Islamophobia in the late twentieth century.

---

[127] Paul Ricoeur, "Perpexlités sur Israël," *Esprit* 262, no. 6 (June 1958): 868–876.
[128] Bruno Frei, *Israel zwischen den Fronten: Utopie und Wirklichkeit* (Vienna: Europa-Verlag, 1965); David Pryce-Jones, *Next Generation: Travels in Israel* (London: Weidenfeld and Nicholson, 1964); Giovanni Russo, L'atomo et la Bibbia: viaggio in Israele (1963), op. cit.
[129] Hazel Erskine, "The Polls: Western Partisanship in the Middle East," *The Public Opinion Quarterly* 4, no. 33 (Winter 1969–1970): 627–640; Michael Suleiman, "Development of Public Opinion on the Palestine Question," *Journal of Palestine Studies* 13, no. 3 (Spring 1984): 87–116; Connie de Boer, "Attitudes toward the Arab-Israeli Conflict," *The Public Opinion Quarterly* 47, no. 1 (1983): 121–131.
[130] Yvan Gastaut, "La Guerre des Six jours et la question du racisme en France," *Cahiers de la Méditerranée* 71 (2005): 15–29.

Until 1967, however, left-leaning philosemitism and pro-Zionism went hand in hand. For the thirty-nine-year-old German novelist and SPD intellectual Günter Grass, the Arab Israeli war miraculously improved the odds of German-Jewish reconciliation. "For the first time since the Nazi persecution," declared Grass in July 1967, "Germans are doing something more than lamenting the past or trying to atone for it with reparation payments." The famed author of *Tin Drum* (1959), who visited Israel in May 1967, alluded to the thousands of German intellectuals, clergymen, students, and trade unionists who mobilized in favor of the Jewish state before and during the short war. This "spontaneous upsurge of sympathy for the bravery of the Jews in their struggle to protect their homeland and have a dignified life," rejoiced Grass, earned Germans new standing in their relation to the Jewish people: "the possibility to express our solidarity for Israel and the fate of the Jews without our feelings being hindered by the past."[131] Jean-Paul Sartre, to the contrary, clung to the legacy of Nazism to explain his position on the Arab–Israeli conflict. Although in May–June 1967 his review *Les Temps Modernes* framed the conflict as right against right, Sartre took a stand: "We are allergic to anything that could in the least resemble anti-Semitism. To which many Arabs would respond: 'We are not anti-Semitic but anti-Israeli.' Doubtless they would be right, but can they change the fact that, for us, the Israelis are also Jews?"[132] Sartre's position frustrated his many admirers in the Arab and decolonized world. How could the celebrated anti-colonial thinker, they pondered, "surrender to Zionist propaganda"?[133] The Parisian intellectual moved closer to their cause at the start of the 1970s when he justified Palestinian "counterterror against established [Israeli] terror." On the eve of the Six-Day War, however, the philosopher felt "affective" solidarity with Israel.[134] "We are all bound to the Jew," his pledge issued twenty-two years earlier in *Réflexions sur la question juive*, remained in effect. His secular philosemitic *engagement* intersected with epochal winds of change: The mid-to-late 1960s was also the moment when the Church professed its own special esteem for Jews, God's first love.

---

[131] "Günter Grass Says Jews Gain German Respect," *The New York Times*, July 3, 1967.
[132] Jean-Paul Sartre, "Pour la vérité," *Les Temps Modernes* 22, no. 253 bis (June 1967): 5–11.
[133] Yoav Di-Capua, *No Exit: Arab Existentialism, Jean-Paul Sartre, and Decolonization* (Chicago, IL: University of Chicago Press, 2018), 241.
[134] John Gerassi, *Talking with Sartre: Conversations and Debates* (New Haven: Yale University Press, 2009), 191; Farouk Mardam-Bey, "Sartre, Israël, et les Arabes: la 'détermination affective'," *Matériaux pour l'histoire de notre temps* 4, no. 9 (2004): 38–41.

5 Birth Pangs
"Judeo-Christian Europe" (1945–1965)

"The common 'Judeo-Christian heritage'," wrote the Israeli Orthodox thinker Yeshayahu Leibowitz in 1968, "(...) has never existed. The very concept is absurd, no less so than that of a square circle." Educated in Berlin in the early 1920s, Leibowitz followed in the footsteps of the German-Jewish philosopher Franz Rosenzweig who after World War I exposed essential differences between Judaism and Christianity. Jews already live in a face-to-face relationship with God, contended the author of *Star of Redemption* (1921), whereas Christians waiting for salvation are never at home in the world. Unlike Rosenzweig or the philosopher Martin Buber, however, Leibowitz ruled out theological reconciliation between "two types of faith." Championed by "Reform or assimilated Jews, especially in the United States," the Judeo-Christian concept was nothing but an abdication of Judaism.[1]

Evocations of shared heritage similarly grated on Jewish thinkers in the United States. In a notorious essay first published in 1957 and reissued in *Commentary* in 1969, the religious scholar Arthur A. Cohen leveled the most systematic criticism at the "myth of the Judeo-Christian tradition." His quarrel was with the post-Holocaust invention of a dubious consensus. "It is in our time," he wrote, "that, Jews and Christians have conspired together to promote a tradition of common experience and common belief."[2] The Jewish-American writer reflected on the popularity of political, cultural, and theological Judeo-Christianism in the United States. "A dishonest compact of love and admiration," this alliance not only papered over fundamental differences between Christians and Jews. It also erased the distinctiveness of Judaism in the North American religious landscape.

---

[1] Yeshayahu Leibowitz, "The Common Judeo-Christian Heritage" (1968) in Eliezer Goldman (ed.), *Judaism, Human Values, and The Jewish State* (Cambridge, MA: Harvard University Press, 1992), 256–262.
[2] Arthur A. Cohen, *The Myth of the Judeo-Christian Tradition* (New York: Schocken Books, 1971), xix.

The triumph of the "Judeo-Christian tradition," however, facilitated the successful incorporation of Jews in postwar America: their transformation from "non-quite-white Jews" into "quite white folks."[3] The influential Reformed theologian Reinhold Niebuhr wrote in 1955 that "to be a Protestant, a Catholic or a Jew is very definitely a part of the American way of life."[4] As public opinion polls revealed since 1945, antisemitism regularly decreased in Cold War America. Waged in the name of Judeo-Christian morality, the struggle against atheistic communism weakened the "Judeo-Bolshevik" myth still vivid during the Rosenberg Trial and Joseph McCarthy's witch-hunt. Judeo-Christian kinship also endeared the image of the new state of Israel to the public. Under the umbrella of Judeo-Christian alliance, American Jews safely identified with the Jewish state without suspicion of dual loyalty. Postwar philosemitism in the United States, in short, was propelled by the very "Judeo-Christian tradition" debunked in Cohen's critical essay.[5]

That the "tradition" fostered unprecedented Jewish inclusion in the United States did not deter the provocative writer from challenging its premises. Western Europe, in Cohen's eyes, offered a welcome alternative to fabricated unity. "Europeans," he noted, "are not addicted as we are here to proclaiming a tradition in which distinctions are fudged (…) by sloppy and sentimental approaches to falling in love after centuries of misunderstanding and estrangement."[6] The fierce critic of the Judeo-Christian construct in the United States ignored that through the Christianization of the Holocaust, prominent French Catholic intellectuals had already imagined Judeo-Christian symbiosis in the 1940s and 1950s. Cohen also downplayed the persistence of theological anti-Judaism in Europe after 1945. The lack of continental addiction to "a tradition in which distinctions are fudged" did not simply result from courageous acknowledgment of irreducible differences: It also stemmed from Christian resistance to

---

[3] Karen Brodkin, *How Jews Became White Folks and What That Says about Race in America* (New Brunswick, NJ: Rutgers University Press, 1998).

[4] Reinhold Niebuhr cited in Michelle Mart, "The 'Christianization' of Israel and Jews in 1950s," *Religion and American Culture: A Journal of Interpretation* 14, no. 1 (Winter 2004): 109–147.

[5] Mark Silk, "Notes on the Judeo-Christian Tradition in American," *American Quarterly* 36, no. 1 (1984): 65–85; K. Healan Gaston, *Imagining Judeo-Christian America: Religion, Secularism, and the Redefinition of Democracy* (Chicago, IL: University of Chicago Press, 2019).

[6] Arthur A. Cohen, David Stern, and Paul Mendes-Flohr (eds.), *An Arthur Cohen Reader: Selected Fiction and Writings on Judaism, Theology, Literature, and Culture* (Detroit, MI: Wayne State University Press, 1998), 211. See also Emmanuel Nathan and Anna Topolsky, "The Myth of a Judeo-Christian Tradition: Introducing a European Perspective" in Nathan and Topolsky (eds.), *Is there a Judeo-Christian Tradition? A European Perspective* (Berlin and Boston: De Gruyter, 2016), 1–14.

philo-Judaism. Cohen nonetheless identified a key transatlantic contrast. While the Judeo-Christian tradition "has particular currency and significance in the United States," he wrote, "it is not as commonplace in Europe as it is here."[7] His observation captured the limited appeal of the phrase in Cold War Europe: Until the "defense of Judeo-Christian culture" became a shibboleth of Islamophobia after 1989, the "Judeo-Christian tradition" in the European Economic Community (EEC) never reached the popularity it enjoyed on North American shores.

Yet from 1945 to the *Nostra Aetate* declaration issued by the Vatican in 1965, a cluster of Christian intellectuals and clergymen committed to a new relation with Jews searched for Judeo-Christian affinities: Contrary to the United States, the difficult construction of a "Judeo-Christian tradition" in Western Europe amounted to an internal Christian philosemitic effort, not to a coalition of faiths. During this period, of course, Jewish representatives participated in dialogue with Catholics and Protestants. Yet the project of Judeo-Christian rapprochement dictated by Christians was also met with fierce Jewish opposition. "It is not enough to call Jesus Yechou and Rabbi to bring him closer to us," wrote the French-Jewish philosopher Emmanuel Levinas in 1953. "For us," he added, "we who are without hatred, there is no friendship. It remains far off."[8] Despite resistances on both sides, however, the "tradition" came into being through Christian theological renewal. In France, the Judeo-Christian symbiosis had other promoters: Catholic intellectuals who turned the Holocaust into a foundational Judeo-Christian event.

Unsuccessful Graft

First espoused by liberals and then appropriated by conservatives, the "Judeo-Christian tradition" remained ubiquitous in Cold War America. The concept, however, did not travel well to Europe. The economic and cultural impact of the Marshall Plan enacted in 1948 was already palpable in the early 1950s, especially in West Germany. But the "Judeo-Christian tradition" found few takers across the Atlantic. Financed by the Ford Foundation and covertly supported by the CIA, the Congress for Cultural Freedom founded in Berlin in June 1950 invited anti-Stalinist European intellectuals to join the ideological Cold War. Its *Freedom Manifesto* denounced neutrality as an "abdication of the free mind."[9]

---

[7] Arthur Cohen, *The Myth of the Judeo-Christian Tradition*, op. cit., xviii.
[8] Emmanuel Levinas, *Difficult Freedom* (Baltimore, MD: The Johns Hopkins University Press, 1997), 105.
[9] Giles Scott-Smith, *The Politics of Apolitical Culture: The Congress for Cultural Freedom, the CIA and Post-War American Hegemony* (London: Routledge, 2002), 112.

Yet Arthur Koestler, Ignazio Silone, Raymond Aron, Manès Sperber, and the other liberals or repentant communists who introduced antitotalitarianism in European political thought, kept their distance from Americanism. Like the Congress's supported publications, they took a hard line against communism without trumpeting the superiority of Judeo-Christian civilization. That most Cold War liberals were Jewish intellectuals who saw in communism a utopian political religion also explains their reluctance to champion another grand narrative. The American Jewish thinker Gertrude Himmelfarb saw in Christianity a bulwark against totalitarianism, but her conservative defense of religion never amounted to militant "Jewish Christianity."[10]

In West Germany, however, the transatlantic export of the "Judeo-Christian tradition" achieved better results. Created at the behest of American authorities in July 1948, the *Societies for Jewish-Christian Cooperation* were modeled after the National Conference for Christian and Jews, the organization founded in 1927 to promote religious diversity against Protestant hegemony. General Lucius D. Clay, the military governor of the US occupation zone, found encouragement "forthcoming from German churchmen, educators and civic leaders (...) to proceed with the project." The Left Catholic essayist Eugen Kogon, a Buchenwald survivor who reported on the Nazi concentration camps system in *Der SS-Staat* (1946), was one of them. "We are gradually beginning to recognize," wrote Kogon in February 1949, "that what we share in common is more important than what differentiates us."[11] Yet while they "joined in a path of belief based on the creator God the Father," the thirteen Societies established in major German cities between 1948 and 1953 had limited ambitions. Their goal was to encourage collaboration between Protestants, Catholics, and rare Jews interested in campaigns for tolerance and public education. For this reason, the Jewish chairman of the Berlin society, who admitted that "Jews view this cooperation skeptically," favored the term "interfaith" over "Christian-Jewish" to best define the organization.[12]

---

[10] Malachi Haim Hacohen, "The Jewishness of Cold War Liberalism" in Abigail Green and Simon Levis Sullam (eds.), *Jews, Liberalism, Antisemitism: A Global History* (Cham: Palgrave Macmillan, 2020), 387–410; on Himmelfarb's "Jewish Christianity," see Samuel Moyn, *Liberalism against Itself: Cold War Intellectuals and the Making of Our Times* (New Haven: Yale University Press, 2023), 89–113.

[11] Kogon cited in Steven M. Schroeder, *To Forget It All and Begin Anew: Reconciliation in Occupied Germany, 1944–1954* (Toronto: University of Toronto Press, 2013), 70.

[12] Frank Stern, *The Whitewashing of the Yellow Badge: Antisemitism and Philosemitism in Postwar Germany* (New York: Oxford University Press, 1992), 323; Joseph Foschepoth, *Im Schatten der Vergangenheit: Die Anfänge der Gesellschaften für Christlich-Jüdische Zusammenarbeit* (Göttingen: Vandenhoeck und Rupprecht, 1993), 82.

The Societies, however, found in the returning émigré Hans-Joachim Schoeps an expedient Jewish voice pleading for spiritual unity between Jews and Christians. Associated with the Munich chapter, the conservative historian of early Christianity advertised to the German public his "two covenants" thesis based on the complementarity of the two religions. But the eccentric Schoeps, who in the early 1950s oddly called for the return to power of the Hohenzollern monarchy, only achieved notoriety thanks to best-selling histories of the Old Prussian kingdom.[13] The Societies' constitution drafted in 1948 was unambiguous: It valued the "brotherhood of all people" but opposed "fusing the different beliefs of the members." As the German émigré Norbert Muhlen observed during his visit of the Federal Republic in 1960, cooperation simply meant pro-Jewish apologetics through "lectures on tolerance, or on a Jewish artist or philosopher, or on a famous Christian's view of Judaism."[14] For a circle of economists associated with the ruling Christian Democratic Union (CDU), interfaith reconciliation fulfilled another purpose. By improving "human relations" in German society, religious dialogue strengthened the flourishing "social market economy." Franz Böhm, the cofounder of the Societies' Frankfurt chapter and a key supporter of the 1952 reparation agreement with Israel, was also an ordo-liberal thinker who saw the state as the guarantor of free market competition.[15]

Christian claims of Hebraic heritage, however, were not uncommon during the four years of Allied occupation and the early Federal Republic. On several occasions, Protestant clergymen reverted to the Old Testament to compare occupied Germans to captives in the land of Egypt; or ethnic German refugees from Eastern Europe to exiles in Babylon. Even exemplary clergymen imprisoned during the war for helping Jews drew such analogies. In 1961, the former Sachsenhausen and Dachau inmate Heinrich Grüber was the only German witness invited to Jerusalem to testify against Adolf Eichmann. That same year, however, the Lutheran pastor told the Jewish-American theologian Richard Rubinstein that Germans had been punished "far worse than the people of the Lord." The inhabitants of divided Berlin, he

---

[13] Hans-Joachim Schoeps, *Theologie und Geschichte des Judenchristentums* (Tubingen: J.C.B. Maur, 1949); "A Religious Bridge between Jews and Christians: Shall We Recognize Two Covenants?," *Commentary* 9 (1950): 129–131. On Schoeps, see also Steven Schroeder, *To Forget It All and Begin Anew*, op. cit., 90–91.

[14] Norbert Muhlen, *The Survivors: A Report on the Jews in Germany Today* (New York: Thomas Crowell Company, 1961), 168.

[15] Noah B. Strote, "Sources of German-Jewish Cooperation in Early Cold War Germany" in Emmanuel Nathan and Anya Topolski (eds.), *Is there a Judeo-Christian Tradition?*, op. cit., 75–100.

added, were now "in the same situation as the Jews."[16] This appropriation of biblical Judaism bolstered feelings of German victimhood. Christianity alone, however, remained the spiritual hallmark of democratic Germany. Admittedly, a small network of Protestant and Catholic figures entered in dialogue with Jews interested in collaboration. Both published in 1961, two specialized volumes explored differences and commonalities between the two religions.[17] The re-Christianization of German society nevertheless remained the priority of Adenauer-era pastors and priests. Only through a return to Christian teachings could the Federal Republic close the book on Nazism and inoculate itself from communism.[18]

A catholic forefather of European integration, the Christian Democrat and first chancellor of West Germany Konrad Adenauer also yearned for a unified continent embodying the "Christian heritage shared by all peoples of Europe." Their duty to protect human dignity and individual freedom from communism, argued Cologne's former mayor, similarly derived from the "spirit of Christianity."[19] Likewise, the Christian Democrat and conservative framers of the European Convention of Human Rights (1950) sought to contain socialism and the almighty state on behalf of a common Christian inheritance: The recent murder of European Jews did not require Judeo-Christian rapprochement. Although the genocide of the Jews was discussed during the drafting of the United Nations Universal Declaration of Human Rights (1948), the Holocaust had no bearing on the birth of the first European human rights legal instrument.[20] Similarly, the EEC founded in Rome in 1957 did not concern itself with the moral legacies of the Final Solution: Continental

---

[16] Susannah Heschel, "Confronting the Past: Post-1945 German Protestant Theology and the Fate of the Jews" in Jonathan Frankel and Ezra Mendelsohn (eds.), *The Protestant-Jewish Conundrum: Studies in Contemporary Jewry*, vol. XXIV (Oxford: Oxford University Press, 2010), 46–70.
[17] H. J. Schultz, *Juden-Christen-Deutsche* (Stuttgart: Kreuz-Verlag, 1961); Wolf-Dieter Marsh and Karl Thieme (eds.), *Christen und Juden: Ihr Gegenüber von Apostelkonzil bis Heute* (Mainz: Matthias-Grünewald Verlag, 1961); on these initiatives, see also Hannah-Vilette Dalby, "Jewish Women Sociologists and Post-War Jewish-Christian Dialogue in West Germany: Eva G. Reichmann and Eleonore Sterling," *Jewish Culture and History* 6, no. 2 (2012): 43–54.
[18] Till van Rahden, "Fatherhood, Rechristianization, and the Search for Democracy in 1950s Germany" in Dirk Schumann (ed.), *Raising Citizens in the 'Century of the Child'* (New York: Berghahn Books, 2010), 141–164.
[19] Speech by Konrad Adenauer on the Possibilities of European Unification, Brussels, September 25, 1956, available at: www.cvce.eu/content/publication/2006/10/25/ea27a4e3-4883-4d38-8dbc-5e3949b1145d/publishable_en.pdf.
[20] Marco Duranti, *The Conservative Human Rights Revolution: European Identity, Transnational Politics, and the Origins of the European Convention* (New York: Oxford University Press, 2017), 404.

integration was premised on reconciliation with democratic Germany, not on Holocaust memory.

The American "Judeo-Christian tradition" received however some measure of support in postwar Britain. Gathered in Oxford in August 1946 at the behest of the National Conference of Christian and Jews, Anglican, Catholic, and Jewish representatives issued a *Declaration of the Fundamental Postulates of Judaism and Christianity in Relation to the Social Order*. "The primary affirmation of both creeds," stated the manifesto, "stands as the bulwark against every kind of materialism, whether 'dialectical' or of the older fashion."[21] The famed historian of world cultures Arnold Toynbee, however, did not chime in. For Judeo-Christianity to exist as civilization, he claimed, Jews would need to have survived centuries of "penalization" unscathed. Yet as Toynbee famously reiterated in 1946, Judaism was merely a "fossil of Syriac civilization." In his grand scheme of world history, other ethnic groups subjected to religious persecution similarly fossilized into extinction. But the "most notable" of all, insisted Toynbee, was the "fossil remnants of Syriac Society, the Jews."[22] In his best-selling *A History of Western Philosophy* (1945), however, Bertrand Russell challenged Toynbee's fossilization narrative. The blood of the "Maccabean martyrs" who in the second century BCE saved Judaism from extinction, wrote the still pro-Zionist philosopher, "ultimately became the seed of the Church": Christianity, according to Russell's philosemitic revisionism, did not supersede inert Judaism but inherited its vitality.[23] The Anglo-Catholic poet T. S. Eliot, for his part, did not waste time on Judeo-Christian ruminations. Lending his voice to British denazification policies in occupied Germany, Eliot reaffirmed the traditional conception of European civilization. "It is against the background of Christianity," he declared in a broadcast recorded in 1946, "that all our thought has significance."[24] In a lecture at Yale University delivered in 1970, the Jewish literary critic George Steiner reflected on Eliot's occultation of the Holocaust. "How was it possible to detail and plead for a Christian order," asked Steiner, "when the Holocaust had put in question the very nature of Christianity and its

---

[21] Council for Christians and Jews, *The Foundations of Civilization* (London: The Council for Christians and Jews, 1947), 3; William W. Simpson, "Jewish-Christian Relations since the Inception of the Council of Christian and Jews," *Transactions & Miscellanies (Jewish Historical Society of England)* 28 (1981–1982): 89–101.

[22] Arnold Toynbee, *A Study of History: Abridgement of Volumes I–VI by D.C. Somervell* (Oxford: Oxford University Press, 1946), 135.

[23] Bertrand Russell, *A History of Western Philosophy* (New York: Simon & Schuster, 1945), 316.

[24] T. S. Eliot, *Notes towards a Definition of Culture* (Broadcast in 1946, first edition 1948) (New York: Houghton Mifflin Harcourt, 2014), 200.

role in European history?"[25] But in 1946 Britain, where the Holocaust was not yet perceived as a singular crime, the genocide of the Jews did not taint the reputation of Christian civilization.

The Labour party in power since July 1945, for its part, dreamed of transforming Britain into an egalitarian New Jerusalem. Borrowed from William Blake's romantic poetry, this allegory did not celebrate Judeo-Christian affinities. New Jerusalem only translated the language of Christian prophecy into socialist politics. In 1951, Winston Churchill's return to power brought back to 10 Downing Street a self-identifying "old Zionist" more than a Judeo-Christian rhetorician. Contrary to American Cold Warriors, Churchill did not invoke the "Judeo-Christian tradition" to contain Soviet expansionism. In his famous Iron Curtain address of March 5, 1946, the Conservative leader only portrayed Communist parties in Europe as a "growing challenge and peril to Christian civilization." At the Congress of Europe gathered in The Hague on May 7, 1948, Churchill extolled Christian culture and tradition. In 1949, the aging Tory told scientists at the Massachusetts Institute of Technology that "the flame of Christian ethics is still our higher guide."[26]

The "Judeo-Christian tradition" was also foreign to Charles de Gaulle's "certain idea of France" outlined in the opening lines of his War Memoirs [1954]. Wary of American hegemony, the French head of state between 1958 and 1969 was more concerned with the restoration of Gallic *grandeur* than with the defense of the Judeo-Christian West. De Gaulle extolled instead France's own Christian identity. As he confided to an American journalist in 1959, "my country is a Christian country and for me the history of France began when a Christian king bearing the name of the Franks acceded to the throne." Judeo-Christian rhetoric was similarly absent from postwar Italian political discourse. In accordance with the Lateran Pacts signed in 1929 between Mussolini and the Vatican, the Italian Constitution declared Roman Catholicism a state religion. Politically dominant for the next four decades, the *Democrazia Christiana* (DC) had scant interest in Judeo-Christian idealizations. Some of its members, such as the mayor of Florence Giorgio La Pira, pioneered friendly contacts between Catholics and Jews. Yet for the DC, anticommunism did not mandate the enlistment of Judeo-Christian ideology to the cause. In Italy, "Judeo-Christian roots" only entered the

---

[25] George Steiner, *In Bluebeard's Castle: Some Notes towards the Redefinition of Culture* (New Haven: Yale University Press, 1971), 34.
[26] Marco Duranti, *The Conservative Human Rights Revolution*, op. cit., 112; Jonathan Sandys and Wallace Henley, *God & Churchill* (Carol Stream, IL: Tyndale Momentum, 2016), 92.

political lexicon thanks to late twentieth-century right-wing populism. In the Netherlands too, political invocations of Judeo-Christianism likewise awaited the end of the Cold War.[27]

Yet if the "Judeo-Christian tradition" failed to take root in Europe's political culture, a constellation of small organizations promoted interfaith amity in the aftermath of the Holocaust. The *Societies for Jewish-Christian Cooperation* in West Germany, the *Council of Christian and Jews* founded in Britain in 1942, the *Amitié Judéo-Chrétienne* in France (1948), the *Amicizia Ebraico Cristiana di Firenze* in Italy (1950), the *Katholieke Raad voor Israel* (1951) in the Netherlands, or the *Koordinierungsausschuss für christlich-jüdische Zusammenarbeit* (1956) in Austria, ignited the Jewish–Christian dialogue in postwar Europe. On the catholic side, however, these discrete initiatives did not represent the Vatican's position. In France, the legal wrangle over the custody of two Jewish boys orphaned during the Holocaust known as the Finaly Affair showed the limits of Jewish Christian entente. The children baptized in 1948 were ultimately returned to their Jewish relatives in 1953, yet not without efforts from the Vatican to keep them within the Christian fold. Before the revision of age-old teachings initiated during the Second Vatican Council (1962–65), interfaith rapprochement ran against theological resistance to accommodation with Judaism.

Resisting Judeo-Christian Proximity

Unfolding between 1945 and 1958, the last thirteen years of Pius XII's pontificate were characterized by doctrinal and political conservatism. Issued in 1950, the encyclical *Human Generis* [On the Human Race] reminded believers that "error and discord ... is only to be expected outside the fold of Christ." In August 1947, the participants in the interfaith conference on antisemitism held in the Swiss village of Seelisberg had already witnessed the Holy See's inflexibility. The persecution of the Jews, insisted the Vatican's envoy Calliste Lopinot, needed to be counterbalanced with the harm inflicted by the Synagogue

---

[27] Andrea Molle, "Religion and Right-Wing Populism in Italy: Using 'Judeo-Christian Roots' to Kill the European Union," *Religion, State and Society* 47, no. 1 (2019): 151–168; Ernst van den Hemel, "(Pro)claiming Tradition: The 'Judeo-Christian' Roots of Dutch Society and the Rise of Conservative Nationalism" in Rosi Braidotti et al. (eds.), *Transformations of Religion and the Public Sphere: Postsecular Publics* (Basingstoke: Palgrave Macmillan, 2014), 33–76; Amanda Kluveld, "Secular, Superior and Desperately Searching for its Soul: The Confusing Political-Cultural Reference to a Judeo-Christian Europe in the Twenty-First Century" in Emmanuel Nathan and Anya Topolski (eds.), *Is there a Judeo-Christian Tradition?* op. cit., 243–267.

upon the Church.²⁸ Pius XII himself cultivated ambiguity. In his postwar allocutions, the pope never pronounced the words "Jew(s)" or "Judaism."²⁹ He preferred instead euphemisms such as "those who wait patiently but in vain," an allusion to Jews in his 1949 Christmas address. Even when greeting Holocaust survivors at the Vatican on November 29, 1945, the pontiff carefully avoided the "J" word. "The abyss of discord, the hatred and the folly of persecution," he told his visitors, "have engulfed an *incomparable numbers of innocent victims, even among those who took no active part in the war.*"³⁰ This passing reference to the Holocaust remained in any case an exceptional occurrence. During Pius XII's papacy, the Vatican never issued a single explicit statement on the genocide. Likewise, the European Catholic press of the 1950s avoided the subject. This was especially the case in Italy where the Jesuit journal *La Civiltà Cattolica*, in keeping with the Holy See, skirted discussion of the Jewish catastrophe.³¹

Founded in Amsterdam in 1948, the Protestant-dominated World Council of Churches (WCC) followed a more amicable path. Contrary to the Vatican under Pius XII, the umbrella organization of Protestant denominations called for "a special approach to the Jews." Its founding members also pledged a "special solidarity linking our destinies together in His design." Unlike the Catholic church, the WCC acknowledged Christian responsibility for propagating "an image of the Jews as the sole enemies of Christ." The Protestant representative body also explicitly remembered the "extermination of six million Jews."³² But this friendly tone went hand in hand with ongoing proselytism: The Holocaust had not relieved Christians from the obligation to preach the Gospel to Jews. Likewise, the German Protestant church persevered in its *Judenmission*. More than ever, wrote German churchmen in 1949, Protestants owed Jews "Christian witness which alone can lead

---

²⁸ Carol Iancu, "Le cheminement de Jules Isaac" in Annette Becker, Danielle Delmaire, and Frédéric Gugelot (eds.), *Juifs et Chrétiens: entre ignorance, hostilité et rapprochement 1898–1998* (Université Charles-de-Gaulle Lille 3, 2002), 161–177.
²⁹ A complete list of Pius XII's speeches and encyclical is available at: https://w2.vatican.va/content/pius-xii/it/speeches/1949/documents/hf_p-xii_spe_19490925_grand-coeur.html.
³⁰ Michael Marrus, "A Plea Unanswered: Jacques Maritain, Pope Pius XII, and the Holocaust" in Eli Lederhendler (eds.), *Jews, Catholics, and the Burden of History*. Studies in Contemporary Jewry (New York: Oxford University Press, 2005), 3–11.
³¹ Elena Mazzini, "Transforming Anti-Semitism: The Civiltà Cattolica after the Shoah (1945–1965)" in James Bernauer and Robert A. Maryks (eds.), *"The Tragic Couple": Encounters between Jews and Jesuits* (Leiden: Brill: 2014), 233–245.
³² "The Christian Approach to the Jews" (1948) in Franklin Sherman (ed.), *Bridges: Documents of the Christian-Jewish Dialogue. Volume One: The Road to Reconciliation 1945–1985* (New York: Paulist Press, 2011), 47–51.

to Christ itself."[33] A philosemitism of pity justified conversion: only the gift of Christian faith could relieve "lost sheep" from divine curse. Even clergymen who felt "deep shame" for the "forceful extermination of Jewry" believed that their debt to Jewish survivors included preaching the Gospel of Jesus.[34]

Dissenting German Protestants, however, pushed for reform. At the Berlin Kirchentag, a national church meeting held in 1961, they urged patient dialogue instead of aggressive proselytism. God had not rejected the chosen people, they argued: This "unabrogated alliance" begged for a more collaborative approach to mission, especially among Holocaust survivors.[35] This tolerant tone drew the ire of hard-liners. Quoting the Book of Revelation, the theologian J. G. Mehl referred to Jews as the "Synagogue of Satan." Only through conversion could the Jewish people "again become part of the chosen people." Others warned that the abandonment of the *Judenmission* would amount to "a betrayal of the Gospel."[36] Divided on this issue, the majority wing of the Protestant church only renounced its "service to the Jews" in 1980. The neighboring Dutch Reformed Church followed suit in 1988.[37]

Despite fierce missionary resistance, signs of greater Protestant acceptance of Judaism in West Germany were noticeable in 1950. The Berlin-Weissensee Synod amended the traditional conception of Jews as a rejected people: "We believe God's promise to be valid for its Chosen People even after the crucifixion of Jesus Christ." This statement was counterbalanced with missionary hopes for the "triumph of Jesus Christ together with saved Israel." Yet such language softened the substitution doctrine alleging the replacement of Judaism by Christianity.[38] The synod also improved upon previous declarations of repentance. More explicitly than in previous years, the church recognized "the outrage which has been perpetrated against the Jews by people of our nation." Although faithful Christians filled the ranks of the genocidal Wehrmacht in the

---

[33] John Conway, "Changes in Christian-Jewish Relations since the Holocaust" in Konrad Kwiet and Jürgen Matthäus (eds.), *Contemporary Responses to the Holocaust* (Westport, CT: Praeger Publishers, 2004), 61–87.
[34] See "Declaration of Guilt toward the Jewish People" (Synod of the Lutheran Church of Saxony, April 1948) in *Bridges*, op. cit., 46–47.
[35] D. Goldschmidt and H.-J. Kraus, *Der ungekündigte Bund: Neue Begegnung von Juden und christlicher Gemeinde* (Stuttgart: Kreuz Verlag, 1962).
[36] On the Berlin Kirchentag controversy, see Elizabeth Fleischner, *Judaism in German Christian Theology since 1945: Christianity and Israel Considered in Terms of Mission* (Metuchen, NJ: Scarecrow Press, 1975), 71–73.
[37] Geert H. Cohen Stuart, "The Attitude of the Dutch Reform Church to *Israel: People, Land and State*," *Immanuel* 22, no. 23 (1989): 146–161.
[38] Matthew Hockenos, *A Church Divided: Germans Protestants Confront the Nazi Past* (Bloomington, IN: Indiana University Press, 2004), 154.

East, however, the synod only limited German culpability to "omission and silence before the God of mercy." But in 1950 these words challenged pervasive denial. Returning then from five years of captivity in the Soviet Union, the Protestant theologian Helmut Gollwitzer discovered that "unrepentance was definitely a characteristic of our society."[39] In December 1949, the Federal Amnesty Law passed in the German parliament had spelled the end of denazification. At a time when former Nazi officials and members of the SS were allowed to reintegrate society, the synod reckoned with German responsibility. Christian expiation, however, also offered redemptive benefits. "In judgment," stated the clergymen, "God's mercy searches for the repentant." To that end they implored Germans "not to balance what has come upon us as God's judgment" with the incomparable "outrage" perpetrated against Jews.

Self-pity stood in the way of this pious injunction. Even liberal churchmen such as Martin Niemöller compensated guilt with evocations of German suffering. "I have sinned, and my people has sinned against thy people and against thyself," the pastor declared to Jews in 1946.[40] Niemöller's admission of personal responsibility constituted a remarkable about-face. Before his arrest in 1937, followed by imprisonment in Sachsenhausen and Dachau until 1945, the pastor from Berlin-Dahlem had opposed Hitler's church policies without renouncing anti-Judaism. In a sermon delivered in 1935, for instance, he still portrayed Jews as an accursed people with a "dark and sinister" history."[41] In 1946, Niemöller's change of heart made him unpopular among remorseless Germans. His contrition, however, did not preclude feelings of victimhood. Under the Third Reich, wrote the pastor, the church had also "passed through a sea of affliction and persecution."[42] Niemöller drew further attention to German suffering during a lecture tour in the United States in early 1947. Occupied Germans, he complained, received quantities of food similar "to the lower ration ever heard of in a Nazi concentration camp."[43] But his famous confession of guilt – "First they came for the socialists (...) then they came for the Jews and I did not speak out" – overshadowed this shocking comparison. Modified numerous times,

---

[39] Gollwitzer cited in Michael Phayer, *The Catholic Church and the Holocaust, 1930–1965* (Bloomington, IN: Indiana University Press, 2000), 184.
[40] Martin Niemöller, *Of Guilt and Hope (Über die deutsche Schuld, Not, und Hoffnung)* (New York: Philosophical Society, 1947), 18.
[41] Matthew D. Hockenos, *Then They Came for Me: Martin Niemöller, the Pastor Who Defied the Nazis* (New York: Basic Books, 2018), 117.
[42] Martin Niemöller, "Introduction" in Stewart Herman (ed.), *The Rebirth of the German Church* (London: SCM, 1946), 7.
[43] Cited by Hockenos, *Then They Came for Me*, op. cit., 204.

these poetic lines earned Niemöller the status of "good German" and international moral figure.⁴⁴

The nascent Protestant culture of guilt did not, however, affect German Lutheran theologians resolutely opposed to the confluence of Christian and Judaic beliefs. In the 1950s, they mounted fierce resistance against the idea of shared tradition. Expectedly, unreformed *German Christians* sympathetic to Nazism between 1932 and 1945 continued to seek the elimination of Judaic traces from the Christian dogma. "The primary role of Jesus research is clear: De-Judaizing the Jesus tradition," stated the New Testament scholar Ethelbert Stauffer in 1957.⁴⁵ The Heidelberg theologian Martin Dibelius died in 1947, but his widely read *Jesus* (1939) reprinted several times in German and English after the war similarly questioned the Son of God's "pure Jewish race."⁴⁶ Dibelius did not indulge in the Nazi fantasy of Aryan Jesus. But whether the Messiah "belonged to this or that race or people," he claimed, should not be of importance to the Christian faith. Like the famed theologian from the university of Marburg Rudolf Bultmann, Dibelius portrayed Jesus as a dehistoricized figure severed from his Jewish background: In the Federal Republic, a significant subset of Christian thinkers continued after 1945 to challenge the Jewish roots of Christianity.⁴⁷

Equally opposed to the "Judeo-Christian tradition" were German theologians who glorified the mythical Jews of the Old Testament at the expense of postbiblical Judaism. In 1950, the famed biblical scholar Martin Noth concluded his influential *History of Israel* with an unequivocal verdict. After the destruction the Second Temple in 70 CE, "Israel thereby ceased to exist and the history of Israel came to an end."⁴⁸ Noth dismissed continuities between the Hebrew religion and its exilic offspring. It would be "thoroughly misguided," he wrote, "to regard later Judaism and [biblical] Israel as one and the same." As the New Testament exegete Leonhard Goppelt similarly argued in 1954, Judaism

---

⁴⁴ Harold Marcuse, "The Origin and Reception of Martin Niemöller's Quotation 'First they came for the Communists ....'" in Michael Berenbaum et al., *Remembering for the Future, Armenia, Auschwitz and Beyond* (Saint Paul, MN: Paragon House: 2016), 173–201.
⁴⁵ Cited in Ernst Klee, *Das Personenlexikon zum Dritten Reich* (Frankfurt am Main: Fischer Taschenbuch Verlag, 2005), 598.
⁴⁶ Martin Dibelius, *Jesus* (Philadelphia, PA: The Westminster Press, 1949), 41–43; on Dibelius's Jesus, see also Anders Gerdmar, *Roots of Theological Anti-Semitism: German Biblical Interpretation and the Jews, from Herder and Semler to Kittel and Bultmann* (Leiden: Brill, 2009), 353–357.
⁴⁷ Charlotte Klein, *Anti-Judaism in Christian Theology* (Philadelphia, PA: Fortress Press, 1974).
⁴⁸ Martin Noth, *History of Israel: Biblical History* (London: Adam & Charles, 1958), 445.

"usurped the Old Testament revelation."[49] Like other bible scholars appointed after the war in German universities, both were veterans of the Wehrmacht. So was the theologian from Göttingen Eduard Lohse who in his *Israel and Christianity* [Israel und die Christenheit, 1960] introduced himself as a veteran "naval officer and speed boat commander."[50] Service in Hitler's army left its mark on Christian biblical scholarship. As proof of "philosemitic" reverence, Goppelt portrayed Old Testament Jews as a noble "folk community." But remnants of Nazi rhetoric were also traceable in his disdain for Judaism. As he wrote in 1954, Jesus brought about the "ruination of Pharisaic legalism," "exploded the idea of the Sabbath law," and "meant the end of Judaism."[51]

Like their Protestant peers, prominent German Catholics dismissed the value of Judaism after Jesus. Although he cultivated a personal friendship with the Jewish philosopher Martin Buber, the Italian-born theologian Romano Guardini maintained that God's covenant with Jews became extinct after its accomplishment in Christ.[52] In 1959, the expert in Christian dogmatic Michael Schmaus, mentor of the future pope Joseph Ratzinger at the university of Munich, similarly declared Israel "obsolete, and its existence meaningless."[53] In 1963, he still found odd that the "people of the Old Testament, despite its obsolescence, should continue to exist simultaneously with the people of the New Testament."[54]

Yet other German Catholic figures, such as the founders of the "Freiburg Circle" Gertrud Luckner and Karl Thieme, renounced claims of Christian superiority through dialogue and brotherhood with Jews. Luckner was a social worker and a rescuer of Jews who survived incarceration at Ravensbrück. A lay anti-Nazi religious thinker, Thieme

---

[49] Leonard Goppelt, *Jesus, Paul and Judaism: An Introduction to New Testament Theology* (London: Thomas Nelson, 1964), 52. (English translation of Christentum und Judentum im ersten und zweiten Jahrhundert. Ein Aufriss der Urgeschichte der Kirche (C. Bertelsmann Verlag Gütersloh, 1954)). On Goppelt's theology, see Klein, Anti-Judaism ..., op. cit., 30–31.

[50] Eduard Lohse, *Israel und die Christenheit* (Göttingen: Vandenhoeck & Ruprecht, 1960), 2.

[51] Goppelt, *Jesus, Paul and Judaism*, op. cit., 59, 61, and 63. On legacies of Nazism in postwar German theology, see also Bjorn Krondorfer, Katharina von Kellenbach, and Norbert Reck (eds.), *Mit Blick auf die Täter: Fragen an die deutsche Theologie nach 1945* (Gütersloher Verlaghaus, 2006).

[52] Robert A. Krieg, *Romano Guardini: A Precursor of Vatican II* (Notre Dame, IN: University of Notre Dame Press, 1997), 130–131; "Martin Buber and Romano Guardini. Case Study in Jewish-Catholic Dialogue" in Michael A. Signer, *Humanity at the Limit: The Impact of the Holocaust Experience on Jews and Christians* (Bloomington, IN: Indiana University Press, 2000), 138–147.

[53] Cited in Klein, *Anti-Judaism*, 32.

[54] Ibid., 8.

yearned for a new relationship with Judaism. Although he still called Jews "enemies of the Christian name" in 1945, Thieme argued in 1950 that the Jewish people remained under divine "merciful guidance even in their distance from Christ."[55] On the Protestant side, trailblazers such as the pastors Adolf Freudenberg and Helmut Grüber, the Heidelberg churchman Herman Maas, or the theologian Helmut Gollwitzer, advocated at the start of the 1950s a friendly approach to Judaism. But as the bible scholar Heinz Kremers discovered in 1972, the books and articles used by students of religion since 1945 remained overwhelmingly anti-Judaic.[56] A younger generation of Protestant scholars led by Friedrich-Wilhelm Marquardt began in the late 1960s to reframe Auschwitz as a judgment on Christianity. Yet prior to the 1970s, the Holocaust did not leave a discernible imprint on German Protestant scholarship.[57]

Philosemitism and Reconciliation

In West Germany, pockets of anti-Judaism delayed the theological rapprochement of Christian and Jews to the late twentieth century. In England, however, the Anglican reverend James Parkes had long recognized the continuing validity of Judaism alongside Christianity. Known since the early 1930s for his critique of the Church's anti-Judaic tradition, Parkes contemplated, immediately after World War II, the possible "union of the two religions." He found prudent, however, to postpone Judeo-Christian fusion to a more propitious future. For the time being, he admitted, "a religion made out of (...) superficial syntheses would be a monster lacking the very qualities which give each tradition its permanent value to humanity."[58] He nonetheless devised an imaginative Judeo-Christian amalgamation. To replace the Christian doctrine of God-in-three-persons, Parkes envisioned three "channels" through

---

[55] Thieme cited in Elias H. Füllenbach, "Shock, Renewal, Crisis: Catholic Reflexions on the Shoah" in Kevin Spicer (ed.), *Antisemitism, Christian Ambivalence and the Holocaust* (Bloomington, IN: Indiana University Press, 2007), 201–237. On the catholic Freiburg circle, see John Connelly, *From Enemy to Brother: The Revolution in Catholic Teachings on the Jews 1933–1965* (Cambridge: Cambridge University Press, 2012), 179.

[56] Heinz Kremers, 'Das Judentum im Evangelischen Religionsunterricht' in Hans Kallengach and Willi Schemel (eds.), *Judentum im christlichen Religionsunterricht* (Frankfurt, 1972), 46–76; see also Hans Erich Jung, "Darstellung des Judentums in Schulbüchern zum Katholischen Religionsunterricht" in Thomas Lange (ed.), *Judentum und jüdische Geschichte im Schulunterricht nach 1945* (Vienna: Böhlau Verlag, 1994), 181–223.

[57] K. Hannah Hotlschneider, *German Protestants Remember the Holocaust: Theology and the Construction of Collective Memory* (Münster: Lit Verlag, 2001), 105–139.

[58] James Parkes, *Judaism and Christianity* (London: Victor Gollancz, 1948), 12 (Charles W. Eliot lectures delivered in New York in late 1946 and early 1947).

which deity could be uncovered. The Mosaic covenant, the advent of Christ, and the scientific revolution formed his alternative Judeo-Christian trinity.[59] As in other instances, the Church of England ignored Parkes's speculations. Only in 1988 did Anglicans affirm that Christians and Jews share a common "mission to the world."[60] But Parkes's unorthodox thought revealed that beyond compassion or guilt, a "theology of Jewish-Christian relationship" informed his lifelong philosemitism and pro-Zionist sympathies.[61]

On the continent, the vanguard of Catholic thinkers who between 1945 and 1962 reappraised the theological function of Jews for the Church exerted decisive influence. In November 1961, John XXIII's inclusion of "the Jewish question" in the agenda of the upcoming Second Vatican Council resulted from their efforts. Like Karl Thieme in Germany, the priests Paul Démann in France, Anton Ramselaar and Johannes Willebrands in the Netherlands, the Dominican Giorgio La Pira and the religious scholar Maria Vingiani in Italy, as well as the Central European émigré in the United States Johanness Oesterreicher, challenged the idea of divine curse placed upon the Jews.[62] The so-called Apeldoorn Memorandum, an influential blueprint for the future *Nostra Aetate* declaration sent to the Vatican in September 1960, exemplified this new approach. After European Jewry endured the "most monstrous of persecutions," the duty of Christians was "to learn about, to reflect about, the subject of Jews." Their recent "return to the land and the language of the bible" likewise begged for "rapprochement and reconciliation with the Jewish people."[63]

---

[59] James Parkes, *God at Work in Science, Politics and Human Knowledge* (New York: Philosophical Library, 1952).

[60] Michael Ipgrave, "Remembering the Covenant: Judaism in Anglican Theology of Interfaith Relation," *Anglican Theological Review* 96, no. 1: 39–55.

[61] James Parkes, "A Theology of Jewish Christian Relationship" in James Parkes (ed.), *Prelude to Dialogue: Jewish Christian Relationships* (New York: Schocken Books, 1969), 188–201.

[62] On the main "pioneers of Vatican II," including numerous converts from Judaism, see John Connelly, *From Enemy to Brother*, op. cit. On La Pira, see Silvia Baldi Cucchiara, "Giorgio La Pira e le relazioni ebraico-christiane" in Luciano Martini (ed.), *Giorgio La Pira e la vocazione di Israele* (Firenzi: Giunti, 2005), 88–105. On Maria Vignani, see Marialuisa-Lucia Sergio, "Oecuménisme et dialogue: une prophétie feminine" in N. Breton et al. (eds.), *Les dialogues inter-religieux, lieux et acteurs* (Rennes: Presses Universitaires de Rennes, 2017), 167–182. On the Dutch Anton Ramselaar and Johaness Willebrands, see Marcel J. M. H. Poorthuis, "The Diplomat and the Pioneer in Jewish-Catholic Relations Prior to Nostra Aetate: Jo Willebrands and Toon Ramselaar," *Journal of Ecumenical Studies* 49, no. 3 (Summer 2014): 471–488.

[63] Gathered in Apeldoorn (central Holland) in 1958 and 1960, "pioneers of Vatican II" drafted an influential memorandum transmitted to the Vatican. See Poorthuis, "The Diplomat and the Pioneer," op. cit.; Connelly, *From Enemy to Brother* ..., op. cit., 179–180.

Before the Vatican's turn to interfaith dialogue after 1965, however, the question of ecumenical relations with Judaism remained internal to the church. If Jews were no longer reprobate, asked the precursors of *Nostra Aetate*, what is their new role for Christianity? Their answer challenged established doctrine: Relieved from their "carnal" status and ennobled with spiritual value, Jews were more than ever relevant to Christians. The French-Jewish philosopher Emmanuel Levinas took notice of this evolution. A new generation of Christians, Levinas observed on the eve of the Second Vatican Council, considered Jews "significant to the future and to life. This significance can transform the very meaning of Judaeo-Christian relations."[64] This position opened new ecumenical possibilities. As Karl Thieme wrote in 1950, the Jewish–Christian relationship was now premised on coexistence between Christians and the "God's pleasing" Jewish people. The "Jewish person," he contended, pleased God not only as a "pious individual," but "also and especially as a Jew."[65] Although ecumenists never abandoned hope for the return of Jews to the Christian fold, the prospect of life side by side tempered old missionizing ambitions. "I demand that time be given us to know each other again, through practical, positive, daily, organic reunion," wrote the French Catholic playwright and poet Paul Claudel in 1950.[66] An ecumenical relationship with Judaism afforded Christians precious eschatological time. Judaism and Christianity could now contemplate a long and peaceful future before the arrival of the messianic age. This pacified climate, however, did not lead to reckoning with a thorny question: the potential responsibility of Christian teachings in the recent destruction of European Jews.

Jesus and Israel

As exemplified by the Vatican's silence on the Holocaust under Pius XII, the Jewish genocide had little immediate effect on the European Christian conscience. French Catholic intellectuals, as detailed at the end of this chapter, empathized with the Jewish tragedy in uniquely Christian terms. Yet in the first postwar decade, as the former Catholic resister and future "righteous among the nations" Germaine Ribière reminisced, "Jewish affliction was not Christian affliction: It only found place in a few Christian hearts."[67] In France, however, the publication

---

[64] Emmanuel Levinas, "Judaeo-Christian Friendship" in *Difficult Freedom*, op. cit., 202.
[65] Thieme cited in Fullenbach, "Shock, Renewal, Crisis," op. cit., 212.
[66] Paul Claudel, *Une Voix sur Israël* (first edition 1950) (Paris: Les Provinciales, 2016), 22.
[67] Germaine Ribière cited in Pierre Pierrard, *Juifs et Catholiques français. D'Edouard Drumont à Jacob Kaplan* (Paris: Cerf, 1997), 331.

in April 1948 of Jules Isaac's notorious *Jesus and Israel* [*Jésus et Israël*] offered churchgoers a point of entry into Holocaust accountability. A milestone in the history of Jewish–Christian relations, *Jesus and Israel* was a "cry of an outraged conscience, of a lacerated heart" from an afflicted man whose wife and daughter perished in Auschwitz. In his refutation of the Church's anti-Jewish doctrine, the French-Jewish historian famously blamed "the teaching of contempt (...) which has been perpetuated for eighteen hundred years." The theology of divine curse, he contended, justified centuries of persecutions culminating "in the gas chambers and crematory ovens of Nazi Germany." Isaac did not however accuse Christianity of direct culpability for the Holocaust. His book exposed the Christian roots of modern antisemitism but only challenged "a certain Christian teaching, a certain tradition, a certain apologetics," not the whole body of scriptures: Isaac offered his readers a provocative but digestible critique of the Christian anti-Judaic tradition.[68]

Jesus and Israel nonetheless provoked defensive Catholic reactions. The future cardinal Jean Daniélou wrote in March 1948 that regarding the Jewish people, a Christian can only have "respect for its glory and compassion for its suffering." The churchman nonetheless chided Isaac for refusing to acknowledge Jewish responsibility for the killing of Christ.[69] The French Protestant leader Charles Westphal accepted blame with more ease. Of Calvinist obedience, the French Reformed Church did not inherit Lutheranism's animosity toward Judaism.[70] Contrary to Luther's doctrine of "salvation through faith alone," the Huguenots' descendants believed in the saving of souls through acceptance of responsibility. This theological tradition made them particularly receptive to Karl Barth's teachings. The principal author of the anti-Nazi *Barmen Declaration* of 1934, the Swiss Reformed thinker opposed the subordination of German Protestantism to Hitler's regime. The church, claimed Barth, should make "its knowledge of Jesus the Lord its criterion for discerning between the just and the unjust state." Although the Barmen Declaration failed to properly condemn antisem-

---

[68] Jules Isaac, *Jesus and Israel* (New York: Holt, Rinehart and Winston, 1971). On Isaac, see among others André Kaspi, *Jules Isaac: Historien, auteur du rapprochement judéo-chrétien* (Paris: Plon, 2002); Norman C. Tobias, *Jewish Conscience of the Church: Jules Isaac and the Second Vatican Council* (Cham: Palgrave Macmillan, 2017); Philip Nord, *After the Deportation: Memory Battles in Postwar France* (Cambridge: Cambridge University Press, 2020), 269–276.

[69] Carol Iancu, "Les réactions des milieux chrétiens face à la Shoah," *Catholiques et protestants français après la Shoah, Revue d'histoire de la Shoah* 192 (2010): 159–193; see in the same issue Paula Berger Marx, "Jean Daniélou, les Juifs, et la Shoah," 81–100.

[70] Patrick Cabanel, "Le Protestantisme français face à la Shoah et l'antisémitisme, de 1945 à nos jours" in *Catholiques et protestants français après la Shoah*, op. cit., 47–77.

itism, Barth's doctrine of dissidence helped French Protestants speak out against anti-Jewish persecutions in 1941.[71] After the war, they also readily admitted the responsibility of the Church in the "teaching of contempt." Jules Isaac took notice of this disposition in the wake of the interfaith Seelisberg conference held in August 1947: "The movement continues and broadens on the Protestant side. Catholics are not there yet."[72]

Jesus and Israel antagonized Catholic traditionalists, but sympathetic clergymen and lay writers came to its defense. The book also earned Isaac international reputation. On October 16, 1949, Pius XII gave the aging historian a courteous but inconsequential audience. In Italy, however, the Dominican Giorgio La Pira, mayor of Florence between 1950 and 1956, entertained a long correspondence with Isaac. In June 1960, La Pira also arranged a decisive meeting between the French author and Pope John XXIII, the initiator of the Second Vatican Council.[73] The German-born priest of Jewish origin Gregory Baum, for his part, wrote in 1958 a refutation of Isaac's thesis. *Jesus and Israel*, he alleged, tarnished parts of the Gospel. Baum felt nonetheless that Isaac successfully "shattered" the traditional Christian attitude and later rallied to his defense.[74] The French scholar, he acknowledged, "produced a critical movement in the church that mediated a certain critical culture."[75]

Jesus and Israel indeed prodded Christians to reconsider their relationship with Judaism after the Holocaust. This demand did not stem from anti-Christian animus: The book provided instead ample Judeo-Christian reassurances. Isaac, to be sure, did not identify with either faith. "The reader may wonder to what religion the author belongs," he wrote in his preface. "This is easy to answer: none." Neither observant Jew nor baptized Christian, Isaac stirred up Judeo-Christian emotions. "This whole book," he added, "witnesses to the fervor that inspires and guides [its author], fervor for Israel, fervor for Jesus, son of Israel."[76] Isaac would have surely disagreed with Catholics who after his death

---

[71] Karl Barth, "Lettre aux Protestants de France," *Esprit et le Voltigeur* 8:91 (April 1940), 73–80. On Barth's influence on French Protestantism, see Patrick Cabanel, "Les protestants français" in Denis Pelletier and Jean-Louis Schlegel (eds.), *À la gauche du Christ: Les chrétiens de gauche en France de 1945 à nos jours* (Paris: Seuil, 2012), 184–185.

[72] Cited in Iancu, "Les réactions des milieux chrétiens," op. cit., 171.

[73] Elena Mazzini, "Jules Isaac e il dialogo ebraico-christiano" in L. Marini (ed.), *Giorgio La Pira e la vocazione di Israele*, op. cit., 147–159.

[74] Gregory Baum, *Is the New Testament Anti-Semitic? A Re-Examination of the New Testament* (Mahwah, NJ: Paulist Press, 1965), 12–15.

[75] Baum cited in Norman C. Tobias, *Jewish Conscience of the Church: Jules Isaac and the Second Vatican Council*, op. cit., 210.

[76] Jules Isaac, *Jesus and Israel*, op. cit., xxiv.

in 1963 hailed him as "an assimilated Jew who reasons as if he is a Christian."[77] But his reverence for Jesus was hard to miss: "that the one year, Jesus's single year, was enough to kindle a flame in the world which would never be extinguished thereafter is a miracle; they are none more convincing."[78] Isaac's fascination with the figure of Jesus secured his status as the "Jewish conscience of the Church." His book nonetheless demanded substantial efforts from Christians. Isaac enjoined them to embrace Jesus's Jewishness, abandon the accusation of deicide, and read the Gospel in the light of the Old Testament: These ideas were only incorporated in Catholic teachings after 1965. But the so-called pioneers of Vatican II – the network of Catholic clergymen who advocated a friendly approach to Judaism after the Holocaust – were now theologically equipped to meet these demands: Their new interpretation of Paul's *Letter to the Romans* 9–11 helped them forge closer bonds with the Jewish "olive tree" upon which the Church's "grafted" itself.

Pauline Philosemitism

Until the mid twentieth century, Christians derived from *Romans 9–11* the justification of discontinuity between Judaism and its successor. Gentiles obtained righteousness through faith; the people of Israel, in its obstinate following of the law, lost its special election to the Church (Romans 9:30). But Paul's epistle famously intertwined enmity with love. Romans 11:28 exemplifies these dialectics: "As regards to the Gospel, they are your enemies for your sake; but as regards to election, they are beloved for the sake of their forefathers (9:28)." God did not cast-off disobedient Israel, announced Paul, and regarding salvation Christians and Jews remained equals. For centuries *Romans 9–11* presented its readers with a daunting challenge: how to reconcile antagonism and affection?

Christian teachings responded by placing limits on Pauline love: Carnal Jews were only worth preserving in anticipation of their salvation "in Christ." Such an interpretation was faithful to the text. God's mercy will save disobedient Israel at the end of the world, preached Paul. But only "children of the promise" – the first-century Jews who like him embraced Christ – remained "God's children" (Romans 9:8). Jews of merely "physical descent," for their part, were condemned to witness the triumph of the Church until "hardening" and jealousy leads them back to Christ. After 1945, this negative view continued to appeal to

---

[77] See John M. Oesterreicher's *Eulogy The Thomist: A Speculative Quarterly Review* 36, no. 1 (January 1972): 179–184.

[78] Isaac, *Jesus and Israel*, op. cit., 97.

German Protestant theologians. Although Paul anguished over "those of my own kin" (Romans 9:3), *Romans 9–11* revealed to the Church its missionary obligation toward "unbelieving Israel." The *Letter* also offered proof that Judaism in its contemporary form is the "opposite counterpart of the ancient people of the covenant." For the German Protestant theologian Leonhard Goppelt, it was, at best, "a prime example of pre-Christian humanity."[79]

In the late 1930s, however, anti-Nazi Central European Catholics such as Karl Thieme, Johannes Oesterreicher, or Waldemar Gurian returned to Paul's *Letter to the Romans* to expose the sinfulness of anti-semitism. If God's love to the Jews was "irrevocable," as Paul promised, Nazi racism violated a core Christian tenet.[80] In *The Living Thoughts of Saint Paul* published in the United States in 1941, the French Catholic philosopher Jacques Maritain similarly retrieved pro-Judaic arguments from Paul's thought. The apostle, argued the exiled French intellectual during the somber days of the Holocaust, felt both "love" and "sorrow" for the Jewish people."[81] Paul's true goal, Maritain told American Jews in 1941, was not the conversion of Israel but its "plenitude" through the unification of the Synagogue and the Church.[82] The hyphen uniting the "Judeo" to the Christian, Paul offered hope for a "Judeo-Christian civilization" in which both faiths "will perceive the vital part each one plays in its total pattern."[83]

After the war, Maritain accepted the co-chairmanship of the International Council for Christian and Jews created in 1946. Paul's teachings, he wrote in August 1947, offered the best antidote against antisemitism: "How much longer (...) will Christians repudiate [the teachings of] Saint Paul, which tell us that we have been grafted upon Israel's olive tree?" Only through Paul could Christians rediscover "the mysterious solidarity uniting them with the elderly race."[84]

---

[79] Leonhard Goppelt, *Jesus, Paul and Judaism*, op. cit., 166–167; see also Goppelt, "Israel and the Church in Today's Discussion and in Paul," *Lutheran World* X, no. 4 (1963): 352–372.
[80] John Connelly, *From Enemy to Brother*, op. cit., 129–130. Elias H. Füllenbach, "Shock, Renewal, Crisis," op. cit., 206–207.
[81] Jacques Maritain, *The Living Thoughts of Saint Paul* (New York: David McKay Company, 1941), 80 and 87.
[82] Jacques Maritain, *The Healing of Humanity* (1941), available at: www3.nd.edu/~maritain/jmc/jm0402a.htm. Olivier Rota, *Essai sur le philosémitisme catholique. Entre le premier et le second Vatican. Un parcours dans la modernité chrétienne* (Arras: Artois Presse Université, 2012), 77.
[83] Cited in Richard F. Crane, *Passion of Israel: Jacques Maritain, Catholic Conscience and the Holocaust* (Scranton, PA: University of Scranton Press, 2010), 81.
[84] Jacques Maritain's letter to Charles Journet, July 28, 1947, available at: www.ajcf.fr/Lettre-de-Jacques-Maritain-a-la-Conference-de-Seelisberg.html.

In 1949, Karl Thieme similarly identified in *Romans 9–11* the root of Christian esteem for Jews. In 1952, the German catholic thinker also noticed with satisfaction a renewed engagement with Paul among postwar Christian thinkers.[85] Growing interest for the Jewish-born apostle was likewise observed among French Catholic worshippers. "[Catholics] who are now reading the Old Testament more than they once did," reported a religious scholar in 1955, "are also reading more frequently St. Paul's Epistle."[86]

The postwar rediscovery of the Pauline canon did not of course dispel its ambiguity. Maritain's optimistic reading of *Romans 9–11* allowed him to blame crucifixion on sinful humanity instead of Jews, but Paul himself never minced words on the people who "killed the Lord Jesus." One could also extend a friendly hand to Jews and resent, like Maritain's close friend and future cardinal Charles Journet, their refusal to enter "the supranational kingdom of God."[87] The question of "reintegration" still weakened Pauline empathy: If salvation only comes from Jewish reunification with Christ, the followers of the Torah, beloved as they may be, remained disbelievers.[88] Paul indeed revered his Jewish kinsmen but announced the replacement of Mosaic Law with a new "Law of Christ." During the Second Vatican Council, the catholic pioneer in Jewish-Christian dialogue Gregory Baum defended the cause of ecumenism through reliance on Paul's teachings. But as he later recognized, this exercise required a healthy dose of "wishful thinking."[89]

The French-Hungarian priest and convert from Judaism Paul Démann, for his part, tried to overcome Pauline contradictions through hope in *mutually agreed* Judeo-Christian reunification. Like Karl Barth, Démann viewed the separation of Jews and Christians as a parting of ways within the same people. This schismatic view challenged the Church's narrower conception of ecumenism, which until then meant collaboration with non-Roman Christians only. Démann, to the contrary, urged "the Church and Israel (...) to enter in communion in shared prayer and shared hope pointing toward Unity."[90] Judeo-Christianity, in his

---

[85] Karl Thieme, "Paulinismus und Judentum: Ein Literaturbericht" (1952), cited in John Connelly, *From Enemy to Brother*, op. cit., 208.
[86] Jacqueline Plantié, "The Rediscovery of Israel in Contemporary Catholicism," *The Ecumenical Review* 7, no. 3 (April 1955): 238–242.
[87] Charles Journet, *Destinées d'Israël: à propos du Salut par les Juifs* (Paris: 1945), 199–201.
[88] On "Pauline philosemitism" and its ambiguities, see Alan T. Davies's *Anti-Semitism and the Christian Mind: The Crisis of Conscience after Auschwitz* (New York: Herder and Herder, 1969), 102–103.
[89] See Baum's introduction to Rosemary R. Ruether, *Faith and Fratricide: The Theological Roots of Antisemitism* (New York: The Seabury Press, 1974), 6.
[90] Paul Démann, "Israël et l'Unité de l'Église" in *Cahiers Sioniens* 1, March 1953, 1–24.

eyes, realized itself in a "people of God" encompassing both Jews and Christians. This idea had already gained currency in Christian circles after the war. In Germany, the unofficial Schwalbach Theses issued in May 1950 envisioned one people "brought together as the new people of God."[91] Démann, however, ruled out missionizing to achieve this goal. The product of voluntary convergence, his people of God resulted from the sole triumph of "God's love (…) one and Unitary."[92] Hope for reintegration was not abandoned but this creative formulation invited Jews to unity as *equals* to Christians.

Démann indeed expanded the boundaries of what passed as philosemitism in postwar catholic circles: an abhorrence of antisemitism combined with persisting hope for Jewish conversion.[93] He yearned instead for intimate proximity with Jews who continued to live as Jews. "Their existence in our midst, their destiny and their faith," he wrote in 1961, "affect us at the deepest level of our being." Observant or not, they formed an "entity whose cohesion, permanence, and personality stand with extraordinary vigor."[94] These exceptional words alienated Démann from his own religious order, the Congregation of Notre Dame de Sion committed to evangelization among Jews. But on the eve of the Second Vatican Council, they reflected growing Catholic willingness to welcome contact with Judaism.

The French Jesuit and future Roman cardinal Jean Daniélou, for his part, returned to the history of early Christianity to highlight the benefits of Jewish spirituality for the Church. Published in 1958, his monumental *Théologie du Judéo-Christianisme* [*The Theology of Jewish Christianity*] offered a bold reinterpretation of Christianity's Jewish origins. In this influential work, Daniélou delved into the thought of Jewish Christians who in the first and second centuries recognized Jesus as the redeemer while still maintaining Jewish traditions. Contrary to German Protestant scholars, the French Jesuit did not view Jewish Christianity as a transition period between a declining "later Judaism" and the victorious advent of the Church. It was instead the moment when Jewish "theological, liturgical and ascetical structures" entered Christianity. Encouraged by the recent discovery of the Dead Sea Scrolls, Daniélou portrayed Jewish Christianity as "a type of Christian thought

---

[91] The Schwalbach Theses (1950) are available at: www.ccjr.us/dialogika-resources/documents-and-statements/roman-catholic/second-vatican-council/naprecursors/schwalbach. See also John Connelly, *From Enemy to Brother*, op. cit., 216–217.
[92] Démann, *Israël et l'Unité de l'Église*, op. cit., 24.
[93] Olivier Rota, "Dépasser les cadres du philosémitisme. La vision oeucuménique de Paul Démann," *Archives Juives* 40, no. 1 (2007): 117–130.
[94] Paul Démann, *Les Juifs, foi et destinée* (Paris: Fayard, 1961), 7, 10.

expressing itself in forms borrowed from Judaism." Early Christian worship, he claimed, was akin to a "Judaistic religion."[95] Far from extinct, "a Judaism contemporary with Christ" imparted itself on the Christian mind. Rabbinical Judaism and early Christianity, of course, remained in "open war." But forms of "Later Judaism" (the Pharisees, the Essenes, and the Zealots) shaped the Christian faith: The distant Old Testament was not Christianity's only Jewish ancestry.

Daniélou, however, qualified his philosemitic retrieval of Judaic sources with a return to the doctrine of substitution. Judaism migrated to early Christianity, but the first Christian worshippers categorically rejected the Law. Jewish Christians were therefore "men who had broken completely with the Jewish world, but who continued to think in its terms."[96] Daniélou's *judéo-chrétien* was indeed the prototype of the true Christian: The first followers of Jesus carried the torch of Judaism after Jews refused entry into "the authentic people of God." The Church, in other words, did not just supersede Judaism: *verus Israel* [true Israel] became more Jewish than the Jews.

Although tactical, Daniélou's reinterpretation of early Christianity infused a dose of Judaism into the Church's post-Holocaust identity. The French-Jewish writer Edmond Fleg, another forefather of the *Amitié judéo-chrétienne*, had since 1946 identified a "semitic ferment" in Daniélou's thought. Although Fleg took offense at Daniélou's harsh words on the Jews' rejection of Jesus, he applauded his recovery of Christianity's Judaic roots. "Yes, Reverend-Father, you are *rejudaizing* the Church," Fleg wrote to Daniélou, "and I can only rejoice."[97] Daniélou's catholic opponents, for their part, faulted him for excessive Judaization. Early Christians may not have been "extricated from the swaddling clothes of Judaism," they claimed, but Daniélou's Jewish-Christianity, oblivious of Hellenic origins, was decidedly "too Jewish."[98] This criticism hit the mark: "re-Judaization" reconnected the Church with its Jewish origins. Daniélou, of course, stressed the Jewish essence of early Christianity to ultimately claim superiority over Judaism. But fifteen years after the words *verjudung* or *enjuivement* ("Jewification") connoted Jewish pollution in Nazi rhetoric or French collaborationist parlance, "Judaization" lost its repulsive meaning.

---

[95] Jean Daniélou, *Theology of Jewish Christianity* (Chicago, IL: Henry Regnery Company, 1964), 9; Marcel Simon, *Verus Israel: Étude sur les relations entre chrétiens et juifs dans l'Empire Romain 135–425* (Paris: 1948).
[96] Daniélou, *Theology of Jewish Christianity*, 9.
[97] Jean Daniélou, *Dialogue avec Israel* (Paris: La Palatine, 1963), 118.
[98] See the review of Daniélou's Magnus opus *Revue des sciences religieuses* 35, no. 1 (1961): 62–64.

The postwar rediscovery of Christianity's Jewish roots took another form with the re-Judaization of the apostle Paul in the Christian imagination. In 1948, the Welsh Congregationalist scholar W. D. Davies (1911–2001) challenged the Protestant tradition until then dismissive of Paul's Jewishness. Although a Hellenic Jew, argued Davies, the apostle "baptized" Jewish concepts "unto Christ." As the future Princeton University professor contended, "Paul belonged to the mainstream of first-century Judaism and elements of his thought, which are often labeled as Hellenistic, might well be derived from Judaism."[99] Paul replaced the Torah with faith in Jesus, but his mental universe remained Judaic: The "rabbi become apostle" only regarded Christ "in the light of a new Moses." Even more provocative was Davies's contention that "Paul is grounded in a rabbinic mode of the thought": His reappraisal paved the way for a "New Perspective on Paul" in Protestant theology three decades later.[100]

Considered the most important Protestant theologian of the twentieth century, Karl Barth too promoted the "re-Judaization" of Christianity. In 1946, amid the ruins of Bonn University, the Swiss-born scholar reminded Germans that Jesus was "of necessity a Jew." Christ's Jewishness, the doctrinal foundation of his complex writings on Judaism, also preconditioned German regeneration: "the man who is ashamed of Israel is ashamed of Jesus Christ and therefore of his own existence."[101] In his essay *The Jewish Question and Christian Answers* (1949), Barth placed an additional Jewish burden on the German citizenry. Since Jews alone "and not the Germans" were God's elect, "in order to be chosen we must, for good or ill, either be Jews or else be heart and soul on the side of the Jews."[102] He once again claimed the mantle of Jewishness in 1950: "In order to be elect ourselves, for good or evil we must either be Jews *or belong to this Jew*" [i.e., Christ].[103] Yet for Barth, Israel's main function was to draw gentiles into God's election. After the accomplishment of this goal, the New Covenant fulfilled in Christ was irrevocable: The persistence of Judaism remained for him a permanent irritant. "The existence of the synagogue beside the church," he wrote in 1953,

---

[99] W. D. Davies, *Paul and Rabbinic Judaism: Some Rabbinic Elements in Pauline Theology* (first published in 1948) (New York: Garper & Row, 1967), 1, 144, 16.

[100] Mathew V. Novenson, "Anti-Judaism and Philo-Judaism in Pauline Studies, Then and Now" in Arjen F. Bakker et al. (eds.), *Protestant Bible Scholarship: Antisemitism, Philosemitism, and Anti-Judaism* (Leiden: Brill, 2022), 106–124.

[101] Karl Barth, *Dogmatics in Outline* (first published in German in 1947) (New York: Harper Perennial, 1959), 76.

[102] Karl Barth, "The Jewish Problem and the Christian Answer" in *Against the Stream: Shorter Post-War Writings 1946–1952* (London: SCM Press, 1954), 193–201.

[103] Karl Barth, *Church Dogmatics* 3/3, cited in Mark. R. Lindsay, *Barth, Israel, and Jesus: Karl Barth's Theology of Israel* (Aldershot, UK: Ashgate, 2007), 83.

"is something like an ontological impossibility, a wound, yes a gaping hole, in the body of Christ Himself, that is simply unbearable."[104]

As theological abstractions, mythical Jews fulfilled a positive function in Barth's theology. Christians are "one with the Jews," he declared in his broadcast of 1949. The real Jews Barth encountered during his life fared differently. As he candidly admitted in 1967, their proximity always inspired in him feelings of "irrational personal aversion." In a letter to the rising star of Protestant scholarship Friedrich-Wilhelm Marquardt, Barth avowed that he was "decidedly not a philosemite."[105] Although soul-searching, his confession was excessively harsh. During his exile in Switzerland, Barth denounced Nazi persecutions and called upon the Vatican to intervene in favor of Hungarian Jews. After the war, he confronted the church's wartime passivity, greeted the creation of the state of Israel, and called for "Jewish-Christian solidarity, today!" But even if "one with the Jews," Barth's doctrine of Israel still denied Judaism the right of existence on its own terms.[106]

From Aversion to Esteem: The *Nostra Aetate* Declaration

Two decades after the Holocaust, however, the Catholic hierarchy departed from theological animosity toward "disobedient" Jews. The end of the Second Vatican council marked indeed a turning point in Catholic–Jewish relations. Promulgated on October 28, 1965, the *Nostra Aetate* declaration issued by the Vatican was part of the council's Declaration on The Relation of the Church to Non-Christian Religions.[107] But while tolerant Catholicism now rejected "nothing that is holy" in Islam, Hinduism, and Buddhism, it acknowledged in a separate paragraph a special bond with Jews and Judaism. In fifteen Latin sentences, *Nostra Aetate* articulated a shift from antagonism to esteem. Jewish authorities at the time of Jesus, the document still claimed, "pressed for the death of Christ." Yet the crucifixion could no longer be "charged against all the Jews, without distinction, then alive, nor against

---

[104] Karl Barth, *Junge Kirche* (1953) cited in Dagmar Herzog, "The Death of God in West Germany: Between Secularization, Post-Fascism and the Rise of Liberation Theology" in M. Geyer and Lucian Hölscher (eds.), *The Presence of God in Modern Society* (Göttingen: Wallstein Verlag, 2006), 431–467.

[105] Cited in Mark. R. Lindsay, *Barth, Israel, and Jesus: Karl Barth's Theology of Israel*, op. cit., 31.

[106] Katherine Sonderegger, *That Jesus Christ Was Born a Jew: Karl Barth's Doctrine of Israel* (University Park, PA: The Pennsylvania University Press, 1992), 141–142.

[107] Nostra Aetate [In Our Times] (1965), available at: www.vatican.va/archive/hist_councils/ ii_vatican_council/documents/vat-ii_decl_19651028_nostra-aetate_en.html.

the Jews of today." The Vatican also shied away from "the teaching of contempt" in favor of the teaching of respect. Although Jews did not accept the Gospel, *Nostra Aetate* instructed Christians that "God holds the Jews most dear": no longer accursed or rejected, revalorized Jews were no longer enjoined to convert to Christianity. Friendliness was likewise conveyed through the condemnation of "hatred, persecutions, displays of anti-Semitism, directed against Jews at any time and by anyone." Cautiously avoiding mention of the state of Israel, the Vatican called for "mutual understanding and respect" between Christians and Jews through the deepening of religious dialogue.[108]

The Declaration's other breakthrough was its explicit affirmation of a "Judeo-Christian tradition." Acknowledging its special proximity with Judaism, the Church remembered "the bond that spiritually ties the people of the New Testament to Abraham's stock." This recognition of Christianity's Judaic roots was no longer compensated with anti-Judaic triumphalism. The humbler Church drew instead "sustenance from the root of that well-cultivated olive tree onto which have been grafted the wild shoots, the Gentiles." Common patrimony, of course, did not eliminate hopes for the end of Jewish particularism. Christ "reconciled Jews and Gentiles," stated *Nostra Aetate*, "making both one in Himself." But the document softened the traditional narrative of rupture accounting for the "parting of ways" in Christian doctrine: the irreconcilability of Jewish carnality and Christian spirituality; the vengeful God of the Old Testament and the God of Love of the New Testament; the Law and Christ; and the disobedient Synagogue and the Church. The Vatican now adopted the language of continuity and coexistence: With *Nostra Aetate*, the "Judeo-Christian tradition" finally found a theological anchor on the European continent.

The declaration's immediate effect was not only the expansion of the Jewish–Christian dialogue during Paul VI's pontificate (1963–78). The document also helped propagate the "tradition" beyond the Church. One of its first disseminators was the distinguished Austrian catholic historian Friedrich Heer. As "God's First Love," Heer argued in 1967, the Jews persecuted throughout 2,000 years of Christianity deserved special respect from the followers of Jesus. But the former anti-Nazi activist went far beyond Nostra Aetate's purview. Heer's provocative history of Christian attitudes toward Jews also sought to explain the "genesis of the

---

[108] On the drafting of Nostra Aetate, see among others Connelly, *From Enemy to Brother*, 239–272; Neville Lamdan and Alberto Melloni (eds.), *Nostra Aetate: Origins, Promulgation, Impact on Jewish–Catholic Relations* (Berlin: LIT Verlag, 2007); Kail C. Ellis (ed.), *Nostra Aetate, Non-Christian Religions, and Interfaith Relations* (Cham: Palgrave Macmillan, 2021), 67–88.

Austrian catholic Adolf Hitler": Such introspection was not part of the Vatican's new discourse of esteem.[109]

Although hailed as an aggiornamento of anti-Judaism, Nostra Aetate remained silent on the Holocaust. The Vatican officialized the Judeo-Christian tradition through theological reform, not confrontation with the Jewish catastrophe. Advocates of a friendly approach to Judaism, to be sure, invoked the murder of European Jews to justify doctrinal revision. The German cardinal Augustin Bea, a key protagonist of Jewish Christian understanding, wrote to John XXIII in 1962 that after the "appalling crimes of National-Socialism against six million Jews," the Church was under obligation to engage in the "purification of spirit and conscience."[110] Yet while *Nostra Aetate* condemned anti-Judaism, it was not a statement on the Jewish genocide: The age of Catholic repentance will await John Paul II's papacy (1978–2005).

In France, however, prominent Catholic intellectuals took a different route in the aftermath of World War II. "When it targeted Judaism," wrote Emmanuel Mounier in September 1945, "the [Nazi] persecutor stroke at the very heart of Judeo-Christian civilization." The extermination of the Jews, added the director of *Esprit*, was also an assault on Judeo-Christianity's "incorruptible sources of life."[111] Mounier's portrayal of Nazi criminality as antithetic to Judeo-Christian values was already in vogue in the United States. In 1940, the Jewish American writer Maurice Samuel depicted Judaism and Christianity as bulwarks against Nazi paganism, a popular theme during the war before its redirection toward Soviet communism during the cold war.[112]

Yet between 1945 and 1960, members of the French Catholic intellectual milieu modified this Judeo-Christian conception. The destruction of European Jewry, in their mind, was less a violation of Judeo-Christianism than its foundational event. "Like strange companions," Jacques Maritain already wrote from the United States in 1943, "Jews and Christians have traveled the way of calvary together."[113] If Nazi antisemitism was displaced "Christophobia," as Maurice Samuel contended, then Jews and

---

[109] Friedrich Heer, *God's First Love: Christians and Jews over Two Thousand Years* (New York: Weybright and Talley, 1970). See also William M. Johnston, "Friedrich Heers' Place in the Debate of Austrian Identity" in G. Bischof, A. Pelinka, and F. Karlhofer (eds.), *The Vranitzky Era in Austria* (New Brunswick, NJ: Transaction Publisher, 1999), 244–253.
[110] Augustin Bea is cited in Connelly, *From Enemy to Brother*, op. cit., 249.
[111] Emmanuel Mounier, "Les juifs parlent aux nations," *Esprit* (September 1945), 457.
[112] Maurice Samuel, *The Great Hatred* (New York: Alfred A. Knopf, 1940), 109, cited in Richard Crane, *Passion of Israel: Jacques Maritain, Catholic Conscience and the Holocaust* (Scranton, PA: University of Scranton Press, 2010), 80.
[113] Robert A. Ventresca, "Jacques Maritain and the Jewish Question: Theology, Identity and Politics," *Studies in Christian-Jewish Relations* 2, no. 2 (2007): 58–69.

Christians were bound in common victimhood. Maritain's comment confirmed that Christological imagery helped followers of Jesus in the United States and Europe make sense of the Judeocide, both during and after the war.[114] In France, the Christianization of the Holocaust took a specific form: The unification of humiliated Jews and Christians.

Humiliated Jews, Humiliated Christians

On July 12, 1946, the recently appointed French ambassador to the Vatican Jacques Maritain sent a personal letter to Giovanni Montini, the future Paul VI and a close aide to Pius XII. A papal statement on the Holocaust, pleaded the Catholic philosopher to no avail, was of utmost urgency after an "unprecedented fury of humiliation and cruelty descended upon the People of Israel."[115] When Hitler rose to power in 1933, however, Maritain only anguished over the humiliation of Christians in the age of fascism. His concern was for "the multitudes of men whom a profound resentment, born of their humiliation and offended dignity, has turned against Christianity."[116] But the Holocaust, which he anxiously followed from his North American exile, led him to ponder the meaning of Jewish humiliation for Christians. As grim news arrived from Europe, Maritain recognized in Jews "unwillingly thrown onto the road of Calvary" a reenactment of the Passion. "Jesus Christ suffers in the Passion of Israel," he wrote in 1941. He reiterated this argument in a broadcast to the Free French in 1944: "In our days the Passion of Israel takes more and more distinctly the form of the Cross." The destruction of European Jewry, in his eyes, was tantamount to "mass crucifixion."[117]

Invoking the suffering of Christ to convey solicitude was not exceptional for a Catholic believer. Since the Middle Age, *humilatio dei*, Jesus's agony, constituted the original scene of Christian compassion. In the medieval social order based on honor and exclusion, public shame or destitution remained normative practices. But through the figure of the humiliated, medieval Christians were also able to visualize the humility

---

[114] Tom Lawson, "Shaping the Holocaust: The Influence of Christian Discourse on Perceptions of the European Jewish Tragedy," *Holocaust and Genocide Studies* 21, no. 3 (Winter 2007): 404–420.

[115] Michael Marrus, "A Plea Unanswered: Jacques Maritain, Pope Pius XII, and the Holocaust," in Eli Lederhendler (eds.), *Jews, Catholics, and the Burden of History. Studies in Contemporary Jewry* (New York: Oxford University Press, 2005), 3–11.

[116] Maritain cited in Joseph Frank, *Responses to Modernity: Essays in the Politics of Culture* (New York: Fordham University Press, 2012), 31.

[117] On Maritain's wartime evocations of the Holocaust as crucifixion, see Richard Crane, *Passion of Israel: Jacques Maritain, Catholic Conscience and the Holocaust* (Scranton, PA: University of Scranton Press, 2010), 69–99.

of the crucified Messiah.[118] Mid twentieth-century Christian humanists like Maritain revolted against man's degradation and loss of dignity. But like their medieval ancestors they also made virtue out of humiliation. Maritain viewed Jewish suffering along similar lines: The humiliation of the Holocaust revealed the innermost humility of Jewish victims. Through its Passion, the Jewish people earned the status of Christ's co-sufferer. This common fate did not detract from God's salvation plan. "In the passion of Israel," Maritain wrote in 1941, "Christ suffers (...) in order gradually to conform His people to Him."[119]

The French catholic thinker nonetheless departed from Augustine's doctrine of Jewish testimony which for centuries helped Christians define the role of Jews for their faith – suffering Jews as witnesses to the truth of Christianity. As custodians of Scriptures, Augustine's Jews also preserved in their subjugation the proof of prophecies announcing Jesus the Messiah. The idea of Jews as witness-people, of course, prominently figured in Maritain's thought. But the French Catholic thinker voided Augustine's doctrine of its punitive dimension. The Holocaust transformed the nature of Jewish humiliation: no longer the suffering of reprobates, it reenacted Christ's own agony. With the influential Maritain, the Holocaust became an existential war on Christians and Jews. "It is our God who is attacked too," he noted in 1944, "it is Him who is humiliated, targeted, insulted, and spat upon by antisemitic persecution. From now on Christ does not separate but unite Jews and Christians."[120]

Talk of equality between Jewish humiliation and the Passion, to be sure, outraged anti-Judaic Catholics. Pity for the Jew as "witness and martyr," conceded in 1945 the French essayist and historian Daniel-Rops, was a Christian duty. The "persecuted face of Israel," however, should not overshadow "this other face soiled by blood and spit, and for which the Jewish crowd did not show pity." Daniel-Rops doubled down on anti-Judaism in his preface to the first French edition of *The Diary of Anne Frank* (1950). When the Jewish girl wrote that "God has never abandoned me," claimed the Catholic intellectual, she intimated that contrary to the cruel God of Israel, Jesus always remained at her side.[121]

Yet in France the first Catholic interpreters of the Holocaust saw in the "Passion of Israel" a sign of Judeo-Christian convergence. The journalist,

---

[118] On the function of humiliation in Medieval Europe, see Michel Zink, *L'humiliation, le Moyen Âge et nous* (Paris: Albin Michel, 2017).
[119] Richard Crane, *Passion of Israel*, op. cit., 74.
[120] Jacques Maritain, *La Passion d'Israël* (1944) cited in Samuel Moyn, "Bearing Witness: Theological Roots of a Secular Morality" in Dan Stone (ed.), *The Holocaust and Historical Methodology* (New York: Berghahn Books, 2012), 127–142.
[121] Daniel-Rops, *Histoire Sainte: Jésus en son temps* (Paris: Fayard, 1945); see also Daniel-Rops's preface to *Le journal d'Anne Frank* (Paris: Calmann-Lévi, 1950), x.

politician, and sympathizer of Zionism Jacques Madaule offered a vivid comparison: "If we could recognize in every Jew persecuted as a Jew the image of [Christ], his face covered with spit, his forehead bleeding from a crown of thorns, the time of reconciliation shall arrive faster."[122] The famed novelist and essayist François Mauriac, winner of the Nobel Prize for literature in 1952, made ample use of Christological metaphors. In October 1940, Mauriac had already likened the Vichy regime's antisemitic laws to crucifixion. "Do not think," he clandestinely wrote, "that the Jews crucified by your police might dispense you from paying your last dime in tribute to the victor."[123] In May 1948, a few days before the creation of the state of Israel, Mauriac again yoked crucifixion to the murder of the Jews. "After receiving so much spit on their face and walking up the road of Calvary," he hoped, Jews will recognize their "eternal conformity" with the Messiah.[124] In 1951, he compared the extermination of European Jewry to an "immense cross" in his preface to Léon Poliakov's pioneering history of the Holocaust, *Le bréviaire de la haine* [*Harvest of Hate*]. In 1954, he drew analogies with the Passion to denounce the use of torture in French Algeria.[125] In 1958, Mauriac famously returned to the theme of Jewish humiliation in his memorable preface to Elie Wiesel's *La Nuit*, the future *Night* (1960), and contemporary emblem of the global Holocaust canon.

"A Crucified Jewish Child"

Moved by "the young Jew" who came to Paris to interview him in May 1955, Mauriac arranged for the publication of Wiesel's testimony of Auschwitz and Buchenwald. The manuscript until then only existed in Yiddish under the name *And the World Kept Silent*. Shorter than its Yiddish precursor, *La Nuit* was also purged of its original rage against Christian indifference to Jewish suffering. In French, Wiesel's anguished but meditative account better suited Catholic sensitivities.[126]

---

[122] Jacques Madaule, "La tragédie juive et le mystère d'Israel" in *Témoignage Chrétien*, June 4, 1948. On early Christian reactions to the Holocaust in France, see François Azouvi, *Le mythe du grand silence: Auschwitz, les français, la mémoire* (Paris: Fayard, 2012), 73–84.
[123] Cited in Nathan Bracher, *François Mauriac on Race, War, Politics & Religion* (Washington, DC: The Catholic University of America Press, 2015), 65.
[124] Mauriac in *Le Figaro*, May 4, 1948.
[125] François Mauriac, *Qu'est-ce que l'homme* (Semaine des intellectuels catholiques, 1954), 245–246.
[126] See Naomi Seidman's seminal article "Elie Wiesel and the Scandal of the Jewish Rage," *Jewish Social Studies* 3, no. 1 (1996): 1–19; Philip Nord, *After the Deportation: Memory Battles in Postwar France* (Cambridge: Cambridge University Press, 2020), 237–247.

Yet Mauriac's preface offered Christian readers additional incentives to identify with the young Jewish writer. Overwhelmed with emotions, the elderly novelist recognized in Wiesel's gaze "Lazarus risen from the dead" and "perhaps" Jesus himself. In 1958, Mauriac dedicated his book *Son of Man* [*Le fils de l'homme*] to "Elie Wiesel, a crucified Jewish child."[127]

A fervent Catholic, Mauriac reacted to the Holocaust through vivid Christian imagery. But he also derived from Wiesel's ordeal a new validation of Christian belief. "Outraged and humiliated beyond all that heart and spirit can conceive of," the child from Seghet saw his entire family "disappear in a furnace fueled by living creatures." His humiliation, however, was above all religious. The horrors of Auschwitz reduced a young boy who until then "lived only for God" to defy "a divinity who was blind and deaf." That the extermination camp forced apostasy upon the observant Wiesel was a "striking abomination (...) yet the worst of all for those of us who have faith." But if Auschwitz became the "stumbling block" to Wiesel's faith, added Mauriac, "it also became the cornerstone of mine."

The Catholic intellectual, however, did not celebrate the replacement of obsolete Judaism with Christianity. In his preface to *La Nuit*, the Nobel Prize recipient departed from a still popular Christian understanding of the Holocaust as God's wrath against a renegade people. In Italy, the play *Processo a Gesù* [*The Trial of Jesus*] authored by the Catholic playwright Diego Fabbri and staged in 1955 before its adaptation for television, perpetuated this interpretation. Its plot revolved around a group of contemporary Jews reflecting on the killing of Christ in front of a Christian audience. Instead of Judeo-Christian amity, *Processo a Gesù* put on display Jews publicly coming to terms with their guilt. But in the play only one Jewish character is absolved from sin: the absent Daniele, who during the war embraced Christ the day the Germans arrested and then murdered him.[128]

Mauriac, to the contrary, did not expect Wiesel to convert to Catholicism. He already saw the truth of Christianity in the young Holocaust survivor: *La Nuit* indeed reassured Mauriac of "the conformity between the Cross and the suffering of men." In keeping with the Augustine tradition, the Jew in Mauriac's thought revealed Christianity to itself. But Mauriac's Wiesel was not an inert proof of Christian triumph, only salvageable through Jewish return to the Church.

---

[127] François Mauriac, *Le fils de l'homme* (Paris: Grasset, 1958).
[128] Emiliano Perra, *Conflicts of Memory: The Reception of Holocaust Films and TV Programmes in Italy, 1945 to the Present* (Bern: Peter Lang, 2010), 38–39.

The Auschwitz survivor, to the contrary, was a source of Christian regeneration, the "cornerstone" of postwar Christian spirituality. Quarantined in Augustine's thought, the Jewish witness was no longer kept at bay. "But I could only embrace him, weeping," Mauriac wrote in the conclusion of his preface. Reprinted to this day in all international editions, his introduction to *Night* prodded Christian readers to enter in communion with Jewish survivors. It also enticed them to visualize the Holocaust as a comprehensible Judeo-Christian event: Several Jewish figures helped them in this endeavor.

Jews for Jesus

In France, Catholic writers who after the Liberation reckoned with the Final Solution through the image of the cross also drew inspiration from Jews attracted to the Passion. Before the war, Marc Chagall already blended images of pogroms with a portrayal of Christ draped in a Jewish prayer shawl (*White Crucifixion* 1938). Exiled in the United States in 1941 before his return to France in 1948, the painter from Vitebsk intertwined evocations of Jewish suffering with images of Jesus on the cross – a cultural response to pogroms not infrequent in Yiddish literature and arts.[129] In the postwar years, Chagall's glass windows and mosaics displayed images from the Hebrew bible in European cathedrals and churches. Admired and befriended by Jacques Maritain and his wife Raïssa, Chagall also exposed a wider Christian public to visual Judeo-Christian themes.

The historian Jules Isaac offered similar allegories. In the last lines of *Jesus and Israel*, Isaac compared the "glow of the Auschwitz crematorium" to the suffering of Christ. "Do you not think," he asked Jews and Christians, "that it mingles with another glow, that of the Cross?"[130] In his best-selling *Le dernier des justes* [*The Last of the Just*, 1959], the Jewish writer and Goncourt Prize recipient André Schwarz-Bart likewise helped Christians grapple with the Jewish tragedy in their own terms.[131] A chronicle of persecution from the Crusades to the Third Reich, the novel portrayed Jewish history through the sacrifice of *tzadikim* or "Just Men"

---

[129] See *Chagall, Love, War and Exile*, Jewish Museum of New York, 2014; Ziva Amishai-Maizels, "Christological Symbolism of the Holocaust," *Holocaust and Genocide Studies* 3, no. 4 (1988): 457–481. On "Jews on the Cross" in Yiddish literature and arts, see David G. Roskies, *Against the Apocalypse: Responses to Catastrophe in Modern Jewish Culture* (1984), 258–313.

[130] *Jesus and Israel*, op. cit., 400. See also Nina Valbousquet, "Conscience historique et mémorielle du génocide: Jules Isaac et Jésus et Israël, rescapés de la Shoah," *Archives Juives* 51, no. 2 (2018): 78–98.

[131] André Schwarz-Bart, *Le dernier des justes* (Paris: Seuil, 1959).

across generations. Ending with the assassination of Ernie Lévy, the last of a long succession of Just, Schwarz-Bart's narrative inspired Christian compassion: Ernie's voluntary deportation to Auschwitz to accompany Jewish children to their death unmistakably evoked Jesus's humility. "There, my little lambs," Ernie tells the young victims before sharing their fate in the gas chamber. Neither Schwarz-Bart's catholic admirers nor his offended Jewish critics missed the Christian signposts interspersed throughout the novel.[132] But 1 million readers in France alone did not close the book with supremacist Christian thoughts. Through themes rooted in Christian culture, Schwarz-Bart led them to philosemitism through the lens of Holocaust sacrifice.

Paradoxically, however, the most effective Jewish contribution to the "Judeo-Christianization" of the Holocaust was silence: The invisibility of humiliation in the first survivor testimonies collected after the war left this theme ripe for Christian taking. European Jews, of course, recognized from the start of the Nazi onslaught the humiliating dimension of their catastrophe. "Jews have been humiliated to the level of lepers, of fourth-class citizens," already wrote in 1938 the historian and future chronicler of the Warsaw Ghetto Emmanuel Ringelblum. After the War, Polish or Soviet Jewish survivors recognized that the cruelty they endured broke them psychologically. Some of their testimonies are replete with accounts of humiliation and powerlessness.[133]

The trope of humiliation did not, however, prominently appear in the first interviews conducted among Jewish survivors in Central and Western Europe. In July 1946, the American psychologist David Boder crossed the Atlantic to record their experiences, "not only in their own language but in their own voices."[134] Only a few of his 130 interlocutors in France, Germany, Switzerland, and Italy admitted to feelings of humiliation. "The years of German occupation," recounted a French Jew who survived in hiding, "will remain for the rest of our lives the bitterest memory of shame, despair and humiliation." In David Boder's collection of testimonies, humiliation was implicit yet seldom expressed.[135] Primo Levi's *If This Is a Man*, first published in 1947 and reissued in 1958, exemplified the inadequacy of "humiliation" when attempting to speak

---

[132] Philip Nord, *After the Deportation*, op. cit., 247–256.
[133] Natalia Aleksiun, "Holocaust Testimonies in Eastern Europe in the Immediate Postwar Period" in Kata Bohus et al. (eds.), *Our Courage: Jews in Europe 1945–48* (Oldenbourg: De Gruyter, 2021), 28–43.
[134] Cited in Alan Rosen, *The Wonder of Their Voices: The 1946 Holocaust Interviews with David Boder* (Oxford: Oxford University Press, 2010), 50.
[135] David Boder's interviews, published by the *Voices from the Past* project at the University of Illinois, are available at: https://voices.library.iit.edu.

about Auschwitz. Levi's narrative features the word only once: "We have to ask permission to go to the latrines with humiliating frequency." But the camp experience, while humiliating, transcended humiliation. Levi's iconic Muselmann, the prostrated "Muslim" prisoner passively awaiting death, symbolized post-humiliation: a moral atrocity no longer representable through shame, guilt, or torture. In Auschwitz, Mauriac wrote in his preface of *La Nuit*, Wiesel was "humiliated" beyond human comprehension. But in his account of Auschwitz Wiesel never used the word: "Humiliation" leaped to the Christian philosemitic eye, but like Primo Levi, the future canonical author deemed the word unsuitable to represent the abyss.

Although cognizant of German dehumanization tactics, the first Jewish historians of the Holocaust contributed to the marginalization of humiliation in Jewish memory, while Judeo-Christian Catholics conversely harped on the theme. In 1947, the Polish Jewish scholar Philip Friedman, one of the founders of Holocaust research, pleaded for the collection of oral testimonies to "reconstruct the humiliation, the deportations, the massacres."[136] Friedman's chronological sequence revealed, however, the limited importance of humiliation in early Holocaust historiography – only the first step toward extermination. From Léon Poliakov's *Bréviaire de la haine* (*Harvest of Hate*, 1951), through Gerald Reitlinger's *The Final Solution* (1953) to Raul Hilberg's *The Destruction of European Jews* (1961), the Holocaust received an overarching meaning of death machinery. In the first decade of the state of Israel's existence, to be sure, collective humiliation found a place in Israeli remembrance: It remained the central meaning ascribed to the catastrophe. But in early Israeli representations of the genocide, the disgrace of the Holocaust was also erased through the heroism of ghetto fighters, the struggle of Jewish partisans, and the creation of a Jewish state. After 1961, the documentary evidence produced during the Eichmann Trial redirected Israeli memories toward the trope of industrial extermination.[137]

That Nazism simultaneously sought the humiliation and the annihilation of Jews only became apparent in Holocaust historiography after the Cold War. In 1991, the literary scholar Lawrence Langer discovered in oral testimonies a "humiliated memory" buried for decades.

---

[136] Dan Michman, *Holocaust Historiography: A Jewish Perspective: Conceptualizations, Terminology, Approaches and Fundamental Issues* (London: Vallentine Mitchell, 2003), 130.
[137] Idit Gil, "The Shoah in Israeli Collective Memory: Changes in Meanings and Protagonists," *History and Memory* 32, no. 1 (2012): 76–101; see also Orna Kenan, *Between Memory and History: The Evolution of Israeli Historiography of the Holocaust, 1945–1961* (Bern: Peter Lang, 2012).

"Besieging the self," argued Langer, humiliation "recalls an utter distress." In a seminal essay published in 1996, Avishai Margalit and Gabriel Motzkin argued that the uniqueness of the Jewish genocide was not its unprecedented scale but the combination of humiliation and extermination, two complementary forms of exclusion from humankind. "Since the Nazis had a unique conception of their racial enemies," wrote the two scholars, "they devised a unique fusion of humiliation and death in order to destroy them."[138] French Catholic thinkers in the 1940s and 1950s knew this all along. Calvary and Crucifixion prepared them to see Christian humiliation in the darkness of Jewish destruction. For them, as for the few Jews who helped them insert the genocide into a Christian framework, the Judeo-Christian narrative of Jewish suffering already amounted to Holocaust memory: a "Holocaust consciousness" predating its secularization during the long 1960s.

---

[138] Lawrence Langer, *Holocaust Testimonies: The Ruins of Memories* (New Haven: Yale University Press, 1991), 77–121; Avishai Margalit and Gabriel Motzkin, "The Uniqueness of the Holocaust," *Philosophy & Public Affairs* 25, no. 1 (1996): 65–83.

6   "The Long 1960s" and the Jews (1960–1980)

The 1960s enjoy a place of choice among decades deemed "long" in historical scholarship. The period of unprecedented affluence in Western Europe began in the late 1950s; the aftershock of generational rebellion was still felt in the late 1970s. The "long 1960s," however, were also a pivotal period for postwar philosemitism. Although legal means against defamation already existed before 1960, the criminalization of anti-Jewish incitement strengthened the moratorium on antisemitism enforced since 1945. The weakening of antisemitism in public opinion also coincided with the redeployment of racism toward non-European immigrants; and with the entry of the Holocaust into public culture. In West Germany, the student protests of 1967–68 mounted the first postwar challenge against the Federal Republic's official philosemitism. Yet as in France, the 1968 antiauthoritarian revolt generated critical discussions on guilt and complicity. The "year of the barricades" also included a vocal anti-Zionist component. But if the left of the left delegitimized the Jewish state, a new Western European consensus on Israel emerged at the dawn of the two-state solution era.

Antisemitism as Hate Speech

"Antisemitism has now ceased to be the main problem of World Jewry," announced the representative of the World Jewish Congress at the United Nations in 1959.[1] But the 1960s began with a spate of antisemitic vandalism in West Germany, a "Swastika Epidemic" soon to spread across borders. After two neo-Nazi youth defaced the Cologne synagogue on Christmas eve 1959, Jewish houses of worship and cemeteries were desecrated in other cities. By mid February, hundreds of antisemitic incidents had been recorded across all West German states. Potentially instigated

---

[1] The British rabbi and World Jewish Congress representative Maurice Perlzweig is cited in James Loeffler, *Rootless Cosmopolitans: Jews and Human Rights in the Twentieth Century* (New Haven: Yale University Press, 2018), 232.

by the Soviet KGB, which sought to discredit the Federal Republic by enlisting far-right radicals, the Swastika Epidemic revived the specter of Nazism fifteen years after Hitler's defeat. For the Central Council of Jews in Germany, this episode revealed "a mystical avowal of the Nazi past" and a "hatred without Jews" after the Holocaust.[2]

Fears of international repercussions, however, prompted Bonn to reassure "the whole world that the Germany of today totally rejects anti-Semitism." In a televised address delivered on January 16, 1960, Konrad Adenauer pledged to his "fellow Jewish citizens" that the "state is behind them with all its power." Antisemitism, in Adenauer's view, was not an endemic problem but the disease of marginal hoodlums. Student protests in Cologne, Frankfurt, Munich, and West Berlin nonetheless kept the *Schmierwelle* ("wave of outrage") on the national agenda. The parliamentary socialist opposition, for its part, pressured Adenauer to not minimize German responsibility. In May 1960, the Bundestag unanimously modified article 130 of the German Penal Code to make incitement against "a national, racial, religious group or a group defined by their ethnic origins" a criminal offense. Thousands of former Nazis had since 1949 obtained amnesty and government pensions, or occupied leading positions in civil service and public life. Yet the anti-incitement bill opened a new avenue for the prosecution of antisemitic libel in the Federal Republic.[3] In post-Fascist Italy, by comparison, a tribunal acquitted a magistrate from Turin who in May 1961 called Jews "God-killers deprived of morality." The defendant claimed in his defense that as an antifascist partisan he had personally saved Jews during the war. The court ruled that his statement was of strict religious nature and "did not constitute an offense." Proposed amendments to the 1930 Penal Code drafted under Mussolini reassured the small Italian Jewish community, but the first law prohibiting hate speech was only passed in 1975.[4]

While simultaneously reaching North America and other parts of the globe, the Swastika Epidemic also swept through Western Europe.

---

[2] On the likely involvement of the KGB, see Thomas Rid, *Active Measures: The Secret History of Disinformation and Political Warfare* (New York: Farrar, Straus, and Giroux, 2020), 184–199; *American Jewish Yearbook (AJYB)* 62, no. (1961): 261.

[3] Peter Schönbach, *Reaktionen auf die antisemitische welle im Winter 1959–1960* (Frankfurt am Main: Europäischeverlaganstalt, 1961); Werner Bergmann, *Antisemitismus in öffentlichen Konflikten: Kollektives Lernen in der politischen Kultur der Bundesrepublik 1949–1989* (Frankfurt am Main: Campus Verlag, 1997), 235–250.

[4] On the Giovanni Durando affair (1961–1963), see AJYB (63), 1962, 326; Annalisa Capristo, "Tullia Zevi, la stampa cattolica e il processo Eichmann," *La Rassegna Mensile di Israel* 85, no. 3 (September–December 2019): 23–49; Stephen Skinner, "Tainted Law? The Italian Penal Code, Fascism and Democracy," *International Journal of Law in Context* 7, no. 4 (2011): 723–746.

Antisemitic inscriptions were spotted in thirty Italian cities; threatening letters were sent to Jewish community leaders in Amsterdam; Nazi scribblings appeared in Brussels and Antwerp; 119 youth were arrested for neo-Nazi activities in Austria; similar incidents were reported in Switzerland, Scandinavia, and Greece.[5] In France, hundreds of anti-Jewish slogans scrawled on synagogues, schools, or the hallways of the Parisian subway sparked public indignation. As in West Germany, the upsurge of antisemitism directed attention to the penalization of hate speech. The existing Marchandeau Law technically allowed courts to prosecute attacks in the press against racial and religious groups. But the burden placed on plaintiffs to prove that injurious statements also intended to incite limited the law's applicability. Over the next decade, the left-wing Movement against Racism, Antisemitism and for Peace (MRAP) lobbied lawmakers for more stringent legislation. In 1972, the landmark Pleven Law unanimously adopted by the French parliament offered broad criminal and civil remedies against antisemitic and racist slander: a legal interventionism contrasting with the First Amendment protections liberally afforded to hate speech in the United States.[6]

In London, a series of synagogue profanations began in Notting Hill on December 30, 1959 and peaked in February 1960. The radicalization of fringe extreme right organizations, however, allowed antisemitic agitation to persist. On July 1, 1962, Colin Jordan's National Socialist Movement attempted to hold a rally in Trafalgar Square under the slogan "Free Britain from Jewish control." Between March and July 1965, Jordan's followers attacked fifteen synagogues in London and the provinces.[7] Passed under Harold Wilson's Labour government, the 1965 Race Relations Act chiefly penalized discrimination against Blacks and South Asians "in places of public resort." One of its sections, however, also outlawed "any intent to stir up hatred against any section of the public (...) distinguished by colour, race, or ethnic, or national origins." The absence of religious groups from the list of protected categories raised doubts about the law's intent. Wary of the categorization of British Jews

---

[5] Paola Bertilotti, "Anatomie d'une crise: Les épisodes antisémites de l'hiver 1959–1960 en Italie," *Laboratoire italien* 11 (2011), available at: http://journals.openedition.org/laboratoireitalien/576; Sidney Liskofsky, "International Swastika Outbreak," *American Jewish Yearbook* (AJYB), 62 (1961): 209–213.
[6] Emmanuel Debono, *Le racisme dans le prétoire: Antisémitisme, racisme et xénophobie devant la justice* (Paris: Presses Universitaires de France, 2019), 575–587; Eric Bleich, *Race Politics in Britain and France: Ideas and Policymaking since the 1960s* (Cambridge: Cambridge University Press, 2003), 127–141.
[7] Nigel Copsey, "A Defining Decade? Swastikas, Eichmann and Arson in 1960s Britain" in Tom Lawson and Andy Pearce (eds.), *The Palgrave Handbook of Britain and the Holocaust* (Cham: Palgrave Macmillan, 2020), 303–324.

as a racial or ethnic group, the Board of Jewish Deputies wondered if the Act effectively covered the implicitly "white" Anglo-Jewish community. Despite its ambiguous wording, however, the 1965 Race Relations Act denied written or spoken antisemitic propaganda the privilege of freedom of speech.[8] Founded in 1967, the far-right National Front initially eschewed blatant anti-Jewish rhetoric but the fringe party, like other neo-fascists and Holocaust revisionists in Western Europe, rapidly learned how to circumvent prohibition.[9] Yet in West Germany (1960), Britain (1965), France (1972), and most member states of the EEC soon after, hate-speech laws not only criminalized anti-Jewish incitement but also defamatory or provocative language: An "anti-antisemitic" legal architecture later enriched by memory laws against Holocaust denial passed within the European Union.[10]

Antisemitism on the Wane

Despite their ominous beginnings, the 1960s also confirmed the decline of overt antisemitic sentiment in public opinion. Progress, to be sure, was only relative in the Federal Republic. In 1965, 19 percent of respondents to a survey answered "yes" to the question "Would Germany be better off without Jews?" – in a country in which the Jewish population did not exceed 35,000 people. This result indicated improvement from a similar poll conducted in 1952, yet nearly half of the interviewees cautiously declined to answer. Although the number of antisemitic hate crimes dropped after 1960, the defacement of Jewish cemeteries continued to make headlines. Public outrage, however, grew more vocal. In Bamberg, for instance, flags were flown at half-mast and 5,000 residents "assembled in a rainstorm to express their horror" after Jewish tombstones were profaned in June 1965.[11] The nationalist weekly *Deutsche National-Zeitung* still had over 100,000 readers in the mid 1960s, but loud condemnations of far-right hooliganism showed the world that democratic Germans rejected extremism.

---

[8] Gavin Schaffer, "Legislating against Hatred: Meaning and Motive in Section Six of the Race Relations Act of 1965" *Twentieth Century British History* 25, no. 2 (2014): 251–275; Christopher Hilliard, "Words That Disturb the State: Hate Speech and the Lessons of Fascism in Britain, 1930s–1960s," *The Journal of Modern History* 88, no. 4 (December 2016): 764–796; Raphael Langham, *250 Years of Convention and Contention: A History of the Board of Deputies of British Jews, 1760–2010* (London: Vallentine Mitchell, 2010), 245–246.

[9] Michael Billig, *Fascists: A Social Psychological View of the National Front* (London: Academic Press, 1976), 164–184.

[10] Erik Bleich, "The Rise of Hate Speech and Hate Crimes Laws in Liberal Democracies," *Journal of Ethnic and Migration Studies* 6, no. 37 (July 2011): 917–934.

[11] AJYB, Vol. 67 (1966), 353.

As public opinion research regularly confirmed, however, "secondary antisemitism" – the defense mechanism against guilt identified since the mid 1950s by Frankfurt School researchers – substituted the tabooed racism of the Third Reich era. Directed against Jewish disrupters of German good conscience, "secondary antisemitism" flourished because of guilt feelings needed to be repressed. "It seems the Germans will never forgive us Auschwitz," stated the German-Jewish publicist Hilde Walter in 1967 – a phrase later popularized by other critics of the phenomenon.[12] Yet if Jews – or mere thought of them – inspired resentment, displays of Israeli Jewishness in West German popular culture did not trigger similar defensiveness. In 1966, the public elected the twenty-five-year-old Esther Ofarim singer of the year. The photogenic Daliah Lavi elicited in turn similar fascination.[13] Enthusiasm for exotic Israeli female performers, or for Ephraim Kishon's satirical essays translated from Hebrew, confirmed that for many citizens of the Federal Republic in the mid-to-late 1960s, distant Jews from Israel felt more *heimlich* or "familiar" than the puny Jewish community.

In Austria, the first governmental study of antisemitism was carried out in October 1966. A surprising 39 percent of respondents to a questionnaire agreed then that "the massacre of the Jews was the greatest shame of our century."[14] The acquittal by jury courts of Austrian Nazis charged for wartime crimes nonetheless revealed hostility to the punishment of Holocaust perpetrators. Franz Razesberger, accused of ordering the killing of hundreds of Jews in Ukraine, walked free in July 1961. Charges against ghetto commander Franz Murer, known as the "Butcher of Vilnius," were dropped in June 1963. Erich Rajakowitsch received a two-and-a-half-year prison sentence in March 1965 for his role in the deportation of Dutch Jews but only spent six months in jail. In February 1966, a jury in Salzburg acquitted Johann and Wilhelm Mauer for their active part in the execution of 12,000 Polish Jews from the Stanislaw ghetto. The two brothers were, respectively, sentenced to twelve and eight years in prison a few months later. But in October 1966, Viennese jurors exculpated Franz Novak, Adolf Eichmann's railroad timetable expert, on behalf of his "obligation to obey binding orders."[15]

---

[12] Hilde Walter cited in Leo Katcher, *Post Mortem: The Jews in Germany Now* (London: Hamish Hamilton, 1968), 89.
[13] Michael Brenner (ed.), *A History of Jews in Germany since 1945* (Bloomington, IN: Indiana University Press, 2018), 281–282.
[14] Paul Lendvai, "The Old Austria and the New Nazis," *Commentary* (September 1967): 81–88.
[15] Thomas Albrich, Winfried R. Garscha, and Martin F. Polaschek (eds.), *Holocaust und Kriegsverbrechen vor Gericht. Der Fall Österreich* (Innsbruck: StudienVerlag, 2006).

The Novak ruling, like the scandal caused in 1965 by the unrepentant Nazi and economics professor Taras Borodajkewycz, stirred up protests in leftist ranks as well as among resistance veterans and concentration camps survivors. "Front stage," democratic and republican Austria firmly stood against antisemitism, despite slips of the tongue in political discourse or in the press. "Backstage," a study group found in 1970, negative stereotypes of Jews, in a country where the Jewish community amounted to 0.1 percent of the population, coexisted with democratic norms.[16] The appointment of the Jewish-born Bruno Kreisky to the chairmanship of the socialist party in February 1967 nonetheless suggested that antisemitism was on the wane. Appointed federal chancellor in April 1970, Kreisky was not only the first Jew to ever govern a German-speaking country. He also became the first Jewish head of government in post-Holocaust Western Europe to hold office for a long period of time. Before him, the French Jewish prime ministers Léon Blum, René Mayer, and Pierre Mendès-France only completed short tenures during the unstable Fourth Republic (1946–58). Upon Kreisky's reelection in 1971, the *New York Times* did not hesitate to declare that "anti-Semitism has ceased to be a decisive factor in Austrian politics."[17]

Surveys of public opinion were less optimistic. A poll conducted in 1973 indicated that 70 percent of the Austrian population above the age of sixteen held antisemitic feelings. But depending on the type of questions asked, an equal proportion expressed either strong or mild "philosemitic tendencies." Antisemitic animus and admiration for imputed Jewish traits – "intelligence," "group solidarity," and "contributors to culture" – complemented each other.[18] The popular Kreisky, in any case, always minored down his Jewish roots. Far-right politicians never forgot his origins but forgave them in exchange of political benefits. Kreisky voters, for their part, did not elect a public Jew: Despite his recognizable Viennese Jewish humor, the socialist prime minister in office between

---

[16] Christian Fleck and Albert Müller, "Front-Stage and Back-Stage: The Problem of Measuring Post-Nazi Antisemitism in Austria" in Stein U. Larsen and Bernt Hagtvet (eds.), *Modern Europe after Fascism, 1943–1980s* (Boulder, CO: University of Colorado Press, 1995), 436–454; Ruth Wodak, "Turning the Tables: Antisemitic Discourse in Post-War Austria," *Discourse & Society* 2, no. 1 (1991): 65–83.

[17] Herbert Pierre Sacher, "Kreisky and the Jews" in Günter Bischof and Anton Pelinka (eds.), *The Kreisky Era in Austria* (New Brunswick, NJ: Transaction Publishers, 1994), 10–31.

[18] See figures in "Antisemitismus in Österreich 1968–1982," *Journal für Sozialforschung* 23, no. 2 (1983): 205–244; Gerhard Botz, "Non-Jews and Jews in Austria" in Michael A. Signer (ed.), *Humanity at the Limit: The Impact of the Holocaust on Jews and Christians* (Bloomington, IN: Indiana University Press, 2000), 265–279.

1970 and 1983 always denied any connection to a Jewish people whose existence he denied. His controversial defense of politicians with a Nazi past, acrimonious relationship with Simon Wiesenthal, misgivings about Zionism, and amicable relationship with Yasser Arafat did not earn him many Jewish friends – even if the chancellor also facilitated the transit of Soviet Jews through Vienna. To Austrians, "Kaiser Bruno" offered an unthreatening "non-Jewish-Jewishness" compatible with social democratic tolerance and the postwar "victim thesis." In traditionally socialist Vienna, surveys revealed in 1973 and 1976, the population harbored less prejudice than in other parts of the country: 30 percent of the city's inhabitants even fell under the "strong philosemite" category. Yet Viennese or not, Kreisky sympathizers also belonged to the 67 percent of Austrians who still opposed any acknowledgment of the country's responsibility in the Holocaust, let alone the compensation of spoliated Jewish survivors.[19]

Throughout the 1960s, correspondents for the *American Jewish Yearbook* in Belgium, the Netherlands, and Italy, regularly reported on the appearance of antisemitic articles in Flemish, far-right or Catholic publications.[20] Swastika daubings, neofascist activism, and the profanation of tombstones also remained a matter of concern. But for the small Jewish communities in these countries, as well as larger ones in France and Britain, the decade of modernization, secularization, and mass consumption, was also a period of security and belonging. Approximately 250,000 Jews from decolonized North Africa successfully resettled in France from the late 1950s to the mid 1960s, even if antagonistic feelings subsided in part of the population. According to a poll conducted in December 1966, one out of every three French citizens objected to having a Jewish son or daughter-in-law; one out of two did not want a president of Jewish origin. But progress was registered in other areas: 17% now believed that Jews "were not really French," as opposed to 37% in 1946. Few respondents avowed feelings of hostility in the presence of Jews, while 82% remained indifferent to this issue. In the wake of France's defeat in Algeria, negative views of Arabs were far more prevalent: In 1966, 60% of the French public had a "negative opinion" of Algerian, Moroccan, and Tunisian labor migrants, while 62%

---

[19] Marin, "Antisemitismus in Österreich 1968–1982," op. cit., 228. For statistical data on antisemitic and philosemitic attitudes in Austria, see also *Antisemitismus in Österreich. Historische Vergleichsdaten 1968–2018* (Vienna: Braintrust GmbH, 2019), available at: www.antisemitismus2018.at/wp-content/uploads/Antisemitismus-in-Österreich-2018_Historische-Vergleichsdaten.pdf.

[20] See for Italy Alfonso M. Di Nola, *Antisemitismo in Italia 1962–1972* (Florence: Vallecchi, 1973).

found them "too numerous."[21] The emergence of a "Muslim problem" in postcolonial France coincided with the growing legitimation of Jewish identity in French society. As the sociologist Georges Lévitte observed in 1966, "it is now possible for a Jew to be a Frenchman (...) and be different at the same time."[22] On November 27, 1967, Charles de Gaulle's unpleasant evocation of a "Jewish people (...) sure of itself and domineering" shocked French Jews precisely because it appeared to roll back two decades of progress: The delegitimization of antisemitism in the public domain, and the ongoing normalization of Jewish difference in a Republic until then expecting polite confessionalism from its *israélite* citizenry.[23]

In Britain, observed the Jewish historian Edgar Samuel in 1967, "overt antisemitism is out of fashion." Jews still heard snide remarks about them, but racism was now "mostly directed against colored immigrants, particularly in areas suffering from severe housing shortages." The Polish-born Isaac Deutscher was more pessimistic. "I know that looking for a flat in London, in Hampstead, say," the Marxist scholar commented, "you can be told that the neighbors would object to a Negro tenant or a Jew moving in, but they would certainly welcome you as an 'exception'."[24] Yet like Arabophobia in France, xenophobia directed against Afro-Caribbeans and South Asians symmetrically reinforced the "whiteness" of British Jews. In April 1968, Enoch Powell's notorious *Rivers of Blood* speech stoked fears of "actual domination, first over fellow immigrants and then over the rest of the population." Powell's racially charged address, however, did not warn Britons against a potential Jewish peril: For the Tory forerunner of "great replacement theory," Jews stood on the right side of the color line. The Labour politician Tony Benn countered that despite Powell's avoidance of anti-Jewish rhetoric, "anti-Semitism is waiting to be exploited as Mosley exploited it before."[25] But Powell's racialism did not posit incompatibility between Jewishness and Englishness: The conservative rising star Margaret Thatcher was already convinced

---

[21] Doris Bensimon and Jeannine Verdès-Leroux, "Les Français et le problème juif," *Archives de sociologie des religions* 29 (1970): 53–91; Yvan Gastaut, *L'immigration et l'opinion francaise en France sous la Ve Republique* (Paris: Seuil, 2000), 77–78.
[22] Cited in Bernard Wasserstein, *Vanishing Diaspora: The Jews of Europe since 1945* (London: Penguin Books, 1996), 82.
[23] Gadi Heimann, "From 'Irresponsible' to 'Immoral': The Shifts in de Gaulle's Perception of Israel and the Jews," *Journal of Contemporary History* 46, no. 4 (October 2011): 897–919.
[24] AJYB 68 (1967), 305; Isaac Deutscher, *The Non-Jewish Jew*, op. cit., 58.
[25] Cited in Tony Kushner, "Offending the Memory? The Holocaust and Pressure Group Politics" in Tony Kushner and Nadia Valman (eds.), *Philosemitism, Antisemitism and "the Jews"* (London: Routledge, 2004), 246–265.

of their special affinities.[26] Anglo-Jewry, however, did not merely owe its "whiteness" to anti-foreigner sentiment. Since the late 1950s, suburbanization and upward mobility secured its place within the affluent white middle class. That the image of Israel in public opinion remained predominantly positive before and in the immediate aftermath of the Six-Day War also contributed to a favorable climate. In a BBC television debate held in June 1968 on whether "the Arab case is more powerful than the Israeli," a panel of thirty lawyers returned a three to one verdict in favor of the Jewish state.[27]

Twenty years after the end of the war, *public* antisemitism in Western Europe was no longer significant while anti-immigrant sentiment deflected attention from the "Jewish problem." In West Germany, hate crimes substantially decreased after 1960, although neo-nationalist weeklies and the far-right regularly dog-whistled antisemitism to their readers and followers.[28] In 1967, however, the French historian Léon Poliakov noted in Western Europe a "regression [of antisemitism] compared to the first half of the current century."[29] The mid-to-late 1960s also witnessed a shift from confessionalism to public Jewishness, most notably in France where newly transplanted North African Jews departed from the assimilationist French Jewish tradition. In ethnocentric England, Jews did not express their religious or cultural distinctiveness demonstratively. Yet in the wake of the Six-Day War, a new generation of Jewish leaders shied away from anglicization in favor of a consciously articulated Jewish identity.[30]

This favorable climate did not prevent the return of old forms of Judeophobia believed to have disappeared from the collective psyche. In France, the "Orléans Rumor" of May 1969 demonstrated that in the midst of "thirty glorious years" of economic growth and modernization, devilish images of Jews resurfaced effortlessly. The contagious rumor about local Jewish business owners trafficking in Christian women, wrote then the sociologist Edgar Morin, indicated the subterranean existence of a "modern Middle Age." Anti-Judaism similarly survived the modernist spirit of Vatican II. In 1969, as in earlier years, the inhabitants of the Bavarian village of Oberammergau fiercely opposed revisions to their

---

[26] Robert Philpot, *Margaret Thatcher: The Honorary Jew* (London: Biteback Publishing Ltd, 2011), 12–13.
[27] AJYB 70 (1969), 327.
[28] Theodor Adorno, *Aspects of the Right-Wing Extremism (1967)* (Cambridge: Polity Press, 2020), 22–23.
[29] Cited in Joëlle Allouche-Benayoun et al., *L'antisémitisme en France: rémanences ou émergences?* (Paris: Hermann, 2022), 9.
[30] Todd M. Endelman, *The Jews of Britain, 1656 to 2000* (Berkeley, CA: University of California Press, 2002), 237–238.

notoriously anti-Judaic Passion Play. On Italian television, the series *The Acts of the Apostles* directed by Roberto Rossellini (1969) did nothing to challenge old accusations of deicide.[31] Yet even historians convinced that "the virus of antisemitism is embedded in the heart and the very bloodstream of European society and culture" have had to pause. The "longest hatred," according to this eternalist view, only took a brief vacation after the Holocaust. For proponents of the "new Judeophobia" thesis, the rise of radical anti-Zionism after the Six-Day War spelled the end of this short respite. Yet the 1960s, conceded a leading representative of this school of thought, nevertheless remained "one of the most philo-Semitic in European and Western history."[32]

Holocaust Memory and Public Culture (1961–1967)

The period ranging from the 1961 Eichmann trial to the Six-Day War was also a transitional moment in the encounter between West European societies and the Holocaust. Although its impact differed from country to country, the televised court proceedings made the realities of the Final Solution comprehensible to a wider public.[33] In the Federal Republic, however, many still championed the idea of German victimhood. After the Soviets built the Berlin Wall in 1961, sixty-one percent of the population believed that "what the communists do today is just as bad as, or even worse than, what Eichmann is accused of." His prosecution in Jerusalem, followed by the landmark Auschwitz Trial held in Frankfurt between 1963 and 1965, nevertheless forced the image of German perpetrators on a population reluctant to admit culpability. Although less publicized, court cases against the German personnel of Treblinka (1964), Sobibor (1965), Belzec (1965), and Chelmno (1962–65), also fulfilled a pedagogical function. They nonetheless encouraged demands for an end to accountability. Proceedings against former concentration camp personnel, demanded a majority of respondents to a poll conducted in 1965, should draw a final line under the Third Reich era.[34]

Since the late 1950s, however, a cohort of male academics, writers, and social commentators born in the 1920s and the early 1930s – the so-called 1945ers who like Günther Grass, Jürgen Habermas, Martin

---

[31] Edgar Morin, *La rumeur d'Orléans* (Paris: Seuil, 1969), 13; AJYB 71 (1970), 452–453 and 440.
[32] Robert S. Wistrich, "Anti-Semitism in Europe after 1945" in *Terms of Survival: The Jewish World since 1945* (London: Routledge, 1995), 269–296.
[33] David Cesarani (ed.), *After Eichmann: Collective Memory of the Holocaust after 1961* (London: Routledge, 2014).
[34] Caroline Sharples, *Postwar Germany and the Holocaust* (London: Bloomsbury, 2016), 78–79.

Walser, or Hans-Magnus Enzensberger experienced the collapse of the Third Reich as young adults – redirected memories of the war from exculpation to criticism.[35] Signs of change were also discernable in visual culture. In 1960, Gerhard Schoenberner's photobook *Der gelbe Stern* [*The Yellow Star*] put into circulation images of Holocaust atrocities unseen by the public since the Nuremberg Trials.[36] In schools, history teaching underwent slow transformation. But compared to the evasive curriculum of the 1950s, the revised or new history textbooks introduced in the early 1960s became more explicit on German crimes against the Jews.[37] Meanwhile, three documentaries on the Nazi era including footage of ghettos and extermination camps were shown on West German television in 1960–61.[38] Other television programs such as *Jews in Germany Today: Taking Stock of a Loss* (1963) contributed to a "fashionable philo-Semitism" noticed within the educated public.[39] In 1964, the exhibition *Monumenta Synagoga: 2000 Years of History and Culture of the Jews Along the Rhine* organized in Cologne attracted 67,000 visitors. Curiosity for the vanished German Jewish past went hand in hand with increased interest in the planned murder of European Jews. In Frankfurt, exhibitions on the Warsaw Ghetto (1963) and Auschwitz (1964), respectively, drew 61,000 and 88,000 predominantly young visitors.[40] In October 1965, Peter Weiss's *Die Ermittlung* [*The Investigation*], based on statements made during the Auschwitz Trial, was performed in twelve theater stages

---

[35] Konrad H. Jarausch, "Critical Memory and Civil Society: The Impact of the 1960s on German Debates about the Past" in Philipp Gassert and Alan E. Steinweiss (eds.), *Coping with the German Past: West German Debates on Nazism and Generational Conflict, 1955-1975* (New York: Berghahn Books, 2006), 11–30. On "1945ers," see Dirk A. Moses, *German Intellectuals and the Nazi Past* (Cambridge: Cambridge University Press, 2007), 55–73.

[36] Robert Sackett, "Visions of Atrocity: Public Discussion of *Der gelbe Stern* in Early 1960s West Germany," *German History* 24 (Winter 2006): 526–556.

[37] Bodo von Borries, "The Third Reich in German History Textbooks since 1945," *Journal of Contemporary History* 38, no. 1 (2003): 45–62; Brian M. Puaca, "Mastering the Past? Nazism and the Holocaust in West German History Textbooks of the 1960s" in Zehavit Gross and E. Doyle Stevick (eds.), *As the Witnesses Fall Silent: 21st Century Holocaust Education in Curriculum, Policy and Practice* (Cham: Springer, 2015), 357–373.

[38] Christiane Fritsche, *Vergangenheitsbewältigung im Fernsehen: Westdeutsche filme über den Nationalsozialismus in der 1950er und 60er Jahren* (Munich: Martin Meidenbauer Verlag, 2003); 100–132; Christoph Classen, *Bilder der Vergangenheit. Die Zeit des Nationalsozialismus im Fernsehen der Bundesrepublik Deutschland 1955–1965* (Cologne: Böhlau Verlag, 1999), 115–127; Julie Maeck, *Montrer la Shoah à la television de 1960 à nos jours* (Paris: Nouveau Monde, 2009), 43–54 and 63–82.

[39] Norbert Muhlen, *The Survivors: A Report on the Jews in Germany Today* (New York: Thomas Y. Cowell, 1962), 150–172; Wulf Kansteiner, "What Is the Opposite of Genocide? Philosemitic Television in Germany, 1963–1995" in Jonathan Karp and Adam Sutcliffe (eds.), *Philosemitism in History*, 289–313.

[40] On these two exhibitions, see Cornelia Brink, *Auschwitz in der Paulskirche: Erinnerungspolitik in Fotoaustellungen der sechziger Jahre* (Marburg: Jonas, 2000).

(as well as four others in East Germany) and broadcast on national radio. The play documented the horrors of the camp and attacked German hypocrisy. In keeping with New Left interpretations of Auschwitz, *Die Ermittlung* also blamed the extermination of Jews on a "capitalist society driven to the most extreme perversion – exploitation even of blood, bones, ashes": The Jewish identity of the victims mattered less than neo-Marxist theory.[41] Weiss's anonymization of Jews in favor of "late capitalist" Auschwitz prefigured an attitude soon prevalent among radical students. Yet within the intellectual Left, a critical memory culture predicated on the integration of "Our Auschwitz" into national identity was already discernable before the Holocaust became "the Holocaust" of a later era.[42]

In Austria, the one-act satire *Der Herr Karl* (1961), plays shown on national television between 1963 and 1967, or the provocative song *Weg zur Arbeit* written in 1968 by the Jewish cabaret artist Georg Kreisler, questioned the dominant "victim thesis" without noticeable consequences for societal soul-searching. Literary authors who criticized historical amnesia, such as Ingeborg Bachmann or Ilse Aichinger, wrote and resided outside the country.[43] In schools, history textbooks in use in the 1960s only referred to the Holocaust allusively. One of them simply informed pupils that "tens of thousands [of Austrians] were tortured to death or executed in the torture chambers of the concentration camps."[44] Austrian socialists and communists, for their part, subsumed crimes perpetrated against the Jews within the memory of Mauthausen and its sub-camps. For the left, remembering the war during the 1960s meant honoring the anti-Nazi resistance movement against the commemoration of fallen soldiers who served in the Wehrmacht. This task was devolved to the *Documentation and Resistance Archive* founded in Vienna in 1963. But despite evidence compiled by Simon Wiesenthal's one-man research center in 1966, public debates over Austrian co-responsibility in the killing of European Jews did not occur before the

---

[41] Cited in Robert Cohen, *Understanding Peter Weiss* (Columbia, SC: University of South Carolina Press, 1993), 88–89.
[42] Martin Walser, "Our Auschwitz (1965)," in Thomas Kovach and Martin Walser (eds.), *The Burden of the Past: Martin Walser on German Identity* (Rochester, NY: Camden House, 2008), 5–22.
[43] Eva Waibel, "Zeitkritik im Hautabendprogramm. Fascismus und krieg im frühen österreichichen Ferhsehspiel" in Judith Keilbach et al. (eds.), *Völkermord zur Prime Time: Der Holocaust in Fernsehen* (Vienna: New Academic Press, 2019), 23–46; Dagmar C. G. Lorenz, "Austrian Responses to National Socialism and the Holocaust" in Katrin Kohl and Ritchie Robertson (eds.), *A History of Austrian Literature 1918–2000* (Rochester, NY: Camden House, 2006), 181–200.
[44] Peter Utgaard, "Remembering and Forgetting the Holocaust in Austrian Schools, 1955–1996" in Günther Bischof, Anton Pelinka, and Ferdinand Karlhofer (eds.), *The Vranitzky Era in Austria* (New York: Routledge, 2017), 201–215.

Friedrich Peter scandal (the far-right politician exposed as former SS infantry officer in 1975), the screening of the *Holocaust* TV miniseries in 1979 and above all, the Kurt Waldheim affair in the mid-to-late 1980s.[45]

The Holocaust, on the contrary, was a recurrent topic in French public conversations. In 1961, the Eichmann trial covered at one time by forty press correspondents highlighted the Jewish tragedy as a unique subject of memory. French society, observed Léon Poliakov in the aftermath of the trial, had "heard the message."[46] Three high-profile polemics involving prominent French intellectuals further familiarized the educated public with specific aspects of the Holocaust. One revolved around Rolf Hochhut's provocative play *Le vicaire* [*Der Stellvertreter*, 1963], an indictment of Pope Pie XII's failure to speak out against the annihilation of the Jews. The second followed the publication of Jean-François Steiner's *Treblinka* (1966), a scandalous yet best-selling account of the death camp prefaced by Simone de Beauvoir. A third controversy similarly revolving around the themes of Jewish passivity or complicity erupted in the wake of Hannah Arendt's *Eichmann in Jerusalem* translated into French in late 1966. "Auschwitz," as the Holocaust came to be named in the mid 1960s, found itself at the forefront of public discussion. A "Vichy syndrome" still prevented the examination of the French state's responsibility in the Final Solution, but the Jewish catastrophe itself already attracted significant attention.[47]

In the Netherlands, the twenty-one-episode series *De Bezetting* [*The Occupation*], Lou de Jong's historical documentary featured on black-and-white television between 1960 and 1965, raised the issue of the Dutch Jewish tragedy. In 1962, the Jewish academic and community leader Salomon Kleerekoper took notice of a "strong philosemitic current" in society, which he attributed to feelings of guilt now afflicting

---

[45] Margit Reiter, "Latenzen der Erinnerung: Der Holocaust im Gedächtnis der österreichischen Linken" in Jan Gerber, Phillipp Graf, and Anna Pollmann (eds.), *Geschichtsoptimismus und Katastrophenbewusstsein: Europa nach dem Holocaust* (Göttingen: Vandenhoeck & Ruprecht, 2022), 39–64; Oliver Rathkolb, *The Paradoxical Republic: Austria 1945–2020* (New York: Berghahn, 2021), 258–259; Heidemarie Uhl, "From Victim Myth to Co-Responsibility: Nazi Rule, World War Two, and The Holocaust in Austrian Memory" in Richard Ned Lebow, Wulf Kansteiner, and Claudio Fogu (eds.), *The Politics of Memory in Postwar Europe* (Durham: Duke University Press, 2006), 40–73.

[46] Cited in François Azouvi, *Le mythe du grand silence: Auschwitz, les Français, la mémoire* (Paris: Fayard, 2015), 267.

[47] On Holocaust memory in France from the Eichmann Trial to the Six-Day War, see Azouvi, *Le mythe du grand silence*, op. cit., 255–336; Philip Nord, *After the Deportation: Memory Battles in Postwar France* (Cambridge: Cambridge University Press, 2020), 287–307; Samuel Moyn, *A Holocaust Controversy: The Treblinka Affair in Postwar France* (Waltham, MA: Brandeis University, 2005).

his countrymen. A year later, the national commemoration of the war traditionally held on May 4 was rescheduled one day earlier day to allow the participation of Orthodox Jews without violation of the Shabbat.[48] A key milestone in the trajectory of Holocaust memory in the Netherlands was the publication of Jacques Presser's two-volume *Ondergang* [*The Destruction of the Dutch Jews*] in 1965. "The book concerns the history of a murder," announced the Jewish historian, "the murderers were Germans and the murdered, Jews." But Presser also exposed the role of part of the population in abetting the Final Solution. His narrative of the war, in which Jewish victimization no longer took the back seat to Dutch rescue and heroism, especially appealed to a young generation born in the 1940s: 140,000 copies of the book were sold in 1965 alone.[49] Written from the victims' perspective, *Ondergang* inscribed the Jewish tragedy into Dutch history. In the Netherlands as in Western Europe, no other scholarly study had until then placed the wartime experiences of Jews at the head of the public agenda.

In Italy, to be sure, Renzo de Felice's *History of Italian Jews under Fascism* (1961) heightened the profile of Fascist antisemitism in the public domain. But the historian also claimed that Mussolini's racial laws were unanimously rejected by the Italian population; and that even if facilitated by Fascists, the deportation of Jews carried out during the German occupation was a crime unrelated to Italy.[50] The closely watched Eichmann trial, during which the Israeli prosecutor Gideon Hausner praised the Italian people for its benevolence toward Jews, reinforced this favorable view. The case against Eichmann elicited interest in Jewish victims without redirecting attention toward the role of Italian functionaries or civilians in the persecution, round-up and deportation of approximately 8,000 Jews.[51] Newspapers of the Italian

---

[48] Kleerokoper cited in Evelien Gans and Remco Emsel (eds.), *The Holocaust, Israel and 'the Jew': Histories of Antisemitism in Postwar Dutch Society* (Amsterdam: Amsterdam University Press, 2016), 146; Bart Wallet, "The Battle for Jewish Sympathy: The House of Orange, The Dutch Jews, and Postwar Morality" in David J. Wertheim (ed.), *The Jew as Legitimation: Jewish-Gentile Relations beyond Antisemitism and Philosemitism* (Cham: Palgrave Macmillan, 2017), 256–274.

[49] On the impact of *Ondergang* on Dutch society, see Deborah Dwork and Robert-Jan van Pekt, "The Netherlands" in David Wyman (ed.), *The World Reacts to the Holocaust* (Baltimore, MD: The Johns Hopkins University Press, 1996), 45–80.

[50] Guri Schwarz, *After Mussolini: Jewish Lives and Jewish Memories in Postwar Italy* (London: Vallentine Mitchell, 2012), 160–167; Giuseppe Parlato, "Renzo de Felice and the 'Jewish Question' in Fascism" in Giovanni Orsina and Andrea Ungari (eds.), *The "Jewish Question" in the Territories Occupied by Italians, 1939–1943* (Rome: Viella, 2019), 23–36; Rebecca Clifford, *Commemorating the Holocaust. The Dilemmas of Remembrance in France and Italy* (Oxford: Oxford University Press, 2013), 103–104.

[51] Manuela Consonni, "The Impact of the Eichmann Event in Italy, 1961" in David Cesarani (ed.), *After Eichmann*, op. cit., 90–99; "Split at the Root: Italian Jewish Identity between Anti-Zionism and Philo-Semitism, 1961–1967" in Uzi Rebhun and

left opened their pages to Jewish testimonies or stressed the moral depravities of Nazism. The political heirs of the Italian resistance, however, still viewed the murder of European Jews as part of the battle between antifascism and fascism.[52] Nevertheless, through a series of films starting with Gillo Pontecorvo's controversial *Kapò* (1960); the success of Giorgio Bassani's autobiographical novel *The Garden of the Finzi-Continis* (1962); RAI television documentaries; the publication of thirty new survivor memoirs by the end of the decade; the translation of historical scholarship from English and French; and Primo Levi's growing prestige, the Holocaust made its first entry into Italian public culture over the course of the 1960s.[53]

In Britain, the Eichmann trial brought new information on the Final Solution but had scant effect on commemoration or historical research. In the 1960s, the niche field of Holocaust memorialization only existed thanks to Anglo-Jewish efforts. Jewish activists also invoked the Holocaust in their campaigns against neo-Nazi agitators.[54] Centered on the sacrifices needed to defeat Nazism on the home front and overseas, British collective remembrance of the war paid little attention to Jewish survivors who like the Polish-born refugee Kitty Hart felt that "they were not supposed to embarrass people by saying a word." As in the first fifteen postwar years, however, awareness of the Holocaust was preserved across a variety of media.[55] National television provides a case in point. Except for

---

Eli Lederhendler (eds.), *Research in Jewish Demography and Identity* (Brookline, MA: Academic Studies Press, 2015), 98–123; Valeria Galimi, "The Image of 'All Good Italians': The Eichmann Trial Seen from Italy," *Journal of Modern Italian Studies* 24, no. 1 (2009): 115–128.

[52] Alexandra Tarquini, "Left-Wing Intellectuals and the Representation of the Shoah in Italy: From the Second World War to the 1970s, Between Anti-Fascism and the Frankfurt School" in Alexandra Tarquini (ed.), *The European Left and the Jewish Question 1848–1992: Between Zionism and Antisemitism* (Cham: Palgrave Macmillan, 2021), 157–174.

[53] Robert Gordon, *The Holocaust in Italian Culture, 1944–2010* (Stanford, CA: Stanford University Press, 2012), 155–157; Millicent Marcus, *Italian Film in the Shadow of Auschwitz* (Toronto: University of Toronto Press, 2007), 35–45; Emiliano Perra, *Conflicts of Memory: The Reception of Holocaust Films and TV Programs in Italy, 1945 to the Present* (Oxford: Peter Lang, 2010), 74–75; Damiano Garofalo, "Breaking the Paradigm: Visualizing the Holocaust in Three of Liliana Cavani's TV Documentaries" in *Völkermord zur Prime Time*, op. cit., 241–252.

[54] Andy Pearce, *Holocaust Consciousness in Contemporary Britain* (New York: Routledge, 2014), 26–27; Joshua Cohen, "Somehow Getting Their Own Back on Hitler": British Antifascism and the Holocaust, 1960–1967" *Fascism* 9 (2020): 121–145.

[55] Tony Kushner, "Loose Connections? Britain and the 'Final Solution'" in Caroline Sharples and Olaf Jensen (eds.), *Britain and the Holocaust: Remembering War and Genocide* (Houndmills, Basingstoke, Hampshire: Palgrave Macmillan, 2013), 51–70; David Cesarani, "Challenging the Myth of Silence: Postwar Responses to the Destruction of European Jewry" in David Cesarani and Eric J. Sundquist (eds.), *After the Holocaust: Challenging the Myth of Silence* (London: Routledge, 2012), 15–38.

Warsaw Ghetto (1965) or *The Joel Brand Story* (1965), the BBC did not produce Holocaust-specific programs. But before the *World at War* series shown on Thames TV in 1973–74, which included a distinct episode on "genocide," the topic of Jewish persecution already had a regular presence in BBC documentaries on World War II. The catastrophe of European Jews was merely an add-on to war memories and only became a subject of public historical commemoration at the end of the twentieth century. Yet even if "in Britain, nothing has been done" to mark the Holocaust, as the Israeli historian Yehuda Bauer regretted in 1979, knowledge of German crimes against the Jews was already availed to a public on the whole uninterested in the details of the Final Solution.[56]

The Six-Day War and Holocaust Memory

In Britain as on the continent, mounting tensions between Israel and Egypt on the eve of the Six-Day War (June 5–10, 1967) sprang the Holocaust into consciousness through the lens of the Arab–Israeli conflict. Demystified historical scholarship has since illuminated the complexities of the road to confrontation. Gamal Abdel Nasser's long view was always to settle accounts with Israel at the appropriate time, but before his brinkmanship went over the brink, his goal was to improve Egypt's strategic position without immediate recourse to war. American and British military experts, in any case, doubted the possibility of Israeli defeat. And while intense fears of "second Auschwitz" gripped Israeli society, a confident military elite saw in Nasser's moves an opportunity to both smash the Egyptian army and enlarge the country's "Auschwitz borders."[57] Yet for anguished diaspora Jews, the prospect of Israel's annihilation awakened traumatic memories of the Nazi era – a watershed moment for Jewish communities across the world and for assimilated Jews who awakened to Jewishness in June 1967. Like other bellicose Arab statements relayed to the Western press by the Israeli Foreign Ministry, Nasser's announcement that in the event of "hostile action against Egypt or Syria (…) our objective goal will be the destruction of Israel" added to the angst-ridden

---

[56] James Jordan, "Beyond the Cesspit Beneath: The BBC and the Holocaust" in Tom Lawson and Andy Pearce (eds.), *The Palgrave Handbook of Britain and the Holocaust* (Cham: Palgrave Macmillan, 2020), 243–260.
[57] See among others William Roger Louis and Avi Shlaim (eds.), *The 1967 Arab-Israeli War: Origins and Consequences* (Cambridge: Cambridge University Press, 2012); Tom Segev, *1967: Israel and the War That Transformed the Middle East* (New York: Holt and Company, 2008); Idith Zertal, *Israel's Holocaust and the Politics of Nationhood* (Cambridge: Cambridge University Press, 2005), 115–127; Guy Laron, *The Six Day War: The Breaking of the Middle East* (New Haven: Yale University Press, 2017), 106–117.

atmosphere.[58] That in this speech Nasser conditioned "total battle" to an Israeli first strike did not diffuse tensions. "If Israel were destroyed," summarized on June 2 the future director of *Shoah* Claude Lanzmann, "it would be more serious than the Nazi Holocaust."[59]

The superposition of a Holocaust narrative on the Middle East crisis, however, was not only traceable in emotionally charged Jewish reactions. In France, the looming conflagration activated a vocabulary already rooted in public discourse. "Should [the Jews] lose Israel," stated a lead article in *Le Monde* on June 3, 1967, "it will never return. It is Auschwitz that will return."[60] Critics of triumphant Israel soon protested the "cynical exploitation of the dead of Dachau, Auschwitz and Treblinka" at the expense of occupied Palestinians. Yet on the eve of the conflict, both Jewish and non-Jewish defenders of Israel dramatized the escalation as a reenactment of Hitler's war against the Jews. Jean-Paul Sartre, for his part, found "unbearable to imagine that a Jewish community, no matter where or what it is, might again have to endure such torment and offer up martyrs to a new massacre."[61] Such rhetoric was less audible in Italy where Christian Democrats worried about ties with Arab countries and Leftist parties had long criticized Zionism. Reformist socialists warned against a "threat of genocide" on June 5. Statements of solidarity with the Jewish state, signed among others by Federico Fellini or the philosopher Norberto Bobbio, also appeared in national newspapers. The filmmaker and unorthodox Marxist Pier Paolo Pasolini nonetheless remained a rare figure from the cultural Left to invoke the Holocaust as a reason to side with Israel.[62] In West

---

[58] Elie Podeh, "Demonizing the Other: Israel Perceptions of Nasser and Nasserism" in Elie Podeh and Onn Winkler (eds.), *Rethinking Nasserism: Revolution and Historical Memory in Modern Egypt* (Gainesville, FL: University Press of Florida, 2004), 72–99. Nasser's speech of May 26, 1967, often misquoted, is available in Arabic at: http://nasser.org/Speeches/list.aspx?search=false&lang=en&page=253#Gallery. I thank Abed Takriti for his translation.

[59] Cited in Joan B. Wolf, *Harnessing the Holocaust: The Politics of Memory in France* (Stanford, CA: Stanford University Press, 2004), 34.

[60] Ibid., 25.

[61] Azouvi, Le mythe du grand silence, op. cit., 336–359; Laurence Coulon, *L'opinion française, Israël et le conflit israélo-arabe, 1947–1987* (Paris: Honoré Champion, 2009), 79–82; Samir Kassir and Farouk Mardam Bey, *Itinéraires de Paris à Jérusalem: La France et le conflit israélo-arabe* (Washington, DC: Palestinian Studies Institute, 1993), vol II, 127–131.

[62] Claudio Brillanti, *Le sinistre italiane e il conflitto arabo-israelo-palestinese* (Roma: Sapienza Università Editrice, 2018), 210; Alexandra Tarquini, "Left-Wing Intellectuals and the Representation of the Shoah in Italy," op. cit., 175–176; Robert S. C. Gordon, "Pasolini as Jew, between Israel and Europe" in Luca di Blasi et al. (eds.), *The Scandal of Self-Contradiction: Pasolini's Multistable Subjectivities, Traditions, Geographies* (Vienna: Turia + Kant, 2012), 37–58.

Germany, however, talk of "second assassination attempt" against the Jews proliferated in the Springer press and among guilt-stricken Protestants or socialists. Expressed from Vienna, support for Israel validated a national narrative of victimhood. "Austria itself," declared the socialist politician Bruno Pittermann on June 7, "knows what happens when a small state is being attacked and when democratic powers ignore such a situation" – a reference to the annexation of the country to the Third Reich in March 1938.[63]

"Within days," generalized the French-Jewish historian Pierre Vidal-Naquet on June 13, "Europe exonerated itself from collective guilt in the drama of the Second World War." The scholar of ancient Greece whose parents perished in Auschwitz in 1944 had defended on June 3 "the absolute, uncontestable right of Israel to live." Yet the former campaigner against torture in colonial Algeria also viewed the sudden surge of Holocaust imagery as Europe's absolution "on the back of the Arabs." On June 20, 1967, the Marxist-Jewish historian Isaac Deutscher similarly stated that "Arabs paid the price for the crimes committed by the West against the Jews," a view shared by the Jewish literary critique Franco Fortini in Italy. In addition to leftist Jews critical of Israel, however, Arab intellectuals such as the Paris-based Egyptian journalist Loftallah Soliman also explained to the public that "assigning to Arabs the unspoken antisemitism of others" was nothing but a "transference of culpability."[64] This argument likewise prominently featured in the rhetoric of radical protesters in West Germany. A month after the conclusion of the Six-Day War, the *Konkret* journalist Ulrike Meinhof still claimed that "there is no reason for the European Left to abandon solidarity with those who were persecuted," namely, Jews in the diaspora and Israel. But the future cofounder of the Red Army Faction also denounced the "questionable reconciliation" of Germans with Jews "not because we acknowledged our own crimes but (...) in solidarity with brutality, with actions that drive citizens from their homes, and with conquest." Germans claimed to love "Jews,"

---

[63] Daniel Marwecki, *Germany and Israel: Whitewashing and State-Building* (New York: Oxford University Press, 2020), 115. Bruno Pittermann is cited in Kathrin Bachleitner, "Ontological Security as Temporal Security: The Role of 'Significant Temporal Others' in World Politics," *International Relations* (2021): 1–23.

[64] Pierre Vidal-Naquet, "Après" in *Le Monde*, June 13, 1967, cited in Michel Winock, *La France et les Juifs de 1789 à nos jours* (Paris: Seuil, 2004), 320; Isaac Deutscher, *The Non-Jewish Jew* (New York: Oxford University Press, 1968), 137; Franco Fortini, *The Dogs of the Sinai (1967)* (London: Seagull Books, 2013), 70; Lotfallah Soliman, 'Un transfert de culpabilité', in 'Le Conflit israélo-arabe', *Les Temps Modernes*, special issue 253 (1967), cited in Gilbert Achcar, *The Arabs and the Holocaust: The Arab-Israeli War of Narratives* (London: Saqi Books, 2010), 241.

Meinhof added, not because of their humanity, but out of admiration for their ferocious "blitzkrieg."[65]

Such images, retorted critics of leftist anti-Zionism appalled by the comparison of Jews to Nazis, erased the Final Solution from public memory. "In the consciousness of the West," the historian Saul Friedländer wrote in 1969, "June 1967 cancelled the import of the Holocaust."[66] But the opposite proved true. The Six-Day War, of course, encouraged transgressive Holocaust inversion within radical subcultures, most notably in West Germany. The permissive Nazification of Arabs in strands of pro-Israel advocacy, however, preceded ultra-leftist (and ultra-rightist) equations of Zionism with Nazism. More frequently, New Left veterans of the 1967–68 student protests charged that invoking the Holocaust to defend the Israeli state whitewashed European guilt at the expense of Palestinians. Yet in the long run, the "year of the barricades" also propelled Holocaust memory to the forefront of public conversation: a key legacy of 1968 in West Germany and France.

The Long March of Philosemitism through the Institutions

"The students have taken on a bit the role of the Jews," observed Theodor Adorno on June 5, 1967. Three days earlier, the killing of the twenty-six-year-old demonstrator Benno Ohnesorg during the visit of the Iranian shah in West Berlin marked the beginning of the student movement in the Federal Republic. Although Adorno later dissociated himself from activists "degenerating into abominable irrationalism," he initially sympathized with allegorical Jewish protestors subjected to the police's "social sadism" and the taunts of onlookers.[67] The twentysomething baby boomers who turned against their parents' "Auschwitz generation," however, could also pass as metaphorical Jews through symbolic filiation with German Jewish spiritual fathers. Max Horkheimer's aphorisms on the "authoritarian state," and above all the writings of Theodor Adorno and Herbert Marcuse, educated

---

[65] Ulrike Meinhof, "Three Friends of Israel" (July 1967) in Karin Bauer (ed.), *Everybody Talks about the Weather ... We Don't: The Writings of Ulrike Meinhof* (New York: Seven Stories Press, 2008), 172–176.

[66] Saul Friedländer, *Réflexions sur l'avenir d'Israël* (1969), 155, cited in Gilbert Achcar, *The Arabs and the Holocaust*, op. cit., 241.

[67] Theodor Adorno cited in Wolfgang Kraushaar (ed.), *Frankfurter Schule und Studentenbewegung: Von der Flaschenpost zum Molotowcocktail 1946–1995*, Volume 1 (Hamburg: Rogner & Bernard, 1998), 254.

young intellectuals in antiauthoritarianism.[68] None of the Frankfurt school stalwarts claimed that Nazism and the Federal Republic were absolute equivalent. Yet Adorno's warnings about the persistence of "authoritarian character structures" within democracy, like Marcuse's thoughts on "repressive tolerance" in advanced capitalist societies, afforded Jewish legitimacy to the idea of enduring fascism. Under the influence of the charismatic Rudi Dutschke, the Socialist German Student League (SDS) shied away from quiet theory in favor of direct action. But the initial "67ers" not only drew inspiration from New Left ideology and a transatlantic language of protest: They also resisted "fascism" with theoretical ammunition obtained from German-Jewish witnesses of the Holocaust.[69]

1968 in the Federal Republic, however, was also a revolt against German philosemitism. In 1964, the German-Israeli Study Groups, an organization both sympathetic to the Jewish state and close to the New Left, had already derided "the ease with which most people in Germany" subverted "Jewish sub-humans" into "fellow human beings."[70] Coinciding with the outbreak of the Six-Day War, the nascent protest movement added a new component to the discourse of antiphilosemitism. While older left-leaning intellectuals pledged solidarity with Israel, SDS spokesmen distanced themselves from the "unlimited support of the Israeli government that came from West German public opinion." Effusive pro-Israel reactions, the SDS Chairman Reimut Reiche wrote on June 13, 1967, exemplified the "reversed antisemitism that is being produced in the Federal Republic today."[71] Three months later, the SDS officially veered toward anti-Zionism. A blend of Marxism, Third Worldism, and revolutionary internationalism, as well as close contacts with Arab students in West German

---

[68] Christoph Schmidt, "The Return of the Dead Souls: The German Students' Movement and the Ghosts of Auschwitz," *Journal of Modern Jewish Studies* 13, no. 1 (March 2014): 75–86; *Israel und die Geister von '68: Eine Phänomenologie* (Göttingen: Vandenhoeck & Ruprecht, 2018).

[69] Hans Kundnani, *Utopia or Auschwitz: Germany's 68 Generation and the Holocaust* (New York: Columbia University Press, 2009), 17–28; Michael Schmidtke, "The German New Left and National Socialism" in *Coping with the German Past*, op. cit., 176–193.

[70] Thomas Käpernick, "Die Studentenrevolte von 1968: Vom Philosemitismus zum Antizionismus? Anmerkungen zur Geschichte der Deutsch-Israelischen Studiengruppen" in Irene A. Diekmann and Elke-Vera Kotowski (eds.), *Geliebter Feind, Gehasster Freund: Antisemitismus und Philosemitismus in Geschichte und Gegenwart* (Berlin: Verlag für Berlin-Brandenburg, 2009), 439–466.

[71] Cited in Jeffrey Herf, *Undeclared Wars with Israel: East Germany and the West German Far Left, 1967–1989* (New York: Cambridge University Press, 2016), 81; Reiche's letter to *Der Spiegel* (June 13, 1967) is cited in Martin W. Kloke, *Israel und die deutsche Linke: Zur Geschichte eines schwierigen Verhältnisses* (Frankfurt: Haag + Herchen, 1990), 72.

universities, accounted for this evolution. At a national meeting held in early September 1967, at least one section of the movement declared the "Zionist state entity" illegitimate.[72] A call for the "rehabilitation of hundreds of thousands of Arab refugees back to their homeland" likewise testified of a generational shift: Unlike old left intellectuals, young activists released themselves from obligatory commitment to the state of Holocaust survivors.

This reversal shocked Jewish commentators who like the Vienna-born writer Jean Améry only saw "virtuous antisemitism" in the New Left's anti-Zionism. For the former Auschwitz prisoner until then indifferent to Israel, the "sanctuary for deeply exhausted survivors" in existence since 1948 deserved the solidarity of "any left not intent of abrogating itself and there is no reason why it should ignore the unbearable fate of Arab refugees to honor this commitment." Against the students' "anti-Zionist furor," Améry drew a comparison destined to weaponization: "Antisemitism resides in anti-Israelism and anti-Zionism as the thunderstorm does in the cloud." West German intellectuals offended by the students' "doctrinaire anti-imperialism" likewise lashed out at their "unacknowledged anti-Judaism." The SDS Chairman Reimut Reiche, however, had already fended off this accusation in June 1967 when he announced that "we do not have a problem with racism and do not have any antisemitism to overcome."[73] Double dissociation from the sins of their parents and from the guilt of the old left not only afforded 68ers the benefit of "militant innocence and moral superiority," as veterans of the movement later admitted.[74] It also allowed them to reverse the terms of leftist solidarity. In 1967–68, Palestine did not yet supersede other anti-imperialist causes but the direction was clear. Throughout the 1970s, far-left support for the Palestinian revolution was more pronounced in the Federal Republic than in any other West European country. As the observer of West German radical politics Moishe Postone noted at the end of the 1970s, "no western Left was as philo-Semitic and

---

[72] Herf, *Undeclared Wars with Israel*, op. cit., 82–85; Kloke, *Israel und die deutsche Linke*, op. cit., 77; Aribert Reimann, "Letters from Amman: Dieter Kunzelmann and the Origins of German Anti-Zionism during the Late 1960s," in Ingrid Gilcher-Holtey (ed.), *A Revolution of Perception? Consequences and Echoes of 1968* (New York: Berghahn Books, 2014), 69–90.

[73] Jean Améry, "Virtuous Antisemitism" (1969) and "The New Left's Approach to Zionism" (1969) in Marlene Gallner (ed.), *Essays in Antisemitism, Anti-Zionism, and the Left* (Bloomington, IN: Indiana University Press, 2021), 34–40 and 41–45; Kloke, *Israel und die deutsche Linke*, op. cit., 72 and 74.

[74] The historian and former 68er Gerd Koenen is cited in Ruth Wittlinger, "Taboo or Tradition? The "Germans as Victims" Theme in the Federal Republic until the Mid-1990s" in Bill Niven (ed.), *Germans as Victims* (Houndmills, Basingstoke, Hampshire: Palgrave Macmillan, 2006), 62–75.

pro-Zionist prior to 1967. Probably none subsequently identified so strongly with the Palestinian cause."[75]

Fringe but disproportionately important splinter groups went further. Emancipation from philosemitism, wrote the leader of the West Berlin Tupamaros Dieter Kunzelmann on November 27, 1969, meant freedom from *Judenknax*: the "Jewish tick" affecting postwar Germans, including fellow leftists. Hang-ups about Jews, Kunzelmann lamented upon his return from Palestinian guerilla bases in Jordan, "dominate all questions and discussions." At first glance, the brain behind the failed firebomb attack against the West Berlin Jewish Community Center three weeks earlier only demanded the replacement "of our simple philosemitism with (...) clear solidarity with AL FATAH." But in a leaflet issued four days after the act of violence in Berlin, its perpetrators had already called a spade a spade. "The Jews," they explained, "have themselves become fascists who, in collaboration with American capital, want to eradicate the Palestinian people." The fedayeen, on the other hand, waged a vanguard battle against "the Third Reich."[76] Here redress of historical injustice mattered less than psychological relief. The question of Palestine was more salient in Berlin and Frankfurt than in Paris and Berkeley, yet like Israel for the old left, it still functioned as projection screen for German guilt. For a fringe minority, the fight against "sacred cow Israel" also entailed lethal attacks against Jews in Germany, such as the anonymous arson of a Jewish retirement home in Munich which killed seven concentration camps survivors on February 13, 1970.[77] Members of the Red Army Faction perfected this mechanism of psychic reversal. In 1972, the imprisoned Ulrike Meinhof revived Nazi terminology when in defense of Black September hijackers, she blamed Israel for the "incineration" of its own athletes at the Munich Olympics. Like her comrade Gudrun Ensslin, she also compared her incarceration to the "gassing" of Jews in extermination camps. "It turns out that my Auschwitz fantasies were realistic," Meinhof wrote during her harsh solitary confinement in Cologne.[78]

Culminating in the bloody autumn of 1977, paranoid violence was only one outcome of the student movement in the Federal Republic.

---

[75] Moishe Postone, "Anti-Semitism and National Socialism: Notes on the German Reaction to 'Holocaust'" *New German Critique* 19, no. 1 (Winter 1980): Germans and Jews (Winter 1980), pp. 97–115.

[76] Kunzelmann is cited in Herf, *Undeclared Wars*, op. cit., 105–106; Kloke, *Israel und die deutsche Linke*, op. cit., 103–105.

[77] Wolfgang Kraushaar, "Wann endlich beginnt bei Euch der Kampf gegen die heilige Kuh Israel?" in *München 1970: über die antisemitischen Wurzeln des deutschen Terrorismus* (Reinbeck bei Hamburg: Rowohlt Verlag, 2013), 86–96.

[78] Ulrike Meinhof cited in Kundnani, *Utopia or Auschwitz*, op. cit., 121.

A quantitative lens reveals another trajectory. Before its dissolution in 1970, the SDS only represented 10 percent of the student body. Until its rapid decline in the second half of 1968, the mass protest movement included a wide array of participants united above all against the authoritarianism they saw in society. Most followed a nonrevolutionary path: While former 68ers populated the Marxist–Leninist or anarchist groupings formed in the early 1970s, 100,000 students joined the Social Democratic Party after Willy Brandt became federal chancellor in October 1969. His pledge to "dare more democracy" paid off. By 1972, the SPD had received 200,000 additional young members seeking, in their own words, "democratization of all areas of life in society."[79]

Their migration to reformist socialism brought with it an obsession with "Auschwitz" peculiar to the 1968 generation. The emblematic site of extermination, however, always had elastic meaning in the eyes of the New Left. In 1965, the writer and poet Hans Magnus Enzesberger severed Auschwitz from its German context to warn against nuclear Armageddon, a generalization repaid by a scolding from Hannah Arendt. Student protestors, for their part, proclaimed like anti-war demonstrators in the United States that "Vietnam is the Auschwitz of America."[80] Whether the transnationalization of Auschwitz was "escapism," as Arendt claimed, or a point of entry into other forms of genocide, later became a cardinal question in debates on the singularity of the Holocaust. But on December 7, 1970, Willy Brandt's spontaneous "knee fall" in front of the Warsaw Ghetto memorial in the Polish capital redirected "Auschwitz" toward Judeocentric guilt: The diplomatic thaw between the Federal Republic and its Iron Curtain neighbors started with a solemn commemoration of Jewish martyrdom.[81] Back home, half of the public disapproved of the chancellor's "overdone" repentance. The memorable Warsaw genuflection nonetheless introduced the idea

---

[79] Harold Marcuse, "The Revival of Holocaust Memory in West Germany, Israel, and the United States" in Carole Fink, Philipp Gassert, and Detlef Junkert (eds.), *1968: The World Transformed* (Cambridge: Cambridge University Press, 1998), 421–438; Andrei S. Markovits and Philip S. Gorski, *The German Left: Red, Green, and Beyond* (New York: Oxford University Press, 1993), 94–95.

[80] A. Dirk Moses, *The Problems of Genocide: Permanent Security and the Language of Transgression* (New York: Cambridge University Press, 2021), 416; Wilfried Mausbach, "Auschwitz and Vietnam: West German Protest against American War in the 1960s" in Andreas W. Daum et al. (eds.), *America, the Vietnam War, and the World: Comparative and International Perspectives* (Cambridge: Cambridge University Press, 2003), 279–298.

[81] On Brandt's "knee fall," see among others Kristina Meyer, *Die SPD und die NS-Vergangenheit 1945–1990* (Göttingen: Wallstein Verlag, 2015), 344–348; Ute Frevert, *The Politics of Humiliation: A Modern History* (Oxford: Oxford University Press, 2020), 192–197; Bernhard Giesen, *Triumph and Trauma* (London: Routledge, 2014), 132–135.

of inescapable responsibility in a social democratic party bolstered by the arrival of pacified rebels. Unthinkable before the student movement threw open the taboos of the "fascistoid" Federal Republic, Brandt's gesture created a template for a still distant age of official atonement. Deeper reckoning with the genocide awaited the post-reunification era, but the domestication of 1968 into a Holocaust-centered memory culture had tentatively begun.

"Citizens' initiatives," alternative scenes, and new feminist and environmental social movements were other offshoots of the German student protests. The immediate afterlife of 1968, however, invigorated "participatory democracy" but did not generate immediate interest in the singularities of the Holocaust. Whether orthodox or unorthodox, young leftists entered the 1970s with an understanding of Nazism inherited from the previous decade: a variation of fascism associated with capitalism, bureaucracy, or authority, but devoid of a unique anti-Jewish driving force. Defensive comparisons between Nazi Germany and Vietnam, or between Nazism and "National-Zionism," likewise deterred confrontation with the Jewish dimensions of German history. And despite the near disappearance of the German-Jewish population, swathes of the hard left remained hostile to Jews perceived as irritating reminders of moral vulnerability, or complicit with the "bridgehead of imperialism" in Palestine.[82] Contrary to the critique of Zionism developed in the late 1970s by Edward Said in the United States, West German leftism did not concomitantly reflect on "what anti-Semitism has meant for the Jews."[83] Such question was cast aside in favor of fervent identification with the Palestinian liberation movement precluding empathy for the Jewish victims of Nazism – and for Palestinians as a people with history instead of proxy revolutionaries. After a German hijacker separated Jewish hostages from non-Jews at the Entebbe airfield in late June 1976, the sociologist, former SDS member, and advocate of Palestinian rights Detlev Claussen denounced the "ahistorical anti-Zionism" of his leftist peers. In 1983, the self-critical intellectual also recognized that the subversive "Never Again Auschwitz postulate" had failed to translate into serious confrontation with the burdens of the German past.[84]

While 1968 did not revolutionize memory culture, the inflationary use of the epithet "Nazi" in the vociferous public sphere of the 1970s

---

[82] Martin Kloke, "Das zionistiche Staatsgebilde als Brückenkopf des Imperialismus," *Merkur* 697 (June 2007): 487–497.
[83] Edward Said, *The Question of Palestine* (New York: Vintage Books, 1979), 60.
[84] Detlev Claussen, "Im Hause des Henkers" in Dietrich Wetzel (ed.), *Die Verlängerung von Geschichte* (Frankfurt: Verlag Neue Kritik, 1983), 113–125.

nonetheless turned the past into a political present.⁸⁵ The mainstreaming of the student movement's rebellious spirit likewise heightened public awareness of the Nazi era. "More democracy," in Willy Brandt's eyes, distinctively entailed a "neither easy nor hasty" reckoning with a dark history. It did not imply, however, wholesale abandonment of the "Germans as victims" narrative or the goal of "final line" under the nation's past. His socialist successor Helmut Schmidt became in December 1977 the first sitting West German chancellor to visit Auschwitz. There he told his Polish hosts that "we Germans of today are not guilty as individual persons, but we must bear the political legacy of those who were guilty." A year later Schmidt called the *Reichskristallnacht* of November 1938 a symbol of "bitterness and shame" for all Germans. In Auschwitz, however, the word "Jew" was not heard once in the speech he delivered at the site.⁸⁶

Yet under two successive social–liberal coalitions, "more democracy" resulted in an unprecedented dissemination of knowledge on the Nazi era. Between 1970 and 1978, observed the historian Martin Broszat in 1979, the twenty-two largest West German universities offered 650 classes on the 1933–45 period. Only twenty-two of them specifically dealt with antisemitism and just two focused on the genocide of European Jews. A dominant view of Nazism as top-down totalitarian dictatorship, or debates on intentionality and structure in Nazi policymaking, still obscured the victim perspective.⁸⁷ A new generation of students nevertheless discovered the Hitler years through history instead of *fascismustheorie*: a more likely conduit to "Holocaust consciousness" than abstract conceptions of National Socialism.

Outside of academic institutions, activists turned the memorialization of the Third Reich into public history. At the end of the decade, veterans of the student protests joined by amateur historians conducted local research, organized exhibits, or mapped out sites of Nazi persecution. Like the more scholarly "History of Everyday Life," the History

---

⁸⁵ Belinda Davis, "New Leftists and West Germany: Fascism, Violence, and the Public Sphere, 1967–1974" in *Coping with the Nazi Past*, op. cit., 210–237.

⁸⁶ Kristina Meyer, "Mehr 'Mut zur Warheit' Wagen"? Willy Brandt, die Deutschen und NS-Vergangenheit" in Axel Schidlt and Wolfgang Schmidt (eds.), *"Wir wollen mehr Demokratie wagen": Antriebskräfte, Realität und Mythos eines Versprechens* (Hamburg: Dietz, 2019), 41–58; Shlomo Shafir, "Helmut Schmidt: Seine Beziehungen zu Israel und den Juden," *Jahrbuch für antisemitismusforschung* 17 (2008): 297–232.

⁸⁷ Martin Broszat, "'Holocaust' und Geschichtswissenschaft," *Vierteljahrhefte für Zeitgeschichte* 27, no. 2 (1979): 285–298, is cited in Harold Marcuse, *Legacies of Dachau: The Uses and Abuses of a Concentration Camp, 1933–2001* (Cambridge: Cambridge University Press, 2001), 342. On historiographical trends in the 1970s, see among others Wolf Kansteiner, *In Pursuit of German Memory: History, Television, and Politics after Auschwitz* (Athens, OH: Ohio University Press, 2006), 41–45.

Workshop movement close to the Green Party approached the Nazi period from the standpoint of ordinary Germans, not their Jewish victims. Their propensity to "historicize" Nazism, or fragment its study through local histories, provoked fierce controversies. And while the "history from below" phenomenon made its way to television programs, its impact paled in comparison to representations of the Jewish genocide imported from the United States. Watched by 20 million viewers in January 1979, the Hollywood TV miniseries *Holocaust* did far more to sensitize the public to the murder of Jews than grassroot historical initiatives. Yet in 1982, at the dawn of the center-right Helmut Kohl chancellorship, "coming to terms with the past" was no longer the commitment of old left intellectual elites. A cohort of younger educators, museum workers, junior academics, journalists, lawyers, and public sector employees – as well as thousands of high-schoolers who entered essay competitions on the history of their hometowns under Nazism – also made critical memory the centerpiece of political engagement.[88]

Neonationalism, of course, was not foreign to "new social movements." The Green Party's antinuclear environmentalism, like the peace movement's struggle against the deployment of American missiles in the country, rejuvenated the discourse of German victimhood. Within fifteen years, however, 1968 had spawned enough civil society actors unwilling to partake in "the grace of late birth." The activist memory boom of the early 1980s admittedly challenged Helmut Kohl's conservative national narrative without special focus on crimes perpetrated against the Jews. Its goal was to inscribe "the topography of [Nazi] terror" into the public space. But sites of destroyed synagogues were now increasingly marked across West German cities; and before the *Stolpersteine* of later years, more plaques or memorials commemorating murdered Jews appeared in West Berlin between 1980 and 1990 than during all preceding decades. Meanwhile, parents who named their children David, Jakob, Judith, or "Sarah" (as the Nazis called their female Jewish victims) resurrected a ghostly yet symbolic Jewish presence in West Berlin and other cities: The deradicalization of the student movement entailed acceptance of the Holocaust as touchstone of German identity.[89]

---

[88] Geoff Eley, "Contemporary Germany and Denial: Is 'Nazis' All There Is to Say?," *History Workshop Journal* 84 (Autumn 2017): 44–66; Eley, "Foreword" in Alf Ludtke (ed.), *The History of Everyday Life: Reconstructing Historical Experiences and Ways of Life* (Princeton, NJ: Princeton University Press, 1995), vii–xi.

[89] Jenny Wüstenberg, *Civil Society and Memory in Postwar Germany* (Cambridge: Cambridge University Press, 2017), 63; Susan Neiman, *Learning from the Germans: Race and the Memory of Evil* (New York: Farrar, Straus, and Giroux, 2019), 147.

After the fall of the Berlin Wall, observers of reunification feared that surging nationalism would forever relegate the Holocaust to the depths of German history. But as discussed in Chapter 7, the opposite took place. "Coming to terms with the past," the moral imperative of progressives only until 1989, morphed into state-sponsored "remembrance culture." This was, however, more continuity than rupture: Some of the key actors of Holocaust memorialization in the 1990s had entered the field of memory activism during the last decade of the Cold War.[90] Such an outcome looked improbable before 1990, but "the long march through the institutions" envisioned by Rudi Dutschke in 1968 to transform society from within would also result in the institutionalization of philosemitism in reunified Germany.

May '68 and Its Jews

While student activists in the Federal Republic occasionally portrayed themselves as "long-haired substitute Jews," one of the most memorable May '68 slogans in Paris remains to this day the iconic "We are all German Jews." In addition to their uneven popularity, however, the two phrases also differed in meaning. When they self-identified as new Jews, West German 68ers only drew attention to their own victimization. Ulrike Meinhof had already devised her own substitution theory several years prior to the student protests. "The only possible response to anti-Semitism," she wrote in 1961, "is the rejection of every kind of political terror [against] those who think differently, those who believe differently, and those who feel differently."[91] Rudi Dutschke followed suit in 1968. Rabid anticommunism in the Bonn Republic, argued the former East German citizen, had become the new antisemitism. This comparison allowed him to portray participants in the movement as the "Jews of anticommunism." Police brutality, argued other SDS members, was akin to "pogroms." In lieu of murdered Jews, *ersatzJuden* bore the brunt of fascist oppression.[92]

---

[90] Harald Schmid, "Von der 'Vergangenheitsbewältigung' zur 'Erinnerungskultur': Zum öffenlichen Umgang mit dem Nationalsozialismus seit ende der 1970er Jahre" in Gerhard Paul and Bernhard Schoßig (eds.), *Öffentliche Erinnerung und Medialisierung des Nationalsozialismus: Eine Bilanz der letzten dreißig Jahre* (Göttingen: Wallstein Verlag, 2010), 171–202.

[91] Ulrike Meinhof, "Hitler Within You" in Karin Bauer (ed.), *Everybody Talks about the Weather ... We Don't*, op. cit., 131–137.

[92] Gerhard Kade, "Langhaarige ErsatzJuden" (1968) and Rudi Dutschke, "Vom Antisemitismus zum Antikommunismus" (1968), are cited in Michael Schmidtke, "The German New Left and National Socialism," op. cit., 180.

First shouted in Paris on May 24, 1968, "We are all German Jews" suggested similar usurpation. But unlike radicals across the Rhine, French protesters did not simply substitute themselves for assassinated Jews. The rallying cry conveyed solidarity with the de facto leader of the revolt Daniel Cohn-Bendit, the son of German Jewish refugees born in France, a West German citizen on a student visa now declared "undesirable" in the country of his birth. The defiant chant heard in his defense, the twenty-three-year-old sociology student commented on June 12, 1968, "was the most important thing we had in France in the last days."[93] In a notorious essay, the French Jewish intellectual Alain Finkielkraut retrospectively charged that such "facile and flashy" generosity reduced Jewishness to an empty symbol. Whether Jewish like him or not, 68ers draped themselves "with the torture that others underwent."[94] Thirty years after the uprising, however, Cohn-Bendit still wished the phrase "a long life." The 50,000 to 70,000 protesters who in late May claimed the mantle of Jewishness were not despoiling it, as Finkielkraut lamented, but subverted a "racist anathema (…) into antiracist anathema." On the fiftieth anniversary of the revolt, the former far-left activist and long-time editor of the newspaper *Libération* Serge July avowed that among all the movement's slogans, "We are all German Jews" remained for him "the most beautiful of all."[95]

Figural or real, however, the Jewish dimensions of May '68 in France did not immediately jump to the eye. Far-left splinter groups, to be sure, counted several Jews in their leadership. Yet if Jewish radicals later invoked identity or second-generation Holocaust trauma to explain their involvement, conscious Jewishness remained invisible in the *gauchiste* movement. "Had people told me in May, you are doing this because you are Jewish," recalled the former Maoist Alain Geismar in 1978, "I would have thought of them as completely crazy." Cohn-Bendit himself reiterated in 2018 that being Jewish played "no role" at the time.[96]

---

[93] Daniel Cohn-Bendit's interview with the BBC (June 12, 1968) cited in Richard Ivan Jobs, "Youth Movements: Travel, Protest, and Europe in 1968" *The American Historical Review* 114, no. 2 (April 2009): 376–404.

[94] Alain Finkielkraut, *Le juif imaginaire* (Paris: Seuil, 1980), 25–45.

[95] Cohn-Bendit, "Nous sommes tous des juifs allemands" in *L'Express*, April 15, 1998, available at: www.lexpress.fr/informations/nous-sommes-tous-des-juifs-allemands_628699.html; Serge July in *Libération*, March 21, 2018, available at: www.liberation.fr/france/2018/03/21/serge-july-le-22-mars-1968-personne-ne-voulait-de-leaders_1637975/.

[96] Cited in Yaïr Auron, *Les juifs d'extrême gauche en Mai 1968: Une génération révolutionnaire marquée par la Shoah* (Paris: Albin Michel, 1998), 25; Daniel Cohn-Bendit in *Jüdische Allgemeine*, March 26, 2018, available at: www.juedische-allgemeine.de/politik/ich-essemazzen-das-ganze-jahr/. For a discussion of May '68 from the perspective of Jewish identity, see Sebastian Voigt, *Der jüdische Mai '68: Pierre Goldman, Daniel Cohn-Bendit und André Glucksmann im Nachkriegsfrankreich* (Göttingen: Vandenhoeck & Ruprecht, 2015).

"We are all German Jews" has now achieved celebrity status, yet the shout only erupted one week before a massive pro-Gaullist rally on the Champs-Élysées spelled the end of the uprising. Had Cohn-Bendit received authorization to reenter France after a short absence, May '68 would not have been "German Jewish" at all. Two posters gave visual form to the slogan, one of them featuring the alternative inscription "We are all Jews and Germans." Both were abandoned in favor of "We are all undesirables," a subversive badge of honor no longer explicitly grounded on Jewishness. In the chronology of May '68, German Jews arrived late on the scene and only for a brief moment.[97]

Although ephemeral, their appearance in the vocabulary of protest nonetheless stunned some of the first commentators of the events. For the French Jewish political philosopher Raymond Aron, of course, May '68 only amounted to an "elusive revolution." In his anti-utopian analysis of the uprising, Aron did not detect in the "We are all" chant any seismic change in the perception of Jewishness in France. The phrase, he noted in passing, merely signified youthful rejection of the Gaullist "dream of French grandeur."[98] The literary critic Maurice Blanchot, to the contrary, waxed lyrical about "an inaugural speech event, opening and overturning borders, opening and overthrowing the future." Identification with the Jewish outcast de-ostracized all outcasts: an emancipatory politics which the enthusiastic Blanchot called "communism without heritage." His friend Emmanuel Levinas interpreted the slogan differently. Parisian students, the philosopher of alterity suggested in 1969, encountered the Other through "German Jews in 1933 (…) that which is most fragile and most persecuted in the world."[99] While Blanchot embraced the phrase for its liberating promise, Levinas paid attention to its historical connotation. If German Jews conjured up the Final Solution, or the Vichy regime's complicity, then not only the Jewish outsider but also the Holocaust itself loomed behind the "We are all" proclamations.

In the summer of 1968, students at the London School of Economics imported the German Jew template to chant "We are all foreign scum"

---

[97] Béatrice Fraenkel, "Les affiches de Mai: l'Atelier Populaire des Beaux-Arts" in Philippe Artières and Michelle Zancarini-Fournel (eds.), *68: une histoire collective* (Paris: La Découverte, 2008), 276–280.
[98] Raymond Aron, *La révolution introuvable* (1968) (Paris: Calmann Lévy, 2018), 186.
[99] Maurice Blanchot (1968) cited in Sarah Hammerschlag, *The Figural Jew: Politics and Identity in Postwar French Thought* (Chicago, IL: University of Chicago Press, 2010), 197–198. On Blanchot and Jewishness, see also Maxime Decout, "Nous sommes tous des Juifs allemands: l'universalisme juif en question," *Revue des sciences humaines*, no. 320 (October–December 2015): 129–140. Emmanuel Levinas (1969) is cited in Michael L. Morgan, *The Cambridge Introduction to Emmanuel Levinas* (Cambridge: Cambridge University Press, 2011), 30.

in solidarity with the Pakistani-born organizer Tariq Ali. In Paris, the Maoist *Gauche Prolétarienne* positioned the Palestinian cause under the tragic aura of German Jews with "We are all Fedayeen."[100] Over the next decades, "We are all foreigners" or "We are all undocumented" would similarly impart the shadow of the Holocaust on pro-immigrant advocacy in France. The Jewish victim as a metaphor of moral force had already appeared in French anti-colonial writings during the late stages of the Algerian war, when revulsion from torture and police violence conjured up images of "ghettos" and "Auschwitz."[101] What developed in the wake of May '68, however, is less "multidirectional memory" than Holocaust totemism: the Jewish genocide as supreme standard of atrocity and trauma.

French humanitarian activists played a key part in this evolution. When *sans-frontiérisme* – the "Without Borders" ideology – displaced revolutionary Third Worldism as a form of radical engagement, the Holocaust began its new career as historical referent for the Western humanitarian movement.[102] Founded in 1971, Doctors Without Borders (MSF) was not a direct heir of May '68. Some of its progenitors, including the future celebrity "French doctor" Bernard Kouchner, served as Red Cross volunteers in Biafra while French students confronted riot police in the streets. Yet the birth of *sans-frontiérisme* in France coincided with the propagation of iconoclastic narratives of the wartime period. Released in 1971, Marcel Ophül's film *Le chagrin et la pitié* [*The Sorrow and the Pity*] challenged the heroic myth of collective anti-German resistance. Two years later, Robert Paxton's bombshell *La France de Vichy: 1940–1944* revealed how wartime rulers initiated anti-Jewish policies without pressure from German occupiers. A pivotal juncture in the history of the "Vichy syndrome," the years 1968–73 paved the way for an "obsession" with Jewish memory in literature, film, and scholarship.[103]

---

[100] Abdellalli Hajjat, "Les comités Palestine (1970–1972). Aux origines du soutien pour la cause palestinienne en France," *Revue d'études palestiniennes*, no. 98 (2006): 74–92; Samir Kassir and Farouk Mardam-Bey, *De Paris à Jérusalem: La France et le conflit israélo-arabe* (Washington, DC: Institut des études palestiniennes, 1992), 169–174.

[101] Michael Rothberg, *Multidirectional Memory: Remembering the Holocaust in the Age of Decolonization* (Stanford, CA: Stanford University Press, 2009), 227–266; Ethan Katz, "Sartre's Algerian Jewish Question" in Manuela Consonni and Vivian Liska (eds.), *Sartre, Jews, and the Other: Rethinking Antisemitism, Race, and Gender* (Berlin: Walter de Gruyter, 2020), 62–74.

[102] Elizabeth Davey, *Idealism beyond Borders: The French Revolutionary Left and the Rise of Humanitarianism, 1954–1988* (Cambridge: Cambridge University Press, 2015), 161–170.

[103] Henry Rousso, *The Vichy Syndrome: History and Memory since 1944* (Cambridge, MA: Harvard University Press, 1991), 132–167.

Doctors Without Borders, for its part, bound the legacy of the Holocaust to a new humanitarian imperative. "Bearing witness" to human rights abuses, the organization's distinctive concept, echoed other political speech acts born in May '68. For the group of volunteer physicians who had returned from Biafra, however, witnessing or *témoignage* was also a response to the Red Cross's public silence during the Holocaust era. Such passivity, they charged, was once again on display when the Nigerian federal army starved the secessionist Ibo population without public protest from Red Cross officials.[104] Bernard Kouchner popularized this version of MSF's origins. After learning that the wartime Red Cross "had chosen not to reveal the existence of extermination camps," he explained in 1979, the French doctors in Biafra "refused collusion with the executioner."[105] During the first years of MSF's existence, "bearing witness" lost ground to a more neutral commitment to care in far-flung conflict zones. But the Holocaust continued to inform *sans-frontiériste* portrayals of humanitarian emergencies. As the 1970s drew to a close, MSF activists referred to atrocities in Khmer Rouge Cambodia, and to the exodus of boat people in the region, as "Auschwitz in Asia." Nonintervention, they warned, would replicate the world's silence during the Holocaust.[106] A decade after May '68, the condition of victimhood in the French humanitarian imagination was grounded on similitude with the abandonment of the Jews during the 1930s and 1940s. Unbeknownst to them, humanitarian subjects in South East Asia also all became German Jews.

Contrary to the rise of *sans-frontiérisme*, the "breakthrough" of human rights ideology in the decade following May '68 stemmed from heightened consciousness of the Gulag more than Auschwitz. Disillusionment with Marxism and the appeal of Eastern European dissidence prompted a disparate group of French intellectuals to search for moral renewal through rejection of revolutionary politics. In the mid 1970s, an antitotalitarian front comprised of former *gauchistes* and late discoverers of liberal political thought found in Eurocentric human rights – the denunciation of oppression across the Iron Curtain – a political commitment

---

[104] Michal Givoni, "Holocaust Memories and Cosmopolitan Practices: Witnessing between Humanitarian Emergencies and the Catastrophe" in Amos Goldberg and Haim Hazan (eds.), *Marking Evil: Holocaust Memory in the Global Age* (New York: Berghahn, 2015), 121–145.

[105] Bernard Kouchner (1979) cited in Shai M. Dromi, *Above the Fray: The Red Cross and the Making of the Humanitarian NGO Sector* (Chicago, IL: Chicago University Press, 2020), 125.

[106] Elizabeth Davey, *Idealism without Borders*, op. cit., 39–42; Stephen Hopgood, *The Endtimes of Human Rights* (Ithaca, NY: Cornell University Press, 2013), 56.

unsullied by radical utopianism.[107] The French contribution to the surge of (selective) human rights talk in the West during the 1970s, however, also had Jewish dimensions. The twenty-nine-year-old Bernard-Henri Lévy and the older André Glucksmann, the two best-selling "new philosophers" whose books published in 1977 assailed the Left's philo-Marxism, were not only abjurers of revolution turned anti-totalitarian absolutists. They also belonged to a new generation of Jewish writers who openly assumed their cultural identity. In the aftermath of May '68, homosexual activists, feminists, immigrant and regionalist groups clamored for "the right to difference": a valorization of identity also conducive to greater affirmation of Jewishness in the public sphere.[108]

The media-friendly Lévy and Glucksmann added to this "coming out" a touch of Jewish chic, and not only because of their telegenic looks. Although derided by its numerous critics as shallow posturing, the "new philosophy" phenomenon elicited voguish interest for the Jewish intellectual as irreverent moral voice and metaphorical dissident. On television sets especially, "BHL" and Glucksmann excelled in this role. The Polish-born Marek Halter and from 1980 onward, the essayist Alain Finkielkraut, followed on their footsteps. Jewish "media intellectuals" in the 1970s and early 1980s almost single-handedly resurrected the old-fashioned French universalist intellectual, indefatigable crusader for justice since the Dreyfus Affair.[109] Away from the spotlights, the belated consecration of Emmanuel Levinas and Vladimir Jankélévitch as major ethical thinkers focused attention on Jewish philosophers "as Jews." The turn from "revolution to ethics" in post-1968 thought, interlaced with the rise of human rights ideology and Holocaust memory, elevated the moral appeal of Jewishness in the French intellectual sphere.[110]

"Rabbi Jacob": Bursting Jewishness on Screen

The long May '68 also affected the representation of Jews – and the Holocaust – in French film. The 1970s *mode rétro*, unlike the

---

[107] Jan Eckel and Samuel Moyn (eds.), *The Breakthrough: Human Rights in the 1970s* (Philadelphia, PA: University of Pennsylvania Press, 2014); Michael Christofferson, *French Intellectuals against the Left: The Antitotalitarian Moment of the 1970s* (New York: Berghahn Books, 2004), 113–155.

[108] On literary Jewishness in post-1968 France, see among others Maxime Decout, *Écrire la judéité* (Seyssel: Champ Vallon, 2015), 177–182; Judith Friedlander, *Vilna on the Seine: Jewish Intellectuals in France since 1968* (New Haven: Yale University Press, 1990).

[109] Jonathan Judaken, "Alain Finkielkraut and the Nouveaux Philosophes: French-Jewish Intellectuals, the Afterlives of May '68 and the Rebirth of the National Icon," *Historical Reflections / Réflexions Historiques* 32, no. 1 (Spring 2006): 193–223.

[110] Julian Bourg, *From Revolution to Ethics: May 1968 and Contemporary French Thought* (Montreal: McGill Queen's University Press, 2007), 309–315.

New German Cinema of the same period, revisited the Nazi era by featuring lead Jewish characters. Contrary to the simultaneous vogue of sexualized and psychoanalytical films on Nazism in Italy, the French *mode rétro* fixated on the occupation years without obsession with sadomasochism or scandalous eroticism.[111] With the exception of François Truffaut's *Le dernier métro* [*The Last Metro*, 1980], however, Jewish-themed *rétro* films only achieved moderate box-office success. More than 7 million movie-goers, on the other hand, saw *Les aventures de Rabbi Jacob* [*The Mad Adventures of Rabbi Jacob*] upon its release on October 18, 1973. Many more enjoyed the movie over the next decades, leading the Prime Minister Dominique de Villepin in office between 2005 and 2007 to hail Rabbi Jacob as "the patrimony of French families."[112] In this satire featuring France's favorite actor Louis de Funès, the film director of Jewish origin Gérard Oury used the character of Victor Pivert, a bigoted bourgeois Catholic turned imposter rabbi, to tackle the problem of racism in French society. Stereotypes abound in this comedy, yet remarkably without stigmatization of Jewishness. To the contrary, it is the distinctively ethnic Jews from Paris's rue des Rosiers who expose Pivert's narrow-mindedness and educate him in pluralism. Concluding the film, a famous klezmer dance scene cements their reconciliation. Donning a *shtreimel* and dressed in a caftan, Pivert-de Funès overcomes bigotry through the healing power of Hassidic joy. *Les aventures de Rabbi Jacob*, according to its cowriter Josy Eisenberg, won over the public with a "sympathetic, warm, welcoming" image of Judaism. But it also allowed French audiences to laugh at *franchouillard* or "typically French" racism without need for soul-searching. The comedy became an instant blockbuster because of de Funès's politically incorrect outbursts, not worries about antisemitism. For the star actor, however, Rabbi Jacob proved transformative. This experience, he confided, "scrubbed the dirt off my soul."[113] The film did not have such a radical effect on French society. Yet this burst of Jewishness on screen inaugurated the normalization of Jewish difference in French popular culture. The mid 1970s was also the moment when the Yiddish-accented stand-up comedian Popeck, followed by

---

[111] Saul Friedländer, *Reflections on Nazism: An Essay on Kitsch and Death* (Bloomington, IN: Indiana University Press, 1993), 74–81.

[112] Cited in Michael Mulvey, "What Was So Funny about *Les Aventures de Rabbi Jacob* (1973): A Comedy Film between History and Memory," *French Politics, Culture and Society* 35, no. 3 (Winter 2017): 24–43. See also Rémi Fournier Lanzoni, *French Comedy on Screen: A Cinematic History* (New York: Palgrave Macmillan, 2014), 129–133; Julien Gaertner, "1973, deux comédies françaises face au racisme: La Valise et Les aventures de Rabbi Jacob," *Hommes & Migrations* 1330 (2020): 68–70.

[113] Samuel Blumenfeld, "Rabbi Jacob: le film qui métamorphosa Louis de Funès" in *Le Monde*, March 20, 2020.

the Tunis-born humorist Michel Boujenah, endeared ethnic Jewishness to a wide public – all the while popular entertainers like Pierre Péchin enjoyed success with the mockery of Maghrebi accent.

Arab difference was also on display in *Les aventures de Rabbi Jacob*. Released during a year rife with racist attacks on North African immigrants, the slapstick comedy sought to combat xenophobia through laughter. The only Arabs featured in the film, however, are not Algerians, Moroccans, or Tunisians – their presence in mainstream French cinema was still negligeable – but assassins dispatched by a dictatorial North African regime to kill the revolutionary Mohamed Larbi Slimane. Violent, conniving, or seducing, postcolonial Arabs are still portrayed through colonial stereotypes. The secular and well-mannered Slimane admittedly receives better treatment. Disguised like Pivert as orthodox Jew to escape a bloodthirsty "colonel Fares" and the French police, Slimane does not share the prejudiced views of his accomplice. He is above all the story's "good Arab," however, because of his embrace of Jewish "distant cousins." Unintentionally released during the Arab–Israeli war of October 1973, the blockbuster film did not directly address the Middle East conflict. It nonetheless recycled the myth of ancestral struggle between Arab and Jews while evacuating the question of Palestine through caricatural terrorists. Played by a French actor, Slimane epitomized for millions of viewers the progressive but moderate Arab capable of peace with Israel in the name of "Semite" brotherhood. Jews in *Les aventures de Rabbi Jacob*, contrary to foreign Arabs, come across as equally ethnic and French. But like Slimane, they also fraternize with their supposed historical enemy. This influential representation of the Arab–Israeli conflict as Arab–Jewish family quarrel kept the question of Palestine at bay: The celebration of tolerance also blurred the distinctiveness of Palestinian national aspirations.

Public opinion polls released during the Arab–Israeli war of October 1973, however, revealed that in France as in the EEC, the majoritarian pro-Israel sentiment of June 1967 declined in favor of growing neutrality. More respondents still supported Israel over Arab countries, but with the exception of West Germany, Austria, and more surprisingly Italy, an equal or greater number did not take side. In Britain, 47.5% were favorable to Israel at the end of the first week of the war, 5% supported the Arab bloc, but 48% remained noncommittal. Even in Israel-friendly Norway, Denmark, and the Netherlands, neutrality gained ground. The Palestinian cause, publicized a year later with Yasser Arafat's "gun and olive branch" speech at the UN General Assembly, simultaneously began to receive attention. Before a sharper pro-Palestinian swing in the wake of the 1982 Israeli invasion of Lebanon, surveys conducted in the mid 1970s already indicated widespread support for Palestinian self-determination in territories conquered by Israel in June 1967. This was not an endorsement of the "one democratic state" to replace the "Zionist entity," the solution to the conflict promoted by Yasser Arafat at the United Nations on November 13, 1974. This option, in any case, did not figure in the list of questions presented to poll respondents. Support for Palestinian rights nonetheless gained a foothold in public opinion.[114] The new resonance of the Palestinian issue, however, did not sound the death knell of Israelophilia: The dawn of the two-state solution era not only salvaged but strengthened Israel's legitimacy in mainstream European politics.

Israelophilia: The Post-1967 Sequel

At the start of the 1970s, the pre-1967 harmonious relations between Western Europe and Israel already looked like a distant past. The reversal of the country's image from David to Goliath, the threat of terrorist attacks by Palestinian groups, and awareness of the Middle East's economic potential, accounted for this change of course. In 1971, the EEC "Schuman Document" set a new tone by calling for the withdrawal of Israel from territories occupied in June 1967 with only minor border corrections, the internationalization of Jerusalem, the return of Arab refugees to their home or their indemnification.[115] Like his predecessor Charles de Gaulle, the French president Georges Pompidou (1969–74) yearned for French "radiance" in the Arab world – as well as for increased arms sales and manufactured exports. In Britain, the conservative prime minister Edward Heath (1970–74) cultivated vital commercial ties with the Middle East. In Italy, ephemeral ruling coalitions dominated by Christian-Democrats continued to view good relations with Arab states a matter of national interest. In West Germany, Willy Brandt's Ostpolitik (1969–74) ended the prohibition of contacts with governments who recognized the German Democratic Republic: Conciliation with the Eastern European bloc also meant rapprochement with Arab League members. In June 1973, Brandt's landmark visit to

---

[114] For public opinion polls in Britain, West Germany, The Netherlands, and Denmark, see Connie de Baer, "The Polls: Attitudes toward the Arab-Israeli Conflict," *The Public Opinion Quarterly* 47, no. 1 (Spring 1983): 121–131. For Belgium and Italy, see AJYB (75), 1974–1975, 441, 458. On France, see L. Coulon, *L'opinion française, Israël et le conflit israélo-arabe 1947–1987*, op. cit., 298–299; and more generally Michael W. Suleiman, "Development of Public Opinion on the Palestinian Question," *Journal of Palestine Studies* 13, no. 3 (Spring 1984): 87–116.
[115] Sharon Pardo and Joel Peters, *Israel and the European Union: A Documentary History* (Lanham, MD: Lexington Books, 2012), 101.

Israel was not another display of Holocaust contrition. To interlocutors still incensed by the failure of West German security forces to rescue Israeli athletes at the 1972 Munich Olympics, the chancellor signified that Bonn favored "even-handedness" in the Arab–Israeli conflict. Brandt also turned down demands for additional reparation payments. The Federal Republic, he declared, sought with Israel a "normalized relation with a special character." While certainly not abolished, the "special relationship" entered troubled waters.[116]

The outbreak of the Arab Israeli war on October 6, 1973, forced EEC members to take a stand. Two days after the joint Egyptian–Syrian attack in the Sinai and the Golan Heights, Pompidou's foreign minister Michel Jobert wondered if "trying to repossess one's land" should be considered "unexpected aggression." Like France, Britain refused to condemn the Arab military campaign. Invoking impartiality, Heath declared an embargo on arms sales to both sides of the conflict. Despite dissent within Tory ranks and protest from the Labour opposition, the prime minister also denied American airplanes ferrying weapons to Israel the use of British airfields in Cyprus. West Germany allowed American supplying vessels to used its ports. Bonn nonetheless reversed course on October 25 when news of the discrete arrangement became public: Since October 17, the oil embargo enforced by Arab members of OPEC against countries supportive of Israel accelerated Western Europe's diplomatic reorientation.[117]

Cutbacks in the supply of oil most severely punished the Netherlands for its delivery of material assistance to the Israeli army. The socialist minister of defense and former resistance fighter Henk Vredeling invoked the persecution of Dutch Jews to justify the transfer of ammunition and spare parts to Israel. "I had seen the Jews drift away once," he later explained, "and then I could not prevent it. I thought that would not happen to me a second time."[118] Oil shortages only lasted a few weeks, but this experience earned the Netherlands the admiration of Israel's supporters. Amsterdam's progressive atmosphere likewise established the country's philosemitic reputation. The Dutch government, however, swiftly fell in line with the EEC. On December 14, 1973, the European

[116] Carole Fink, *West Germany and Israel: Foreign Relations, Domestic Politics, and the Cold War, 1965–1974* (Cambridge: Cambridge University Press, 2019), 238–244; Jenny Hestermann, *Inszenierte Versöhnung. Reise Diplomatie und die deutsch-israelischen Beziehungen von 1957 bis 1984* (Frankfurt am Main: Campus, 2016), 184–203.

[117] Howard Sachar, *Israel and Europe: An Appraisal in History* (New York: Vintage Books, 2000), 282–309; Rory Miller, *Inglorious Disarray: Europe, Israel and the Palestinians since 1967* (New York: Columbia University Press, 2011), 27–62.

[118] Peter Malcontent, "The Netherlands, the EU and the Israeli-Palestinian Conflict," *European Review of International Studies* 2, no. 9 (2022): 270–299.

Nine reiterated their support for UN Security Council Resolution 242 interpreted as full Israeli withdrawal from territories occupied since 1967. Whereas the UN resolution only called for "a just settlement of the refugee problem," EEC heads of government also demanded that the "legitimate rights" of Palestinians be "taken into account": enough to placate Arab oil-producing countries, intimate to Israel that concessions would be compensated by security guarantees, and watch *pax americana* condemn the so-called Euro-Arab dialogue to irrelevance.

Other EEC statements culminating in the 1980 Venice Declaration reaffirmed this position. The Palestinian problem was no longer "one of refugees"; Israeli settlements presented a "serious obstacle" to peace; dialogue with the PLO was indispensable to secure a "just solution." Although the declaration recognized "the right to exist of all states in the region, including Israel," it did not express particular sympathy for the Jewish state. Emphasis on "the Palestinian people, conscious to exist as such" testified to this change of tone. The European mediation attempt, however, did not address the details of border arrangements. It also conveyed to Palestinians that sovereignty in or parts of the West Bank, the Gaza strip, and East Jerusalem, was the most they could expect. The declaration was nonetheless anathema to the right-wing Israeli prime minister Menachem Begin always keen to compare the PLO to "Arab SS." Torn between armed struggle and diplomacy to defeat Zionism, the Palestinian leadership in Beirut rejected the proposal for its evasiveness on statehood.[119] The document, in any case, had little practical value: The Camp David Accords signed in 1978 between Israel and Egypt had already secured Washington's control over a PLO-less peace process. It nonetheless laid out the parameters of the US-backed Oslo Accords (1993). The Venice Declaration already symbolized the late 20th century Western consensus on Zionism: a recognition of its historical legitimacy compensated by overtures to Palestinian claims.

Reactions to UN General Assembly Resolution 3379 which on November 10, 1975, determined that "Zionism is a form of racism and racial discrimination," had already demonstrated the resilience of Western support for Israel. Twenty-eight years after the United Nations adopted the partition plan of Palestine, the question of Zionism was back on the agenda. Decolonization, however, changed the balance of power on the UN floor: a Soviet, Arab, and Non-Aligned coalition passed resolution 3379 by 72 votes against 35 and 32 abstentions. Ideologically, the motion condemned Zionism as part of a broader campaign against "neocolonialism, foreign occupation, apartheid and racial discrimination."

---

[119] Miller, *Inglorious Disarray*, op. cit., 81–95.

Diplomatically, the maneuver sought to isolate Israel on the international stage a year after South Africa's suspension from the United Nations. Like the United States, EEC countries unanimously opposed the resolution. Yet they justified their vote without American hyperbole. In a fiery speech, the US ambassador to the United Nations Daniel Patrick Moynihan led the Western charge against "the terrible lie that has been told here today." The Cold War hawk inveighed against the granting of "symbolic amnesty – and more – to the murderers of 6 million Jews" – a phrase which even Secretary of State Henry Kissinger found "just wrong." The General Assembly, added Moynihan, gave "the abomination of anti-Semitism (...) the appearance of international sanction." With the passing of Zionism-is-Racism, Antizionism-is-Antisemitism officially entered the vocabulary of US foreign policy.[120]

Western Europeans kept their distance from such equivalence. They nonetheless concurred with the overall American position. Resolution 3379 undermined "the right of the State of Israel to exist and the United Kingdom (...) will oppose any such move," declared the Labour-appointed British ambassador Ivor Richard. "The equation of Zionism with (...) racial discrimination is devoid of any foundation," stated the West German Rüdiger von Wechmar, a former lieutenant in Erwin Rommel's Afrika Korps. A Free French during World War II, Paris's envoy Louis de Guiringaud condemned an "initiative (...) directed against those who were not very long ago the victims of the most odious form of racism." Public opinion in their respective countries supported this view. In December 1975, a Gallup poll showed that only 25% of the British and French public agreed with resolution 3379, and less than 20% in West Germany and Switzerland.[121] Thousands of Dutch or Scandinavian young adults did not see Israel as racist either. Jobless at home since the 1973 oil shock, they enjoyed the countercultural lifestyle of volunteers in kibbutzim. Goodwill was also perceptible at the level of economic relations. Private companies seeking contracts in the Middle East continued to abide by the Arab boycott, but in May 1975 a trade agreement turned the EEC into Israel's largest commercial partner.[122]

Historians have portrayed the European left's change of heart about Israel after 1967 as a fateful "divorce": Responses to resolution 3379 nonetheless show that the categorical delegitimization of Zionism only

---

[120] UN General Assembly 2400th Plenary Meeting, November 10, 1975, available at: https://ecf.org.il/media_items/1396; See also Gil Troy, *Moynihan's Moment. America's Fight against Zionist as Racism* (New York: Oxford University Press, 2013), 132–158.
[121] AJYB (77), 1977, 361.
[122] Pardo and Peters, *Israel and the European Union*, op. cit., 133–134.

took place within the militant but electorally weak radical left.[123] Zionism-is-Racism was nothing new to the Marxist-Leninist groupings which since the 1967–68 student protests threw their lot with the Palestinian revolution. In France, however, second thoughts about revolutionary violence contributed to the self-dissolution of the pro-Palestinian *Gauche Prolétarienne* in the wake of the 1972 Munich Olympics. A sympathizer of the violent Revolutionary Cells in the Federal Republic, the future Green Party foreign minister Joschka Fischer began a two-decade journey toward liberal-Atlanticism in the wake of the 1976 Entebbe hijacking. Yet Zionism remained unquestionably racist for West German radicals, *Lotta Continua!* in Italy, French far-left *groupuscules*, British Trotskyist students – and the Palestine solidarity committees active on university campuses since the start of the decade.

The two largest communist parties in Western Europe differed on resolution 3379. In France, the PCF accepted it with qualifying "nuances." The party's mouthpiece *L'Humanité*, however, reaffirmed that "French communists support without ambiguity the existence of the state of Israel" alongside "an independent and pacifist Palestinian state." Italian communists, for their part, disagreed with the UN condemnation. Zionism was a "reactionary and conservative ideology," stated the PCI, "but on grounds of principle we do not equate Zionism with racism." Although more successful in Italy than in France, "Eurocommunism" distanced both parties from Soviet orthodoxy: For the heirs of the anti-Nazi resistance struggle, calling Israel "racist" was a Rubicon too symbolically charged to cross.[124] Midway between social democracy and the far left, the non-Marxist New Left denounced Israel's ethnonationalism or oppression of Palestinians without categorical anti-Zionism. In Paris, *Le Monde*'s editorial on resolution 3379 typified this position better defined as anti-Israelism. The prestigious newspaper called Zionism a "nationalist doctrine (…) which often established questionable distinctions among human beings" yet still deplored the "harmful" UN decision.[125]

Left flanks of socialist parties, including Labour's left wing in Britain, shared in the anti-Israelism described above. Bruno Kreisky, who from 1973 to 1977 led a peace mediation in the Middle East on

---

[123] See among others Paul Kelemen, *The British Left and Zionism: History of a Divorce* (Manchester: Manchester University Press, 2017); Colin Shindler, *Israel and the European Left: Between Solidarity and Delegitimization* (2012); Robert S. Wistrich, *From Ambivalence to Betrayal: The Left, the Jews, Israel* (Lincoln, NE: University of Nebraska Press, 2012).

[124] *L'Humanité*, November 12, 1975; *L'Unità*, November 12, 1975. See also Claudia de Martino, "Israel and the Italian Communist Party (1948–2015): From Fondness to Enmity," *Communist and Post-Communist Studies* 48 (2015): 281–290.

[125] *Le Monde*, November 12, 1975.

behalf of the Socialist International, never hid his dislike of Zionist ideology which he called "a mysterious racism in reverse." His Third-Worldist Swedish colleague Olof Palme stood among the most vocal socialist sympathizers of Palestinians.[126] Yet if the defeat of the Israeli Labor party in April 1977 ended an already fading romance with socialist Israel, mainstream social democracy never delegitimized Zionism: The preservation of a perfectible but esteemed Jewish state through compromise with Palestinians became the new version of socialist Israelophilia. From 1974 to 1979, the British Labour prime ministers Harold Wilson and James Callaghan embraced the two-state platform with a flexible interpretation of UN resolution 242 allowing for border arrangements. They also insisted on the PLO's official recognition of the Jewish state as precondition for peace. Wilson later portrayed himself as the "best friend Israel had in the Western world,"[127] yet the emblematic philo-Zionist socialist of the 1970s remained François Mitterrand. In 1972, the head of the new Parti Socialiste entered into electoral alliance with Communists. His long history of friendship with Israel, however, did not end in divorce. While premised in his eyes on the "equal right of Palestinians and Israelis to self-determination," the two-state solution allowed him to pledge attachment to a Jewish state he always held in high regard. Equity demanded the realization of Palestinian self-determination, Mitterrand already claimed in the mid 1970s. Yet he simultaneously drew the limits of his pro-Palestinianism. Zionism-is-Racism, commented the future French president, only deserved "scorn."[128]

Mitterrand's indignation was not unique to social democrats. In West Germany, it was not only chancellor Helmut Schmidt or SPD intellectuals who bristled at the condemnation of Zionism. Liberal coalition members, as well as the CDU/CSU opposition, also joined in outrage. The Societies for Christian-Jewish Cooperation (to which virtually no Jews belonged) hurried to dedicate their yearly Brotherhood Week to "Zionism: Liberation Movement of the Jewish People."[129]

---

[126] Robert S. Wistrich, *Anti-Zionism and Antisemitism: The Case of Bruno Kreisky* (Hebrew University of Jerusalem: Vidal Sassoon Center for the Study of Antisemitism, 2007), 13.

[127] Harold Wilson in *The Jewish Chronicle* (1982), cited in Paul Kelemen, *The British Left and Zionism*, op. cit., 162.

[128] François Mitterrand, *L' Unité*, November 12, 1975. See also *L'abeille et l'architecte* (Paris: Flammarion, 1978), 100, cited in Jean-Pierre Filiu, *Mitterrand et la Palestine* (Paris: Fayard, 2005), 46.

[129] Rolf Vogel, *Der deutsch-israelische Dialog: Dokumentation eines erregenden Kapitels deutscher Außenpolitik*, Part 1, Volume 2 (Munich: K.G Saur, 1988), 603–606; AJYB (78), 1978, 434–435.

On November 13, 1975, the European parliament rebuked the UN decision without a dissenting vote. No detailed rebuttal was offered. For the assembly seated in Luxemburg, the "profound" differences between Zionism and racism were simply too "obvious" to be spelled out. The UN resolution was above all an affront to the post-Holocaust conscience: The "unacceptable" suggestion that Jewish victims of racism became enforcers of racism. The Italian Christian Democrat who tabled the anti-3379 motion reminded his colleagues that "the people of Europe (.) had direct experience of the cost in blood and tears of the tragic confrontation between Zionism and the most merciless racism." Since the Third Reich exterminated "Zionists," he seemed to believe, the vilification of Zionism at the UN was a continuation of Nazism by other means. Other speakers similarly viewed the resolution as an unbearable breach of morality. This was not only true of parliament members who considered Zionism-is-Racism a perversion of antiracism. Communists abstained, yet for them too resolution 3379 "incomprehensibly linked [Zionism] to racism." The French Gaullist Louis Terrenoire, a vocal anti-Israeli since 1967 and leader of the Progressive Democrats faction, was also a former resister and survivor of Dachau. Like other politicians of his generation, Terrenoire still associated racism with Nazism, not apartheid-like racial oppression. Even for the future founding member of the France–Palestine association (1979), branding Zionism as racism was uncomfortable terrain. The "legitimate rights of the Palestinian people" awaited vindication, but the "regrettable" UN decision only delayed the achievement of peace.[130]

In Britain, 160 members of the Houses of Parliament called on the UN "to repudiate all attempts, racialist in themselves, to pillory the democratic state of Israel." In France, Italy, and West Germany, signatories of open letters where not all self-declared "friends of Israel." What they similarly defended from the charge of racism, however, was the "the aspiration of Jews persecuted by racism to recover a national identity."[131] That the 1975 Nobel Peace Prize recipient Andrei Sakharov entered the fray added weight to their protest. In his Oslo lecture read by his wife Elena Bonner, the Soviet prisoner of conscience sympathetic to Jewish *refuzniks*

---

[130] Official Journal of the European Communities, Debates of the European Parliament 1975–1976 Session, *Report of Proceedings from 10 to 14 November 1975*, 243–245.

[131] In Britain, Conservative, Labour and Liberal Friends of Israel issued a joint statement in *The Observer* on December 7, 1975. In France, prominent figures signed the "Appel contre la résolution de l'ONU condamnant le sionisme" published in several dailies. In Italy, ninety-eight intellectuals appealed to the government to denounce the resolution: AJYB (77), 1977, 416. For reactions in the West German press, see Rolf Vogel, *Der deutsch-israelische Dialog*, op. cit., 607–615.

in his country affirmed that "all impartial persons know that Zionism (...) is not directed against any other people."[132] Like other opponents of resolution 3379, Sakharov applauded the "national rebirth of the Jewish people" from the point of view of Zionist ideology. Palestinian spokesmen offered another perspective. "The policy of the Zionist state," retorted from Paris the PLO representative at UNESCO Ibrahim Souss, "seeks to systematically separate the Jew from the non-Jew, to prepare the evacuation of the non-Jew." The "Judaization" of Palestine, he added, was tantamount to "racial discrimination, if not plain racism."[133]

Yet as Sakharov's address confirmed, the explosion of human rights language and activism in the West afforded Zionism a moral shield against disrepute. Since the late 1960s, to be sure, Amnesty International clashed with the Israeli government over its treatment of Palestinian prisoners. To the dismay of Jewish critics decrying double standards or a dubious obsession, the transnational NGO did not spare Israel from shaming. In its anti-totalitarian version, however, the North Atlantic "breakthrough of human rights" offset the delegitimization of Zionism at the United Nations or within the hard left. Not only could Israel's reputation be defended by exposing the human rights violations committed by its Soviet-bloc, Arab, or African accusers: Zionism itself preserved its status of just cause in the Western liberal imagination. A new form of sympathy contributed to this resilient esteem.

Pourquoi Israël

Released to international audiences on the eve of the 1973 Arab–Israeli war, Claude Lanzmann's *Pourquoi Israël* [Israel, Why] exemplified the mutation of cultural philo-Zionism after 1967. Gone was the romance with blooming deserts and socialist achievements. "In no way a work of propaganda," assured its author, the film sought to capture "the awe-inspiring wonder of a normal, Jewish state." Three years in the making, Lanzmann's unambiguously pro-Zionist directorial debut showcased everyday Israelis: intellectuals and workers, new immigrants from the Soviet Union, older ones from North Africa, Holocaust survivors, Mizrahi Black Panthers, or one of the first Jewish settlers in al-Khalil/ Hebron. Dominating the film, however, is the figure of the introspective liberal, of Ashkenazi origin or leftist kibbutz member, reflecting in fluent English on the challenges of nation-building or the prospect of peace. Against the triumphalist mood of the post-1967 years, *Pourquoi Israël*

---

[132] Andrei Sakharov, "Peace, Progress, Human Rights" (Nobel Lecture, December 11, 1975) is available at: www.nobelprize.org/prizes/peace/1975/sakharov/lecture/.
[133] Ibrahim Souss, Le racisme en Palestine, *Le Monde*, December 25, 1975.

portrayed the twenty-five-year-old state as an uncertain yet extraordinary quest for Jewish normality. "We have never seen anything like this before," exclaimed the German-Israeli thinker Gershom Scholem after the film was shown in Jerusalem.[134]

Lanzmann's exploration of Israel's social and political tensions nonetheless shared a common trait with earlier representations of the Jewish state on screen: the conspicuous absence of Arabs over more than three hours of interviews. Palestinians in a Gaza refugee camp briefly appear as the director follows an Israeli army patrol. An elderly man exchanges a few untranslated words with an officer; silent coffee-drinkers avert their eyes from Lanzmann's intrusive camera; children are seen from a distant alley; a passer-by carrying a basket is stopped at gun point: This is the extent of the Arab presence in *Pourquoi Israël*. Fascinated with the "reappropriation of violence by the Jews" after centuries of victimhood, the future creator of *Shoah* did not seek to hear what Palestinian onlookers might think of this historical reversal. With noticeable empathy for "an army unlike any other," he instead gave voice to Israeli conscripts dissatisfied with "being in Gaza ... playing cat and mouse, but this is our duty, we have to finish off the terrorists."[135]

Like other reviewers of the film in West Germany, Italy, or the United States, the French historian François Furet questioned Lanzmann's "strangely marginal" treatment of the Palestinian issue. But like other film critics enthralled by the "unique tonality of Israeli existence," the preeminent scholar of the French revolution found logic in Lanzmann's partiality: "Is it not (...) because the Arab problem, and this is its tragedy, is ultimately lateral and almost accidental in relation to Israeli consciousness?" The depth of "human meanings" in *Pourquoi Israël*, he observed, conveyed a "profound historical truth" independent of other considerations. Despite their one-sidedness, Lanzmann's interviews illuminated "a 'return' which is not only historical and sentimental, but also spiritual and metaphysical." For the former communist intellectual now committed to rescue the historiography of the French revolution from Marxist "catechism," the film raised questions hitherto ignored by the anti-colonial left: "What is a Jew? What does the resurrection of a Jewish state in Palestine mean? What is the historical identity of an Israeli?"[136]

---

[134] Claude Lanzmann, *Le lièvre de Patagonie. Mémoires* (Paris: Gallimard, 2009), 427–428.
[135] On *Pourquoi Israël*, see Rocco Giansante, "Israel through the Viewfinder: Claude Lanzmann and Susan Sontag Film the Jewish State" in Rocco Giansante and Luna Goldberg (eds.), *Imagined Israel(s): Representation of the Jewish State in the Arts* (Leiden: Brill, 2023), 145–160.
[136] François Furet, "Arabes, si vous saviez ..." (October 1973) in *Penser le XXe siècle* (Paris: Robert Laffont, 2007), 260–262.

Furet's approval of *Pourquoi Israël* reflected a liberal-centrist turn in both pro-Zionism and philosemitism. After a short romance with the young state of Israel, argued the former Communist, the left now reduced "the Exodus passengers" to colonial settlers perhaps unaware of their sins, "yet colonial settlers nonetheless." Empathy for persecuted Jews after World War II, he added, did not erase all traces of "latent antisemitism" within the progressive camp. But Furet above all criticized the left's inability to accept Jewish particularism, whether national or religious: two categories about which Marxism or philo-Marxism "never had much to say." The "Jewish problem," he countered in 1979, is not "normalizable" through revolution or universalism. Only a left emancipated from utopia and Manichean anti-fascism could comprehend the complexities of the Jewish reality, "live with it, as it is, and at the present time." Confrontation with this "immense question," wrote the scholar fascinated with "the Jewish destiny in the 20th century," was a cardinal feature of post-Marxist liberal politics.[137] Furet's intellectual trajectory, of course, only exemplified a rightist inflection among members of the French left reconciled with market society and Republicanism. But a decade before 1989, his import of philosemitism into late twentieth-century centrist-liberalism proved prophetic for Europe as a whole. Politically situated between center-left and center-right, Euro-optimists yearned for a union transcending the boundaries of economic community: They also discovered unique affinities between Europeanism and Jewishness.

---

[137] "Entre Israël et la gauche française: trente ans de malentendus" (Mai 1978) in *Penser le XXe siècle*, op. cit., 267–270. On Furet's philosemitism, see Christophe Prochasson, *François Furet: Les chemins de la mélancolie* (Paris: Stock, 2013), 470–482; Gil Mihaely, "Révolution sans table rase: François Furet et le sionisme" in Denis Charbit (ed.), *Les intellectuels français et Israël* (Paris: Editions de l'éclat, 2009), 121–127.

7 Archetypal Friends
Euro-Philosemitism (1980–2020)

Three weeks after her electoral victory of May 1979, Margaret Thatcher lauded "the very qualities (...) Jews have always cherished." Self-help, hard work, and "reverence for education" were not only characteristics the long-time Member of Parliament for Finchley had observed among her north London Jewish constituents. These traits also dovetailed with the core principles of the Thatcher revolution: the new prime minister brought to Downing Street a philosemitism tailored to her conservative philosophy. What Thatcher called "the Jewish way of life" exemplified the Victorian middle-class ethics she championed against the welfare state. In 1986, Britain's Chief Rabbi Immanuel Jakobovits claimed that according to Judaism "cheap labor is more dignified than a free dole": This controversial statement only validated Thatcher's pro-Jewish sentiments.[1] Predicated in her own words on "Judeo-Christian values," esteem for Israel, and admiration for imputed Jewish morals, her lifelong Judeophilia contrasted with the mild Judeophobic snobbery still traceable among Tory grandees. Commenting on the presence of Jews within Thatcher's inner circle, the former Conservative prime minister Harold McMillan remarked that there were "more Estonians in the cabinet than Etonians." But from 1979 to 1990, supporters of the Iron Lady approvingly pronounced Judaism "the new creed of Thatcherite England."[2] This positive image continued to inhabit the Tory mind decades after the end of the Thatcher era. "So many Jewish values are conservative values and British values too," Liz Truss told a Manchester synagogue in August 2022. On the eve of her ephemeral premiership, she extolled

---

[1] Sir Immanuel Jakobovits, *From Doom to Hope: A Jewish View on 'Faith in the City'* (London: Michaelson, 1986), 10.
[2] "Judaism Is the New Creed of Thatcherite England," *Sunday Telegraph*, January 10, 1988, cited in Roger Philpot, *Margaret Thatcher the Honorary Jew: How Britain's Jews Helped Shape the Iron Lady and Her Beliefs* (London: Biteback Publishing, 2017), 4. On Thatcher's and Jews, see also Eliza Filby, *God & Mrs Thatcher: The Battle for Britain's Soul* (London: Biteback Publishing, 2015), 249–255; Geoffrey Alderman, *Modern British Jewry* (New York: Oxford University Press, 1992), 347–352.

once again the "Jewish family unit" and its purported ethics of self-reliance and entrepreneurship.³

Neoliberalism in post-1979 Britain not only pushed philosemitism to the right. The new era also consecrated the whiteness of Jews in British race politics. "People are really afraid that this country might be rather swamped by people with a different culture," Thatcher declared a year before her election. Anglo-Jews, in her mind, unquestionably belonged to a primordial nation fearful of onslaught on "the British character [which] had done so much for democracy, for law, and (…) throughout the world." Long suspicious of the "race relations industry," an increasing number of Jewish voters responded in kind: Their migration from the Labour party to Conservatism both stemmed from socioeconomic factors and agreement with Thatcherite monoculturalism.⁴ Immanuel Jakobovits's views reflected this new orientation. Afro-Caribbeans, lamented the Chief Rabbi with the urban riots of 1981 and 1985 still in mind, wanted to give British society a "multi-ethnic form." While sympathetic to the hardships of the underclass, Jakobovits advised inner-city Blacks to learn from past Jewish experiences. In London's East End, he reminded them, Jewish immigrants lifted themselves out of poverty and integrated into the host culture.⁵ It is no surprise that the prime minister cultivated a friendship with the Orthodox rabbi upon whom she bestowed the peerage in 1988: Sir Immanuel exemplified unique affinities between Englishness and Jewishness. Thatcher, of course, did not describe unity in the language of racial kinship. But the British-Jewish symbiosis dear to her heart confirmed the position of Anglo-Jews at the heart of white Britain. Jewish communal leaders, for their part, never proclaimed Jews white. Yet faithful to its Anglophile tradition, the Board of Deputies resisted ethnicization. Britain's Jews stood ready to help discriminated non-whites, the representative body had already stated in the late 1960s, but they did not constitute a distinct racial group. During the Thatcher years, only young Jewish leftists allied with antiracist activists advocated the alignment of Anglo-Jews with Britain's ethnic minorities.⁶

Claiming Jewish difference across the Channel did not require similar radicalism. Elected president in May 1981, François Mitterrand ushered

---

³ *Haaretz*, August 14, 2022.
⁴ Geoffrey Alderman, "The Political Conservatism of the Jews in Britain" in Peter Y. Medding (ed.), *Values, Interests and Identity: Jews and Politics in a Changing World* (New York: Oxford University Press, 1995), 101–116.
⁵ Sir Immanuel Jakobovits, *From Doom to Hope*, op. cit., 7.
⁶ I am here indebted to Joseph Finlay's seminal research: *Between Religion and Ethnicity: How Jews Navigated Race Relations in Postwar Britain*, PhD dissertation, University of Southampton (UK), 2023, Chapters 5 and 6 especially.

an era of cultural pluralism in traditionally assimilationist France: not a multiculturalism of separate communities but "the right to be different" in an otherwise integrationist republic. Jewish particularism, of course, had already burst into the French public sphere in the wake of the 1967 Six-Day War. But the arrival of the Union of the Left to power encouraged young French Jews to embrace identity politics in alliance with the daughters and sons of Maghrebi immigrants. The creation of *SOS Racisme* in 1984 cemented this coalition. Under the umbrella of the socialist-dominated antiracist organization, Jewish students and second-generation North Africans affirmed their religious or cultural distinctiveness while jointly fighting antisemitism and xenophobia. This partnership, however, foundered at the end of the 1980s. Although both sides claimed that "we cannot solve the Israel-Palestinian problem on the banks of the Seine," Israel's invasion of Lebanon in 1982 and the outbreak of the First Intifada in 1987 drew a wedge between Jews often critical of Israel yet affectively Zionists, and pro-Palestinian youths of Arab immigrant background. The "problem" of Islam, above all, fractured Jewish-Muslim interethnicity. During the first "scarf affair" of 1989, *SOS Racisme* still defended the right of Muslim girls to wear the hijab in public schools. But as the question of Islam's compatibility with national identity travelled from the far-right to the mainstream, the simultaneous representation of Jews as models of civic integration, and of Muslims as problem minority, entered public discourse.[7] Exemplar Republicans in France, ideal neo-Victorians in Britain, or custodians of untainted *kultur* in the West German philosemitic imagination: Various iterations of model Jews already circulated before the end of the Cold War. Three decades later, postcolonial critics named this phenomenon "state philosemitism," a phrase connoting the cooptation of "white" Jews in the national project at the expense of racialized Arabs, Muslims, or Palestinians.[8]

The 1980s, however, also witnessed the emergence of postnational philosemitism: Jews – yet again – as litmus test of European cosmopolitanism. The modish rediscovery of Central Europe "as an idea, a state

---

[7] Maud S. Mandel, *Muslims and Jews in France: History of a Conflict* (Princeton, NJ: Princeton University Press, 2014), 125–152; Daniel A. Gordon, "Antisemitism, Islamophobia and the Search for Common Ground in French Antiracists Movements since 1898" in James Renton and Ben Gidley (eds.), *Antisemitism and Islamophobia in Europe: A Shared Story?* (London: Palgrave Macmillan, 2017), 165–186; Rita Chin, *The Crisis of Multiculturalism in Europe: A History* (Princeton, NJ: Princeton University Press, 2017), 166–178.

[8] Houria Bouteldja, *Les Blancs, les Juifs et nous: Vers une politique de l'amour révolutionnaire* (Paris: La Fabrique, 2016); Alana Lentin, *Why Race Still Matters* (Cambridge: Polity Press, 2020).

of mind, a worldview" helped vehiculate this trope.⁹ With his much-discussed essay first published in French in 1983, Milan Kundera almost single-handedly sparked a Western intellectual romance with Mitteleuropa. "The tragedy of Central Europe," argued the Czech writer established in France since 1975, was its separation from Europe's consciousness after 1945. The Soviets absorbed the region into Eastern Europe while the West ignored its disappearance. Despite communist oppression, "small nations between Germany and Russia" remained Europe's spiritual center.¹⁰ Kundera's melancholic ruminations, however, were also an ode to Jewish Central Europe. "No other part of the world," he observed, "has been so deeply marked by the influence of Jewish genius." This was not only a tribute to the Jewish writers, composers, or artists who prior to the Holocaust disproportionately contributed to modernist culture. "Aliens everywhere and everywhere at home," added Kundera, "the Jews in the twentieth century were the principal cosmopolitan, integrating element in Central Europe." His warm feelings for Jews stemmed in part from the identification of Czech dissidents with a twin "small nation."¹¹ But the novelist above all paid homage to vanished Jewish cosmopolitans: Premised on culture instead of borders, the Jews' portable identity was the "condensed version" of Central Europe's spirit.

Kundera, to be sure, offered readers particularly admirative in Paris a mythical Mitteleuropa devoid of antisemitic and authoritarian traditions. Many received license to imagine the former Habsburg lands as a lost paradise of cultural diversity.¹² The influential essay nonetheless reshaped their mental map of the continent. Europe's civilizational heart, they learned, was its geographical core. The rediscovery of "arch-European Europe" also meant the rediscovery of quintessential Europeans: The Jews who made Central Europe "a culture or a fate." Admittedly, Kundera's "love for the Jewish heritage" did not include the teachings of the Tora or the Yiddish-speaking world. Yet his idealization of Jewish cosmopolitanism inverted the vilification of Jewish wanderers alien to Europe – and the demonization of "rootless

---

⁹ Tony Judt, "The Rediscovery of Central Europe," *Daedalus* 119, no. 1 (Winter 1990): 23–54.
¹⁰ Milan Kundera, "The Tragedy of Central Europe" in *A Kidnapped West: The Tragedy of Central Europe* (New York: Faber & Faber, 2023), 18–37.
¹¹ Peter Hallama, "Vergangenheitsbewältigung auf Tschechisch: Der Holocaust im tschechischen Samizdat" in Peter Hallama and Stephan Stach (eds.), *Gegengeschichte: Zweiter Weltkrieg und Holocaust im ostmitteleuropäischen Dissens* (Leipzig: Leipziger Universitätsverlag, 2015), 237–260.
¹² Carl Tighe, "Kundera's Kidnap Revisited," *Journal of European Studies* 44, no. 2 (2014): 112–133.

cosmopolitans" common to Nazism and Stalinism. Kundera also distanced himself from postmodern adulation of Jewish nomads "whose Being-together depends not on the authenticity of any primary roots."[13] His remarkable Jews belonged to Central Europe: Their virtue was not nomadism but their role as cultural cement.

The Czech writer, however, succumbed to romanticization. What attracted him to Franz Kafka, Joseph Roth, or Bruno Schultz, was not their alienness "everywhere" but their capacity to feel "everywhere at home." Enthralled by Jews without borders, Kundera glossed over the tragic side of their predicament. For his heroes, as for assimilated Jewish intellectuals across Mitteleuropa, embracing Europe was less a "Jewish" disposition than a flight from outsideness – an escape to a cosmopolitan world still primarily composed of Jews.[14] Like Kundera, Hannah Arendt had earlier noted that the "fatherland" of early twentieth-century Jewish intellectuals was Europe, "something that could be said of no other group." But their universalism unmoored from Jewishness was only "self-deception," argued Arendt, not the noblest form of European identity.[15] Kundera's "Kidnapped West" nonetheless inserted Jewish memory into liberal visions of Europe's future. To imagine supranationalism was to think of supranational Jews; to envision a pluralistic community required valorization of the Jewish cosmopolitan experience.[16] In a lecture delivered in Jerusalem in 1985, the Czech émigré went one step further: Not only dead Central European Jews but Israel itself was "the true heart of Europe – a peculiar heart located outside the body." The Israeli state, in Kundera's eyes, was neither supremacist nor ethnonational, but the heir of cosmopolitan Europe in the Middle East.[17]

The transition from the Common Market to the European Union, however, proceeded without fantasies of Jewish Mitteleuropa. Jacques Delors,

---

[13] Jean-François Lyotard, *Heidegger et "les juifs"* (Paris: Galilée, 1987), 52, cited in Sarah Hammerschlag, *The Figural Jew: Politics and Identity in Postwar French Thought* (Chicago, IL: University of Chicago Press, 2010), 8.
[14] Ilse Josepha Lazaroms, "Hotel Patriots or Permanent Strangers? Joseph Roth and the Jews of Inter-War Central Europe" in Cathy S. Gelbin and Sander L. Gilman (eds.), *Jews on the Move: Modern Cosmopolitanist Thought and Its Others* (London: Routledge, 2018), 46–59; Malachi Haim Hacohen, "Dilemmas of Cosmopolitanism: Karl Popper, Jewish Identity, and 'Central European Culture'" *The Journal of Modern History* 71, no. 1 (March 1999): 105–149.
[15] Hannah Arendt, *Men in Dark Times* (New York: Harcourt Brace Jovanovic, 1968), 42. On Arendt's "rooted cosmopolitanism," see Natan Sznaider, *Jewish Memory and the Cosmopolitan Order* (Cambridge: Polity Press, 2011).
[16] For a discussion of Jews in late twentieth-century cosmopolitanist thought, see Cathy S. Gelbin and Sander L. Gilman (eds.), *Cosmopolitanisms and the Jews* (Ann Arbor, MI: University of Michigan Press, 2017).
[17] Milan Kundera, "Jerusalem Address: The Novel and Europe" in *The Art of the Novel* (London: Faber, 1990), 157–165.

president of the European Commission between 1985 and 1995 and the last pioneer of continental integration, rightfully called himself a "militant European." Yet his dream was not cosmopolitanism but federalism. "The joint exercise of sovereignty," declared the French social democrat in 1989, was the best antidote to nationalism, not "a conspiracy against the nation-state."[18] Stefan Zweig's pre-Holocaust cosmopolitan enthusiasm – "To me the greatness of Judaism is to be supra-national" – or George Steiner's more recent idealization of Central European Jewish intellectuals as Europe's lost leaven, had no bearing on Delors's roadmap to the 1992 Maastricht Treaty.[19] For the visionary but technocratic policymaker, the "quantum leap" from economic community to the European Union necessitated the removal of internal barriers and "the principle of subsidiarity," not conversion to Jewish Europeanness. Fifteen years later, however, this idea had made its way into official EU pronouncements. "We can learn a lot from the history of the Jews of Europe," declared the European Commission president Romano Prodi in 2004. "New Europeans," explained the center-left Italian politician, "are just starting to learn the complex art of living with multiple allegiances." But Jews, "the first, old Europeans," have been forced "to master this art since antiquity."[20] They now offered the EU a model to emulate: "the values that have guided them through the centuries have provided a reference for us." To become European, in this logic, was to become allegorically Jew.

Speaking in Brussels at a seminar on antisemitism, Prodi may not have realized that his praise for "Europe's archetypal minority" still positioned Jews as outsiders. Without mentioning Muslims, he also implied that other minorities should imitate Jews in order to belong to Europe. Yet his remarks above all exemplified the entanglement of Euro-optimism with philosemitism at the start of the twenty-first century. This moment coincided with the peak of Europeanist self-celebration: the ever-enlarging EU as a postnational peace project, a success story of democratic rule and human rights, "a union of diversity where differences are accepted and perceived as enriching the whole."[21] This triumphant account

---

[18] Jacques Delors, "Our Necessary Union" (1989) in Brent F. Nelsen and Alexander C-G. Stubb (eds.), *The European Union: Readings in the Theory and Practice of European Integration* (Boulder, CO: Lynne Rienner Publishers, 1994), 51–64.

[19] On Zweig's and Steiner's cosmopolitanism, see Nick Lambert, *Jews and Europe in the Twentieth Century* (London: Vallentine Mitchell, 2008), 125–129; Adam Sutcliffe, *What Are Jews For? History, Peoplehood, and Purpose* (Princeton, NJ: Princeton University Press, 2020), 284–286.

[20] Romano Prodi, "A Union of Minorities" (2004) in Sharon Pardo and Hila Zahavi (eds.), *The Jewish Contribution to European Integration* (Lanham, MD: Lexington Books, 2020), 85–90.

[21] Ibid.

presupposed that the European idea was now civic/universalist and no longer ethnic/cultural. Such confidence precluded consideration of a less flattering option: the EU as a regional project of "Eurowhiteness" blind to Eurocentrism, oblivious of colonial crimes, and a fortress against Islam.[22] To the contrary, prominent advocates of "new cosmopolitanism" at the start of the twenty-first century imported Euro-optimism into the intellectual sphere. After pleading for a postnational Germany grounded on constitutionalism and democracy, the philosopher Jürgen Habermas saw in the EU the template for a global "postnational constellation." More measured, the sociologist Ulrich Beck portrayed Maastricht Europe as the successful reconciliation between universalism and difference. The cosmopolitan outlook, summarized Beck, was not a substitute for rootedness, but "a break with the hallowed principle of sovereignty."[23]

Contrary to Kundera, Habermas and Beck did not designate Jews as palimpsests of postnationalism. However, the fact that turn-of-the-century German thinkers became Europe's leading theorists of cosmopolitanism was not incidental. Since the fall of the Berlin Wall, they simultaneously witnessed the explosion of "remembrance culture" in their country and the Europeanization of Holocaust memory enshrined in the 2000 Stockholm Declaration.[24] In the ivory tower or among EU officials, Europe's cosmopolitan self-image was the product of recent baptism. At the end of the Cold War, Holocaust remembrance became the birth certificate of a new Europe confident in victory over nationalism, antisemitism, and racism. The memory of colonialism played little role in the rebranding of "the idea of Europe" as cosmopolitan project. Although central-western European states shared a common history of rule on foreign lands, the critical reevaluation of colonialism only occurred – at best – at the national level. Reckoning with ill-digested imperial history, let alone with colonial crimes, had no place in the project of unified European memory.[25] Although a postcolonial turn

---

[22] Hans Kundnani, *Eurowhiteness: Culture, Empire and Race in the European Project* (London: Hurst, 2023); Shane Weller, *The Idea of Europe: A Critical History* (Cambridge: Cambridge University Press, 2021), 247–268.
[23] Jürgen Habermas, *The Postnational Constellation* (Cambridge: Polity Press, 2000); Ulrich Beck, *The Cosmopolitan Vision* (Cambridge: Polity Press, 2006), 69.
[24] Larissa Allwork, *Holocaust Remembrance between the National and the Transnational: The Stockholm International Forum and the First Decade of the International Task Force* (London: Bloomsbury, 2015).
[25] Małgorzata Pakier and Bo Stråth (eds.), *A European Memory? Contested Histories and Politics of Remembrance* (New York: Berghahn Books, 2010); Aleida Assmann, "*Europe: A Community of Memory?* (Washington, DC: German Historical Institute, 2006), available at: https://fsnagle.org/papers/assmann2006printing.pdf.

became noticeable in national historiographies after 2000, the critical memorialization of the colonial past still remained in its infancy at the level of EU institutions.[26]

The Holocaust, on the other hand, was now "seared in the consciousness of Europe." The landmark European Parliament resolution of January 27, 2005, also declared that "the crimes committed at Auschwitz must live on in the memory of future generations."[27] In his 2004 remarks, Romano Prodi assured his audience that Holocaust consciousness had long been part of the European project. "The horror of the Shoah and the terrible loss of life caused by the Second World War," he observed, "deeply marked Europe's founding fathers too." The Treaty of Rome (1957), however, promoted reconciliation and economic integration in response to World War II yet without reference to the annihilation of Jews. Although Konrad Adenauer signed the 1952 Reparations Agreement, his fellow Christian Democrat founding fathers yearned for "an ever-closer union of the peoples of Europe" while keeping – if not by keeping – the Holocaust at bay. The European Union "anti-Holocaust club," by contrast, turned the memory of Jewish extermination into its "foundational past," its "civil religion" or its paradigmatic *lieu de mémoire* ("site of memory"): Scholars have offered various turns of phrases to capture the European sacralization of Jewish victims at the end of the Cold War.[28]

The moral halo of the Holocaust, critics have since argued, also served as "moral alibi" for NATO and American military interventions, subjected Jews to a "new grammar of otherness," impoverished politics in favor of apolitical empathy, and magnified the Final Solution at the expense of colonial crimes. But whether the start of confrontation with historical responsibility, or the presage of Holocaust fundamentalism, the inscription of the Jewish genocide into Europe's core identity fast-tracked philosemitism after 1989. To be sure, the portrayal of Jews as "archetypal" friends; the European Union's official anti-antisemitism;

---

[26] Aline Sierp, "EU Memory Politics and Europe's Forgotten Colonial Past," *Interventions: International Journal of Postcolonial Studies* 22, no. 6 (2020): 686–702.

[27] European Parliament Resolution on Holocaust Remembrance, Anti-Semitism, and Racism (January 27, 2005), available at: www.europarl.europa.eu/doceo/document/TA-6-2005-0018_EN.html.

[28] Wulf Kansteiner uses the expression "Anti-Holocaust Club" in *In Pursuit of German Memory: History, Television, and Politics after Auschwitz* (Athens, OH: Ohio University Press, 2006), 291; Alon Confino, *Foundational Pasts: The Holocaust as Historical Understanding* (Cambridge: Cambridge University Press, 2011); Enzo Traverso, *The End of Jewish Modernity* (London: Pluto Press, 2016), 116–127; Adam Sutcliffe, "Whose Feelings Matter? Holocaust Memory, Empathy, and Redemptive Anti-Antisemitism," *Journal of Genocide Research* 26, no. 2 (2022): 222–242.

or a sympathetic view of Israel as extension of cosmopolitan Europe, were also reactions to a threatening "Muslim Question." Euro-skeptics, including far-right parties and anti-immigrant populists, soon "loved" Jews against Islam with their own vocabulary. Philosemitism met Islamophobia in the course of the 1990s, yet a "surfeit of memory" first enabled its acceleration: the consecration of the Shoah as "the very definition and guarantee of the continent's restored humanity."[29]

"In Remembrance Lies the Secret of Redemption"

For Jewish observers of this historic moment, the fall of the Berlin Wall on November 9, 1989, raised fears of antisemitism more than hopes of philosemitism. "I cannot hide the fact that the Jew in me is troubled, even worried," wrote Elie Wiesel on October 17.[30] The desecration of 327 Jewish cemeteries in Germany between October 1990 and the summer of 1992 vindicated his pessimism. Although Third World asylum seekers, refugees from Eastern Europe, and Turkish guest workers bore the brunt of neo-Nazi violence, antisemitic incidents soared in the aftermath of German reunification. Few Jews were physically harmed during a wave of hate crimes predominantly committed in the Eastern states between 1990 and 1993. Yet extreme rightists and skinhead youths made no secret of wishing both "foreigners and Jews out." Large crowds, in response, marched against xenophobia and racism. Yet in November 1992, the writer of Jewish descent Ralph Giordano penned an open letter informing chancellor Helmut Kohl that Jews in Germany had no choice but to prepare for armed self-defense.[31]

The 1989 "turning-point," however, elicited above all fears of Holocaust amnesia. The normalization of German history had been since 1982 the central theme of Kohl's national narrative. The Federal Republic learned the lessons of the past, the Christian Democrat chancellor told his Israeli hosts in 1984, but the "grace of late birth" and their vibrant democracy now dispensed Germans from guilt. A year later,

---

[29] Tony Judt, *Postwar: A History of Europe since 1945* (New York: Penguin Press, 2005), 804.
[30] Cited in Sander L. Gilman, "German Reunification and the Jews," *New German Critique* 52, Special Issue on German Unification (Winter 1991): 173–191.
[31] Robert S. Wistrich (ed.), "Xenophobia and Antisemitism in the New Europe: The Case of Germany" in *Demonizing the Other Antisemitism, Racism, and Xenophobia* (London: Routledge, 1999), 349–365; Hermann Kurthen, Werner Bergmann, and Rainer Erb (eds.), *Antisemitism and Xenophobia in Germany after Unification* (New York: Oxford University Press, 1997); Jeffrey M. Peck, "The "Ins" and "Outs" of the New Germany: Jews, Foreigners, Asylum Seekers" in Sander L. Gilman and Karen Remmler (eds.), *Reemerging Jewish Culture in Germany: Life and Literature since 1989* (New York: New York University Press, 1994), 131–147; *American Jewish Year Book*, no. 94 (1994): 310.

Kohl's tribute to fallen Wehrmacht and SS soldiers at the Bitburg cemetery in the company of Ronald Reagan confirmed his determination to free the nation from the stigma of Nazism. The chancellor, however, diffused the Bitburg controversy by mending ties with American Jewish organizations and Jews in Germany.[32] Although the president of the Bundestag Philipp Jenninger delivered an embarrassing speech on the same occasion, Kohl's commemoration of Kristallnacht on November 9, 1988, included acknowledgment of "deep shame" and thankfulness for the "precious" but "fragile" presence of Jews in the Federal Republic.[33] During his visit of Auschwitz on November 14, 1989, Kohl recognized that "unspeakable hurt was inflicted on various peoples here, but above all on European Jews, in the name of Germany": an evocation of Jewish victims absent from Helmut Schmidt's remarks at the site in 1977. A few days after the fall of the Wall, Kohl still signaled that the new Germany in the making had not stepped out of Hitler's shadow.[34]

Proclaimed on October 3, 1990, reunification potentially rid the resurgent nation from the burden of ritualized penitence. The sudden transformation of Germany into Europe's most populous and prosperous country offered a tempting opportunity: the celebration of a healthy national history unencumbered by excessive Jewish memory. In his televised address, Kohl now only made passing reference to Germany's criminal past. He instead announced that "united Europe is our future." It befell on the Easterner Lothar de Maizière to remind revelers in Berlin that "the murder of six million Jews and many other Nazi crimes (...) weighs heavily on us."[35] But like the prominent critics of unification Günther Grass and Jürgen Habermas, Jewish commentators in Germany, the United States, and Israel worried about the future of Holocaust memory. National revival, they feared, could rapidly reduce Auschwitz to a forgettable aberration. Surveys of public opinion justified their concerns. In late 1990, 65 percent of West Germans believed that their country had sufficiently atoned for Nazi crimes. Most citizens of the Federal Republic felt ashamed that "Germans committed so many crimes against the Jews," revealed an opinion poll from January 1992, but as in the past they also wished to "close the file" on

---

[32] Jacob Eder, *Holocaust Angst: The Federal Republic of Germany and Holocaust Memory since the 1970s* (New York: Oxford University Press, 2016), 75–83.

[33] Cited in Jeffrey Herf, *Divided Memories: The Nazi Past in the Two Germanies* (Cambridge, MA: Harvard University Press, 1997), 360.

[34] "Clamor in the East: A Good Will Trip Ends," *The New York Times*, November 15, 1989.

[35] "Two Germanies Merge into One in a Historic Night of Celebration," *The Washington Post*, October 3, 1990.

this dark episode. About 42 percent still believed that Nazism had its good and bad sides.[36] Foreign observers of the German cultural scene nevertheless noted "a fascination for things Jewish" at the dawn of the 1990s. "The Jewish past has become almost folkloric, a lost paradise," cautioned the Dutch-American writer Ian Buruma in 1992. Contrary to previous philosemitic fads, countered the more optimistic American scholar Jack Zipes, Jews in Germany were no longer passive objects of exoticization. They now drew positive attention thanks to a distinctive minority culture created on their own terms. Yet the leading historian of West German philosemitism saw clouds on the horizon. "The philosemitic barriers cautiously accepted by the German intellectual mainstream for so many decades," wrote Frank Stern in 1991, "are now eroding." Others did not hesitate to conclude that "the official philosemitism of the postwar era came to an end on November 9, 1989." For the German Jewish intellectual Mischa Brumlik, philosemitism was already extinct since "the obscene ritual at Bitburg."[37]

Admittedly, the "new uninhibitedness" toward Jews within the conservative right, already palpable during the Historians' Debate (1986–88), suggested that Holocaust exculpation was no longer taboo in the public domain. The dissolution of the German Democratic Republic was also an invitation for the so-called New Right to balance the memory of the Nazi past against the crimes of state socialism.[38] On the left, the fall of the Berlin Wall encouraged intellectuals or politicians to shy away from Jürgen Habermas's constitutional patriotism – a postnational identity grounded on the permanent repudiation of Nazism. "Self-confidence and pride from one's own history," the SPD leader Peter Glotz had already countered in 1986, were equally important.[39] In the first half of the 1990s, however, Helmut Kohl's memorialization initiatives best exemplified the postunification longing for affirmative history. Inaugurated in

---

[36] AJYB (94), 1994, 311.
[37] Ian Buruma, "The Ways of Survival" in *New York Review of Books* (July 16, 1992); Jack Zipes, "The Contemporary Fascination for Things Jewish: Toward a Minor Culture" in *Reemerging Jewish Culture in Germany*, op. cit., 15–45; Frank Stern and Bill Templer, "The 'Jewish Question' in the 'German Question' 1945–1990: Reflections in Light of November 9th, 1989" *New German Critique* 52 (Winter, 1991): 155–172; Robert S. Wistrich, "Xenophobia and Antisemitism in the New Europe: The Case of Germany," op. cit.; Mischa Brumlik, "The Situation of the Jews in Today's Germany" (1990) in Y. Michal Bodemann (ed.), *Jews, Germans, Memory* (Ann Arbor, MI: University of Michigan Press, 1996), 1–18.
[38] Marko Elliot Neaman, "A New Conservative Revolution?: Neo-Nationalism, Collective Memory, and the New Right in Germany since Unification" in *Antisemitism and Xenophobia in Germany after Unification*, op. cit., 190–210.
[39] Peter Glotz cited in Geoff Eley, "Nazism, Politics, and the Image of the Past: Thoughts on the West German *Historikerstreit*, 1986–87" *Past and Present* 121 (1988): 171–208.

1994, the Museum of the Federal Republic in Bonn recounted the success story of democratic West Germany. Opened in 1993, the Central Memorial for the Victims of War and Tyranny in Berlin paid tribute to fallen Wehrmacht soldiers, POWs, civilian victims, German expellees, and Jews. Neither museum ignored the Holocaust but one used the genocide to highlight the redemption of post-1945 Germany. The other lumped perpetrators and victims within a unified narrative of suffering. Both celebrated the restoration of Germany as a normal nation. In the early 1990s, the acceptance of the Holocaust as cornerstone of the German political culture looked like an unrealistic prospect.[40]

Yet the end of German division breathed new life into Holocaust memorial culture. In the East, the disappearance of the GDR spelled the demise of ideological antifascism. In the West, the end of the Cold War eroded the salience of "totalitarian theory" which between 1945 and 1989 allowed democratic Germans to frame Nazism as a mere variant of modern dictatorship: The birth of a unified state in 1990 opened a new space of national remembrance.[41] Normalizers, of course, continued to challenge the "guilt-obsession" of left-leaning intellectuals. But at the high levels of state or within educational or cultural institutions, Holocaust "historicization" and "relativization" never gained the upper hand. Kohl yearned for a usable past no longer dominated by Nazism, but under his administration the House of the Wannsee Conference Memorial Site opened its doors in 1992. Plans were also made to turn Berlin's The Topography of Terror into a permanent museum and documentation center.[42] In 1993, Kohl voiced support for the construction of the Memorial to the Murdered Jews of Europe in Berlin – a project hotly debated since the late 1980s and inaugurated in 2005. No electoral benefit could be expected from this stance. In 1994, 46 percent of CDU/CSU voters considered the Holocaust "irrelevant today" and 43 percent disapproved of plans for a Holocaust memorial.[43]

Yet aware that Germany's image in the US-dominated West depended on its engagement with the memory of Nazi crimes, Kohl

---

[40] Wulf Kansteiner, *In Pursuit of German Memory: History, Television, and Politics after Auschwitz* (Athens, OH: Ohio University Press, 2006), 270–279; Christian Wicke, *Helmut Kohl's Quest for Normality* (New York: Berghahn, 2015), 195–196; Siobhan Kattago, "Representing German Victimhood and Guilt: The Neue Wache and Unified German Memory," *German Politics & Society* 48, no. 3 (1998): 86–104.

[41] Bill Niven, *Facing the Nazi Past: United Germany and the Legacy of the Third Reich* (London: Routledge, 2002), 1–9.

[42] Ibid., 197.

[43] Jennifer Golub, *Current German Attitudes towards Jews and Other Minorities: A Survey of Public Opinion* (American Jewish Committee, 1994), 14, available at: https://access.gesis.org/dbk/2280.

recognized that the Americanization of the Holocaust ongoing since the late 1970s compelled the reunified state to turn the genocide into its central reference point.[44] The positive reception of Steven Spielberg's *Schindler's List* (1993) and Daniel Jonah Goldhagen's *Hitler's Willing Executioners* (1996) likewise revealed the impact of American cultural exports on the German psyche. Unbothered by criticism, Goldhagen declared all "ordinary Germans" who lived between the late nineteenth century and 1945 contaminated by "eliminationist antisemitism." A predominantly young public enthusiastically embraced his thesis. But the "Goldhagen effect" also extended the distance between genocidal Germans and their democratic successors. During his media-hyped book tour, the American scholar reassured packed audiences that they were not "obligated to feel tormented by the past." The "antagonist," observed the Israeli writer Amos Elon, simultaneously played the role of "liberator."[45]

The novelist and public intellectual Martin Walser, to be sure, did not see any liberation in Holocaust remembrance. In a notorious speech delivered in October 1998, the renowned intellectual compared Holocaust commemoration to a "moral cudgel" whose only function was the eternal shaming of Germans. Memory and guilt, argued Walser, were better left to private conscience. The standing ovation he received confirmed that many educated elites shared this sentiment.[46] Competing memories of German suffering – from victims of Allied bombings to ethnic German expellees – likewise challenged the central place of Jewish victims in official remembrance. But at the end of a long chancellorship initially premised on historical conservatism, Helmut Kohl changed course in 1998. Among other incentives, the Americanization of the Holocaust in the age of post-Cold War US hegemony required from reunified Germans to make the memory of the crime the "core of our self-concept as a nation."[47] His successor Gerhard Schröder, head of the Red-Green coalition from 1998 to 2005, reaffirmed this point of view. "No one can excuse

---

[44] Eder, *Holocaust Angst*, op. cit., 160–196.
[45] Atina Grossmann, "The "Goldhagen Effect": Memory, Repetition, and Responsibility in the New Germany" in Geoff Eley (ed.), *The Goldhagen Effect* (Ann Arbor, MI: University of Michigan Press, 2000), 99–123; Amos Elon, "The Antagonist as Liberator," *The New York Times Magazine*, January 26, 1997, cited in the roundtable forum "Holocaust Scholarship and Politics in the Public Sphere: Reexamining the Causes, Consequences, and Controversy of the Historikerstreit and the Goldhagen Debate," *Central European History*, no. 50 (2017): 375–403.
[46] Thomas A. Kovach and Martin Walser, *The Burden of the Past: Martin Walser on German Identity: Texts, Contexts, Commentary* (Rochester, NY: Camden House, 2008), 85–95.
[47] Cited in Eder, *Holocaust Angst*, op. cit., 160.

himself by claiming the grace of the late birth," he announced after his electoral victory.[48] Contrary to his Green foreign minister Joschka Fisher, Schröder adhered to a left-wing nationalism always aspiring to German normality. Yet at the dawn of the twenty-first century, the towering status of the Holocaust in official memory was solidly entrenched. "Remembrance of the war and the genocide perpetrated by the Nazis," Schröder declared a few months before ceding power to Angela Merkel, "is part of our national identity." Even before the radicalization of philosemitism during the Merkel era, the explosion of remembrance culture in the 1990s had already transformed Germans into "memory world champions."[49]

The institutionalization of Holocaust commemoration combined both progressive and conservative aspects. On the one hand, remembrance culture vindicated the left-wing liberal intellectuals who during the 1980s challenged the normalizing impulse. The proliferation of state-sponsored Holocaust memory initiatives in schools, museums, and archives also built upon the grassroot memory activism of the preceding decade. On the other hand, the ritualization of commemoration potentially voided "working through the past" of its self-critical dimension. Academic research on the Holocaust blossomed in the 1990s, but the devolution of ceremonial atonement to politicians and dignitaries allowed large segments of the public to remain indifferent. Remembrance culture, concurred scholars of German memory, fostered both *Betroffenheit* ("show of concern") and detachment.[50] The contrarian Jewish publicist Henryk Broder was more dismissive. Ritualized mourning, he already charged in the mid 1980s, allowed Germany to recover national pride: a self-serving *Sündenstolz* or "pride in confessing one's sin."[51]

The prioritization of the Holocaust in official memory, however, opened a new phase in the history of German philosemitism. The respectability of the Federal Republic always hinged on "reconciliation" with Jews domestically and abroad, as well as on special ties with Israel despite recurrent tensions. Yet the dependency of German absolution on

---

[48] Cited in Jeffrey K. Olick, *The Sins of the Fathers: Germany, Memory, Method* (Chicago, IL: University of Chicago Press, 2016), 411.

[49] Aleida Assmann, *Das neue Unbehagen an der Erinnerungskultur* (Munich: C.H. Beck, 2020), 59.

[50] Ibid., 76–77; Jan-Werner Müller, "Germany's Two Processes of 'Coming to Terms with the Past' – Failures, After All?" in Vladimir Tismeanu and Bogdan C. Iacob (eds.), *Remembrance, History, and Justice* (Budapest: Central European University Press, 2015), 213–238.

[51] Henryk M. Broder, "Jedem sein Mahnmal" in *Jedem das Seine* (Augsburg: Ölbaum, 1999), 168–173.

Holocaust remembrance deepened after 1990. Richard von Weizsäcker's landmark speech of May 8, 1985, had already announced this evolution. Three days after the controversial Bitburg commemoration, the President of Germany declared the surrender of the Third Reich a moment of "liberation." Equally innovative was his plea for redemptive memory. Remembrance of the Jewish genocide, he implored, must become "a part of our very beings." Often overlooked in commentaries of this notorious speech, however, is the mentoring role assigned to Jewish memory. "In remembrance lies the secret of redemption," stated von Weizsäcker in reference to an adage attributed to the Hassidic luminary Baal Shem Tov. "The Jewish nation," he added, "remembers and will always remember." To redeem themselves, intimated the Christian Democrat head of state, Germans should remember like the Jews: The biblical command *Zakhor* ("Remember") also obligated the descendants of Holocaust perpetrators.

The many Germans convinced that "grandpa was not a Nazi" easily ignored this injunction. But von Weizsäcker's address revealed elite-level readiness to ground German morality on the memory of dead Jews. After reunification, however, official philosemitism also entailed the revitalization of Jewish life. In late 1990, the presidents of the sixteen Länder still opposed the mass immigration of Soviet Jews to the Federal Republic. Insensitive to traumatic memories, they instead sought the help of Jewish representatives to select "contingents" of suitable newcomers.[52] Yet after unanimous parliamentary approval, at least 170,000 Jewish "quota refugees" settled in Germany between 1990 and 2010.[53] This special procedure, adopted while Kohl and conservatives otherwise claimed that "we are not a country of immigration," reversed a key feature of migratory philosemitism since the Holocaust. While from 1945 to 1990 the West facilitated the collective relocation of Eastern European and Soviet Jews outside of Europe (in Israel or the United States), reunified Germany revived intracontinental Jewish migration. From the perspective of asylum law, fear of antisemitism in the ex-USSR justified the reception of Soviet Jews unwilling to live in Israel or unable to obtain American visas. Half-a-century after its murderous crusade against Judeo-Bolshevism, Germany was now the "protector of Jews in the East."[54]

---

[52] Frank Stern and Bill Templer, "The 'Jewish Question' in the 'German Question', op. cit., 171.

[53] Yfaat Weiss and Lena Gorelik, "The Russian Jewish Immigration" in Michael Brenner (ed.), *A History of Jews in Germany since 1945* (Bloomington, IN: Indiana University Press, 2018), 379–416.

[54] Dan Diner, "Germany, the Jews, and Europe: History and Memory and the Recent Upheaval" in Y. Michal Bodemann (ed.), *Jews, Germans, Memory*, op. cit., 263–272.

The "reforestation" of Jewish life in the reunified country, however, also accounted for liberal entry regulations. Imagined as replicas of disappeared German Jews, immigrants from the former Soviet Union were entrusted by the political class with the resurrection of German Judaism. In addition to its positive effect on Western public opinion, "expiatory demographic engineering" sought redemptive benefits from the revival of Jewish presence. It also legitimized a peculiar vision of the Holocaust as German self-victimization: the wound the nation inflicted upon itself when it forced out or murdered its upstanding Jewish citizens.[55] The scant interest many Russian-speaking Jews showed for Jewish identity or religious observance, however, tempered hopes for the renaissance of the German-Jewish tradition. Yet by 2018, approximately 225,000 Jews affiliated and nonaffiliated with communities lived in Germany, while the conversion of non-Jews to Reform Judaism became a noticeable phenomenon. This was less than half than in 1933, but Germany now hosted the second largest Jewish population after France in the post-Brexit European Union. After remembrance culture transformed the Berlin Republic into a purported model of "coming to terms with the past," the cultivation of a flourishing yet always "precarious" Jewish life also turned twenty-first-century Germans into world champions in "anti-antisemitism": the protection of Jews from Muslim, Palestinian, and Jewish anti-Zionist "antisemitism," the shielding of the Holocaust from comparability, and a fervent commitment to Israel's security in the name of "reason of state."

Moral dependency on Jewish death and Jewish life, however, was not only peculiar to post–Cold War German identity. From 1989 to the 2010 Eurozone financial crisis – the peak period of Euro-optimism – Holocaust memory and anti-antisemitism became twin pillars of philosemitism in the European Union. Yet like the new remembrance culture envisioned in Richard von Weizsäcker's speech, the turn to Holocaust remembrance and anti-antisemitic governance in the European Union can also be traced to 1985. Released that year, Claude Lanzmann's nine-hour film *Shoah* was only seen by artsy or intellectual audiences. Entirely based on oral testimonies of survivors, bystanders, and perpetrators, the austere documentary revolutionized the representation of the genocide on screen. It also popularized the Hebrew *Shoah* ("disaster") in European

---

[55] Hanna Tzuberi, "'Reforesting Jews': The German State and the Construction of 'New German Judaism'" *Jewish Studies Quarterly* 27, no. 3 (2020): 199–224; see in the same issue, Johaness Becke, "German Guilt, White Guilt: The Politics of Reforestation and the Return of the Gardening State," 225–239; Y. Michal Bodemann and Olena Bagno, "In the Ethnic Twilight: The Path of Russian Jews in Germany" in Y. Michal Bodemann (ed.), *The New German Jewry and the European Context* (Houndmills, Basingstoke, Hampshire: Palgrave Macmillan, 2008), 158–176.

terminology. The word's rise to prominence, only fully apparent in the twenty-first century, was never absolute. "Holocaust" did not disappear from the lexicon and in Britain – as in the English-speaking world – the word retained its preeminence. In its official statements, the European Union continued to privilege "Holocaust" over "Shoah." In post-Communist Eastern Europe, the Hebrew term likewise remained in limited use. But for the academics, memory activists, media professionals, or politicians who especially in France and Germany adopted the short and mysterious "Shoah," naming the genocide in the (imagined) language of the victims not only asserted the uniqueness of their murder. It also reframed the German campaign of annihilation as "the attempt of one group of Europeans to exterminate every member of another group of Europeans, here on European soil."[56]

The proliferation of anti-antisemitic watchdogs institutions within the European Union stemmed from the newly discovered Europeanness of the Jewish genocide: overcoming the European arch crime begged for sustained monitoring of "a very light sleeper."[57] By the end of the 1990s, anti-antisemitism took a more combative turn. For proponents of the term "new antisemitism" who conflated leftist and Muslim anti-Zionism with Judeophobia, hatred of Jews "ceased to be a socially marginal phenomenon." In 2003, the French Jewish writer and media figure Alain Finkielkraut announced "a coming antisemitism" unseen in Europe since 1945.[58] From the center-left to the conservative right, anti-antisemitism now occupied a prominent place in political discourse. For their own purposes, conservative populists and far-right extremists also embraced this rhetoric. The strengthening of anti-antisemitism in the European Union, however, was first prepared by a transnational "politics of regret"[59]: The spread of Holocaust repentance beyond Germany's borders created a psychological space favorable to an intensified "war on antisemitism."

The Atonement Cascade

Although always carefully worded, official expressions of national remorse for the Holocaust remained until the end of the Cold War an exclusive West German ritual. The central place of the Jewish genocide

---

[56] Tony Judt, *Postwar*, op. cit., 804.
[57] The British think-tank Runnymede Trust coined the phrase in 1994: *A Very Light Sleeper: The Persistence and Dangers of Antisemitism* (London: Runnymede Trust, 1994).
[58] Bernard Harrison, *Blaming the Jews: Politics and Delusion* (Bloomington, IN: Indiana University Press, 2020), 3–4; Alain Finkielkraut, *Au nom de l'autre: Réflexions sur l'antisémitisme qui vient* (Paris: Gallimard, 2003).
[59] The sociologist Jeffrey K. Olick coined the phrase in *The Politics of Regret: On Collective Memory and Historical Responsibility* (New York: Routledge, 2007).

in post-1990 German memory only consolidated the status of the Berlin Republic as Europe's "master atoner."[60] Others nonetheless joined the fray: Europe's contribution to a burgeoning "age of apology" was to turn Holocaust contrition into the template for a (partial) politics of repentance in the West. The opening act of the atonement cascade, however, still took place on German soil. On April 12, 1990, the democratically elected East German parliament recognized the "immeasurable suffering" inflicted on Europeans by "Germans during the time of National Socialism." More daring was the admission of responsibility "on behalf of the people for the humiliation, expulsion, and murder of Jewish women, men, and children": The first unqualified confession of guilt by a European country since 1945 unexpectedly came from the socialist East. The GDR's antifascist myth vanished with the state in 1990, but four decades of antifascist culture had nonetheless prepared reformists to accept full responsibility for the Holocaust. In the same statement, the Volkskammer also asked "Jews of the world to forgive us for the hypocrisy and hostility of East German policies towards Israel and also for the persecution (...) of Jewish citizens after 1945 in our country."[61] Like the newborn Federal Republic after 1949, the ephemeral post-Communist East German government sought legitimation through philosemitism – and now penance for anti-Zionism. The mutation of socialist antifascism into Holocaust regret also set a precedent for the process of "democratic transition" in Eastern Europe. Critical examination of the past will not be demanded from former Soviet satellite states seeking membership in the European Union. But despite nationalist resistance and competing memories of Communist victimization, their "return to Europe" in 2004 and after will require at a minimum the payment of lip service to a key EU *acquis communautaire* or "common core": homage to the singular Shoah as prerequisite to Europeanization.

Austria, to the contrary, could until the late 1980s envision entry in the European Union without modification of its foundational myth. The darling of the West during the Cold War, the neutral country clung since 1945 to its "victim thesis." The doctrine initially affirmed Austria's status as "first victim of Hitlerite aggression." From the 1950s onward, it also connoted the patriotic sacrifice of Austrian soldiers and civilians "who only did their duty" under German rule. Both versions of

---

[60] Mischa Gabowitsch, "Replicating Atonement: The German Model and Beyond" in Mischa Gabowitsch (ed.), *Replicating Atonement: Foreign Models in the Commemoration of Atrocities* (Cham: Palgrave Macmillan, 2017), 1–24.
[61] Cited in Herf, *Divided Memories*, op. cit., 375.

the thesis, in any case, marginalized the role of Austrian Holocaust perpetrators and the persecution of Jews.[62] The outbreak of the Waldheim Affair in 1986, however, marked a turning point in Austria's self-perception. Although the federal president accused of misrepresenting his Wehrmacht service enjoyed strong popular support, a network of dissenters (including Jewish activists no longer willing to serve as "alibi Jews of Austria's national lie") challenged the narrative of innocence.[63] Only a predominantly young and progressive segment of the public took part in this grassroot counter-memory movement. Yet change was also perceptible at the level of high politics. On July 8, 1991, the socialist chancellor Franz Vranitzky issued the first non-German declaration of regret in post–Cold War Europe. "We acknowledge all aspects of our history," Vranitzky stated, "but just as we claim the good ones, we have to ask forgiveness for the bad ones – among the survivors and the descendants of the dead." The negative publicity generated by the Waldheim Affair undoubtedly accounted for this repentant tone. In June 1993, however, Vranitzky deepened his remorse during a visit of Israel, "a country whose people and destiny are so close to the hearts and minds of many Austrians." In November 1994, his successor Thomas Klestil told the Knesset that "We Austrians recognize that the acknowledgment of the full truth is long overdue."[64]

In 1995, Austria joined the European Union with an official remembrance culture no longer antithetical to that of guilty Germany. The reopening of Vienna's Jewish Museum in 1993, the Holocaust monument inaugurated in Vienna's Judenplatz in 2000, and a program of restitution of stolen Jewish property finalized in 2001, exemplified this convergence. Simon Wiesenthal's new prestige likewise reflected this evolution. Recurrently vilified as vengeful Jew and defamer of the country since the 1960s, the renowned Nazi hunter became in the liberal press of the late 1990s "the consciousness of the nation," the country's Jewish

---

[62] Peter Pirker, "The Victim Myth Revisited: The Politics of History in Austria up until the Waldheim Affair" in Günter Bishof, Mark Landry, and Christian Karner (eds.), *Myths in Austrian History: Construction and Deconstruction* (New Orleans: University of New Orleans Press, 2020), 153–174.

[63] The Austrian Jewish writer Doron Rabinovici is cited in Matti Bunzl, *Symptoms of Modernity: Jews and Queers in Late-Twentieth Century Vienna* (Berkeley, CA: University of California Press, 2004), 96. See also Helga Embacher, "Controversies over Austria's Past: Generational Changes and Grassroot Awakenings Following the Waldheim Affair and the 'Wehrmacht Exhibitions'" *Nationalities Papers* 51, no. 3 (2023): 644–664.

[64] "Austria Admits Role in Holocaust," *The Washington Post*, July 8, 1991; Vranitzky's speech in Jerusalem (June 1993) is available in German at: https://dasrotewien.at/seite/auszuege-aus-vranitzkys-rede-vor-der-hebraeischen-universitaet-jerusalem; Klestil's address (November 1994) is available at: https://m.knesset.gov.il/EN/activity/Documents/SpeechPdf/klestil.pdf.

guide to morality and truth.[65] The strong showing of Jörg Haider's far-right Freedom Party in the 1999 parliamentary elections, and its governmental alliance with conservatives until 2005, revealed the fragility of the post-innocence turn. Yet the protest culture born out of the Waldheim Affair grew into forceful opposition. The estimated 250,000 people who on February 19, 2000, filled Vienna's Heldenplatz demonstrated above all against a "coalition with racism." But the anti-Haider movement was not a return to old left antifascism. It signaled instead a generational shift in interpretations of the past. This was not only true of the young and left-leaning segment of civil society: In the early twenty-first century, the Shoah moved from the periphery to the center of official Austrian memory.[66] As in Germany, the explosion of commemorative projects in Vienna and other cities after 2005 will be accompanied by heightened monitoring of "both existing and the new imported antisemitism," in the words of Sebastian Kurz pronounced in Israel in 2018. Like Angela Merkel a decade earlier, the young center-right chancellor also committed his country to Israel's security, "our moral obligation that is part of our Staatsräson [reason of state or national interest]."[67] In Austria as in other EU member states, the liberal impulse initially behind the memorialization of the Shoah yielded distinctive forms of conservative – and far-right – pro-Israelism.

The gold standard of Holocaust remorse in post–Cold War Europe was set in France. Speaking at the anniversary of the 1942 Vel d'Hiv round up on July 16, 1995, Jacques Chirac's recognized his country's co-responsibility in the Final Solution. His address still distinguished between the "land of the Enlightenment and Human Rights" and the Vichy regime. Yet contrary to his predecessor François Mitterrand who always refused to "apologize in the name of France," Chirac broke with exculpation. "A collective fault," he acknowledged, the deportation of Jews was "backed up by French people and the French State." In reunified Germany, the phrase "remembrance culture" pertained to the institutionalization of guilt and expiation. In France, *devoir de mémoire* (duty of memory) symbolized the

---

[65] Bunzl, *Symptoms of Modernity*, op. cit., 177–178.
[66] Heidemarie Uhl, "From the Periphery to the Center of Memory: Holocaust Memorials in Vienna," *Dapim: Studies on the Holocaust* 3, no. 30 (2016): 221–242; Peter Pirker, Johannes Kramer, and Mathias Lichtenwagner, "Transnational Memory Spaces in the Making: World War II and Holocaust Remembrance in Vienna," *International Journal of Politics, Culture, and Society* no. 32 (2019): 439–458; Katya Krylova, *The Long Shadow of the Past: Contemporary Austrian Literature, Film, and Culture* (Rochester, NY: Camden House, 2017), 96–134.
[67] "Kurz vows Vienna to support Israel's security needs in 'tough neighborhood'," *The Jerusalem Post*, June 11, 2018.

new place of the Shoah in the national narrative.[68] The expression began to circulate in the early 1970s, but Chirac's speech revealed its hegemonic meaning in the mid 1990s. "To transmit the memory of the Jewish people (...) to bear witness again and again," was now a new moral standard. The life-long Gaullist who nevertheless shied away from de Gaulle's "resistancialist myth" did not speak in isolation. In late July 1995, 72 percent of the public approved of his declaration.[69] Chirac's successors, in turn, expanded the place of the Shoah in French memory. "There is nothing to add or remove from Jacques Chirac's speech," declared Nicolas Sarkozy at Paris's Shoah Memorial in 2007. In the name of "transmission," however, the conservative president proposed to pair every ten-year-old pupil with a Holocaust survivor (the project deemed potentially traumatic was ultimately aborted.) In 2012, François Hollande's own Vel d'Hiv address was a trenchant admission of French responsibility. "The truth," stated the one-term socialist president, "is that this crime was perpetrated in France, and by France." Yet unlike Chirac, Hollande also declared the murder of European Jews "an enterprise without precedent and which cannot be compared to anything else."[70] The exceptionality of the crime was already the cornerstone of German atonement. Overcoming the "Vichy syndrome" in France likewise entailed affirmation of the Shoah's incomparability: In both countries, the stage was set for a standoff between Holocaust and postcolonial memory.

Although directed at the French public, Chirac's epoch-making speech also offered leaders of former German-occupied countries in Western Europe a template for public penance. Despite Denmark's reputation as protector of Jews, the Prime Minister Anders Fogh Rasmussen apologized in 2005 for "the active cooperation of the Danish authorities" with German occupiers. That same year, the Dutch head of government Jan Peter Balkenende called the deportation of Jews a "pitch-black" chapter in the history of the Netherlands – a reference to collaboration and passivity departing from the cult of heroic Dutch rescuers. "We have to recognize [state collaboration] and say sorry," similarly declared the Belgian prime minister Guy Verhofstadt in 2007. The socialist premier Elio di Rupo sought "forgiveness" from the Belgian Jewish community in 2012. Collaborationist authorities "and through them the Belgian state,"

---

[68] On the history of the phrase, see Sébastien Ledoux, *Le devoir de mémoire: Une formule et son histoire* (Paris: CNRS, 2016).
[69] Rebecca Clifford, *Commemorating the Holocaust: The Dilemmas of Remembrance in France and Italy* (Oxford: Oxford University Press, 2013), 199.
[70] "Une entreprise qui n'a pas eu de précédent et qui ne peut être comparée à rien." François Hollande's address of July 22, 2012 is available at: www.vie-publique.fr/ discours/185557-declaration-de-m-francois-hollande-president-de-la-republique-sur-la.

he acknowledged, "were complicit in the most abominable crime." Like Chirac before him, the Walloon socialist avowed an "unforgivable debt" and pledged "to do all I can to never let it fall into oblivion."[71] No state-level apology for Belgian atrocities during the country's rule over Congo had until then been issued.

The French *devoir de mémoire* migrated to the Low Countries but crossed the Alps with more difficulties. In July 2000, the Italian Parliament instituted a Day of Memory to be observed every year on the anniversary date of the liberation of Auschwitz (January 27, 1945). The event was to commemorate "the extermination and persecution of the Jewish people and of Italian political and military deportees in the Nazi camps." The balancing of "Jewish" victimhood with "Italian" suffering distinguished Italian memory politics from Chirac's exclusive attention to the Final Solution. The absence of the word "Fascism" from the language of the law was another singularity. Two years after the Vatican's landmark "We Remember" declaration, the "Day of Memory" paid homage to Jewish victims, but alongside others and without designation of domestic perpetrators. For its critics, the project conveniently "de-Fascistized" the Shoah.[72] The law nonetheless specifically recognized "Italy's persecution of its Jewish citizens," a first official deviation from the "good Italian" myth. Although devoid of a unifying theme, the Day of Memory generated public discussions on Italy's role in the Holocaust, a topic until then only addressed in scholarly studies of antisemitism under Mussolini. A project initiated in 2006 to commemorate Fascist crimes in Ethiopia and the Balkans, on the other hand, never materialized.[73]

In Britain, the first Holocaust National Day marked on January 27, 2001, showed that the incorporation of the Shoah into European civic calendars was not limited to the former satellite states of Hitler's empire. "The Holocaust deserves a permanent place in our collective memory," announced Tony Blair on that day. Although a striking departure from the marginal place of the Jewish genocide in British memory, Blair's

---

[71] *Haaretz*, "Belgium's PM Apologizes for State's Holocaust-Era Complicity," September 11, 2012.

[72] Robert Gordon, *The Holocaust in Italian Culture, 1944–2010* (Stanford, CA: Stanford University Press, 2012), 182–183; Ruth Nattermann, "Italian Commemoration of the Shoah. A Survivor-Oriented Narrative and Its Impact on Politics and Practices of Remembrance" in Małgorzata Pakier and Bo Stråth (eds.), *A European Memory?*, op. cit., 204–218.

[73] Rebecca Clifford, *Commemorating the Holocaust*, op. cit., 230–246; Michele Sarfatti, "Notes and Reflections on the Italian Law Instituting Remembrance Day: History, Remembrance and the Present," in *Quest: Issues in Contemporary Jewish History*, December 12, 2017, available at: www.quest-cdecjournal.it/wp-content/uploads/file/Q12/Q12F5%20-%20Sarfatti.pdf.

statement avoided Britain's own historical relation to the Holocaust. The universal and dehistoricized Shoah, in the mind of the New Labour leader, was an invitation to "recommit (...) to the best, most decent values of humanity and compassion." Blair made no mention of Britain's "Late Victorian Holocausts" or its history of imperial violence: The Shoah remained the exclusive moral lesson for "the kind of society we believe in." Two years later, the Holocaust as Western paradigm of atrocity also justified the export of "decent values" to the Middle East through British participation in the American-led invasion of Iraq.[74]

In July 2001, Alexander Kwasniewski's address at the north-eastern Polish village of Jedwabne demonstrated that the Holocaust apology cascade also reached post-Communist Europe. During visits of Israel in 1995 and 1998, Lithuanian and Latvian heads of states had already expressed regret – before facing uproar at home. Issued in Poland, Kwasniewski's powerful declaration was also a domestic acknowledgment of guilt. A year after the publication of Jan T. Gross's *Neighbors* (published in Poland in 2000), the center-left president apologized "in the name of those Poles whose conscience is shattered by that crime." In Jedwabne, he stated, "Polish citizens were killed at the hands of fellow citizens." Like Kwasniewski, liberal politicians, academics, and journalists recognized that parts of the Polish population, while victimized by the Third Reich, also participated in the killing or persecution of Jews. On the seventieth anniversary of the pogrom (July 2011), Poland's president Bronislaw Komorowski apologized again for the crime.

Polish reactions to *Neighbors*, however, epitomized a chasm between the politics of regret in Western Europe and in post-Communist states. Jan T. Gross's bombshell provoked unprecedented soul-searching on violence committed by ethnic Poles against Jews during and after the war. The Jedwabne issue, however, divided liberals who remembered "to remember," conservatives who remembered "to benefit," and populists and nationalists who remembered "to forget."[75] As in other former communist states, Holocaust memory in Poland alternatively meant critical introspection, the start of a mutually beneficial relationship with Jews and Israel, or a tyrannical imposition of guilt on the martyred nation.

---

[74] Tony Blair Cited in Andy Pearce, "Britain's Holocaust Memorial Day: Inculcating 'British' or 'European' Holocaust Consciousness?" in Caroline Sharples and Olaf Jensen (eds.), *Britain and the Holocaust: Remembering War and Genocide* (Houndmills, Basingstoke, Hampshire: Palgrave Macmillan, 2013), 133–164; Mark Levene, "Britain's Holocaust Memorial Day: A Case of Post-Cold War Wish-Fulfillment or Brazen Hypocrisy?" *Human Rights Review* 3, no. 7 (2006): 26–59.

[75] John-Paul Himka and Joanna Betta Michlic (eds.), *Bringing the Dark Past to Light. The Reception of the Holocaust in Post-Communist Europe* (Lincoln, NE: University of Nebraska Press, 2013), 11.

Whereas the "Paxton effect" in France or the "Goldhagen effect" in Germany ultimately yielded elite consensus on remembrance culture or *devoir de mémoire*, the "Jan Gross effect" in Poland unleashed memory wars unseen in Western Europe after 1989. The right-wing populist Law and Justice party in power between 2015 and 2023 only widened the rift between patriotic memory and critical remembrance: For the guardians of the martyrdom narrative, the politics of regret was only a "pedagogy of shame," when not a "crime against the Polish nation."[76]

Polish responses to *Neighbors* from 2000 to 2015, and Law and Justice's ideological war against revisionist historians during its eight-year rule, confirmed that the addition of Eastern members to the European Union did not easily translate into the "Europeanization of Holocaust memory." Post-Communist states, to be sure, signed the 2000 Stockholm Declaration which singled out the Holocaust as a singular breach of civilization. They supported numerous European Parliament resolutions calling for Holocaust education and research at the continental level. In 2005, they recognized January 27 as "European Holocaust Memorial Day." By 2015, most of the former peoples' democracies had joined the International Holocaust Remembrance Alliance (IHRA) founded in 2000.[77] Although a prerequisite for EU membership, their gravitation toward Shoah memory was not a "zero hour" of Holocaust consciousness in the region. From 1945 to 1989, socialist antifascism did not hermetically suppress discussions of Jewish victimhood. Despite the insertion of the Holocaust into a scripted antifascist narrative, historians, artists, and writers carved out a space of memorialization in the communist bloc. In the wake of the 1989 revolutions, ethnonationalists resisted Jewish memory but pro-European liberals who grew in the shadow of antifascism did not always discover the Holocaust thanks to Western moral education. While buried under communist ideology until 1989, its memory was nonetheless kept alive in parts of the intelligentsia and dissident networks.[78]

Commitment to Holocaust remembrance, however, was also the prize to pay to commemorate "our own" suffering under Nazism and Communism. At the start of the twenty-first century, acceptance of the Shoah as foundational European event aligned the East with the West.

---

[76] Jörg Hackmann, "Defending the 'Good Name' of the Polish Nation: Politics of History as a Battlefield in Poland" in Ljiljana Radonić (ed.), *The Holocaust/Genocide Template in Eastern Europe* (New York: Routledge, 2020), 194–203.

[77] Marek Kucia, "The Europeanization of Holocaust Memory and Eastern Europe," *East European Politics and Societies and Cultures* 1, no. 30 (2016): 97–119.

[78] Kata Bohus, Peter Hallama, and Stephan Stach (eds.), *Growing Up in the Shadow of Antifascism: Remembering the Holocaust in State-Socialist Europe* (Budapest: Central European University Press, 2022).

But the post-Communist states who joined the European Union in 2004, 2007, and 2013, pursued their own mnemonic agenda. They either equalized the Shoah and Communist crimes, celebrated brave rescuers while forgetting complicity, or used the Jewish genocide to highlight other forms of victimization. The Holocaust undoubtedly entered Eastern Europe's official memory culture after 1989, but governments retained control over the way in which it is "remembered, understood, and interpreted": The project of unified Shoah memory resulted instead in memory divergence.[79] Yet in East-Central Europe, the Balkans, and the Baltic States, the multiplication of Holocaust museums, research centers, and memorial sites also pointed to institutional convergence. Despite the conflation of "our suffering" with the Holocaust, or the prioritization of Communist oppression, the musealization of the Shoah in the former communist realm extended Western commemorative practices to the East. The "return to Europe" of post-Communist states did not elicit a consensus of regret across the former Iron Curtain: Enlargement to the East nonetheless bolstered the European Union's "anti-Holocaust club."[80]

Resurrecting the Jew?

The arrival of Shoah memory in Eastern Europe coincided with the emergence of grassroot "Jewish" revivalism in the region. The production and consumption of Jewish culture by predominantly non-Jews was already a phenomenon noticed in Germany after reunification. The Klezmer boom in Berlin during the 1990s, for instance, brought to life a musical genre foreign to the German Jewish experience yet marketed as authentically Jewish. The Klezmer wave also rolled through the former Yiddish-speaking East where the sound of Jewish music filled the void of absence.[81]

---

[79] See among others Jelena Subotić, *Yellow Star, Red Star: Holocaust Remembrance after Communism* (Ithaca, NY: Cornell University Press, 2019), 20, 56; Éva Kovács, "Limits of Universalization: The European Sites of Genocide" in *The Holocaust/Genocide Template in Eastern Europe*, op. cit., 22–55; Emmanuel Droit, "Le Gulag contre la Shoah: Mémoires offcielles et cultures mémorielles dans l'Europe élargie," *Vingtième Siècle: Revue d'histoire* 2, no. 94 (2007): 101–120.

[80] Ljiljana Radonić, "World War II and the Holocaust in Post-Communist Memorial Museums" in Paul Srodecki and Daria Kozlova (eds.), *War and Remembrance: World War II and Memory Politics of Post-Socialist Europe* (Paderborn: Brill, 2023), 205–224.

[81] Liliane Weissberg, "The Sound of Music: Jews and the Study of Jewish Culture in the New Europe," *Comparative Literature* 4, no. 58 (2006): 403–417; Raysh Weiss, "Klezmer in the New Germany: History, Identity, and Memory" in Jay Geller and Leslie Morris (eds.), *Three-Way Street: Jews, Germans and the Transnational* (Ann Arbor, MI: University of Michigan Press, 2016), 302–319; Eleanor Shapiro, "The Sound of Change: Performing 'Jewishness' in Small Polish Towns," *Polin: Studies in Polish Jewry* 32 (2020): 477–498; and in the same issue, Magdalena Waligorska, "The Klezmer Revival in Poland as a Contact Zone," 461–475.

In former centers of pre-Holocaust Jewish life, "virtual Jewishness" suddenly resuscitated the vanished Jewish past. Prague's Old Town in the mid 1990s, observed then a Jewish-American visitor, oddly looked like a "Jurassic Park of Judaism (...) a circus of the dead."[82] In Poland, Krakow's historic Jewish quarter became a flourishing center of "Jewish" tourism. Hassidic figurines in souvenir shops, "Jewish" restaurants and cabaret artists, or street performers dressed as *shtetl* Jews, left an impression of kitsch and commercialism. Yet Poland's non-Jewish "Jewish turn" amounted to more than commodification. For liberal revivalists, "resurrecting the Jew" through the learning of Yiddish and Jewish history, attendance of "Jewish" festivals, or the mapping of past Jewish sites, meant resisting Polish-Catholic ethnonationalism. Civic philosemitism did not prevent the Law and Justice party from securing a solid electoral majority in 2015. Since Jan T. Gross's "shock therapy," however, progressive actors defended the idea of secular and multicultural Polishness through "vicarious Jewishness" – their conduit to pluralist democracy.[83]

The arrival of Shoah memory in the European Union's East not only elicited new forms of liberal engagement with "things Jewish." It also added new "Jewish spaces" to a region which prior to 1989 looked like the graveyard of European Jewry. Beautified Jewish quarters or synagogues brought to life a "virtual" Jewish heritage. But the "return" of the Holocaust to East-Central Europe, pointed out the sociologist Diana Pinto in the mid 1990s, also produced "Jewish-friendly neutral spaces": Jewish activities now taking place outside the Jewish world. Memorials, Jewish museums, and Jewish programs in universities, observed the French-Italian scholar, migrated from the Jewish sphere to civil society. Already in existence in the West but a novelty in the post-Communist East, such "friendly neutral spaces" carried out Jewishness to a wider public. Fifty years after the Holocaust, they signaled the mutation of Jews from "intrinsic foreigners" into "integral pieces, *qua Jews*, of an open European continent."[84]

---

[82] Ruth Ellen Gruber, *Virtually Jewish: Reinventing Jewish Culture in Europe* (Berkeley, CA: University of California Press, 2002), 132.

[83] Geneviève Zubrzycki, *Resurrecting the Jew: Nationalism, Philosemitism, and Poland's Jewish Revival* (Princeton, NJ: Princeton University Press, 2022); Erica Lehrer, *Jewish Poland Revisited: Heritage Tourism in Unquiet Places* (Bloomington, IN: Indiana University Press, 2013); Magdalena Waligorska, "In the Cellars and Attics of Memory: Mapping Jewish and Non-Jewish Spaces in Contemporary Poland" in Alina Gromova, Felix Heinert, and Sebastian Voigt (eds.), *Jewish and Non-Jewish Spaces in the Urban Context* (Berlin: Neofelis, 2015), 243–258.

[84] Diana Pinto, "A New Jewish Identity for Post-1989 Europe" in *JPR Reports: Institute for Jewish Policy Research* (June 1996), available at: www.jpr.org.uk/sites/default/files/attachments/new-jewish-identity-post-1989-europe.pdf; "The Third Pillar: Towards a New European Identity" in *Jewish Studies at the Central European University: Public*

Other commentators tempered this enthusiasm. New meeting grounds between Jews and non-Jews emerged in post-1989 Europe, yet as the case of reunified Germany demonstrated, these "Judaizing terrains" also created "distortive imaginations of Jews." From the same German vantage point, scholars countered in the early 2000s that "civil society does not yet acknowledge Jews' entitlement to a distinct place in it (...) since the perpetrator's side has not yet come to terms with their deeds."[85] Delivered in 2004, George Steiner's remarks exemplified the persistence of lachrymosity after 1989. "Until Europe (...) comes to explicit terms with the long prehistory of the gas-ovens," warned the distinguished Jewish intellectual, "many of the stars in our European firmament will continue to be yellow."[86]

The age of Euro-optimism nonetheless gave ground to Jewish optimism. The Europeanization of the Shoah, and in Western Europe the breaking of taboos about complicity, pushed the memory of the crime from the Jewish realm to society at large. Despite unease with ritualistic expiation – "a way *not* to remember" for its fiercest critics[87] – the democratization of the Shoah fostered the normalization of Jewishness in the European Union. At the risk of lachrymose reprimand, Diana Pinto noted that twenty years after the end of the Cold War, "Jewish themes, references, and life now occupy center stage in ways that seemed unimaginable" during the first postwar decades. This was not just overcompensation. The chasm between "Europe" and "Jews" spectacularly narrowed after 1989: The Holocaust, as well as the pre-Holocaust Jewish past, were now officially shared by both sides.[88] In the academic world, the expansion of Jewish history into national or European history testified of this proximity. Populated by Jewish and non-Jewish researchers alike, centers for Holocaust or Jewish history mainstreamed "Jewish" knowledge in universities – even if in Germany debates over ownership

---

Lectures 1996–1999 (Budapest: Central European University, 2000), 177–201; "Negotiating Jewish Identity in an Asemitic Age," *Jewish Culture and History* 2–23, no. 14 (2013): 68–77.

[85] See Y. Michal Bodeman, "A Jewish Cultural Renascence in German?" and Ian Leveson and Sandra Lustig, "Caught between Civil Society and the Cultural Market: Jewry and the Jewish Space in Europe: A Response to Diana Pinto" in Leveson and Lustig (eds.), *Turning the Kaleidoscope: Perspectives on European Jewry* (New York: Berghahn Books, 2006), 164–178 and 187–120. For a critique of Pinto's "Jewish Space" thesis, see also Eszter B. Gantner and Jay Oppenheim, "Jewish Space Reloaded: An Introduction," *Anthropological Journal of European Cultures* 2, no. 23 (2014): 1–10.

[86] George Steiner, *The Idea of Europe* (New York: Overlook Duckworth, 2015), 25.

[87] Manuela Consonni, "The New Grammar of Otherness: Europe, the Shoah, and the Jews," *Jewish History* 24 (2010): 105–126.

[88] Pinto, "Negotiating Jewish Identity in an Asemitic Age," op. cit., 69.

flared up when "Jewish studies without Jews" gained a foothold in the academic landscape.[89] For the first time in its long trajectory, "the idea of Europe" now entailed the unproblematic presence of "Jews qua Jews" into pluralist democracy. In the early 2000s, Jewish advocates of the European project took notice of this friendly context. The "huge success" of the European Union, they felt, empowered Jews to identify "as Jews, Europeans, *and* for example British (…) without any conceptual or logical discomfort."[90]

Yet a parallel discourse of "new antisemitism" poured cold water on Jewish confidence. Contrary to believers in improved conditions for European Jews, alarmists saw an existential threat in the "second great mutation of antisemitism in modern times, from racial antisemitism to religious anti-Zionism."[91] The specter of "new Judeophobia," however, reinforced philosemitism by drawing attention to Jewish vulnerability. On January 27, 2005, the European Parliament condemned "racist violence" on the continent, but "in particular and without reservations all acts or expressions of anti-semitism of whatever kind." The rhetoric of resurgent antisemitism also affected the politics of friendship. In 1989, the victory of European liberalism elicited an epochal rapprochement between "the idea of Europe" and Jewishness: In the twenty-first century, hardline conservatives, right-wing populists, and far-right extremists also became stakeholders in Euro-philosemitism.

---

[89] Klaus Hödl, "Jewish Studies without Jews: The Growth of an Academic Field in Austria and Germany" in Steven Leonard Jacobs (ed.), *Maven in Blue Jeans: A Festschrift in Honor of Zev Garber* (West Lafayette, IN: Purdue University Press, 2009), 198–207; Till von Rahden, "History in the House of the Hangman: How Postwar Germany Became a Key Site in the Study of Jewish History" in Steven E. Aschheim and Vibian Liska (eds.), *The German-Jewish Experience Revisited* (Berlin: De Gruyter, 2015), 171–192; Liliane Weissberg, "Jewish Studies or Gentile Studies: A Discipline in Search for Its Subject" in Y. Michal Bodemann (ed.), *The New Germany Jewry and the European Context: The Return of the European Jewish Diaspora* (New York: Palgrave Macmillan, 2008), 101–110; Dani Kranz and Sarah M. Ross, "Jüdische Selbstermächtigung in der deutschen Wissenschaftslandschaft. Tektonische Verschiebungen in der Judaistik und den Jüdischen Studien nach 1990" in Marina Chernivsky and Friederike Lorenz-Sinai (eds.), *Weitergaben und Wirkungen der Shoah in Erziehungs- und Bildungsverhältnissen der Gegenwartsgesellschaft* (Leverkusen: Barbara Budrich Verlag, 2022), 79–100.

[90] Steven Beller, "Is Europe Good for the Jews? Jews and the Pluralist Tradition in Historical Perspective," *European Judaism: A Journal for the New Europe* 1, no. 42 (2009): 44–55; Anita Bunyan, "Cosmopolitan Europeans? Jewish Public Intellectuals in Germany and Austria and the Idea of 'Europe'" in Cathy S. Gelbin and Sander L. Gilman (eds.), *Jews on the Move: Modern Cosmopolitanist Thought and Its Others*, op. cit., 302–328.

[91] Britain's Chief Rabbi Jonathan Sacks cited in Brian Klug, "The Myth of New Antisemitism" in *The Nation*, January 15, 2004, available at: www.thenation.com/article/archive/myth-new-anti-semitism/.

From New Antisemitism to New Philosemitism

Antisemitism, wrote in 2003 one of its prominent scholars, is always "old-new."[92] But since the outbreak of the Second Intifada in 2000, the UN World Conference Against Racism in Durban (July 2001), and the 9/11 attacks the United States, a network of academics, pundits, and members of watchdog organizations claimed that a "new" antisemitism was "rising from the muck." The novelty of the phenomenon, argued its theoreticians, was the role of "collective Jew" assigned to the state of Israel by its radical opponents.[93] For the prolific French scholar Pierre-André Taguieff, new antisemitism was better defined as "new Judeophobia." Charging the Jewish state of "apartheid" or "genocide," he contended, allowed "the denunciation of the "chosen people" as a people giving itself every right to dominate, conquer, oppress, and destroy." The Zionism-is-Racism rhetoric, in which Israel stands as "the incarnation of absolute evil," expunged antisemitism from the category racism: The path was allegedly clear for the normalization of anti-Jewish animus in antiracist ideology.[94]

In Taguieff's own country, however, "new Judeophobia" did not permeate public opinion. To the contrary, French surveys conducted in the early 2000s showed an uptick in already predominantly favorable perceptions of Jews.[95] Fifteen years into the twenty-first century, the Pew Research Center identified a similar trend in Western Europe – the supposed hotbed of "new" antisemitism while in Eastern Europe antisemitism revived old anti-Judaic, ethnonationalist, or anticommunist tropes.[96] In France (92%), Britain (86%), Germany (80%), and Italy (71%), an overwhelming majority of respondents showed "a positive attitude towards Jews."[97] Similar results were obtained in Spain,

---

[92] Robert Wistrich, "The Old-New Anti-Semitism," *The National Interest*, no. 72 (Summer 2003): 59–70.
[93] Anthony Lerman, *What Happened to Antisemitism? Redefinition and the Myth of the 'Collective Jew'* (London: Pluto Press, 2022).
[94] Pierre-André Taguieff, *Rising from the Muck: The New Anti-Semitism in Europe* (Chicago, IL: Ivan R Dee, 2004), cited in Jonathan Judaken, "So What's New? Rethinking the 'New Antisemitism' in a Global Age," *Patterns of Prejudice* 42, no. 4–5 (2008): 531–560.
[95] Nonna Mayer, "Nouvelle judéophobie ou vieil antisémitisme?" *Raisons politiques* 16, no. 4 (2004): 91–103.
[96] See among others the contributions by Jan T. Gross, András Kovács, and Rafał Pankowski in Christian Heilbronn, Doron Rabinovici, and Natan Sznaider (eds.), *Neuer Antisemitismus? Fortsetzung einer globalen Debatte* (Berlin: Suhrkamp Verlag, 2019), first published in 2004.
[97] The 2015 Pew Research Center survey is available at: www.pewresearch.org/global/2015/06/02/chapter-3-anti-minority-sentiment-not-rising/; 10% of Europeans avowed negative feelings about Jews according to a 2018 CNN/ComRes poll: https://edition.cnn.com/interactive/2018/11/europe/antisemitism-poll-2018-intl/.

although the American Defamation League was able to establish in 2015 that "eleven million Spaniards harbored antisemitic attitudes."[98] Yet in June 2015, the Spanish parliament passed a law enabling Sephardic Jews "descendants of those expelled from Spain in the 15th Century" to swiftly obtain citizenship. An identical bill had earlier come into effect in Portugal (there the ADL only counted 1.8 million antisemites). No similar invitation was extended to the descendants of Muslims driven out or who emigrated from the Iberian Peninsula after 1492. "Philosephardic" Spain and Portugal officially longed for the return of Jews, not that of Arabs.[99]

Despite apparent tolerance, monitors of antisemitism documented since the 2002 a steady rise in anti-Jewish vandalism, as well as verbal and physical attacks on Jews – an increase correlating with Israeli military operations in the West Bank and Gaza. In 2013, the Pew Research Center additionally found – although without precise quantification – that Jews experienced harassment "by individuals or social groups" in most member states of the European Union. Eighteen reports on antisemitism were issued by the Vienna-based European Monitoring Centre for Racism and Xenophobia (and its successor agency) from 2000 to 2022. They confirmed the coexistence of "positive views of Jews" with growing insecurity. From 2009 to 2019, for instance, Jews were the second group of people most readily accepted as potential neighbors or family members, just behind "disabled persons."[100] Britain ranked first in this category despite warnings from antisemitism scholars that the United Kingdom was "sleepwalking into a morass of anti-Israel and anti-Jewish bigotry."[101] In 2019, the Pew Research Center found again that "half of more of surveyed European countries have favorable views of Jews" – between 76 and 92 percent in Western Europe. Across the European Union, Muslims, refugees, and at the bottom of the scale Sinti and Roma, received significantly lower scores.[102]

---

[98] *ADL Global 100 Index*, available at: https://global100.adl.org/country/spain/2015.
[99] Dalia Kandiyoti and Rina Benmayor (eds.), *Reparative Citizenship for Sephardic Descendants: Returning to the Jewish Past in Spain and Portugal* (New York: Berghahn Books, 2023).
[100] European Union Agency for Fundamental Rights (FRA), "Overview of Antisemitic Incidents Recorded in the European Union, 2009–2019," available at: https://fra.europa.eu/sites/default/files/fra_uploads/fra-2020-antisemitism-overview-2009-2019_en.pdf.
[101] Robert Wistrich, "From Blood Libel to Boycott: Changing Faces of British of British Antisemitism" (Jerusalem, 2011), cited by David Feldman, "Anti-Zionism and Antisemitism in Britain," Jewish Museum Berlin (November 8–9, 2013), available at: www.jmberlin.de/sites/default/files/media/documents/antisemitism-in-europe-today_9-feldman.pdf.
[102] Pew Research Center Survey (2019), available at: www.pewresearch.org/global/2019/10/14/minority-groups/.

Yet since the year 2002, data on hate speech and hate crimes revealed a steady rise in anti-Jewish acts including vandalism, online harassment, threats, and physical harm. Many additional cases were believed unreported. "The number of officially recorded incidents [2011–2021] is very low," pointed out the European Union Agency for Fundamental Rights (FRA), yet this did not mean that "antisemitism is not present." Lack of "systematic data collection," added the watchdog organization, further skewed survey results. When taking into account the "experiences and perceptions" of European Jews, assessed the FRA in 2018, antisemitism was both "pervasive" and "normalized" across the EU – a conclusion that American Defamation League, the American Jewish Committee, and new antisemitism scholars had long reached without hesitation.[103] Such discrepancy between reassuring polls and a rising sense of insecurity, explained defenders of the new antisemitism concept, was the peculiar trait of the Judeophobic wave. "Levels of antisemitism in Great Britain are among the lowest in the world," acknowledged the London-based Institute for Jewish Policy Research (JPR) in 2017. Yet "counting antisemites," claimed the think-tank, was different from measuring "elastic" antisemitism. By this standard, "30% of British society" held at least "one antisemitic attitude." The JPR did not hesitate to blame criticism of Israel for this discrepancy. "56% of the general population hold at least one anti-Israel attitude," found its researchers; and "the stronger a person's anti-Israel views, the more likely they are to hold antisemitic attitudes." Scholars of new antisemitism expressed the same view differently. Although limited to "educated people who consider themselves to be politically radical and overrepresented among Muslim people," a unique "ideological-political phenomenon" allegedly threatened Jewish existence in Europe.[104] By designating the "Zio" as the enemy of human emancipation, exacerbating the "competition of victims" to deny the Shoah, and importing Judeophobia from the global south, "antiracist anti-Zionists" on one hand, and "Muslims" on the other, supposedly created "a growing sense of emergency." In 1990,

---

[103] "Experiences and perceptions of Antisemitism. Second Survey on Discrimination and Hate Crime against Jews in the European Union" (2018), available at: https://fra.europa.eu/sites/default/files/fra_uploads/fra-2018-experiences-and-perceptions-of-antisemitism-survey-summary_en.pdf. On "apocalypticism" and "moral panics" in new antisemitism discourse, see Anthony Lerman, *What Happened to Antisemitism?*, op. cit., 240–256.

[104] Institute for Jewish Policy Research, Antisemitism in Contemporary Great Britain (2017), available at: www.jpr.org.uk/reports/antisemitism-contemporary-great-britain. The British sociologist David Hirsch is cited in "What the Data Really Says about Anti-Semitism," *Haaretz*, June 18, 2015; Pierre-André Taguieff, "Retour sur la nouvelle Judéophobie," *Cités* 12, no. 4 (2002): 117–134.

500,000 French Jews and non-Jews had marched together after the desecration of the Carpentras Jewish cemetery. Although in 2006, demonstrations took place after the shocking murder of Ilan Halimi, French Jewish commentators noted that most participants were Jews (although government ministers, Christian and Muslim dignitaries, and politicians joined in). Since 2000, lamented the Jewish thinker Shmuel Trigano in 2015, Jews in France lived in "solitude." David Badiel's *Jews Don't Count* would six years later convey a similar feeling in Britain.[105] New antisemitism, summarized its decipherers, spelled the end of the philosemitic respite in Europe. "Taboos kept antisemitism in check in the post-Holocaust years," but restraints "no longer seem to exercise the full protective power they once had."[106]

Objectors to the new antisemitism thesis charged that the new Judeophobia panic "obscured the far more pressing reality of Islamophobia." For some, Muslim immigrants were Europe's new Jews; for others, antisemitism and Islamophobia remained distinct forms of racism despite their historical entanglement.[107] Yet while new antisemitism scholars proclaimed the return of Europe's "Jewish question," critics saw in this discourse a reflection of Europe's "Muslim question." Synonymous with Muslim antisemitism, new antisemitism reinforced the image of Muslim incompatibility with the European Union – the self-proclaimed antidote to antisemitism since 1992. While no less a threat to Jewish security, retorted analysts of the phenomenon, Judeophobia among Muslim youths expressed "a system of values and a cultural universe very different from those that formerly fed European anti-Semitism."[108] To understand why in immigrant neighborhoods the Jew became a symbol of European or white hegemony and oppression of Palestinians required rigorous sociology, not hysteria over Jew-hating "Eurabia" or the presumed collective mind of Muslims. Antisemitism among youths of immi-

---

[105] Shmuel Trigano, *Quinze ans de solitude* (New York: Berg International, 2015); David Badiel, *Jews Don't Count* (London: TLS Books, 2021).
[106] Alvin H. Rosenfeld (ed.), *Resurgent Antisemitism: Global Perspectives* (Bloomington, IN: Indiana University Press, 2013), 2–3.
[107] Matti Bunzl, *Anti-Semitism and Islamophobia: Hatreds Old and New in Europe* (Chicago, IL: Prickly Paradigm Press, 2007), 3–4, cited in Robert Fine, "Fighting with Fantoms: A Contribution to the Debate on Antisemitism in Europe," *Patterns of Prejudice* 5, no. 43 (2009): 459–479; Brian Klug, "The Limits of Analogy: Comparing Islamophobia and Antisemitism," *Patterns of Prejudice* 5, no. 48 (2014): 442–459; and more generally James Renton and Ben Gidley (eds.), *Antisemitism and Islamophobia in Europe: A Shared History?* (London: Palgrave Macmillan, 2017).
[108] Enzo Traverso, *The End of Jewish Modernity* (London: Pluto Press, 2016), 87; for a rebuttal of Traverso's view from the perspective of "new antisemitism," see Bruno Chaouat, "Good News from France: 'There Is No New Antisemitism'" in Alvin H. Rosenfeld (ed.), *Deciphering the New Antisemitism* (Bloomington, IN: Indiana University Press, 2015), 179–205.

grant background argued the French sociologist Michel Wieviorka, "arises from a logic of the ghetto (...) "and a deep sense of being rejected and trapped in a place of relegation."[109] Taking marginalization into account did not make Judeophobia less repugnant but helped situate the phenomenon within the realities or perceptions of social exclusion. If inattentive to other forms of racism, anti-antisemitism only remained "a pretext for discussing another object: Islam and its "rogue" forms."[110]

Challengers of new antisemitism ideology pointed to another diversionary tactic: the weaponization of antisemitism to stifle systemic criticism of Israel. Anti-Zionist discourse, as in the past, could always devolve into fantasies of Jewish world domination, hold all Jews responsible for Israel's actions, or as in the case of the humorist Dieudonné in France, revel in grotesque Holocaust denial. But even if many of its theorists considered themselves liberal Zionists, new Judeophobia was also new Palestinophobia: the designation of categorical pro-Palestinianism as the main source of antisemitism in the West. Even before the popularity of the "from the river to the sea" slogan, accusations of war crimes, apartheid, settler colonialism, and racism leveled at Israel, as well as the Boycott, Divestment and Solidarity campaign, unsettled believers in the Oslo peace process – let alone hardline supporters of Israeli right-wing governments. No longer contained within the "left of the left," asserted new antisemitism alarmists, anti-Zionism seeped into antiracism, antiglobalism, postcolonialism, neo-humanitarianism, or the Green movement: A threatening coalition which in alliance with predisposed Muslims allegedly declared open season on the "collective Jew," and by extension on all Jews. In accordance with Natan Sharansky's "3D-test" first advertised in 2004, new antisemitism ideologues, supported by Israeli officials and academics, responded by declaring anti-Zionism antisemitic when it engaged in "delegitimization, demonization, and double standards": a bar flexible enough to permanently inject the question of antisemitism in debates on Israel-Palestine, and a "3D-test" never reversely applied to anti-Palestinian rhetoric.[111] When "every anti-Zionist is an anti-Semite," reminded an opponent of this stance, "the concept of anti-Semitism loses its significance."[112]

---

[109] Michel Wieviorka (2005) cited in Traverso, *The End of Jewish Modernity*, op. cit., 88.
[110] Vincent Geisser, *La nouvelle islamophobie* (Paris: La Découverte, 2003), 84.
[111] On the role played by Israeli governmental agencies and institutions in the diffusion of "new antisemitism," see Anthony Lerman, *What Happened to Antisemitism? Redefinition and the Myth of the 'Collective Jew'* (London: Pluto Press, 2022), Chapter 11 especially.
[112] Brian Klug, "The Myth of New Antisemitism" in *The Nation*, January 15, 2004, available at: www.thenation.com/article/archive/myth-new-anti-semitism/.

In Europe, however, new antisemitism ideology did not become unchallenged orthodoxy. "Old" ethnonationalist antisemitism was alive and well, especially in Eastern Europe, argued challengers of the new antisemitism concept. Anxieties over "new" anti-Jewish hostility, however, had more to do with "American, Israeli and Zionist discomfort with strong European criticism of Israeli policy than it has with actual antisemitism."[113] Yet with the help of the Israeli government and think tanks, the American Jewish Committee, and the European Jewish Congress, the discourse of new antisemitism entered the realm of policy-making at the European Union level. Until 2016, to be sure, proponents of the new antisemitism paradigm lamented the EU's "ritual posturing" which in their mind "elided" the true nature of the phenomenon.[114] Yet the EU had since its inception pledged to "combat" antisemitism under the general rubric of "racism and xenophobia." After 2000, anti-antisemitism also became a distinct policy area within the European Commission, but also the OSCE and intergovernmental watchdog agencies.[115] "Governments have overcome their reluctance," approvingly noted a contributor to this effort, "to separate anti-Jewish hatred from other forms of bigotry lest they be seen as creating victimhood hierarchies."[116] The EU's policy record nonetheless failed to impress new antisemitism ideologues who until 2016 denounced Brussel's failure to confront Muslim Judeophobia and counteract the "caricature of the state of Israel" as Nazi regime. A "working definition" of antisemitism reflective of its new form, they complained, was thoroughly lacking. In 2005, the Vienna-based European Monitoring Centre for Racism and Xenophobia had endorsed a "working definition" in which "double standards" on Israel, and the comparison of the Jewish state with Nazism, were categorized as hate speech. Yet its successor agency shelved the document in 2013: proof for critics that in the European Union "the new antisemitism is often glimpsed but rarely grasped."[117]

---

[113] Steven Beller, "In Zion's Hall of Mirrors: A Comment on *Neuer Antisemitismus?*," *Patterns of Prejudice* 2, no. 41 (2007): 215–238. See also Rony Stauber, "The Academic and Public Debate over the Meaning of 'New Antisemitism'" (2007) in Charles Asher Small (ed.), *The Yale Papers: Antisemitism in Comparative Perspective* (New York: ISGAP, 2015), 225–236.

[114] R. Amy Elman, *The European Union, Antisemitism, and the Politics of Denial* (Lincoln, NE: University of Nebraska Press, 2014), 2.

[115] Esther Romeyn, "(Anti) New Antisemitism as a Transnational Field of Racial Governance," *Patterns of Prejudice*, no. 54 (2020): 1–2, 199–214.

[116] Michael Whine, "Can the European Agencies Combat Antisemitism Effectively?" *Israel Journal of Foreign Affairs* (2018): 1–11.

[117] R. Amy Elman, "The EU Responses to Antisemitism: A Shell Game" in Alvin Rosenfeld (ed.), *Deciphering the New Antisemitism*, op. cit., 405–429.

In 2016, however, the International Holocaust Remembrance Agency adopted a "working definition" of antisemitism first endorsed by Britain. In March 2024, at least forty-three countries, including all European Union states except Malta and Ireland, had adopted the IHRA statement. In Europe and the United States, numerous universities, media organizations, or state agencies incorporated the document into their statutes. For its advocates, the IHRA definition only reflected the distinctiveness of antisemitism not sufficiently recognized in existing antiracist legislation. It simply clarified, "for the benefits of governments and administrators at all levels, what kind of activity can be considered as antisemitism and why."[118] But the IHRA definition turned key tenets of new antisemitism ideology into definitional standards. To portray the state of Israel as "racist endeavor," for instance, meant "denying the Jewish people their right to self-determination," not legitimate characterization of Israeli rule over Palestinians. The IHRA statement, to be sure, stipulated that "criticism of Israel similar to that leveled to another country cannot be regarded as antisemitic." Objectors retorted that "there are no effective checks to prevent (…) its abusive application," namely, the censoring of anti-Zionist speech. Authors of an alternative definition pointed out that seven out of eleven examples of antisemitism featured in the document "focus on the state of Israel." Palestinian and Arab scholars, for their part, argued that to label antisemitic "anyone who call the existing state of Israel as racist (…) amounts to granting Israel absolute impunity." A lead drafter of a "working definition" penned in the early 2000s and later reproduced in the IHRA statement, expressed regret. "None of us anticipated that it would be used as this blunt instrument to suppress pro-Palestinian speech," avowed the former American Jewish Committee official Kenneth Stern.[119]

For its challengers, the IHRA "holy writ" was merely "the Zionist definition of antisemitism."[120] Yet despite push-back, the statement

---

[118] Bernard Harrison and Lesley Klaff, "In Defence of the IHRA Definition" in *Fathom* (January 2020), available at: https://fathomjournal.org/in-defence-of-the-ihra-definition/.

[119] Rebecca Ruth Gould, "The IHRA Definition of Antisemitism: Defining Antisemitism by Erasing Palestinians," *The Political Quarterly* 4, no. 91 (October–December 2020): 825–883; Jan Deckers and Jonathan Coulter, "What Is Wrong with the IHRA Definition," *Res Publica* 4, no. 28 (2022): 733–752; The Jerusalem Definition of Antisemitism (2020), available at: https://jerusalemdeclaration.org; "Palestinian Rights and the IHRA Definition of Antisemitism," *The Guardian*, November 29, 2020; Stern cited in Eyal Press, "The Problem with Defining Antisemitism" in *The New Yorker*, March 13, 2024.

[120] Neve Gordon, "Antisemitism and Zionism: The Internal Operations of the IHRA Definition" in *Middle East Critique* (posted online on March 9, 2024), available at: www.tandfonline.com/doi/epdf/10.1080/19436149.2024.2330821?needAccess=true.

imposed itself as standard policy framework in Europe (in addition to Commonwealth countries, North America, and parts of Latin America). The widespread endorsement of the IHRA definition was not merely the result of pro-Israel lobbying, or the weaponization of antisemitism by Israeli governments. The success of a "working definition" of antisemitism issued by an international Holocaust organization above all derived from the support it received from Europe's political mainstream. Center-leftists and moderate conservatives alike recognized in it familiar features of post-1989 philosemitism: Holocaust remembrance, anti-antisemitism, and the defense of Zionism's legitimacy. The European Commission, for its part, viewed the IHRA definition an "essential tool for (...) tackling antisemitism (...) in particular for education and training purposes." Out of attention to the "victims' perspectives," the safeguard of Jews in Europe justified deference to the IHRA guidelines and special attention to critical anti-Israel speech.[121]

The twenty-first-century European Union's policy kit against antisemitism also included "monitoring and research," "legal frameworks," "policies and actions," as well as Holocaust remembrance and education programs. By 2015, however, Brussels was also committed to "fostering Jewish life" in EU member states. Few citizens of the Union likely knew of this policy sphere, but the "promotion of the European Way of Life" entailed both the preservation and cultivation of "Jewish Life" under a coordinator appointed in December 2015. While unknown outside Eurocrat circles, this language testified of the Jews' symbolic status as Europe's archetypal friends, seventy years after the Holocaust. In 2015, to be sure, the Commission also appointed a "coordinator on combatting anti-Muslim hatred." The separation of antisemitism and racism, often decried as betrayal of unitary antiracism, allowed here for a more targeted focus on Islamophobia. The fight against anti-Muslim bigotry, however, proceeded without pledges to "foster" Muslim life as part of the European Way of Life. What was distinctively "European" in the Commission's anti-Islamophobia agenda was its commitment to social inclusion and antidiscrimination.[122] EU anti-antisemitism, by contrast, stressed the value of Jewish life and its unique precariousness. Deadly radical Islamist attacks on Jews in Toulouse (2012),

---

[121] European Commission, "Definition of Antisemitism," available at: https://commission.europa.eu/strategy-and-policy/policies/justice-and-fundamental-rights/combatting-discrimination/racism-and-xenophobia/combating-antisemitism/definition-antisemitism_en.

[122] European Commission, "Combating anti-Muslim Hatred," available at: https://commission.europa.eu/strategy-and-policy/policies/justice-and-fundamental-rights/combatting-discrimination/racism-and-xenophobia/combating-anti-muslim-hatred_en.

Brussels (2014), Paris (2015), or Copenhagen (2015) had already reinforced this perception. "France, without Jews, will no longer be France," declared the French socialist Prime Minister Manuel Valls in the wake of the Hyper Casher attack of January 2015. David Cameron, for his part, avowed that he would be "heartbroken" should British Jews decide that the country is no longer safe for them. "We are glad and thankful that there is Jewish life again in Germany," stated Angela Merkel in February 2015. Six months later, her notorious "We can manage" signaled readiness to accept 800,000 predominantly Muslim refugees in the country. Throughout their integration process, many will be instructed that the unflinching protection of Jewish life in Germany, but also Israel, was now a core tenet of German identity.

New antisemitism, then, produced in return a new philosemitism in which "Jewish life," in the words of Angela Merkel, "is part of our identity and culture." Thankfulness for Jewish presence after the Holocaust had long been part of German atoning pronouncements. But the valorization of Jewish life, and proclamations of its vital necessity for Europe, now transcended the realm of German philosemitism. "To achieve full recognition of Jewish life as part of Europe's society," stated the European Commission in 2021, "awareness and knowledge of Jewish history and culture need to be increased among the general public." This statement may be dismissed as inconsequential Euro-talk, but such official longing for Jewishness in integrated Europe was a novelty of the post-1989 era. In Brussels or Strasbourg at least, Jewish life and European life achieved symbiosis during the first two decades of the twenty-first century.[123]

As philosemitism became *acquis communautaire*, however, left and postcolonial critics denounced the phenomenon as "philosemitic reaction," "Euro-Zionism," "state philosemitism," or Holocaust "catechism."[124] To understand why philosemitism elicited a spate of "anti-philosemitic" writings in the twenty-first century requires paying attention to its reconfiguration. Already noticeable at the end of the 1990s, the hijacking of philosemitism by the populist, Islamophobic, and anti-immigrant far-right positioned a dubious "love for the Jews" on the side of illiberalism:

---

[123] EU Strategy for Combating Antisemitism and Fostering Jewish Life (2021–30), available at: https://eur-lex.europa.eu/legal-content/EN/TXT/PDF/?uri=CELEX:52021DC0615.

[124] Ivan Segré, "The Philo-Semitic Reaction" in Alain Badiou, Eric Hazan, and Ivan Segré (eds.), *Reflections on Anti-Semitism* (London: Verso, 2013), 45–232; Gabriel Piterberg, "Euro-Zionism and Its Discontents," *New Left Review*, no. 84 (November-December 2013): 43–65; Houria Bouteldja, *Whites, Jews, and Us: Towards a Politics of Revolutionary Love* (South Pasadena, CA: Semiotext(e), 2016); A. Dirk Moses, "The German Catechism" (May 23, 2021), available at: https://geschichtedergegenwart.ch/the-german-catechism/.

The antisemites of yesterday converted then to a philosemitism more often than not synonymous with "pro-Israel antisemitism."[125] In Germany, Angela Merkel's "hyper Zionism," uncontested by her red–yellow–green successors, elicited a backlash against "philosemitic McCarthyism." Remembrance culture, avowed a disappointed admirer of Germany's historical reckoning, had gone "haywire."[126] The migration of pro-Jewish "friendship" to the populist far-right, along with its radicalization in twenty-first-century Germany, has exposed "the new European philosemitism" to systematic critique.[127] Meanwhile, the normative liberal pillars of philosemitism in the New Europe – the memory of the unique Holocaust, the war on antisemitism, and acceptance of Zionism's legitimacy – also came under scrutiny.

---

[125] Jelena Subotic, "Antisemitism in the Global Populist International," *The British Journal of Politics and International Relations* 3, no. 24 (2022): 458–474.

[126] Susan Neiman, "Historical Reckoning Gone Haywire" in *The New York Review of Books*, October 19, 2023.

[127] Yitzhak Laor, *Le nouveau philosémitisme européen et le « camp de la paix » en Israël* (Paris: La Fabrique, 2007), translated as *The Myths of Liberal Zionism* (London: Verso, 2009); Brian Klug, "An Emblematic Embrace: New Europe, The Jewish State, and the Palestinian Question" in Bashir Bashir and Leila Farsakh (eds.), *The Arab and Jewish Question: Geographies of Engagement in Palestine and Beyond* (New York: Columbia University Press, 2020), 47–67.

Epilogue
New Philosemitism and Its Critics: From the Turn of the Twenty-First Century to October 7, 2023

A year prior to his death in 2011, the former anti-Nazi resister and non-Jewish Buchenwald prisoner Jorge Semprun was aware of being one of the last survivors of the camp. The elderly Spanish-French writer, however, did not fear oblivion. In the new Europe, he observed, the Shoah represented all the "disappeared, the wrecked and the rescued, the Jews and the goys, men and women." Holocaust remembrance, he intimated, now absorbed the memory of antifascist political internees. The gravely ill Semprun did not lament usurpation. "When all the witnesses, deported resistors, have disappeared," he wrote, "there will remain (...) a memory that will outlive us, and that is the Jewish memory." This prospect gave him solace. "Long live the Jewish memory of our death!," exclaimed the man of letters confident in the future of Shoah consciousness in the unified continent.[1]

Semprun, in his own words, "became a philosemite" at Buchenwald in contact with Jewish prisoners. He died with the belief that liberal Europe shared his lifelong abhorrence of antisemitism, friendship with "peace camp" Israel, and moral imperative to remember the Shoah. Yet philosemitism had since the start of the twenty-first century gained another meaning: the defense of Jews against Islam in the name of "Judeo-Christian civilization." Proponents of this view did not all come from the extreme right. In the Netherlands, the politician Pim Fortuyn assassinated in 2002, and the founder of the Party for Freedom (PVV) Geert Wilders after him, exemplified a philosemitism predicated on "Enlightenment fundamentalism" and anti-Muslim racism. In the mid 1990s, the former Marxist, socialist, and openly gay Fortuyn portrayed "Islamic culture" as an existential danger for "Judeo-Christian humanistic culture: our culture!" Originally a moderate conservative, Wilders similarly trumpeted the superiority of "Judeo-Christian civilization" – a concept now stripped of theological substance and connoting instead

---

[1] Jorge Semprun, "Mon dernier voyage à Buchenwald" in *Le Monde*, March 6, 2010.

a "humanist" culture under threat.[2] Over the course of two decades culminating in stunning electoral victory (2023), the PVV leader availed himself of anti-antisemitism and ultra-Zionism to attack Islam and the multiculturalism tolerating its presence. Threatened by rising Muslim populations, Wilders never ceased to claim, Jews were the prime victims of "Islamization." The state of Israel, he tirelessly repeated, stood at the "frontline against the totalitarian threat of Islam." The Dutch politician, who visited the country dozens of times, called "the Jewish villages and cities of Judea Samaria (…) outposts of freedom," and in 2023 advocated the forcible transfer of Palestinians from Gaza and the West Bank to Jordan, also praised Israel for showing the European Union "how important it is for a people to have its own homeland." Jewish ethnonationalism was the counter-model to emulate. "What we need today," Wilders urged in 2009, "is Zionism for the nations of Europe."[3] Dutch Israelophilia, of course, had a longer history. Favorable sentiment had flourished in government and public opinion even before the 1967 Six-Day War and peaked during the 1973 Arab–Israeli war. Despite a decline in positive attitudes after the 1982 Israeli invasion of Lebanon, the Queen of the Netherlands still celebrated "a special relationship between our peoples" in a speech delivered at the Knesset in 1995.[4] Wilders's PVV redefined this bond at the dawn of the twenty-first century: a pro-Zionism tantamount to Judeo-Christian civilizationism, Islamophobia, and Palestinophobia.

Leaders of far-right parties in Western and Northern Europe did not always match Wilders's uniquely rabid rhetoric. Yet set into motion at the end in the 1990s, the conversion of the post-fascist radical right to populist far-right politics also entailed philosemitic rebranding. In Italy, the head of the National Alliance Gianfranco Fini made acceptance of Holocaust guilt a key feature of normalization. "As an Italian," declared in 2002 Silvio Berlusconi's deputy and coalition ally, "I must accept

---

[2] Cited in Amanda Kluveld, "Secular, Superior and Desperately Searching for Its Soul: The Confusing Political-Cultural Reference to a Judeo-Christian Europe in the Twenty-First Century" in Emmanuel Nathan and Anya Topolski (eds.), *Is There a Judeo-Christian Tradition? A European Perspective* (Berlin: De Gruyter, 2016), 243–267.

[3] Cited in David J. Wertheim, "Geert Wilders and the Nationalist-Populist Turn towards the Jews in Europe" in David J. Wertheim (ed.), *The Jew as Legitimation: Jewish-Gentiles Relations beyond Antisemitism and Philosemitism* (Cham: Palgrave Macmillan, 2017), 275–290. See also Evelien Gans, "Anti-Antisemitic Enthusiasm & Selective Philosemitism: Geert Wilders, the PVV and the Jews," *Proceedings of International Conference "Antisemitism in Europe Today: The Phenomena, the Conflicts"*, Jewish Museum Berlin, November 8–9, 2013, available at: www.jmberlin.de/sites/default/files/media/documents/antisemitism-in-europe-today_6-gans.pdf.

[4] Queen Beatrix's speech (March 28, 1995) is available at: https://m.knesset.gov.il/EN/activity/Documents/SpeechPdf/Beatrix.pdf.

responsibility [for Mussolini's racial laws]. I must do it in the name of all Italians, who are responsible for what happened after 1938." During a trailblazing visit of Israel in 2003, the former leader of the Italian Social Movement (MSI), who in 1994 still called Mussolini "the greatest statesman of the 20th century," completed his decade-long reinvention. At Yad Vashem, Fini announced his "definitive" abjuration of Fascism, an "absolute evil." The Italian politician also declared anti-Zionism the equivalent to antisemitism and pledged support for Prime Minister Ariel Sharon, who in return called him "our closest friend in Europe." Fini's repositioning of neofascism into mainstream conservatism, however, stood out for its atoning tone. His overtures to Jews and Israel to demonstrate ideological *aggiornamento* also came with unexpected acknowledgment of "the shameful chapters in the history of our people."[5]

Filip Dewinter, the Flemish leader of the nationalist and secessionist Vlaams Belang (Flemish Interest), did not follow Fini's remorseful path. In 2005, the journalist and politician from Antwerp reduced pro-Nazi collaboration in Flanders to a mere effort to gain independence. "This was the whole story," Dewinter claimed, "the overwhelming majority were not Nazis." Yet his refusal to condemn Flemish accomplices to Nazi Germany who, he assured, were not all "necessarily antisemitic," did not prevent him from calling contemporary Jews "our brothers-in-arms in the battle against extremist Islam in Antwerp." Like Wilders, Dewinter also lavished praised on Israel, "outpost for Western society (…) protecting common values within a hostile environment." His philosemitism, however, was above all transactional. "There is common interest between Jewish and Flemish people in the struggle against Islam in Europe," Dewinter declared in 2006. Jews, now "part of European culture," received in this bargain protection from Muslim immigrants, collectively imagined as antisemites from birth.[6] What Vlaams Belang sought to obtain in return was not only the vote of Antwerp's 20,000 predominantly ultra-Orthodox Jews. In Flanders as in Western Europe, the far-right's philosemitic reorientation sought to attract a broader electorate looking for moral cover: the disavowal of antisemitism as gateway to anti-Muslim enmity.[7]

---

[5] "Mussolini's Heir on Israel Trip as Italian Party Alters Image," *The Guardian*, November 24, 2003; "Fini Condemns Italy's Past, *Haaretz*, November 25, 2003.

[6] "Belgian Far-Rightist Calls on Jews to Join Battle against Muslims," *Haaretz*, October 8, 2006.

[7] Bodo Kahmann, "The Most Ardent Pro-Israel Party: Pro-Israel Attitudes and Anti-Antisemitism among Populist Radical-Right Parties in Europe," *Patterns of Prejudice* 5, no. 51 (2017): 396–411; Yves Patrick Pallade, "Philosemitismus in rechtspopulistischen und rechts-extremen europäischen Parteien der Gegenwart" in Irene A. Diekmann and Elke-Vera Kotowski (eds.), *Geliebter Feind, Gehasster Freund: Antisemitismus und Philosemitismus in Geschichte und Gegenwart* (Berlin: Verlag für Berlin-Brandenburg, 2009), 409–436.

When in 1999 the Austrian Freedom Party (FPÖ) received an unprecedented 27 percent of the vote under the leadership of Jörg Haider, the European Union responded with a temporary *cordon sanitaire* around the conservative and far-right governmental coalition. Although Haider had a record of positive statements on Nazi Germany, however, FPÖ politicians now expressed concern for "Jewish friends" allegedly threatened by "the high degree of Muslim presence" in the country.[8] At the start of the twenty-first century, the image of the Jew as exemplary victim of Islam not only neutralized old antisemitic instincts. If partner in the fight against Islamization or the looming "great replacement," the far right's historic racialized Others could enjoy the elevated status of ally. In 2010, to be sure, the FPÖ chief Hanz-Christian Strache revealed the limits of this makeover. Courted by Likud party functionaries, Strache visited Israel in December 2010 in the company of other far-rightists united in a "European Freedom Alliance." At Yad Vashem, Strache insisted on donning his *Biertönnchen* – the cap of his student fraternity associated with pan-Germanism and antisemitism – instead of a kippa: a gesture signifying to his supporters at home that "it's not really what you think."[9]

Yet opportunistic or not, philosemitism afforded the Western European far-right unprecedented respectability. In France, the *stratégie de dédiabolisation* ("de-demonization strategy") of the National Front and future National Rally began in the late 1980s. After succeeding her father Jean-Marie Le Pen at the head of the party in 2011, however, Marine Le Pen accelerated the drive to normalization through a series of pro-Jewish pronouncements. Her rhetoric still included dog-whistling attacks on "the power of money, the media, and the banks, which we all know are linked to each other." But under her leadership, the party quickly understood the necessity to "break the lock of antisemitism (…) which prevents people to vote for us."[10] The National Front, she told Jews in 2014, "is without a doubt the best shield to protect you against the true enemy, Islamic fundamentalism."[11] Whereas her father had in 1987 called the Final Solution "a detail in the history of World War Two," in 2020 Marine Le Pen paid homage to the 13,000 Jews rounded up by the French police in July 1942. More than belated acceptance

---

[8] Matti Bunzl, *Symptoms of Modernity: Jews and Queers in Late-Twentieth Century Vienna* (Berkeley, CA: University of California Press, 2004), 222–223.
[9] "Strache, Biertönnen, und das Heilige Land," *Der Standard*, December 22, 2010; "Far-Right Politicians Find Common Cause in Israel" in *Newsweek*, February 27, 2011.
[10] See the interview of the then National Front's Vice-President Louis Alliot (November 6, 2013) in Valérie Igounet, *Le Front National de 1972 à nos jours* (Paris: Seuil, 2014), 420.
[11] "France's Far-Right, Once Known for Antisemitism, Courts Jews," in *The New York Times*, April 5, 2017, cited in Hannah Rose, *The New Philosemitism: Exploring a Changing Relationship between the Jews and the Far-Right* (ICSR: King's College London, 2020).

of Shoah memory, however, the image of "shield" against antisemitic Islam became central to the party's new message. In the aftermath of October 7, 2023, the National Rally's spokesman reaffirmed a now well-established position when he stated that "our compatriots of Jewish confession know who really protect them." Marine Le Pen, for her part, participated on November 13, 2023, in a "march against antisemitism" during which she declared that the demonstration "is precisely where the National Rally needs to be."[12] Her party's successful transition from extremism to mainstreamed national-populism, to be sure, derived from a variety of factors. Yet it was also facilitated by a "philosemitic turn" that across Western Europe gave far-right politics a historic facelift.[13]

The post-1989 radical right in East-Central Europe did not experience similar mutation. Antisemitic narratives and stereotypes – the Judeo-Bolshevik myth, the Jewish manipulation of the Holocaust, the Jews' global financial power – never disappeared from its repertoire. Far-right parties in the European Union's east, to be sure, concealed their anti-Jewish rhetoric through coded anticosmopolitanism and antiglobalism. Some, like the Jobbik leader Gabor Vona in Hungary, nonetheless claimed to change course in 2013, after a decade of explicit antisemitic and anti-Roma statements. In 2020, Jobbik elected a president with partly Jewish roots. But Israel-related philosemitism in Visegrad Group countries – (Poland, Slovakia, the Czech Republic, and Hungary) – flourished instead among populist nationalists during Benjamin Netanyahu's second hold on power (2009–21). "What attracts Eastern European populists to Israel today," observed the political scientist Ivan Krastev in 2019, "is their old dream realized: Israel is a democracy but an ethnic democracy; it defines itself as a state for Jews in the same way East Europeans imagine their countries as a state for Poles, Hungarians, or Slovaks."[14] A role model for ethnonationalists, Netanyahu's Israel offered Euro-skeptics in the region a muscular alternative to the weak cosmopolitanism of the European Union. Until a spat over the "Holocaust speech law" (2018) drew a wedge between the ruling Law and Justice party and Israel, right-wing Polish populists entertained harmonious relations with a government similarly invested in antidemocratic judicial overhaul. Hungary's Viktor Orban, however, best exemplified illiberal pro-Israelism in East-Central Europe.

---

[12] *Le Monde*, "La marche contre l'antisémitisme," November 13, 2023.
[13] Rogers Brubaker, "Between Nationalism and Civilizationism: The European Populist Movement in Comparative Perspective," *Ethnic and Racial Studies* 8, no. 40 (2017): 1191–1226.
[14] Ivan Krastev, "Why Do Central European nationalist Love Israel So Much," in *The New York Times*, March 18, 2019.

Fidesz's leader began to cultivate a personal friendship with Benjamin Netanyahu after his visit of Israel in 2005: Both saw their two countries as small states threatened by adverse demography and hostile surroundings. The so-called migrant crisis of 2014–15 deepened this rapprochement. Orban's vehement anti-refugee campaign, verbally directed against the "poison" of Muslim invaders, aligned Fidesz's rhetoric with that of hotheaded European Islamophobes. But the prime minister in office since 2011 also saw in Israel a twin "illiberal democracy" – a label he proudly applied to his own country. "We do not want our own color, traditions and national culture to be mixed with those of others," declared Orban in 2018 – the year Netanyahu's government passed a law declaring the Jewish state "the nation-state of the Jewish people."[15]

Fidesz's accentuated pro-Israelism in the wake of the migrant crisis, however, went hand in hand with its weaponization of Judeophobic messages. During the 2017 parliamentary election, Orbán's party circulated thousands of posters showing a grinning George Soros with the slogan "Let's not allow Soros to have the last laugh!" Propagators of "anti-Sorosism" portrayed the Budapest-born Jewish financier as puppet-master of global migration, promoter of anti-Magyar "open society," and arch-enemy of the nation.[16] Orban himself referred to Soros as "cunning," "malicious," "not national but international," "vengeful ... and always attacks the heart, especially when it is red, white, and green."[17] Such abundance of antisemitic stereotypes did not deter Orban from professing "zero tolerance when it comes to antisemitism" – a term he reserved to the radical far-right, "Muslims" and pro-Palestinian demonstrators. In February 2019, Benjamin Netanyahu hailed Orban a "true friend of Israel." The Hungarian populist's instrumentalization of the Soros myth, or his admiration for Miklos Horthy and other "great statesmen" of the wartime era, could be easily sidelined in favor of the revival of Jewish life in Budapest, Hungary's commitment to "true and significant Holocaust memory," and above all, unflinching support for Israeli policies: In Netanyahu's eyes, Orban's Hungary was the philosemitic counterweight to the adversarial European Union.[18]

---

[15] Orban cited in Ivan Krastev, "Will 2018 Be as Revolutionary as 1968" in *The New York Times*, February 21, 2018.

[16] Ivan Kalmar, "Islamophobia and Anti-Antisemitism: The Case of Hungary and the 'Soros Plot'," *Patterns of Prejudice* 1–2, no. 54 (2020): 1–7.

[17] Cited in John Richardson and Ruth Wodak, "Anti-Sorosism: Reviving 'the Jewish World Consiracy'" in Massimiliano Demata, Virginia Zorzi, and Angela Zottola (eds.), *Conspiracy Theory Discourses* (Amsterdam: John Benjamins, 2022), 395–420.

[18] Joshua Shanes, "Netanyahu, Orbán, and the Resurgence of Antisemitism: Lessons of the Last Century," *Shofar* 37, no. 1 (2019): 108–120; Dany Filc and Sharon Pardo, "Israel's Right-Wing Populists: The European Connection," *Survival* 3, no. 63 (2001): 99–122.

After its arrival on the German political scene in 2013, *Alternativ für Deutschland* (AfD) similarly illustrated the intersection of Euroskepticism, Islamophobia, Palestinophobia, and philosemitic posture. The novelty, however, was the symbolic dimension of this entanglement: a German nationalist party professing, like its leader Frauke Petry in 2017, that its steady rise to prominence was a "welcome development" for Jews.[19] A moderate when compared to some of her *völkish* colleagues, Petry resigned in 2017. But despite internal divisions, her successors continued to cultivate the image of a Jewish-friendly AfD, "the only party to represent the interest of Jewish citizens," and "only friend of Israel" in the Bundestag. Created in 2018, a small group called "Jews in the Afd" helped propagate this narrative. Yet the party's self-styled rhetoric on Jews, Judaism, and Israel, was only a blend of "philosemitic civilizationism" and "antisemitic nationalism."[20] On the one hand, the AfD claimed to defend "Judeo-Christian culture" and to protect Jews from "immigrant Muslim hatred." Its politicians have also couched their support for Israel in civilizational terms, by framing the Jewish state as a Western bulwark against Islamist extremism, and "a guarantor of human rights [which] deserves full support from Germany and Europe."[21] On the other hand, AfD officials have engaged in antisemitic conspiracies, or manipulated Holocaust interpretative concepts to portray refugee criminality in Germany as "rupture of civilization." They also lashed out at commemorative culture. In 2017, the AfD fraction chief in Thuringia Björn Höcke referred to Berlin's Holocaust memorial as "a monument of shame in the heart of our capital." Anti-Jewish sentiment was likewise perceptible at the grassroot level. In 2018, an Allensbach Institute survey revealed that 55 percent of AfD voters – overrepresented in its eastern bastions – believed that "Jews have too much influence in the world."[22] The heterogenous AfD – part anti-elites and anti-immigrant populist, part *völkisch* national-conservative – has continuously refuted the charge of endemic antisemitism in its ranks. Yet in the course of its decade-long

---

[19] "Frauke Petry, The New Face of Germany's Anti-Immigrant Right" in *Tablet*, February 8, 2017.
[20] Maximilian Selent and Matthias Kortmann, "Philo-Semitic Civilisationism or Anti-Semitic Nationalism? The Ambivalent Stance of the Alternative for Germany towards Judaism, Jews, and Israel" in *German Politics* (published online on May 13, 2023).
[21] Jürgen Braun's declaration (April 27, 2023) is available at: https://afdbundestag.de/juergen-braun-je-linker-desto-feindlicher-gegenueber-israel/.
[22] Michelle Lynn Kahn, "Antisemitism, Holocaust Denial, and Germany's Far-Right: How the AfD Tiptoes around Nazism," *The Journal of Holocaust Research* 2–3, no. 36 (2022): 164–185; Samuel Salzborn, "Antisemitism in the Alternative for Germany Party" in Eric Langenbacher (ed.), *Twilight of the Merkel Era: Power and Politics in Germany after the 2017 Election* (New York: Berghahn Books, 2019), 254–273.

existence, the rising political party has instrumentalized Jews to legitimate racism against other groups, and rehabilitated German nationalism in the name of anti-antisemitism. Such maneuver, however, was not merely another variant of far-right rebranding in the European Union: It was also the illiberal extension of the radicalized philosemitism born out of the Angela Merkel era.

From Remembrance Culture to "Philosemitic McCarthyism"

"We should develop a natural feeling for our whole history," Angela Merkel told a journalist in 2000, "and then say: we are also happy to be Germans."[23] Five years before the start of her chancellorship, the newly appointed chairman of the CDU/CSU reiterated what had been Helmut Kohl's position for most of his long tenure: Past crimes against the Jews deserved special acknowledgment but should not deprive postwar Germans from pride in their otherwise healthy history. In March 2008, however, Merkel's notorious "staatsräson speech" delivered in front of the Knesset revealed a different approach to the past. "I most firmly believe," she declared, "that only if Germany accepts its enduring responsibility for the moral disaster in its history will we be able to build a humane future."[24] Her statement suggested appropriation of what remained until 1990 a progressive moral imperative: the permanent acceptance of criminal responsibility as central tenet of German democracy. It also echoed Richard von Weiszäcker's famous injunction, atypical in 1985 but now normalized in official discourse: "in remembrance lies the secret of redemption." By all appearances, Merkel positioned herself as the inheritor of left-liberal traditions of historical accountability. Three times in her speech, however, she introduced her Israeli audience to new terminology. The development of "a culture of remembrance that will also endure when the survivors of the Shoah are no longer among us," she announced, was now a core task of the German state. Merkel's "remembrance culture" did not only connote the statization of "coming to terms with the past": The term also signified the migration of Holocaust memory from the realm of contested politics to that of national identity.

---

[23] Cited in Frank Brunssen, "The New Self-Understanding of the Berlin Republic: Readings of Contemporary German History" in Stuart Taberner and Frank Finlay (eds.), *Recasting German Identity: Culture, Politics, and Literature in the Berlin Republic* (Rochester, NY: Camden House, 2002), 19–36.

[24] Merkel's speech is available at: https://m.knesset.gov.il/EN/activity/Documents/SpeechPdf/merkel.pdf.

This shift mirrored another reconfiguration. At the start of the twenty-first century, argued the political scientist Hans Kundnani, the universalist meaning of the Holocaust – a legacy of the 1960s New Left – faded from view in favor of a particularist interpretation of the crime. In 1999, the Green foreign minister Joschka Fischer's exclamation "Never again Auschwitz" in support of NATO military campaign in Serbia was the last "universalist aspiration to prevent any genocide in the world" before the Holocaust's particularist shrinking. After that, universal Auschwitz "was never invoked in German foreign policy debates as it had been in the 1990s."[25] Such framing of Fischer's phrase warrants qualification. In the mind of the ex-68er converted to Atlanticism, "Never again Auschwitz" was only a universal creed tailored to Western liberal interventionism. It was also a slogan which neoconservative elites in the United States could have easily made theirs. "Remembrance culture," however, particularized the Holocaust through the nationalization of its moral consequences: a German obligation to cultivate Jewish life, fight *Judenhass* (Jew-hatred), and stand by Israel. These three components of official German philosemitism were already in place prior to the twenty-first century. What took place under Angela Merkel (2005–21) is their radicalization. During this period, a now "obsessive" philosemitism hardened into a code of conduct redefining the parameters of German citizenship: *erinnerungskultur* (remembrance culture) as firewall against *kulturschande* or "cultural infamy."[26]

The outrage in question was the shame of antisemitism – conceived not only as harm done to Jews but also as assault on German decency. In 2000, the socialist chancellor Gerhard Schröder had already called for an "Uprising of the Decent" in reaction to antisemitic and anti-immigrant incidents. Yet anxieties over "new antisemitism" – redefined as anti-Zionist and Muslim Judeophobia – turned the defense of German decency into a war on antisemitism waged through monitoring, research, and educational programs. This intensification, argued the sociologist Anna-Esther Younes, stemmed from elite-level projection of Germanness

---

[25] Hans Kundnani, "Zionism über Alles," in *Dissent*, March 15, 2024, available at: www.dissentmagazine.org/online_articles/zionism-uber-alles/. On the weight of the Holocaust in German responses to genocide prior to the twenty-first-century, see Andrew I. Port, *Never Again: Germans and Genocide after the Holocaust* (Cambridge, MA: Harvard University Press, 2023).

[26] On the transformation of philosemitism into "obsession," see Saba-Nur Cheema, "Die deutsche Debatte ist von Obsessionen geprägt" in *Die Zeit*, June 14, 2022, cited in A. Dirk Moses, "Die deutsche Debatte ist von Obsessionen geprägt": Erinnerungsräumliche Betrachtungen zum Katechismus der Deutschen" in Jürgen Zimmerer (ed.), *Erinerungskämpfe: Neues deutsches Geschitsbewusstsein* (Stuttgart: Reclam, 2023), 264–290.

on Jewishness, according to which "whoever attacks Jews, also attacks German national ethics."[27] In their study of anti-antisemitic discourse during the Merkel era, the ethnographers Irit Dekel and Ezra Öyzürek identified another mutation: a shift "from a public emotion of guilt to a public emotion of shame." Holocaust guilt, of course, was always close to shame in the vocabulary of German atonement. Both words belonged to the repertoire of contrition. Karl Jaspers's emblematic *The Question of German Guilt* (1946), for instance, equally alluded to the "ineradicable shame" of Germans.[28] During the Merkel years, however, the discourse of guilt gave way to a permanent state of alert against the shame of antisemitism. "Germany's duty to remember the Holocaust," wrote Dekel and Öyzürek, continued to occupy a central place in political culture. But it was now primarily fulfilled by "fighting antisemitism." The move from guilt to shame, they added, "was the first and most consequential step in the logic that drives accusations of antisemitism to expand."[29]

Released in November 2022, the "National Strategy against Anti-Semitism and for Jewish Life" turned the containment of shame into policy. Hoping to "assure Jews in Germany that they have its support," the Federal Government reaffirmed its simultaneous "responsibility to remember the Shoah" and to "fight antisemitism." Yet incumbent upon Germans was also the "the protection of Jews everywhere in the world and the security of the state of State of Israel as a component of the German national ethos." Angela Merkel set this precedent in her 2008 address when in reference to "the threats of the Iranian president" against the Jewish state, she declared Israel's security "part of my country's *staatsräson*," or a matter of national interest. But as the 2022 National Strategy demonstrated, by the end of Merkel's tenure all the components of official German philosemitism fell under *staatsräson*: remembrance culture, the preservation of Jewish life, anti-antisemitism, and the deflection of "every attack on Israel's right to exist." Toeing a tenuous line between liberality and censorship, the Federal Government assumed "responsibility for identifying and condemning antisemitic hostility and attacks as well as Holocaust denial and distortion."[30]

[27] Anna-Esther Younes, "Fighting Anti-Semitism in Contemporary Germany," in *Islamophobia Studies* 2, no. 5 (2020): 249–266.
[28] Karl Jaspers, *The Question of German Guilt* (New York: Fordham University Press, 2000), 65–66.
[29] Irit Dekel and Esra Öyzürek, "The Logic of the Fight against Antisemitism in Germany in Three Cultural Shifts," *Patterns of Prejudice* 2–3, no. 56 (2022): 157–187.
[30] Federal Government of Germany, "National Strategy against Antisemitism and for Jewish Life" (English version, 2022), available at: www.bmi.bund.de/SharedDocs/downloads/EN/publikationen/2023/BMI23001.pdf?__blob=publicationFile&v=6.

Although disconnected from public opinion polls revealing hostility or indifference to Holocaust memorialization and Israel, this official language testified of the nationalization of philosemitism in twenty-first-century Germany: not only ritualized repentance but also a demarcation line between "us" and "them," or between redeemed (white) Germans and suspicious (racialized) Others. That the rigidification of German philosemitism coincided with anxieties over the transformation of Germany into a country of immigrants was not incidental. "The multiculturalism concept is a failure, an absolute failure," Merkel declared in 2010, although Germany had only offered citizenship to long-established residents in 2000. That same year, Thilo Sarrazin's bestselling book *Deutschland schafft sich ab* [*Germany Does Away with Itself*] blamed the undoing of Germany on unassimilable Muslim immigrants, only to praise "the average higher intelligence of Jews" passed through a Jewish gene.[31] Merkel, of course, found Sarrazin's blend of anti-Muslim racism and genetic philosemitism "completely unacceptable." Her position was instead in line with that of her liberal conservative counterparts David Cameron and Nicolas Sarkozy in Britain and France, who likewise blamed multiculturalism for its failure to integrate Muslim communities.[32] "Mutti Merkel," to be sure, never opposed ethnic diversity, and five years later put her political career on the line when she opened the door to 800,000 predominantly Middle Eastern refugees. *Willkommenskultur*, however, rapidly morphed into a culture of suspicion. During the last years of Merkel's chancellorship, the dominant perception of antisemitism in political discourse – as well as among the leaders of the Central Council of Jews in Germany – was that of "migrated" Muslim antisemitism, although during her tenure statistics showed that the vast majority of perpetrators of antisemitic incidents remained far-right ethnic Germans.[33] By allegedly threatening Jews, or not expunging antisemitism from their midst, Muslims jeopardized the social contract. Philosemitic encouragement was in order. To instill in Muslim-background Germans the proper form of emotional identification, the state launched Holocaust memory programs to help youth of Turkish, Arab, or Kurdish origin engage in German repentance. These efforts achieved unexpected results. Participants in trips to Auschwitz, observed the anthropologist Ezra Öyzürek, "had strongest feelings when they identified with the victims and likened them (…) to their own status of religious minorities,

---

[31] Sander L. Gilman, "Thilo Sarrazin and the Politics of Race in the Twenty-First Century," *New German Critique*, no. 17 (2022): 47–59.
[32] Rita Chin, *The Crisis of Multiculturalism in Europe* (Princeton, NJ: Princeton University Press, 2017), 237–238.
[33] Irit Dekel and Esra Öyzürek, "The Logic of the Fight against Antisemitism," op. cit.

and to their own feeling of being German but not accepted as German." Holocaust education programs did not "reform" young Muslims but instead encouraged them to reflect on their own positionality.[34] The good Muslim, however, remained one who internalized German values: "sensitivity to Germany's historical responsibility" as precondition to inclusion. The then Foreign Minister Frank-Walter Steinmeier clarified the terms of incorporation at the height of the European refugee crisis. "Arriving in the heart of German society," the future president of the Federal Republic declared in March 2016, "also means accepting the commitment against antisemitism in one's heart."[35]

More than the "dangerous Muslim," however, the figure of the "Palestinian antisemite," and that of her/his accomplices, radicalized German philosemitism during the Merkel era.[36] In 2008, the chancellor's *staatsräson* address did not call for the policing of public opinion. But her elevation of the "special relationship" to the rank of moral and strategic priority justified increased monitoring of "Israel-related antisemitism," the euphemistic rephrasing of "antizionism is antisemitism." In early 2018, the Federal government appointed its first "Commissioner for Jewish Life and the Fight Against Antisemitism" after the burning of an Israeli flag in front of Berlin's Brandenburg Gate. Within five years, all sixteen federal states had their own antisemitic commissioners – the majority of them non-Jewish.[37] With their commitment to counteract "every attack on Israel's existence," state-appointed antisemitism adjudicators have called for the censorship of Israel critics who in their eyes deviated from the IHRA definition or stood in "proximity" to BDS – the Palestinian solidarity campaign declared antisemitic (but not banned) in a Bundestag resolution adopted in 2019.

In a country long committed to the two-state solution, empathy for Palestinians couched in the language of mutual tolerance did not jeopardize the philosemitic ethos: It instead reinforced it.[38] Yet talk of apartheid, settler colonialism, Holocaust comparability, or German historical

---

[34] Esra Özyürek, *Subcontractors of Guilt: Holocaust Memory and Muslim Belonging in Postwar Germany* (Stanford, CA: Stanford University Press, 2023), 200–201.
[35] Steinmeier cited in Irit Dekel, "Philosemitism in Contemporary German Media," *Media, Culture & Society* 44, no. 4 (2020): 746–763.
[36] On the interplay between these two tropes, see Anna-Esther Younes, "Fighting Anti-Semitism in Contemporary Germany," op. cit.; Sindyan Qasem, "'Little More than Terrorists': Eine Reflektion über das Verhältnis von Islamismusprävention und Palästinadiskurs," *Islamophobia Studies Yearbook* 11 (2020): 71–90.
[37] Peter Kuras, "The Strange Logic of Germany's Antisemitism Bureaucrats" in *Jewish Currents* (Spring 2023), available at: https://jewishcurrents.org/the-strange-logic-of-germanys-antisemitism-bureaucrats.
[38] On tolerance as erasure, see Saree Makdisi, *Tolerance Is a Wasteland: Palestine and the Culture of Denial* (Berkeley, CA: University of California Press, 2022).

responsibility for Palestinian dispossession, destabilized the code of honor. "The terms on which Palestine can be discussed are heavily constricted and monitored, resulting in a reduced understanding of Palestinian experiences, perspectives and analysis": that the author of this matter-of-fact statement preferred to stay anonymous revealed the pervasiveness of fear.[39] Palestinians in Germany, observed the German-Palestinian lawyer Nadija Samour, "are a thorn in the side of German memory culture. If you want to prove (…) how civilized you are, or philosemitic or pro-Israel you are, you have a chance to do that by throwing Palestinians under the bus."[40] In 2021 and 2022, Germans of Arab or African background lost public employment, were disinvited from cultural events or found themselves in Germany's "anti-Palestinian crosshairs."[41] International guests, academics or artists, including non-Zionist Jews reprimanded by non-Jewish censors for their betrayal of Jewishness, also stood in the line of fire. Between 2019 and 2022, the removal of the renowned scholar Peter Schäffer from his post of director of Berlin's Jewish Museum, the Achille Mbembe affair, or accusations of antisemitism leveled against the exhibition *Documenta 15*, were only the most publicized instances of suppression of untamed pro-Palestinian voices. "In a paradox typical of the upside-down dynamics surrounding Jews, Arabs, and Germans in contemporary Germany," observed students of this phenomenon, "a questionably conceived anti-antisemitism has become the mechanism for keeping Germanness Aryan."[42] This equation too rapidly conflated the *völkish* philosemitism/antisemitism of the AfD with the liberal philosemitic consensus in government, academia, or part of the media: a self-imposed regulation of speech designed above all to keep Germanness redeemed. Yet in the process of mastering the Nazi past, charged A. Dirk Moses, "Germans ended up reproducing the exclusionary structures and illiberalism they were trying to overcome."[43] The radicalization of philosemitism – whether in its German form or otherwise – simultaneously gave way to radical critique.

---

[39] "Palestine Between German Memory of Politics and (De-) Colonial Thought" (anonymous author), *Journal of Genocide Research* 23, no. 3 (2021): 374–382. See also in the same issue, Aleida Assmann, "A Specter Is Haunting Germany: The Mbembe Debate and the New Antisemitism," 400–411.
[40] Cited in Kuras, "The Strange Logic of Germany's Antisemitism Bureaucrats," op. cit.
[41] Hebh Jamal, "Germany Puts Artists, Academics in Its Anti-Palestinian Crosshairs" in *972 Magazine*, July 3, 2022, available at: www.972mag.com/germany-artists-academics-palestinian-antisemitism/.
[42] See the collective article "Bad Memory" in *Jewish Currents*, Spring 2023, available at: https://jewishcurrents.org/bad-memory-2.
[43] A. Dirk Moses, "The German Campaign against Cultural Freedom: Documenta 15 in Context," *Grey Room*, 92 (Summer 2023): 74–93.

"Anti-Philosemitism"

The discourse of new antisemitism, the appropriation of philosemitism by the populist far right, and the "hyper-Zionism" of the Merkel era, did not develop without opposition. In Europe, however, the critique of philosemitism did not start in 2000. In 1967–68, the German New Left accused the German state of "repressed antisemitism" and denounced its guilty pro-Israelism. Yet the subsequent conversion of aging 68ers to remembrance culture muted their youthful anger at the "fascistoid" Federal Republic. In the 1980s and 1990s, the translation of Edward Said's writings exposed European readers to the way Palestinians and Arab intellectuals conceptualized philosemitism: guilt over Western antisemitism, or deflection of guilt at the expense of the "victims of the victims," expressed through a "transference of animus" from the Jew to the Arab/Palestinian. Yet more attuned to the "secret sharing" between the Othering of Arabs and antisemitism in nineteenth-century Western culture, *Orientalism* (1978) did not dwell on the bifurcation of the (good) Jew and the (bad) Arab in the West – what Gil Anidjar called the naturalization of "the Jew and the Arab as polarized entities."[44] The discourse of "Semitism" embedded in Western Christian thought since the start of the nineteenth century, to be sure, ended in 1945. The Nazis, wrote Anidjar, "at once produced the culmination and carried out the exhaustive demise of the notion of 'Semites'."[45] But what has been termed "the end of the Semites" simultaneously reinforced their polarization after the Holocaust: "two separate categories, Jew/Judaism and Arab/Islam, belonging to two opposing camps in the European understanding of the world: the West and the Orient."[46] The end of "Semitism," concomitant with the discredit of biological race after 1945, paradoxically marked the beginning of the philosemitic era: the Westernization, or Judeo-Christianization, of the Jew against the Arab/Muslim/Palestinian.

Philosemitism as Occidentalism was indeed a key theme in early twentieth-century "anti-philosemitic" interventions. In 2004, Mahmood Mamdani took notice of "a sea change in consciousness." Once at the margins of the West, he wrote, Judaism and Jews now belong "to the heart of Western history and Western civilization." In defense of Jewish

---

[44] Gil Anidjar, *The Jew, The Arab: A History of the Enemy* (Stanford, CA: Stanford University Press, 2003), xvi.

[45] Gil Anidjar, *Semites: Race, Religion, Literature* (Stanford, CA: Stanford University Press, 2008), 19.

[46] James Renton, "The End of the Semites" in James Renton and Ben Gidley (eds.), *Antisemitism and Islamophobia in Europe: A Shared History?* (London: Palgrave Macmillan, 2017), 99–140.

universalism, the French-Jewish philosopher Ivan Segré deconstructed the "reactionary philosemitism" of neoconservative Jewish intellectuals in France, "the cornerstone (...) of a broad ideological operation aiming to impose the slogan of 'defense of the West." The historian Enzo Traverso argued for his part that after the Holocaust the Jew morphed into "the standard against which the democratic West measures its moral virtues." The Israeli poet and writer Itzhak Laor depicted the post-1989 "philosemitic offensive" in Europe in similar vein: "The European subject who, at an earlier epoch, had succeeded so well in distancing himself from the Jew ("he is not like us"), is now eager to demonstrate how much he loves him: first because now "he is like us," and second because he no longer lives here." The West, or Europe, incorporated the Jew after 1945, but preferential "love" also justified neocolonial racism against Muslims and the negation of Israel's treatment of Palestinians.[47]

Decolonial theorists likewise contended that post-Holocaust Jews had been "chosen by the West." This co-optation, argued the French Algerian writer Houria Bouteldja, had three motivations: "to solve the white world's moral legitimacy crisis (...), to outsource [French] republican racism, and finally to be the weaponized wing of Western imperialism in the Arab world." But while the West subcontracted Jews to do its dirty work, "state philosemitism" – the cooptation of Jews by the French republic – dissociated "good" white Jews from racialized minorities, Muslims chiefly among them. "You are losing your historical friends. You are still in the ghetto. Why don't we get out of there together?," Bouteldja asked in a challenge to Jews. The way out of philosemitism, she proposed, was first to metaphorically "shoot Sartre": to do away with a left tolerant of Zionism, and therefore blind to its own whiteness. The second step was for Jews to refuse the role of "stakeholders of Judeo-Christian civilization," and opt instead for "revolutionary love." In front of them was a "binary" choice: "West or Third World, whiteness or decolonization, Zionism or anti-Zionism."[48]

---

[47] Mahmood Mamdani, *Good Muslim, Bad Muslim. America, the Cold War, and the Roots of Terror* (New York: Pantheon Books, 2004), 36; Ivan Segré, "The Philo-Semitic Reaction" (first published in French in 2009) in Alain Badiou, Eric Hazan, and Ivan Segré (eds.), *Reflections on Anti-Semitism* (London: Verso, 2013); Enzo Traverso, *The End of Jewish Modernity* (London: Pluto Press, 2016), 3; Yitzhak Laor, *Le nouveau philosémitisme européen et le « camp de la paix » en Israël* (Paris: La Fabrique, 2007), translated as *The Myths of Liberal Zionism* (London: Verso, 2009), 24, cited in Gabriel Piterberg, "Euro-Zionism and its Discontents," *New Left Review*, no. 84 (November–December 2013): 43–65.

[48] Houria Bouteldja, *Whites, Jews, and Us: Towards a Politics of Revolutionary Love* (South Pasadena, CA: Semiotext(e), 2016). On Bouteldja's radical critique of philosemitism, see among others Ivan Segré, "A Native with a Pale Face" in *Los Angeles Review of Book* (November 14, 2018).

Philosemitism as defense of the Judeo-Christian West; as the "setting apart of Semites in the service of Western-Christian interests"[49]; as "hyper-humanization" of the Jews since the Holocaust[50]; or as "endorsement of white Europeanness"[51]: Such critical framings remained too general or theoretical to elicit public conversations on the function of philosemitism in European politics and memory. Widely covered in the international press and German media, however, A. Dirk Moses's "The German Catechism" (2021) immediately stirred up controversy. The critique of German philosemitism had a long history and the "German Catechism" echoed older New Left arguments. Yet published at the end of the Merkel era, Moses's provocative essay drew particular attention. "The tinder was very dry; only a spark was required to ignite the flame," explained the Australian historian. His fusillades against German memory culture took to task the "high priests" of a new German catechism whose articles of faith were the uniqueness of the Holocaust and its incomparability with other genocides; the Shoah as "rupture of civilization" and moral foundation of the nation; a special responsibility to Jews in Germany, and special loyalty to Israel; the separation of antisemitism, a "distinctly" German prejudice, from racism; and the equation of anti-Zionism with antisemitism. "In short," summarized Moses, "the catechism implies a redemptive story in which the sacrifice of Jews in the Holocaust by Nazis is the premise for the Federal Republic's legitimacy." Unreflective of Germany's diverse population, and complicit with the mistreatment of Palestinians, the catechism had run its course. "The time has come," he concluded, "to set it aside and renegotiate the demands of historical justice in a way that respects all victims of the German state and Germans of all kinds."[52]

Moses's intervention was followed by animated exchanges with scholars or pundits who supported, nuanced, or assailed his "catechism" thesis. Few however understood the text as a plea for a post-philosemitic age – if anything for the sake of Jews. Germany's overidentification with its former victims, Moses wrote, does not erase their alterity. "Philosemitism continues to view Jews (…) as guests, not fully German, and the Jewish community as representing a foreign state." Its redemptive dimension,

---

[49] Gil Hochberg, "Remembering Semitism; or, on the Prospect of Re-membering the Semites," *ReOrient* 1, no. 2: 192–223.
[50] Alana Lentin, *Why Race Still Matters* (Cambridge: Polity Press, 2020), 132.
[51] Steven Friedman, *Good Jew, Bad Jew: Racism, Anti-Semitism, and the Assault on Meaning* (Johannesburg: Wits University Press, 2023), 4.
[52] A. Dirk Moses, "The German Catechism" (May 2021) in *The New Fascism Syllabus*, available at: https://newfascismsyllabus.com/wp-content/uploads/2021/08/The-Catechism-Debate.pdf.

he added, disturbingly mirrors the "redemptive antisemitism" of the Nazi era. Moses did not explain in details how to exit philosemitism, but we can infer that a post-philosemitic age would be one which accepts Jewish life in society for humanist or universalist reasons, away from instrumentalization or fetichization.[53]

This is no doubt a proposition that most Jews would wholeheartedly welcome. This is however the easy part. After 1945, philosemitic Europe, in its liberal or German hypertrophied form, meant the delegitimation of antisemitism; the unprecedented acceptance of Jewishness and Judaism in public culture; the recognition of the Shoah; the acceptance of Jewish statehood as *fait accompli*, if not as ontological just cause irrespective of its consequences for the victims of Zionism; and the possibility for many diaspora Jews to feel symbolic attachment with Israel without accusations of disloyalty. Which elements of this post-Holocaust consensus would the end of philosemitism undo? Will Jewish safety after philosemitism require from Jews the "unlearning" of Zionism – a new demand for "regeneration" in return of solidarity? Will a new generation of young Jews voluntarily drift away from pro-Israelism, co-share "Never Again," and return to the tradition of Jewish universalism without dissolution of Jewish identity? Or will vengeful "anti-philosemitism" function as the antisemitism of the twenty-first century? October 7, 2023, whose consequences for Western philosemitism will be analyzed in a sequel to this study, added urgency to these questions. The state of Israel, which according to Zionist ideology "normalized" Jewish existence, may have now de-normalized the Jewish condition. And whether "after Gaza" the Shoah will remain "the measure of all crimes" in the West, or even in Germany, is in doubt.[54] At the time of writing (March 2024), however, it is still premature to declare philosemitic Europe – the liberal and illiberal identification with "the Jew" documented in this book – a matter of the past. The architecture of philosemitism born out of the post-Holocaust period remains in place within the political establishment. But signs also point to an alternative path. A liberating prospect for some, a dreaded specter for others: Philosemitic Europe contemplates today the potential dawn of its post-philosemitic future.

---

[53] Deborah Feldman, *Judenfetisch* (Berlin: Luchterhand Literaturverlag, 2023).
[54] Pankaj Mishra, The Shoah after Gaza in *London Review of Books*, Vol. 46, 6, March 21, 2024.

Select Bibliography

Adorno, Theodor W. *Zur Bekämpfung der Antisemitismus heute?* [1962] (Berlin: Suhrkamp, 2024).
Adunka, Evelyn. *Die vierte Gemeinde: Die Wiener Juden in der Zeit von 1945 bis heute* (Berlin: Philo, 2000).
Albrich, Thomas, Winfried R. Garscha, and Martin F. Polaschek (eds.). *Holocaust und Kriegsverbrechen vor Gericht: Der Fall Österreich* (Innsbruck: StudienVerlag, 2006).
Allwork, Larissa. *Holocaust Remembrance between the National and the Transnational: The Stockholm International Forum and the First Decade of the International Task Force* (London: Bloomsbury, 2015).
Allwork, Larissa, and Rachel Pistol (eds.). *The Jews, The Holocaust, and The Public: The Legacies of David Cesarani* (London: Palgrave Macmillan, 2019).
Amouroux, Henri. *J'ai vu vivre Israël* (Paris: Fayard, 1958).
Anidjar, Gil. *Semites: Race, Religion, Literature* (Stanford, CA: Stanford University Press, 2008).
Anidjar, Gil. *The Jew, The Arab: A History of the Enemy* (Stanford, CA: Stanford University Press, 2003).
Anthias, Floya, and Cathie Llyod (eds.). *Rethinking Anti-Racisms: From Theory to Practice* (London: Routledge, 2002).
Anthony, Elizabeth. *The Compromise of Return: Viennese Jews after the Holocaust* (Detroit: Wayne State University Press, 2021).
Aschauer-Smolik, Sabine, and Mario Steidel (eds.). *Tamid Kadima – Immer vorwärts: Der jüdische Exodus aus Europa 1945–1948* (Innsbruck: StudienVerlag, 2010).
Assmann, Aleida. *Das neue Unbehagen an der Erinnerungskultur* (Munich: C.H. Beck, 2020).
Azouvi, François. *Le mythe du grand silence: Auschwitz, les Français, la mémoire* (Paris: Gallimard, 2015).
Badiel, David. *Jews Don't Count* (London: TLS Books, 2021).
Bair, Nadya. *The Decisive Network: Magnum Photos and the Postwar Image Market* (Oakland: University of California Press, 2020).
Bakker, Arjen F. et al. *Protestant Bible Scholarship: Antisemitism, Philosemitism, and Anti-Judaism* (Leiden: Brill, 2022).
Baram, Daphne. *Disenchantment: The Guardian and Israel* (London: Guardian Books, 2004).

Bashir, Bashir, and Leila Farsakh. *The Arab and Jewish Question: Geographies of Engagement in Palestine and Beyond* (New York: Columbia University Press, 2020).
Beck, Ulrich. *The Cosmopolitan Vision* (Cambridge: Polity Press, 2006).
Beller, Steven. "Is Europe Good for the Jews? Jews and the Pluralist Tradition in Historical Perspective," *European Judaism: A Journal for the New Europe* 42, no. 1 (2009): 44–55.
Bergmann, Werner. *Antisemitismus in öffentlichen Konflikten: Kollektives Lernen in der politischen Kultur der Bundesrepublik 1949–1989* (Frankfurt am Main: Campus Verlag, 1997).
Bergmann, Werner, and Rainer Erb. *Antisemitismus in der Bundesrepublik Deutschland: Ergebnisse der empirischen Forschung von 1946–1989* (Opladen: Leske + Budrich, 1991).
Bischof, Günter (ed.). *Austria in the European Union* (New Brunswick, NJ: Transaction Publishers, 2002).
Bischof, Günter, Mark Landry, and Christian Karner (eds.). *Myths in Austrian History: Construction and Deconstruction* (New Orleans: University of New Orleans Press, 2020).
Bischof, G., A. Pelinka, and F. Karlhofer (eds.). *The Vranitzky Era in Austria* (New Brunswick, NJ: Transaction Publishers, 1999).
Böhm, Franz, and Marietta Böhm. *Eine Reise nach Israel* (Düsseldorf: Kalima Druck, 1955).
Bodemann, Y. Michal (ed.). *The New German Jewry and the European Context* (Houndmills, Basingstoke, Hampshire: Palgrave Macmillan, 2008).
Bodemann, Y. Michal. *Jews, Germans, Memory* (Ann Arbor, MI: University of Michigan Press, 1996).
Bouteldja, Houria. *Whites, Jews, and Us: Towards a Politics of Revolutionary Love* (South Pasadena, CA: Semiotext(e), 2016).
Brandt, Willy. *People and Politics: The Years 1960–1975* (London: William Collins Sons & Co, 1978).
Brasz, Chaya, and Yosef Kaplan (eds.). *Dutch Jews as Perceived by Themselves and Others* (Leiden: Brill, 2000).
Brillanti, Claudio. *Le sinistre italiane e il conflitto arabo-israelo-palestinese* (Roma: Sapienza Università Editrice, 2018).
Brink, Cornelia. *Auschwitz in der Paulskirche: Erinnerungspolitik in Fotoaustellungen der sechziger Jahre* (Marburg: Jonas, 2000).
Broder, Henryk M. *Jedem das Seine* (Augsburg: Ölbaum, 1999).
Brubaker, Rogers. "Between Nationalism and Civilizationism: The European Populist Movement in Comparative Perspective," *Ethnic and Racial Studies* 8, no. 40 (2017): 1191–1226.
Brenner, Michael (ed.). *A History of Jews in Germany since 1945: Politics, Culture, and Society* (Bloomington, IN: Indiana University Press, 2018).
Brenner, Michael. "'Gott schütze uns vor unseren Freunden' – Zur Ambivalenz des Philosemitismus im Kaiserreich," *Jahrbuch für Antisemitismusforschung* 2 (1993): 174–199.
Bunzl, Matti. *Anti-Semitism and Islamophobia: Hatreds Old and New in Europe* (Chicago, IL: Prickly Paradigm Press, 2007).

Bunzl, Matti. *Symptoms of Modernity: Jews and Queers in Late-Twentieth Century Vienna* (Berkeley, CA: University of California Press, 2004).
Cairns, Lucille. *Francophone Jewish Writers: Imagining Israel* (Liverpool: Liverpool University Press, 2015), 24–29.
Cardaun, Sarah K. *Countering Contemporary Antisemitism in Britain: Government and Civil Society Responses between Universalism and Particularism* (Leiden: Brill, 2015).
Case, Holly. *The Age of Questions* (Princeton, NJ: Princeton University Press, 2018).
Cesarani, David (ed.). *After Eichmann: Collective Memory of the Holocaust after 1961* (London: Routledge, 2014).
Charbit, Denis (ed.). *Les intellectuels français et Israël* (Paris: Editions de l'éclat, 2009).
Clifford, Rebecca. *Commemorating the Holocaust: The Dilemmas of Remembrance in France and Italy* (Oxford: Oxford University Press, 2013).
Cohen, Arthur A. *The Myth of the Judeo-Christian Tradition* (New York: Schocken Books, 1971).
Cohen Weisz, Suzanne. *Jewish Life in Austria and Germany after 1945: Identity and Communal Reconstruction* (Budapest: Central European University Press, 2016).
Confino, Alon. *Foundational Pasts: The Holocaust as Historical Understanding* (Cambridge: Cambridge University Press, 2011).
Connelly, John. *From Enemy to Brother: The Revolution in Catholic Teachings on the Jews 1933–1965* (Cambridge: Cambridge University Press, 2012).
Consonni, Manuela. *L'eclisse dell'antifascismo: Resistenza, questione ebraica e cultura politica in Italia dal 1943 al 1989* (Bari: Gius. Laterza & Figli, 2015).
Consonni, Manuela. "Split at the Root: Italian Jewish Identity between Anti-Zionism and Philo-Semitism, 1961–1967" in Uzi Rebhun, and Eli Lederhendler (eds.), *Research in Jewish Demography and Identity* (Brookline, MA: Academic Studies Press, 2015), 98–123.
Consonni, Manuela. "The New Grammar of Otherness: Europe, the Shoah, and the Jews," *Jewish History*, no. 24 (2010): 105–126.
Consonni, Manuela, and Vivian Liska (eds.). *Sartre, Jews, and the Other: Rethinking Antisemitism, Race, and Gender* (Berlin: De Gruyter Oldenburg, 2020).
Coulon, Laurence. *L'opinion française, Israël et le conflit israélo-arabe* (Paris: Honoré Champion, 2009).
Crane, Richard F. *Passion of Israel: Jacques Maritain, Catholic Conscience and the Holocaust* (Scranton, PA: University of Scranton Press, 2010).
Crossman, Richard. *Palestine Mission: A Personal Record* (New York and London: Harper & Brothers Publishers, 1947).
Czollek, Max. *Desintigriert euch!* (Munich: BtB Verlag, 2018).
Davies, Alan T. *Anti-Semitism and the Christian Mind: The Crisis of Conscience after Auschwitz* (New York: Herder and Herder, 1969).
Debenedetti, Giacomo. *October 16, 1943: Eight Jews* [1944] (University of Notre Dame Press, 2001).
Debono, Emmanuel. *Le racisme dans le prétoire: Antisémitisme, racisme et xénophobie devant la justice* (Paris: Presses Universitaires de France, 2019).

Decout, Maxime. *Écrire la judéité* (Seyssel: Champ Vallon, 2015).
Dekel, Irit, and Esra Özyürek. "The Logic of the Fight against Antisemitism in Germany in Three Cultural Shifts," *Patterns of Prejudice* 2–3, no. 56 (2022): 157–187.
De la Bollardière, Constance Pâris, and Simon Perego. "Les migrations juives d'Europe centrale et orientale en France au lendemain de la Shoah" *Archives Juives* 54, no. 1 (2021): 4–24.
De Saint-Cheron, Michaël. *Malraux et les Juifs: Histoire d'une fidélité* (Paris: Desclée de Brouwer, 2008).
Diekmann, Irene A., and Elke-Vera Kotowski (eds.). *Geliebter Feind, Gehasster Freund: Antisemitismus und Philosemitismus in Geschichte und Gegenwart* (Berlin: Verlag für Berlin-Brandenburg, 2009).
Di Figlia, Matteo. *Israele e la sinistra: Gli ebrei nel dibattito pubblico italiano dal 1945 a oggi* (Rome: Donzelli Editore, 2012).
Droit, Emmanuel. "Le Gulag contre la Shoah: Mémoires officielles and cultures mémorielles dans l'Europe élargie," *Vingtième Siècle. Revue d'histoire* 2, no. 94 (2007): 101–120.
Droz, Jacques. *La création de l'État d'Israël vu par la presse française* (Paris: La Documentation Française, 1993).
Dubnov, Arie M. *Isaiah Berlin: The Journey of a Jewish Liberal* (New York: Palgrave Macmillan, 2012).
Dziaczkowska, Magdalena, and Adele Valeria Messina. *Jews in Dialogue: Jewish Responses to the Challenges of Multicultural Contemporaneity* (Leiden: Brill, 2020).
Eder, Jacob. *Holocaust Angst: The Federal Republic of Germany and Holocaust Memory since the 1970s* (New York: Oxford University Press, 2016).
Eley, Geoff (ed.). *The Goldhagen Effect* (Ann Arbor, MI: University of Michigan Press, 2000).
Eley, Geoff. "Contemporary Germany and Denial: Is 'Nazis' All There Is to Say?," *History Workshop Journal* 84 (Autumn 2017): 44–66.
Ellis, Kail C. (ed.). *Nostra Aetate, Non-Christian Religions, and Interfaith Relations* (Cham: Palgrave Macmillan, 2021).
Endelman, Todd M. *The Jews of Britain, 1656 to 2000* (Berkeley, CA: University of California Press, 2002).
Feldman, Deborah. *Judenfetisch* (Berlin: Luchterhand Literaturverlag, 2023).
Filby, Eliza. *God & Mrs. Thatcher: The Battle for Britain's Soul* (London: Biteback Publishing, 2015).
Filiu, Jean-Pierre. *Mitterrand et la Palestine* (Paris: Fayard, 2005).
Fink, Carole. *West Germany and Israel: Foreign Relations, Domestic Politics, and the Cold War 1956–1974* (Cambridge: Cambridge University Press, 2019).
Finkielkraut, Alain. *Le juif imaginaire* (Paris: Seuil, 1980).
Finlay, Joseph. Between Religion and Ethnicity: How Jews Navigated Race Relations in Postwar Britain. PhD dissertation, University of Southampton, 2023.
Fortini, Franco. *The Dogs of the Sinai* [1967] (London: Seagull Books, 2013).
Foschepoth, Joseph. *Im Schatten der Vergangenheit: Die Anfänge der Gesellschaften für Christlich-Jüdische Zusammenarbeit* (Göttingen: Vandenhoeck und Ruprecht, 1993).

Frei, Norbert. *Adenauer's Germany and the Nazi Past* (New York: Columbia University Press, 2002).
Friedländer, Saul. *Nazi Germany and the Jews, 1939–1945: The Years of Extermination* (New York: Harper Perennial, 2008).
Gabowitsch, Mischa (ed.). *Replicating Atonement: Foreign Models in the Commemoration of Atrocities* (Cham: Palgrave Macmillan, 2017).
Galster, Ingrid (ed.). *Sartre et les Juifs* (Paris: La Découverte, 2005).
Gans, Evelien, and Remco Emsel (eds.). *The Holocaust, Israel and "the Jew": Histories of Antisemitism in Postwar Dutch Society* (Amsterdam: Amsterdam University Press, 2016).
Gassert, Philipp, and Alan E. Steinweiss. *Coping with the German Past: West German Debates on Nazism and Generational Conflict, 1955–1975* (New York: Berghahn Books, 2006).
Geisser, Vincent. *La nouvelle islamophobie* (Paris: La Découverte, 2003).
Gelbin, Cathy S., and Sander L. Gilman (eds.). *Cosmopolitanisms and the Jews* (Ann Arbor, MI: University of Michigan Press, 2017).
Gelbin, Cathy S., and Sander L. Gilman. *Jews on the Move: Modern Cosmopolitanist Thought and Its Others* (London: Routledge, 2018).
Geller, Jay Howard. *Jews in Post-Holocaust Germany, 1945–1953* (Cambridge: Cambridge University Press, 2005).
Giansante, Rocco, and Luna Goldberg (eds.). *Imagined Israel(s): Representation of the Jewish State in the Arts* (Leiden: Brill, 2023).
Giesen, Bernhard. *Triumph and Trauma* (London: Routledge, 2014).
Gilcher-Holtey, Ingrid (ed.). *A Revolution of Perception? Consequences and Echoes of 1968* (New York: Berghahn Books, 2014).
Gilbert, Martin. *Churchill and the Jews: A Lifelong Friendship* (New York: Henry Holt & Company, 2007).
Gilman, Sander L., and Karen Remmler (eds.). *Reemerging Jewish Culture in Germany: Life and Literature since 1989* (New York: New York University Press, 1994).
Gilman, Sander L. "Thilo Sarrazin and the Politics of Race in the Twenty-First Century." *New German Critique*, no. 17 (2012): 47–59.
Goldberg, Amos. "If This Is a Man: The Image of Man in Autobiographical and Historical Writing during and after the Holocaust." *Yad Vashem Studies* 33 (2005): 381–429.
Goldberg, Amos, and Haim Hazan (eds.). *Marking Evil: Holocaust Memory in the Global Age* (New York: Berghahn Books, 2015).
Goldberg, Sol et al. (eds.). *Key Concepts in the Study of Antisemitism* (New York: Palgrave Macmillan, 2021).
Gollwitzer, Helmut. *Israel-Und Wir* (Berlin: Lettner Verlag, 1958).
Gordon, Robert S. C. *The Holocaust in Italian Culture, 1944–2010* (Stanford, CA: Stanford University Press, 2012).
Gould, Rebecca Ruth. "The IHRA Definition of Antisemitism: Defining Antisemitism by Erasing Palestinians." *The Political Quarterly* 91, no. 4 (October–December 2020): 825–883.
Gronauer, Gerhard. *Der Staat Israel im westdeutschen Protestantismus: Wahrnehmungen in Kirche und Publizistik von 1948 bis 1972* (Göttingen: Vandenhoeck & Ruprecht, 2013).

Grossmann, Atina. *Jews, Germans, and Allies: Close Encounters in Occupied Germany* (Princeton, NJ: Princeton University Press, 2007).
Gromova, Alina, Felix Heinert, and Sebastian Voigt (eds.). *Jewish and Non-Jewish Spaces in the Urban Context* (Berlin: Neofelis, 2015).
Gruber, Ruth Ellen. *Virtually Jewish: Reinventing Jewish Culture in Europe* (Berkeley, CA: University of California Press, 2002).
Habermas, Jürgen. *The Postnational Constellation* (Cambridge: Polity Press, 2000).
Hacohen, Malachi Haim. *Jacob & Esau: Jewish European History between Nation and Empire* (Cambridge: Cambridge University Press, 2019).
Hammerschlag, Sarah. *The Figural Jew: Politics and Identity in Postwar French Thought* (Chicago, IL: University of Chicago Press, 2010).
Healan, K. Gaston. *Imagining Judeo-Christian America: Religion, Secularism, and the Redefinition of Democracy* (Chicago, IL: University of Chicago Press, 2019)
Heer, Friedrich. *God's First Love: Christians and Jews over Two Thousand Years* (New York: Weybright and Talley, 1970).
Heestermann, Jenny. *Inszenierte Versöhnung: Reisediplomatie und die deutsch-israelischen Beziehungen von 1957 bis 1984* (Frankfurt am Main: Campus Verlag, 2016).
Herf, Jeffrey. *Divided Memory: The Nazi Past in the Two Germanies* (Cambridge, MA: Harvard University Press, 1997).
Herf, Jeffrey. *Undeclared Wars with Israel: East Germany and the West German Far Left, 1967–1989* (New York: Cambridge University Press, 2016).
Heschel, Susannah. "Confronting the Past: Post-1945 German Protestant Theology and the Fate of the Jews" in Jonathan Frankel, and Ezra Mendelsohn (eds.), *The Protestant-Jewish Conundrum: Studies in Contemporary Jewry*, vol. XXIV (Oxford: Oxford University Press, 2010), 46–70.
Himka, John-Paul, and Joanna Betta Michlic (eds.). *Bringing the Dark Past to Light: The Reception of the Holocaust in Post-Communist Europe* (Lincoln, NE: University of Nebraska Press, 2013).
Himmelfarb, Gertrude. *Philosemitism in England from Cromwell to Churchill* (New York: Encounter Books, 2011).
Hockenos, Matthew D. *A Church Divided: German Protestants Confront the Nazi Past* (Bloomington, IN: Indiana University Press, 2004).
Hockenos, Matthew D. *Then They Came for Me: Martin Niemöller, the Pastor Who Defied the Nazis* (New York: Basic Books, 2018).
Holtschneider, K. Hannah. *German Protestants Remember the Holocaust: Theology and the Construction of Collective Memory* (Münster: Lit Verlag, 2001).
Horn, Dara. *People Love Dead Jews: Reports from a Haunted Present* (New York: W. W. Norton & Company, 2021).
Jacobs, Jack. *The Frankfurt School, Jewish Lives and Antisemitism* (New York: Cambridge University Press, 2015).
Julius, Anthony. *Trials of the Diaspora: A History of Anti-Semitism in England* (New York: Oxford University Press, 2010).
Judaken, Jonathan. *Critical Theories of Anti-Semitism* (New York: Columbia University Press, 2024).

Judaken, Jonathan. *Jean-Paul Sartre and the Jewish Question: Anti-Antisemitism and the Politics of the French Intellectual* (Lincoln, NE: University of Nebraska Press, 2006).
Judaken, Jonathan (ed.). *Race after Sartre: Antiracism, Africana Existentialism, Postcolonialism* (Albany, NY: State University of New York Press, 2008).
Kahn-Harris, Keith. *Strange Hate: Antisemitism, Racism, and the Limits of Diversity* (London: Repeater, 2019).
Kalmar, Ivan. "Islamophobia and Anti-Antisemitism: The Case of Hungary and the 'Soros Plot'," *Patterns of Prejudice* 54, no. 1–2 (2020): 1–7.
Kandiyoti, Dalia, and Rina Benmayor (eds.). *Reparative Citizenship for Sephardic Descendants: Returning to the Jewish Past in Spain and Portugal* (New York: Berghahn Books, 2023).
Kansteiner, Wolf. *In Pursuit of German Memory: History, Television, and Politics after Auschwitz* (Athens, OH: Ohio University Press, 2006).
Kaplan, Amy. *Our American Israel: The Story of an Entangled Alliance* (Cambridge, MA: Harvard University Press, 2018).
Karp, Jonathan, and Adam Sutcliffe (eds.). *Philosemitism in History* (Cambridge: Cambridge University Press, 2011).
Katcher, Leo. *Post Mortem: The Jews in Germany Now* (London: Hamish Hamilton, 1968).
Keilbach, Judith et al. *Völkermord zur Prime Time: Der Holocaust im Fernsehen* (Vienna: New Academic Press, 2019).
Kelemen, Paul. *The British Left and Zionism: History of a Divorce* (Manchester: Manchester University Press, 2012).
Klein, Charlotte. *Anti-Judaism in Christian Theology* (Philadelphia, PA: Fortress Press, 1974).
Klarsfeld, Beate, and Serge Klarsfeld. *Mémoires* (Paris: Flammarion, 2015).
Kloke, Martin W. *Israel und die deutsche Linke: zur Geschichte eines schwierigen Verhältnisses* (Frankfurt am Main: Haag + Herchen, 1990).
Klug, Brian. "The Limits of Analogy: Comparing Islamophobia and Antisemitism," in *Patterns of Prejudice* 48, no. 5 (2014): 442–459.
Knight, Robert. "National Construction Work and Hierarchies of Empathy in Postwar Austria," *Journal of Contemporary History* 49, no. 3 (2014): 491–513.
Koposov, Nikolay. *Memory Laws, Memory Wars: The Politics of the Past in Europe and Russia* (Cambridge: Cambridge University Press, 2018).
Krylova, Katya. *The Long Shadow of the Past: Contemporary Austrian Literature, Film, and Culture* (Rochester, NY: Camden House, 2017).
Kundnani, Hans. "Zionism über Alles." In *Dissent* (March 15, 2024). Available at: Dissent Magazine.
Kundnani, Hans. *Eurowhiteness: Culture, Empire and Race in the European Project* (London: Hurst, 2023).
Kundnani, Hans. *Utopia or Auschwitz: Germany's 68 Generation and the Holocaust* (New York: Columbia University Press, 2009).
Kuras, Peter. "The Strange Logic of Germany's Antisemitism Bureaucrats." In *Jewish Currents* (Spring 2023). Available at: Jewish Currents.
Lambert, Nick. *Jews and Europe in the Twentieth Century* (London: Vallentine Mitchell, 2008).

Langbehn, Volker, and Mohammad Salama. *German Colonialism: Race, The Holocaust, and Postwar Germany* (New York: Columbia University Press, 2011).

Langham, Raphael. *250 Years of Convention and Contention: A History of the Board of Deputies of British Jews, 1760–2010* (London: Vallentine Mitchell, 2010).

Laor, Yitzhak. *The Myths of Liberal Zionism* (London: Verso, 2009).

Lapidot, Elad. *Jews Out of the Question: A Critique of Anti-Anti Semitism* (Albany, NY: State University of New York Press, 2020).

Lassner, Phyllis, and Lara Trubowitz (eds.). *Antisemitism and Philosemitism in the Twentieth and Twenty-First Centuries: Representing Jews, Jewishness and Modern Culture* (Newark, DE: University of Delaware Press, 2008).

Láníček, Jan, and James Jordan (eds.). *Governments-in-Exile and the Jews during the Second World War* (London: Vallentine Mitchell, 2013).

Lanzmann, Claude. *Le lièvre de Patagonie: Mémoires* (Paris: Gallimard, 2009).

Ledoux, Sébastien. *Le devoir de mémoire: Une formule et son histoire* (Paris: CNRS, 2016).

Lebow, Richard Ned, Wulf Kansteiner, and Claudio Fogu (eds.). *The Politics of Memory in Postwar Europe* (Durham, NC: Duke University Press, 2006).

Lehrer, Erica. *Jewish Poland Revisited: Heritage Tourism in Unquiet Places* (Bloomington, IN: Indiana University Press, 2013).

Lendvai, Paul. *Anti-Semitism without Jews: Communist Eastern Europe* (New York: Doubleday, 1971).

Lentin, Alana. *Why Race Still Matters* (Cambridge: Polity Press, 2020).

Lerman, Anthony. *What Happened to Antisemitism? Redefinition and the Myth of the 'Collective Jew'* (London: Pluto Press, 2022).

Levenson, Alan T. *Between Philosemitism and Antisemitism: Defense of Jews and Judaism in Germany 1871–1932* (Lincoln, NE: University of Nebraska Press, 2004).

Leveson, Ian, and Sandra Lustig. *Turning the Kaleidoscope: Perspectives on European Jewry* (New York: Berghahn Books, 2006).

Lindsay, Mark R. *Barth, Israel, and Jesus: Karl Barth's Theology of Israel* (Aldershot, UK: Ashgate, 2007).

Linfield, Susie. *The Lions' Den: Zionism and the Left from Hannah Arendt to Noam Chomsky* (New Haven: Yale University Press, 2019).

Loeffler, James. *Rootless Cosmopolitans: Jews and Human Rights in the Twentieth Century* (New Haven: Yale University Press, 2018).

Lüth, Erich. *Ein Deutscher sieht Israel* (Hamburg: Gesellschaft für Christlich-Jüdische Zusammenarbeit, 1955).

Maeck, Julie. *Montrer la Shoah à la television de 1960 à nos jours* (Paris: Nouveau Monde, 2009).

Makdisi, Saree. *Tolerance Is a Wasteland: Palestine and the Culture of Denial* (Berkeley, CA: University of California Press, 2022)

Makovsky, Michael. *Churchill's Promised Land: Zionism and Statecraft* (New Haven: Yale University Press, 2007).

Mandel, Maud S. *In the Aftermath of Genocide: Armenians and Jews in Twentieth-Century France* (Durham: Duke University Press, 2003).

Marcus, Millicent. *Italian Film in the Shadow of Auschwitz* (Toronto: University of Toronto Press, 2007).

Marin, Bernd. *Antisemitismus ohne Antisemiten: Studien zur Vorurteildynamik* (Vienna: Campus Verlag, 2000).
Marwecki, Daniel. *Absolution? Israel und die deutsche Staatsräson* (Göttingen: Wallstein Verlag, 2024).
Marwecki, Daniel. *Germany and Israel: Whitewashing and State-Building* (New York: Oxford University Press, 2020).
Mardam-Bey, Farouk. "French Intellectuals and the Palestine Question," *Journal of Palestine Studies* XLIII, no. 3 (Spring 2014): 26–39.
Mardam-Bey, Farouk. *L'antiebraismo cattolico dopo la Shoah: Tradizioni e culture nell'Italia del secondo dopoguerra (1945–1974)* (Rome: Viella, 2012).
Marcuse, Harold. *Legacies of Dachau: The Uses and Abuses of a Concentration Camp, 1933–2001* (Cambridge: Cambridge University Press, 2001).
Mazzini, Elena. *L'antiebraismo cattolico dopo la Shoah: Tradizioni e culture nell'Italia del secondo dopoguerra (1945–1974)* (Rome: Viella, 2012).
Meyer, Kristina. *Die SPD und die NS-Vergangenheit 1945–1990* (Göttingen: Wallstein Verlag, 2015).
Moses, A. Dirk. "Die deutsche Debatte ist von Obsessionen geprägt: Erinnerungsräumliche Betrachtungen zum Katechismus der Deutschen," in Jürgen Zimmerer (ed.), *Errinerungskämpfe: Neues deutsches Geschitsbewusstsein* (Stuttgart: Reclam, 2023), 264–290.
Moses, A. Dirk. *The Problems of Genocide: Permanent Security and the Language of Transgression* (New York: Cambridge University Press, 2021).
Morris, Leslie, and Jack Zipes (eds.). *Unlikely History: The Changing German-Jewish Symbiosis, 1945–2000* (New York: Palgrave Macmillan, 2002).
Mounk, Yascha. *Stranger in My Own Country: A Jewish Family in Modern Germany* (New York: Farrar, Straus and Giroux, 2014).
Muhlen, Norbert. *The Survivors: A Report on the Jews in Germany Today* (New York: Thomas Y. Cowell, 1962, 150–172).
Moyn, Samuel. *A Holocaust Controversy: The Treblinka Affair in Postwar France* (Waltham, MA: Brandeis University Press, 2005).
Nathan, Emmanuel, and Anna Topolsky (eds.). *Is There a Judeo-Christian Tradition? A European Perspective* (Berlin and Boston: De Gruyter, 2016).
Neiman, Susan. "Historical Reckoning Gone Haywire." In *The New York Review of Books* (October 19, 2023).
Neiman, Susan. *Learning from the Germans: Race and the Memory of Evil* (New York: Farrar, Straus, and Giroux, 2019).
Niven, Bill. *Facing the Nazi Past: United Germany and the Legacy of the Third Reich* (London: Routledge, 2002).
Niven, Bill (ed.). *Germans as Victims* (Houndmills, Basingstoke, Hampshire: Palgrave Macmillan, 2006).
Nord, Philip. *After the Deportation: Memory Battles in Postwar France* (Cambridge: Cambridge University Press, 2020).
Olick, Jeffrey K. *The Sins of the Fathers: Germany, Memory, Method* (Chicago, IL: University of Chicago Press, 2016).
Olick, Jeffrey K., and Andrew J. Perrin (eds.). *Guilt and Defense: On the Legacies of National Socialism in Postwar Germany* (Cambridge, MA: Harvard University Press, 2010).

Özyürek, Esra. *Subcontractors of Guilt: Holocaust Memory and Muslim Belonging in Postwar Germany* (Stanford, CA: Stanford University Press, 2023).
Pakier, Małgorzata, and Bo Stråth (eds.). *A European Memory? Contested Histories and Politics of Remembrance* (New York: Berghahn Books, 2010).
Panay, Panikos (ed.). *Racial Violence in Britain in the Nineteenth and Twentieth Centuries* (London and New York: Leicester University Press, 1996).
Pardo, Sharon, and Hila Zahavi (eds.). *The Jewish Contribution to European Integration* (Lanham, MD: Lexington Books, 2020).
Parkes, James. *An Enemy of the People: Antisemitism* (Harmondsworth: Penguin Books, 1945).
Pearce, Andy. *Holocaust Consciousness in Contemporary Britain* (New York: Routledge, 2014).
Peck, Jeffrey. *Being Jewish in the New Germany* (New Brunswick, NJ: Rutgers University Press).
Pelletier, Denis, and Jean-Louis Schlegel (eds.). *À la gauche du Christ: Les chrétiens de gauche en France de 1945 à nos jours* (Paris: Seuil, 2012).
Perra, Emiliano. *Conflicts of Memory: The Reception of Holocaust Films and TV Programmes in Italy, 1945 to the Present* (Bern: Peter Lang, 2010).
Pinto, Diana. "Negotiating Jewish Identity in an Asemitic Age," *Jewish Culture and History* 2–23, no. 14 (2013): 68–77.
Pierrard, Pierre. *Juifs et Catholiques français: D'Edouard Drumont à Jacob Kaplan* (Paris: Cerf, 1997).
Piterberg, Gabriel. "Euro-Zionism and Its Discontents," *New Left Review* no. 84 (November–December 2013): 43–65.
Phayer, Michael. *The Catholic Church and the Holocaust, 1930–1965* (Bloomington, IN: Indiana University Press, 2000).
Qasem, Sindyan. "'Little More than Terrorists': Eine Reflektion über das Verhältnis von Islamismusprävention und Palästinadiskurs," *Islamophobia Studies Yearbook*, no. 11 (2020): 71–90.
Rabinbach, Anson, and Jack Zipes (eds.). *Germans and Jews since the Holocaust* (New York: Holmes & Meier, 1986).
Radonić, Ljiljana (ed.). *The Holocaust/Genocide Template in Eastern Europe* (New York: Routledge, 2020).
Rabi, Wladimir. *Anatomie du judaïsme français* (Paris: Les Editions de Minuit, 1962).
Rathkolb, Oliver. *The Paradoxical Republic: Austria 1945–2020* (New York: Berghahn Books, 2021).
Reisigl, Martin, and Ruth Wodak. *Discourse and Discrimination: Rhetorics of Racism and Antisemitism* (London: Routledge, 2001).
Renton, James, and Ben Gidley (eds.). *Antisemitism and Islamophobia in Europe: A Shared History?* (London: Palgrave Macmillan, 2017).
Reuveni, Gideon, and David Franklin (eds.). *The Future of the German Jewish Past* (West Lafayette, IN: Purdue University Press, 2021).
Richardson, John, and Ruth Wodak. "Anti-Sorosism: Reviving 'the Jewish World Conspiracy'" in Massimiliano Demata, Virginia Zorzi, and Angela Zottola (eds.). *Conspiracy Theory Discourses* (Amsterdam: John Benjamins, 2022), 395–420.

Rose, Hannah. *The New Philosemitism: Exploring a Changing Relationship between the Jews and the Far-Right* (London: ICSR, King's College London, 2020).
Romeyn, Esther. "(Anti) New Antisemitism as a Transnational Field of Racial Governance," *Patterns of Prejudice* 1–2, no. 54 (2020): 199–214.
Rosenfeld, Alvin H. (ed.). *Deciphering the New Antisemitism* (Bloomington, IN: Indiana University Press, 2015).
Rosenfeld, Alvin H. (ed.). *Resurgent Antisemitism: Global Perspectives* (Bloomington, IN: Indiana University Press, 2013).
Rothberg, Michael. *Multidirectional Memory: Remembering the Holocaust in the Age of Decolonization* (Stanford, CA: Stanford University Press, 2009).
Royal, Robert (ed.). *Jacques Maritain and the Jews* (Notre Dame, IN: University of Notre Dame Press, 1994).
Rubinstein, William D., and Hilary L. Rubinstein. *Philosemitism: Admiration and Support in the English-Speaking World for Jews, 1840–1939* (Houndmills, Basingstoke, Hampshire: Palgrave Macmillan, 1999).
Said, Edward W. *After the Last Sky: Palestinian Lives* (New York: Columbia University Press, 1986).
Said, Edward. *The Question of Palestine* (New York: Viking Press, 1992).
Samuels, Maurice. *The Right to Difference: French Universalism and the Jew* (Chicago, IL: University of Chicago Press, 2016).
Sartre, Jean-Paul. *Anti-Semite and Jew* (New York: Schocken Books, 1995).
Schmidt, Christoph. *Israel und die Geister von `68: Eine Phänomenologie* (Göttingen: Vandenhoeck & Ruprecht, 2018).
Schroeder, Steven M. *To Forget It All and Begin Anew: Reconciliation in Occupied Germany, 1944–1954* (Toronto: University of Toronto Press, 2013).
Schildt, Axel, and Wolfgang Schmidt (eds.). *"Wir wollen mehr Demokratie wagen": Antriebskräfte, Realität und Mythos eines Versprechens* (Hamburg: Dietz, 2019).
Schwartz, Guri. *After Mussolini: Jewish Life in Post-Fascist Italy* (London: Vallentine Mitchell, 2012).
Segré, Ivan. "The Philo-Semitic Reaction" in Alain Badiou, Eric Hazan, and Ivan Segré (eds.), *Reflections on Anti-Semitism* (London: Verso, 2013), 45–232.
Sharples, Caroline. *Postwar Germany and the Holocaust* (London: Bloomsbury, 2016).
Sharples, Caroline, and Olaf Jensen. *Britain and the Holocaust: Remembering War and Genocide* (Houndmills, Basingstoke, Hampshire: Palgrave Macmillan, 2013).
Shafir, Shlomo. *An Outstretched Hand: German Social Democrats, Jews and Israel 1945–1967* (Hebrew) (Tel Aviv: Zmora Bitan, 1986).
Sonderegger, Katherine. *That Jesus Christ Was Born a Jew: Karl Barth's Doctrine of Israel* (University Park, PA: The Pennsylvania University Press, 1992).
Spicer, Kevin (ed.). *Antisemitism, Christian Ambivalence and the Holocaust* (Bloomington, IN: Indiana Press University, 2007).
Srodecki, Paul, and Daria Kozlova (eds.). *War and Remembrance: World War II and Memory Politics of Post-Socialist Europe* (Paderborn: Brill, 2023).
Steiner, George. *In Bluebeard's Castle: Some Notes towards the Redefinition of Culture* (New Haven: Yale University Press, 1971).
Stern, Frank. *Whitewashing of the Yellow Badge: Antisemitism and Philosemitism in Postwar Germany* (New York: Oxford University Press, 1992).

Stone, Dan. "The Holocaust and 'The Human'," in *The Holocaust, Fascism and Memory: Essays in the History of Ideas* (Houndmills, Basingstoke, Hampshire: Palgrave Macmillan, 2013), 49–63.

Subotić, Jelena. *Yellow Star, Red Star: Holocaust Remembrance after Communism* (Ithaca, NY: Cornell University Press, 2019).

Sutcliffe, Adam. *What Are Jews For? History, Peoplehood, and Purpose* (Princeton, NJ: Princeton University Press, 2020).

Sutcliffe, Adam. "Whose Feelings Matter? Holocaust Memory, Empathy, and Redemptive Anti-Antisemitism," *Journal of Genocide Research* 26, no. 2 (2022): 222–242.

Szafran, Maurice. *Les juifs dans la politique française: De 1945 à nos jours* (Paris: Flammarion, 1990).

Sznaider, Natan. *Jewish Memory and the Cosmopolitan Order* (Cambridge: Polity Press, 2011).

Taguieff, Pierre-André. *La nouvelle judéophobie* (Paris: Fayard, 2002).

Tanzer, Frances. *Vanishing Vienna: Modernism, Philosemitism and Jews in a Postwar City* (Philadelphia, PA: University of Pennsylvania Press, 2024).

Tarquini, Alessandra. *La sinistra italiana e gli ebrei: Socialismo, sionismo e antisemitismo dal 1882 al 1992* (Bologna: Mulino, 2019).

Tarquini, Alessandra (ed.). *The European Left and the Jewish Question 1848–1992* (Cham: Palgrave Macmillan, 2021).

Tarquini, Alexandra (ed.). *The European Left and the Jewish Question 1848–1992: Between Zionism and Antisemitism* (Cham: Palgrave Macmillan, 2021).

Tobias, Norman C. *Jewish Conscience of the Church: Jules Isaac and the Second Vatican Council* (Cham: Palgrave Macmillan, 2017).

Toscano, Mario. *La "Porta di Sion": L'Italia e l'immigrazione clandestina ebraica in Palestina (1945–1948)* (Bologna: Mulino, 1990).

Toscano, Mario (ed.). *Ebraismo, sionismo e antisemitismo nella stampa socialista italiana* (Venice: Marsilio Editori: 2015), 95–161.

Toscano, Mario (ed.). *L'Italia racconta Israele 1948–2018* (Viella: Rome, 2018).

Traverso, Enzo. *The End of Jewish Modernity* (London: Pluto Press, 2016).

Tzuberi, Hanna. "'Reforesting Jews': The German State and the Construction of 'New German Judaism'," *Jewish Studies Quarterly* 27, no. 3 (2020): 199–224.

Uhl, Heidemarie. "From the Periphery to the Center of Memory: Holocaust Memorials in Vienna," *Dapim: Studies on the Holocaust* 3, no. 30 (2016): 221–242.

Ury, Scott, and Guy Miron (eds.). *Antisemitism and the Politics of History* (Waltham, MA: Brandeis University Press).

Van der Knaap, Ewout (ed.). *Uncovering the Holocaust: The International Reception of Night and Fog* (London: Wallflower Press, 2006).

Villani, Cinzia. *Infrangere le frontiere: l'arrivo in Italia delle displaced persons ebree 1945–1948*. PhD thesis, University of Trento, 2010.

Voigt, Sebastian. *Der jüdische Mai '68: Pierre Goldman, Daniel Cohn-Bendit und André Glucksmann im Nachkriegsfrankreich* (Göttingen: Vandenhoeck & Ruprecht, 2015).

Von Hindenburg, Hannfried. *Demonstrating Reconciliation: State and Society in West German Foreign Policy toward Israel, 1952–1965* (New York: Berghahn Books, 2007).

Von Rahden, Till. "History in the House of the Hangman: How Postwar Germany Became a Key Site in the Study of Jewish History." in Steven E. Aschheim, and Vibian Liska (eds.). *The German-Jewish Experience Revisited* (Berlin: De Gruyter, 2015), 171–192.
Wasserstein, Bernard. *Vanishing Diaspora: The Jews of Europe since 1945* (London: Penguin Books, 1996).
Wertheim, David J. *The Jew as Legitimation: Jewish-Gentile Relations beyond Antisemitism and Philosemitism* (Cham: Palgrave Macmillan, 2017).
Wicke, Christian. *Helmut Kohl's Quest for Normality* (New York: Berghahn Books, 2015).
Winock, Michel. *La France et les Juifs de 1789 à nos jours* (Paris: Seuil, 2004).
Wistrich, Robert S. (ed.). *Austrians and Jews in the Twentieth Century: From Franz Joseph to Waldheim* (New York: St. Martin's Press, 1992).
Wistrich, Robert S. (ed.). *Austrians and Jews in the Twentieth Century: From Franz Joseph to Waldheim* (New York: Palgrave Macmillan, 2001).
Wistrich, Robert S. "Anti-Semitism in Europe after 1945." in *Terms of Survival: The Jewish World since 1945*, 269–296 (London: Routledge, 1995).
Wolf, Joan B. *Harnessing the Holocaust: The Politics of Memory in France* (Stanford, CA: Stanford University Press, 2004).
Wüstenberg, Jenny. *Civil Society and Memory in Postwar Germany* (Cambridge: Cambridge University Press, 2017).
Wyman, David (ed.). *The World Reacts to the Holocaust* (Baltimore, MD: The Johns Hopkins University Press, 1996).
Younes, Anna-Esther. "Fighting Anti-Semitism in Contemporary Germany." *Islamophobia Studies Journal* 5, no. 2 (2020): 249–266.
Zubrzycki, Geneviève. *Resurrecting the Jew: Nationalism, Philosemitism, and Poland's Jewish Revival* (Princeton, NJ: Princeton University Press, 2022).
Zuckermann, Moshe. *"Antisemit!" Ein Vorwurf als Herrschaftsinstrument* (Vienna: Promedia Verlag, 2010).

Index

The Acts of the Apostles (1969), 180
Adenauer, Konrad, 52, 57, 68, 131, 140, 172, 222
Adorno, Theodor, 9, 28, 51, 128, 189
Algerian War (1954–1962), 81
allosemitism, 19
Alternativ für Deutschland (AfD), 259
American Jewish Committee, 26, 248
American Jewish Year Book, 26, 32, 34, 36–40
    Austria, 47, 49
    Belgium, 177
    Italy, 43
    West Germany, 53
American Joint Jewish Distribution Committee, 124
Améry, Jean, 191
Anglo-American Committee of Inquiry, 63, 65
Anidjar, Gil, 266
Anti Defamation League (ADL), 244
Apeldoorn Memorandum, 150
Arab–Israeli war (1948), 111–112, 122
Arab–Israeli war (1973), 204, 206
Arafat, Yasser, 204
Arbeiter-Zeitung, 67
Arendt, Hannah, 2–3, 8, 51, 66, 72, 85, 97, 131, 193, 219
    Eichmann in Jerusalem (1963), 183
Aron, Raymond, 199
Arthur, Balfour, 4
Auschwitz Trial (1963–1965), 180–181
Austrian Freedom Party (FPÖ), 256

Badiel, David, 246
Barmen Declaration (1934), 152
Baron, Salo W., 14
Barrault, Jean-Louis, 119
Barth, Karl, 159–160
Bauer, Yehuda, 186
Beck, Ulrich, 221
Belang, Vlaams, 255

Ben-Gurion, David, 117, 128
Berlin, Isaiah, 112, 269
Berlin Wall, 223, 225
Berlin-Weissensee Synod, 145
Bernanos, Georges, 26, 58
Bevin, Ernest, 69
Bibó, István, 66
Bidermanas, Izraels, 126
Bitburg controversy (1985), 224–225, 229
Blair, Tony, 236
Blanchot, Maurice, 199
Bloch, Ernst, 9, 29, 66
Board of Deputies of British Jews, 45, 61, 216
Boder, David, 168
Böhm, Franz, 127, 139
Borodajkewycz, Taras, 176
Bouteldja, Houria, 267
Boycott, Divestment and Solidarity campaign (BDS), 247
Brandt, Willy, 116, 128, 131–132, 193–195
    Ostpolitik (1969–1974), 205
British Union of Fascists. *See* Mosley, Oswald
Broszat, Martin, 195
Buber, Martin, 135, 148
Buruma, Ian, 225

Camp David Accords (1978), 207
Camus, Albert, 96, 107, 116
    The Plague (1947), 108–109
Catholic church, 6, 12
    Nostra Aetate declaration (1956), 22, 137, 151, 160–163
    Pope John XXIII, 42, 150, 153
    Pope Paul VI, 161
    Pope Pius XI, 7
    Pope Pius XII, 7, 42, 75, 143–144, 151, 153, 183
Center of Contemporary Jewish Documentation, 33

284 Index

Central Council of Jews in Germany, 9, 172
Central Memorial for the Victims of War and Tyranny (Berlin), 226
Césaire, Aimé, 92, 98
Chagall, Marc, 167
Chirac, Jacques, 234–235
Christianity, 19, 22
  humilatio dei "Jesus's agony," 163–165
  Pauline canon, 154–160
  Romans 9–11, 154–155
Christian-Jewish dialogue, 71
  Seelisberg conference (1947), 62
Churchill, Winston, 4, 142
Cioran, Emil, 59
Claussen, Detlev, 194
Clay, Lucius D., 138
Cohen, Albert, 25, 27, 29
Cohen, Arthur A., 135–136
Cohn-Bendit, Daniel, 198
Commissariat-General on Jewish Affairs (France), 32, 66
Commissioner for Jewish Life and the Fight Against Antisemitism (Germany), 264
Congress for Cultural Freedom, 137
Conseil Représentatif des Institutions Juives de France, 61
Cordan, Wolfgang, 122
Croce, Benedetto, 41–42
Crossman, Richard, 63–65, 114

Daniélou, Jean, 157–158
Davies, W. D., 159
de Beauvoir, Simone, 100, 105, 183
de Felice, Renzo, 184
de Gaulle, Charles, 142
Debenedetti, Giacomo, 58
Declaration of the Fundamental Postulates of Judaism and Christianity in Relation to the Social Order.
  See National Conference of Christian and Jews
Dekel, Irit, 262
Delors, Jacques, 219
Démann, Paul, 156–157
Democrazia Christiana (DC), 142
Denebedetti, Giacomo, 40
Der gelbe Stern (1960). *See* Schoenberner, Gerhard
Deutsche National-Zeitung, 174
Deutschland schafft sich ab [Germany Does Away With Itself] (2000).
  See Sarrazin, Thilo
Dewinter, Filip, 255
Dialectic of Enlightenment (1944, 1947).
  See Frankfurt School

The Diary of Anne Frank (1950), 164
Dibelius, Martin, 147
displaced persons, 28, 102–103, 124
  Austria, 48
  Exodus (ship), 104–107
  La Spezia incident (1946), 103–104
  West Germany, 50–51
Doctors Without Borders (MSF), 200–201
Documentation and Resistance Archive, 182
Dreyfus Affair, 33, 202
Du Bois, W. E. B., 92
Dutschke, Rudi, 197

Eichmann Trial (1961), 130–131, 139, 169, 183–185
Eight Jews (1944). *See* Debenedetti, Giacomo
Elon, Amos, 227
Eliot, T. S., 141
Entebbe airfield incident (1976), 194
Enzesberger, Hans Magnus, 193
Erhard, Ludwig, 131
Esprit (magazine), 76, 80, 105
European Convention of Human Rights (1950), 140
European Jewish Congress, 248
European Monitoring Centre for Racism and Xenophobia, 244, 248
Eurozone financial crisis (2010), 230

The Fallen Soldier (1936), 124
The Family of Man (1955), 98, 124
Federal Amnesty Law (1949), 146
Figl, Leopold, 46–47
Fini, Gianfranco, 254
Finkielkraut, Alain, 198, 231
First Intifada (1987), 217
Fischer, Joschka, 209, 228, 261
Fleg, Edmond, 158
Fogh Rasmussen, Anders, 235
Forest of Martyrs, 127
Fortuyn, Pim, 253
Fourth Republic (1946–1958), 176
France–Palestine association (1979), 211
Frank, Anne, 39
Frankfurt School, 78
  "Anti-Semitism Project" and "Studies in Prejudice," 79
Frankl, Viktor, 97
French League for a Free Palestine, 105
French National Liberation Committee, 30
Friedländer, Saul, 1
Friedman, Philip, 169
Friedrich Peter scandal (1975), 183

Index

Gauche Prolétarienne, 209
German New Left, 266
German Penal Code article 130, 172
German-Israeli Study Groups, 190
Gerstenmeier, Eugen, 131
Giordano, Ralph, 223
Glotz, Peter, 225
Glucksmann, André, 202
The God That Failed (1949), 65
Goebbels, Joseph, 5–6, 55, 106
Gollwitzer, Helmut, 146
Grass, Günter, 134
Gross, Jan T., 240
Grüber, Heinrich, 139

Habermas, Jürgen, 19, 221, 225
Haider, Jörg, 234, 256
Hausner, Gideon, 184
Heath, Edward, 205
Hedler, Wolfgang, 52
Heidegger, Martin, 95
Heine, Heinrich, 86
Hertzberg, Abel, 37
Himmelfarb, Gertrude, 138
Historians' Debate (1986–1988), 225
History of Italian Jews Under Fascism (1961). *See* de Felice, Renzo
Hitler's Willing Executioners (1996), 227
Hobsbawm, Eric, 15
Höcke, Björn, 259
Hollande, François, 235
Holocaust (TV miniseries, 1979), 183
Holocaust Reparations, 10, 14, 68
    Belgium, 35
    West Germany, 52
Horkheimer, Max, 189
House of the Wannsee Conference Memorial Site, 226
Humboldt, Wilhelm von, 75

If This is a Man (1947). *See* Levi, Primo
Institute for Jewish Policy Research (JPR), 245
International Council for Christians and Jews, 155
International Holocaust Remembrance Alliance (IHRA), 238, 249–250
International League Against Antisemitism (LICRA), 60
Isaac, Jules, 152, 167
Israeli Labor party, 210
Italian Social Movement (MSI), 255

Jakobovits, Immanuel, 215–216
Jaspers, Karl, 99, 132, 262
Jenninger, Philipp, 224

Jesus and Israel (1948). *See* Isaac, Jules
Jewish Central Information Office (JCIO), 44
Jewish immigration, 15, 28, 34–35, 37, 102, 229–230
Jewish Museum of the City of Vienna, 233
The Jewish Question and Christian Answers (1949). *See* Barth, Karl
Jews Don't Count (2021). *See* Badiel, David
Jobert, Michel, 206
Jordan, Colin, 173
"Judeo-Christian tradition," 135–138, 141–143, 147, 150, 161–162, 253, 259

Kessel, Joseph, 111
kibbutzim, 115, 132
    Kielce pogrom (1946), 27
Klarsfeld, Serge, 31
Kleerekoper, Salomon, 183
Kohl, Helmut, 196, 223–227, 229
Komorowski, Bronislaw, 237
Krastev, Ivan, 257
Kreisky, Bruno, 49, 68, 176, 209
Kreisler, Georg, 182
Kundera, Milan, 23, 218–219
Kundnani, Hans, 261
Kunzelmann, Dieter, 192
Kurz, Sebastian, 234
Kwasniewski, Alexander, 237

Labor Zionism, 113
Langer, Lawrence, 169
Lanzmann, Claude, 212–214
Laor, Itzhak, 267
Lateran Pacts (1929), 142
Lattes, Dante, 40
Le bréviaire de la haine [Harvest of Hate]. *See* Poliakov, Léon
Le Pen, Marine, 256–257
Leibowitz, Yeshayahu, 135
Les aventures de Rabbi Jacob, 203–204
Levi, Primo, 97, 102, 168, 185
Levinas, Emmanuel, 137, 151
Lévitte, Georges, 178
Lévy, Bernard-Henri, 202
Life (magazine), 125
Luckner, Gertrud, 148
Lüth, Erich, 129
Luxembourg Agreement (1952), 139, 222

Maastricht Treaty (1992), 220
Madaule, Jacques, 165
Magnum Photos agency (1947), 124–125
Malraux, André, 126
Manchester Guardian, 69, 106
Mann, Thomas, 63

Man's Search for Meaning (1946).
  See Frankl, Viktor
Marchandeau Law, 30
Marcuse, Herbert, 189
Maritain, Jacques, 7, 27, 155, 162–163
  On *humilatio dei*, 164
Marquardt, Friedrich-Wilhelm, 160
Marshall Plan (1948), 137
Mauriac, François, 30, 165
  On *Night* (1960), 165–167
McCloy, John, 50
McMillan, Harold, 215
Meinhof, Ulrike, 192, 197
Merkel, Angela, 13, 23, 228, 251, 260
  multiculturalism, 263
  philosemitism, 252, 261
  staatsräson speech (2008), 260, 262
Merleau-Ponty, Maurice, 100
Merzagora, Cesare, 42
Mitterrand, François, 210, 216
mode rétro, 202–203
Moscow Declaration (1943), 46
Moses, A. Dirk, 265, 268–269
Mosley, Oswald, 43
Movement against Racism, Antisemitism and for Peace (MRAP), 173
Moynihan, Daniel Patrick, 208
Muhlen, Norbert, 9, 139
Munich Olympics (1972), 206, 209
Murer, Franz, 175
Musée de l'Homme, 96
Museum of the Federal Republic (Bonn, Germany), 226

Nasser, Gamal Abdel, 115, 133, 186
National Conference of Christian and Jews, 138, 141
National Front (France), 256
National Socialist Movement (*Britain*), 173
National Strategy against Anti-Semitism and for Jewish Life (2022), 262
Neighbors (2000). *See* Gross, Jan T.
Netanyahu, Benjamin, 257–258
Niebuhr, Reinhold, 136
Niemöller, Martin, 146
Night (1960), 165
Novak, Franz, 175
Nuit et Brouillard (1956), 101
Nuremberg Trial (1945–1946), 99, 181

Ondergang [*The Destruction of the Dutch Jews*] (1965). *See* Presser, Jacques
Orban, Viktor, 257
The Origins of Totalitarianism (1951).
  See Arendt, Hannah

Orléans Rumor (1969), 179
Orwell, George, 43, 87
  anti-antisemitism, 87–91
  anti-Zionism, 89
  Nineteen Eighty-Four (1949), 90
Oslo Accords (1993), 207
Öyzürek, Ezra, 262–263

Palestine Liberation Organization (PLO), 207
Palestine Mission (1946). *See* Crossman, Richard
Palme, Olof, 210
Paris Peace Treaties (1947), 58
Parkes, James, 72–74, 77, 149
Party for Freedom (PVV). *See* Wilders, Geert
Patai, Raphael, 117
Pinto, Diana, 240–241
Pleven Law (1972), 173
Poliakov, Léon, 165, 179, 183
Pompidou, Georges, 205–206
Poujade, Pierre, 33–34
Pourquoi Israël [Israel, Why] (1973).
  See Lanzmann, Claude
Powell, Enoch, 178
Presser, Jacques, 184
Prodi, Romano, 220, 222

The Question of German Guilt (1946).
  See Jaspers, Karl

Rabi, Wladimir, 34, 60, 80, 85
Race Relations Act (1965), 173
Razesberger, Franz, 175
Reagan, Ronald, 224
Red Army Faction, 192
Réflexions sur la question juive. *See* Sartre, Jean-Paul
Reiche, Reimut. *See* Socialist German Student League (SDS)
Renner, Karl, 47–48
restitution of Jewish property, 31
  Austria, 47
Ringelblum, Emmanuel, 168
Rivers of Blood speech. *See* Powell, Enoch
Rodinson, Maxime, 133
Rops, Daniel, 164
Rosenberg, Arthur, 68
Rosenberg Trial (1951), 33, 136
Rosenzweig, Franz, 135
Roth, Cecil, 46
Russell, Bertrand, 141

Said, Edward, 21, 194, 266
Sakharov, Andrei, 211–212

Index

Samour, Nadija, 265
Samuel, Maurice, 162
sans-frontiérisme, 200–201
Sarrazin, Thilo, 263
Sartre, Jean-Paul, 21, 24, 66, 81, 95, 134, 187
   anti-antisemitism, 86
   colonialism, 82
   philosemitism, 77–81, 85
   Zionism, 82–83, 86
Schindler's List (1993), 227
Schmid, Carlo, 128
Schmidt, Helmut, 195, 210, 224
Schneerson, Isaac, 33
Schoenberner, Gerhard, 181
Schoeps, Hans-Joachim, 139
Scholem, Gershom, 3
Schröder, Gerhard, 227–228, 261
Schumacher, Kurt, 57, 68
Schwarz-Bart, André, 167–168
Seelisberg conference (1947), 153
Segré, Ivan, 267
Semprun, Jorge, 253
Seymour, David, 124
Sharansky, Natan, 247
Six-Day War (1967), 129, 132, 134, 179–180
Social Democratic Party (SPD), 68, 114, 193
Socialist German Student League (SDS), 190–191, 193, 197
Socialist International, 114
Socialist Unity Party of Germany (SED), 69
Societies for Christian-Jewish Cooperation, 128, 138–139, 210
SOS Racisme, 217
Steiner, George, 141, 220, 241
Steiner, Jean-François, 183
Steinmeier, Frank-Walter, 264
Stern, Frank, 11, 225
Stern, Kenneth, 249
Stockholm Declaration (2000), 221, 238
Strache, Hanz-Christian, 256
Strauss, Franz-Joseph, 131
Suez crisis (1956), 115–116, 132
Swastika Epidemic, 171–172

Taguieff, Pierre-André, 243
Terrenoire, Louis, 211
Thatcher, Margaret, 113, 178
   philosemitism, 215
Théologie du Judéo-Christianisme. *See* Daniélou, Jean

Thieme, Karl, 148, 150–151
Tin Drum (1959). *See* Grass, Günter
Toynbee, Arnold, 141
travelogues, 121–123
Traverso, Enzo, 267
Treaty of Rome (1957), 222
Treblinka (1966). *See* Steiner, Jean-François
Trigano, Shmuel, 246
Truss, Liz, 215

UN General Assembly resolution 3379 (1975), 207–212
Un peuple de solitaires (1956). *See* Cioran, Emil
UN resolution 242, 210
UN World Conference Against Racism in Durban (July 2001), 243
UNESCO, 95, 99
United Nations Convention on the Elimination of All Forms of Racial Discrimination (1965), 93
United Nations Relief and Works Agency (UNWRA), 123, 125
United Nations Universal Declaration of Human Rights (1948), 140

Valentin, Hugo, 79
Valls, Manuel, 251
Verhofstadt, Guy, 235
von Weizsäcker, Richard, 229–230, 260
Vona, Gabor, 257
Vranitzky, Franz, 233
Vredeling, Henk, 206

Waldheim Affair (1986), 233–234
Walser, Martin, 227
Walter, Hilde, 175
Westphal, Charles, 152
Wiener Zeitung, 67
Wiener, Alfred. *See* Jewish Central Information Office (JCIO)
Wiesel, Elie, 223
Wiesenthal, Simon, 182
Wieviorka, Michel, 247
Wilders, Geert, 253–254
World Council of Churches (WCC), 144
World Jewish Congress, 33, 36, 39, 171

Yad Vashem, 131, 255–256
Younes, Anna-Esther, 261

Zweig, Arnold, 79
Zweig, Stefan, 220

For EU product safety concerns, contact us at Calle de José Abascal, 56–1°,
28003 Madrid, Spain or eugpsr@cambridge.org.

www.ingramcontent.com/pod-product-compliance
Ingram Content Group UK Ltd.
Pitfield, Milton Keynes, MK11 3LW, UK
UKHW022002030326
468620UK00021B/862